CROALL

CRIME AND
SOCIETY IN BRITAIN

Longman

An imprint of **Pearson Education**

Harlow, England · London · New York · Reading, Massachusetts · San Francisco
Toronto · Don Mills, Ontario · Sydney · Tokyo · Singapore · Hong Kong · Seoul
Taipei · Cape Town · Madrid · Mexico City · Amsterdam · Munich · Paris · Milan

Pearson Education Limited
Edinburgh Gate
Harlow,
Essex CM20 2JE
England

and Associated Companies throughout the world

Visit us on the World Wide Web at:
http://www.pearsoneduc.com

First published 1998

ISBN 0 582 29897–0 Paper

British Library Cataloguing-in-Publication Data

A catalogue record for this book is
available from the British Library

Library of Congress Cataloging-in-Publication Data

Croall, Hazel, 1947–
Crime and society in Britain / Croall.
p. cm.
Includes bibliographical references and index.
ISBN 0–582–29897–0
1. Crime—Great Britain. 2. Great Britain—Social
conditions—1945– I. Title.
HV6947.C736 1998
364.941—dc21   97–46850
CIP

10 9 8 7
06 05 04 03 02

Set by 35 in 10/12pt Plantin
Printed in Malaysia, LSP

CONTENTS

LIST OF FIGURES

ACKNOWLEDGEMENTS

Many people have supported and encouraged the author throughout the production of this text. Students and colleagues at both Thames Valley University and the University of Strathclyde have been helpful and have tolerated my being less than attentive to their needs. Considerable thanks are also due to the anonymous referees whose suggestions on the original proposal produced a more comprehensive and well-ordered text and to the readers of successive drafts, not only for their patience in correcting many mistakes but for their invaluable suggestions which enriched the final product. I am also grateful to Brian Willan for his continued support and confidence and also to all the staff at Addison Wesley Longman.

CHAPTER 1

INTRODUCTION: CRIME AND SOCIETY

Crime has become a major area of public policy and political debate, and to politicians and public commentators it is often seen as a sign of underlying problems in society. Governments, academic researchers and other commentators ask many questions about crime. Are levels of crime really rising? What affects crime rates? Why do people commit crime? What actions should be defined as criminal? How should offenders be dealt with? How can crime be reduced? These issues all arouse considerable discussion and debate and an enormous amount of information has been produced in the attempt to measure and understand crime. This book introduces readers to the academic study of crime which will enable them to better understand and critically evaluate these issues. It will examine how we find out about crime and how different theoretical approaches have sought to understand it. It will ask how crime can be related to social inequality in society, to social deprivation and social class and to age, gender and race. It will explore different kinds of crime, from violent and sexual crimes to organized and corporate crime and the crimes of the state.

Firstly, however, it is important to look carefully at the focus of this concern – at crime. What do we mean when we talk about crime? What is crime? How is it different from other kinds of behaviour? How is it related to society? This chapter will start by looking at some of the conflicting feelings aroused by crime before asking how it is defined. It will go on to explore how crime can be related to society and will finally outline the structure and scope of this book.

THE FEAR AND FASCINATION OF CRIME

Our attitudes to crime are complex and contradictory. Dramatic news stories of murder, rape, assault and major frauds horrify and frighten us, while at the same time exciting our curiosity about the criminals and victims involved. We are, therefore, both fascinated by and afraid of crime (Clarke 1996). Criminals can be portrayed as heroes, anti-heroes or villains. We can be appalled by accounts of sensational murders while at the same time have a grudging

1

respect for the bank robber who outwits the police. These mixed emotions are fuelled by dramatic reports of crime in the news, which can distort our images of crime and criminals. Crime is often seen as something which happens to other people – criminals are feared as strangers or outsiders and victims, too, may be seen as different by having done something to provoke a crime. Yet crime is an everyday occurrence – we are victimized every day by crimes we may not even be aware of, and many of us commit crime.

The attractions of crime are illustrated in its domination of newspapers, TV dramas and documentaries, films and literature. Accounts of crimes and criminal trials make headline news. It is a major theme in literature from classics like *Crime and Punishment* to the highly popular *genre* of detective fiction. Some of the most popular TV dramas feature fictional detectives such as Inspectors Frost, Morse, Wexford or Tennyson while police series such as *The Bill* cover more everyday aspects of crime and policing. Criminal trials provide a popular source of documentary and fictional drama. The story lines of popular soaps such as *EastEnders* feature a diet of rape, assault, property crime and attempted murder and characters involved in the shadowy world of professional crime and corruption. While these are dramatic and fictional accounts they do reveal the abiding appeal of crime.

Fear of crime, often prompted by sensational stories, affects our everyday lives. Reports of child murders make parents more protective of their children. People avoid certain streets or areas at particular times of the day or night. Some women and children effectively live under a curfew, being scared of going out alone. We take many other precautions against crime. Every day we lock our doors and carry a bunch of keys to our home, car or workplace. We carry credit cards, identity and membership cards, all of which are designed to prevent theft and fraud. We are surrounded by crime prevention devices. We may face security barriers at home, at work or in the bank and when we are shopping, travelling or walking we may be under the gaze of security cameras. These not only protect us from crime, they also aim to prevent our committing it.

Our image of crime, affected by dramatic stories of atypical crimes, may be misleading. What people tend to fear most of all is the unprovoked attack from the stranger – so much so that we avoid going to places where this might happen. In reality the risk of this is small and dangers lie elsewhere. Many crimes take place not in the public places we avoid but in the home. We are far more likely to be physically and sexually assaulted by family members than by strangers. We can be harmed by pollution, unsafe working environments or the food we eat, which often results from the neglect of criminally enforced regulations. We can be defrauded by family members, local shops or financial advisers. We are indirectly affected by many other forms of crime – we pay higher prices for goods to cover the cost of shoplifting or employee theft and pay more tax to compensate for the activities of people who evade it.

While most of us do not see ourselves as criminals, many of us commit 'crimes' – as motorists we park on yellow lines, as employees we may be less than honest about our incomes to tax inspectors, we may 'borrow' items from work and as passengers we may avoid paying fares on the bus or train. We may conspire in crime by buying cheap goods without asking where they came from, or by 'paying in cash' for services subject to VAT. Most of us would distinguish these activities, all against the criminal law, from the activities of murders, rapists or hooligans. This demonstrates that there is often a very narrow borderline between what is generally regarded as 'criminal' and 'normal', legal or illegal. Crime is therefore very difficult to define.

DEFINING CRIME

As commonly understood, crime includes many different kinds of activities such as theft, fraud, robbery, corruption, assault, rape and murder. Do these activities have anything in common other than that they are all widely accepted as crime? How can crime be defined? As this section will illustrate, there is no one straightforward way of defining crime and differentiating it from other activities. At first sight it seems easy to define crime as it might, for example, be seen as doing something wrong. Crime is often, therefore, related to morality.

There are, however, many difficulties with this. Is there any agreement over what is morally right or wrong? Can, or should, all moral wrongs be crimes? Lying, cheating or deliberately hurting someone might all be considered immoral but not criminal. It could also be argued that poverty, deprivation, or racism are 'crimes against humanity' whereas these would not normally be regarded as crime. It could also be asked whether all crimes are moral wrongs. We can be prosecuted under the criminal law for parking on a yellow line but this is not generally seen as being immoral. The criminal law therefore does not necessarily reflect morality, nor do legal definitions reflect commonsense notions of crime. Furthermore, the criminal law is created in Parliament and there is a political dimension in defining crime. This section will focus on the legal, social and political elements in defining crime.

Crime and the criminal law

The simplest way of defining crime is to see it as 'something which is against the criminal law' and it could be argued that the only common characteristic of 'crimes' is that at some time they have been made subject to the criminal law. This involves using public as opposed to private enforcement and punishment. It is enforced by public agencies like the police, and involves prosecution in criminal courts, findings of guilt and sentencing, whereas private law deals with resolving conflicts between different parties and determining appropriate remedies, which may involve financial recompense (see, for example, Davies et al 1995). Criminal law, therefore, involves a distinctive process of law enforcement. But what characterizes the activities with which it is concerned? Are they different from, or more serious than, other activities? Some of the problems of using legal definitions of crime are outlined below.

Are all crimes really 'crime'?

As has been seen, many people break the criminal law but are not seen as 'criminal'. The criminal law prohibits activities ranging from failing to pay a dog, car, or television licence to assault and murder. While some of these activities are incontestably 'crime', many others are not and the criminal law itself distinguishes different kinds of crime. In English law, for example, some offences such as murder, theft or serious assaults are described as *mala in se* or wrong in themselves. These are often seen as 'real' crimes in contrast to acts which are *mala prohibita*, prohibited not because they are morally wrong but for the protection of the public (see, for example, Lacey et al 1990). Thus the criminal law is used to enforce regulations concerning public health, pollution or the quality or quantity of goods on sale, not because they are universally seen as 'crime' but because it is considered to be the most effective way of ensuring that regulations are complied with. These offences are often distinguished from 'real' crime by saying they are, for example, 'technical' offences. Criminal law is also used to enforce traffic regulations and licensing requirements where offenders would similarly not be seen as 'criminal'.

These distinctions do appear to reflect the seriousness of offences and levels of morality and immorality, however it is not easy to dismiss all 'technical' offences as not 'really' crime. Parking on a yellow line could be seen to be motivated by a selfish disregard for other road users and neglecting health or safety regulations may endanger the lives of consumers, workers or passengers. Selling goods which do not contain the stated or implied ingredients amounts to defrauding consumers. Dog licences aim to protect animals from cruel owners and the public from possibly dangerous dogs. Failing to obtain a licence may, like neglecting other regulations, imply a lack of concern for others.

Legally defining crime – from actions to offences

What is often called 'black letter law' cannot capture the multitude of situations in which specific actions are legally or socially interpreted as crime as this so often depends on the context in which they occur. A simple example is the offence of possessing an offensive weapon. Any item, such as an umbrella, handbag or beer glass, can be offensive if a person uses it in a threatening way. Taking any action which results in someone being injured or killed might also be assumed to be wrong and criminal, yet killing someone is legitimate if that person is threatening the safety of oneself or others. The police, for example, have a legitimate right to use 'reasonable force', but the situations in which that force is reasonable are often highly contested. How much force, for example, should be used to remove someone in a demonstration?

Another set of questions surrounds the intentions of the person committing the act. Did the person intend to harm someone? The drunken driver may not intend to injure anyone, but driving while under the influence of alcohol may reflect recklessness about the consequences of such an action. Is the factory manager who neglects to ensure the safety of workers similarly reckless, making this a 'real' rather than a 'technical' offence? Actions therefore have to be defined as criminal. Thus Howard Becker, whose work will be explored later, argued that crime is not an intrinsic property of any particular action or behaviour – it is the interpretation that others place upon it that makes it criminal (Becker 1963).

Changing legal definitions

Legal definitions of crime change over time and vary across cultures. In some countries the sale and consumption of alcohol is a crime, in others the sale and consumption of opium, heroin or cannabis is perfectly legal. While most criminal codes include murder, assault, theft and fraud, many other activities are subject to what is described as criminalization and decriminalization. In the 1960s so-called liberal legislation decriminalized aspects of homosexuality, abortion and prostitution, making many acts which were formerly criminal no longer so. It was argued, for example, that there were no direct victims and that the activities involved 'consenting adults'. Criminalizing these activities could also lead to participants becoming involved with other forms of crime, and law enforcement was expensive. Currently there have been arguments that the use of some soft drugs such as cannabis should be legalized. On the other hand, there have been recent calls for criminalizing a variety of behaviours such as stalking, racially motivated crime or knowingly passing on the HIV virus. Legal definitions of crime must therefore be considered alongside social constructions and political processes.

The social construction of crime

The legal definition of crime is therefore often distinguished from common-sense definitions, and in everyday speech the words crime or criminal assume a commonly understood or shared meaning. This reflects what sociologists call a social construction, in which 'crime' is a distinctive category constructed around the variety of meanings which are taken for granted in the description of an event, activity or a group of events or activities as 'crime'. They are taken for granted in that they are rarely expressed but widely accepted – everyone more or less knows what they mean by crime. The social construction of crime, or any other category, can be revealed by 'deconstructing', or taking apart, the construct and exploring its meanings. Examples of the kinds of question which do this are outlined below and many more examples will be given throughout this book.

How is 'crime' different?

The construction of crime can be illustrated by looking at what it includes and excludes. To Mars, 'crime', 'theft' and 'offence' are 'hard' words which can be differentiated from 'softer' words such as 'fiddle' or 'perk' which might be used to describe technically criminal activities in the workplace (Mars 1982). Similarly, the word 'con' might be used to describe something which does not quite amount to 'fraud', as might phrases such as 'creative accounting' or 'fiddling the books'. The word abuse, as in for example child abuse, elder abuse or sexual abuse, is often used to describe what are in effect forms of sexual and physical violence, and it distinguishes these acts from violent crime by placing them in a different category. Incidents in which people are killed or injured in a train crash or as a result of using unsafe equipment are generally described as 'accidents' or 'disasters' rather than as 'crimes', albeit they often result from a failure of transport operators or managers to comply with safety regulations (see, for example, Wells 1993). These different words compartmentalize different kinds of crime, with some crimes being excluded from the social construction of crime.

Criminals and victims

Crime is associated with 'criminals' and 'victims'. It has already been seen that not all those convicted of offences would be described as 'criminal'. On the other hand, it will be seen in subsequent chapters that crime is often associated with particular groups such as young men or the unemployed, some of whom can become 'folk devils', and identified with different forms of crime. Criminals are also often seen as 'strangers' or 'outsiders', whereas many crimes are committed by people known to their victims. It will also be seen in Chapter 5 that the concept of the victim is socially constructed. If, for example, someone is assaulted in a fight in which they themselves have participated, they would be seen as having provoked an assault and thus be distinguished from more 'deserving' victims such as a child assaulted by a stranger.

Constructing the 'crime problem'

The social construction of crime is reflected in media discussions and portrayals of crime, particularly in discussions of the 'crime problem'. When, for example, rising crime rates or policies aiming to 'crack down' on crime are discussed, the focus tends to be on rates of burglary or violent crime rather than on environmental crimes like pollution, or corporate crimes and major frauds. Thus they use a narrow definition and construct 'the' crime problem as being made up of particular kinds of crime. Recent discussions of how to 'tackle' crime have centred around tougher policies such as curfews for teenage offenders. This assumes that they are, in effect, 'the' crime problem whereas, as will be seen in Chapter 7, older people may well commit more serious crimes. It will also be seen in subsequent chapters that different kinds of crime such as violent or sexual crime are also socially constructed.

Crime, politics and criminalization

Social constructions and legal definitions are both related to political processes as laws are made in Parliament and social constructions may reflect political interests. Criminalization and decriminalization involve challenging the way in which crime is defined through campaigns undertaken by interested groups. Homosexuals, for example, campaigned to change the criminal status of homosexuality and business groups consult with government on laws which seek to regulate their activities. These may involve law enforcement as well as the law itself as not all laws are enforced with equal vigour and sentences may not reflect the assumed severity of offences. The police may want more powers to enforce some laws and others call for tougher sentencing. Alternatively, it may be argued that police activity is too hard or too soft. They have, for example, been criticized for acting too strongly against young people and demonstrators and for failing to deal strongly enough with domestic violence or racially motivated crime. The criminal law and its enforcement can therefore become hotly contested political issues. Some issues are outlined below, and these factors will also form a major theme in later chapters.

Political power and the law

Legal definitions of crime may reflect the operation of political power. It has often been suggested, for example, that the apparently more lenient treatment of offences committed by business groups reflects their ability to affect both the law and its enforcement. It has also been seen that the crime problem is often associated with young people, and the 1994 Criminal Justice and Public Order Act criminalized elements of squatting and rave parties and restricted the activities of new age travellers. This act, which prompted many demonstrations, was seen as an attack on the lifestyles of the young. The neglect of domestic violence has also been interpreted as reflecting women's relative powerlessness, and the treatment of racially motivated crimes could similarly be seen as indicating the powerlessness of minority ethnic groups.

The ideological construction of crime

Legal definitions and social constructions of crime can be seen as ideological, which means that they are supported and reinforced by a set of ideas and beliefs about crime and what constitutes the crime problem. These also reflect the balance of political power. It was mentioned above that many 'criminal offences' are not seen as part of the 'crime problem' whereas those of the least powerful groups, such as the crimes of young people, are seen as a major crime problem. In addition, as will be seen in later chapters, while the state

7

ultimately defines crime by passing laws against the activities of citizens, the crimes of the state and its agencies, such as war crimes or violence perpetrated by the police or army, are not generally constructed in the same way as other crimes.

CRIME AND SOCIETY IN BRITAIN

Crime and society

The phrase 'crime and society', used in the title of this book and in many sociology and criminology courses, assumes that crime is related to society. It has already been seen that crime is socially constructed and that its definition can be linked to wider structures of power. Crime is often perceived to be threatening the 'fabric of society' or as symptomatic of a breakdown in social order. It is generally seen as a social problem although to some sociologists, as will be seen in Chapter 3, it is inevitable. It can also be asked whether crime is better explained by looking at individual criminals or at their environment, culture or the social structure. This involves relating crime to social and economic change and to social inequality, by looking at whether some groups commit more crime or whether their crimes are more subject to criminalization. This section will introduce these issues, all of which form a major theme of this book.

Crime, culture and social structure

A major issue in the study of crime is the relationship between individual and social problems. In many ways crime appears to be an individual problem – individual offenders choose to commit an offence. This could be related to a number of personal problems, but individual decisions are made in a social context. One sociologist, C Wright Mills, pointed to the close relationship between individual and social problems, between personal troubles and public issues (Mills 1970). Unemployment, for example, may create personal problems such as marital breakdown, depression or suicide. The unemployment causing these problems is, however, linked to wider economic and social problems, and its solution may be beyond the individual's control. Individual choices to commit crime must therefore be seen in the context of their social environment and socio-economic situation.

This can be illustrated in a hypothetical situation in which an individual decides to commit a crime to resolve a short-term financial problem (which in itself may be caused by other problems). They must then consider what kind of crime to commit and how they can justify it. This will depend on their social environment. Within their social group, some offences might be tolerated more than others, and they might consider stealing from work which might be regarded with less disapproval. They can only do this, however, if they have the opportunity and are employed. The unemployed would have to consider other forms of crime such as shoplifting, theft or burglary, a choice which may similarly be affected by their local culture. Some might see shoplifting as more morally acceptable than burglary as it involves less direct harm to individual victims.

Crime and social change

Changes in the social and economic structure of society have often been associated with crime. Economic, social and technological changes affect the opportunities for crime and the forms of crime which are prevalent. Increasing amounts of money or goods in circulation means increasing opportunities for crime. Placing large numbers of consumer goods on display in shops not only tempts people to commit crime but provides a greater range of opportunities. Changes in business, commerce and technology also affect patterns of crime. In pre-industrial times wealthy travellers who carried large amounts of goods and money were vulnerable to the activities of highway robbers. This form of crime subsided as people travelled with less cash and money was held in banks, which then became the target of bank robbers. As money is increasingly transferred electronically, criminals must learn new techniques to cope with new technology (see Chapter 13). The development of cars and computers have created new forms of crime which require new laws to keep pace with them.

Social and economic change can also affect how likely individuals are to participate in crime, and many theories which will be reviewed in subsequent chapters have explored this. In very general terms the massive changes which accompanied the growth of industrial or modern societies were related to crime. These saw the breakdown of small, pre-industrial communities characterized by strong bonds of religion, family and morality. They also saw the rise of materialism and increased economic opportunities. The growth of the consumer society not only increased opportunities for crime, it also led many people to expect more than they could achieve, thereby providing a motivation to commit crime. The latter decades of this century have also seen major social and economic changes, including the decline of manufacturing industries and the growth of long-term unemployment. For many, family, economic, personal or consumer goals can no longer be achieved through legitimate employment. This, as will be seen in Chapter 6, has led to fears of rising crime.

Crime and social inequalities

Social inequalities have often been linked to crime and the majority of convicted offenders have been found to be men from lower-class backgrounds. Accordingly, many theories related crime to many aspects of lower-class life and culture and to poverty and deprivation. Later, the assumption that lower-class individuals were more likely to commit crime was criticized by those pointing to the largely undetected and unprosecuted crimes of upper-class offenders. Men and women have different conviction rates, raising the issue of how crime can be related to gender and conceptions of masculinity or femininity (see Chapter 8). Young people are also convicted of crime in far greater numbers than older people and for different kinds of crime, raising questions about how age may be related to crime and also to criminalization. Young people, being more likely to be 'hanging about' the streets, may be more likely to attract suspicion from the public or police (see Chapter 7). More recently attention has also been drawn to the different patterns of conviction of racial and ethnic groups (see Chapter 9).

These dimensions of inequality also affect victimization, which is not evenly distributed throughout society (see Chapter 5). Those who live in poorer inner city areas have a higher risk of being victimized by many forms of crime, and while the more affluent are not immune they can afford to protect themselves better. Women and men have very different experiences of victimization, with women being more likely to be injured and sexually assaulted at home and men more likely to be victimized in public places (see Chapters 5 and 10). Children, young people and the elderly are also vulnerable to family violence and young people have recently been found to be victims of a wide range of crimes. Members of racial and ethnic minorities are victimized by racially motivated offences.

Social inequalities therefore affect crime in diverse ways and the criminalization process is also relevant. It cannot be assumed that because any group are more likely to be convicted of crime that they actually commit more crime. As we have seen, the social construction of crime, the creation of law and its enforcement are in themselves related to social inequality. Thus the crimes of lower-class youth, mainly street crime, property crime and public disorder, may be subject to greater amounts of public intolerance, media complaint, criminal law and policing than the offences, often not seen as crime, of older people who, if they wish to commit crime, are more likely to embezzle, defraud or evade taxes than resort to street crime.

Crime in Britain

The British focus of this book can be justified on the grounds that it limits the amount of material to be included and it will emphasize British material and the relevance of theories of crime in a British context. But crime in Britain must be seen in both a local and international context. Many theories of crime have developed outside Britain but are nonetheless useful and relevant. Similar crimes occur across the world, albeit in slightly different forms and in different proportions. Crime itself is increasingly international, or global, and some forms transcend national boundaries. The illegal drugs trade and many forms of organized crime are multi-national criminal enterprises (see Chapter 13).

A focus on Britain raises some problems as the very word 'Britain' is in itself controversial especially in a period of devolution. The United Kingdom of Great Britain and Northern Ireland encompasses three different legal systems – those of Northern Ireland, Scotland, and England and Wales. There are also very different 'national' and 'regional' identities, cultural traditions and different experiences of economic change and inequality, all of which may affect crime. While popular and academic work often talks about crime in Britain, it often refers, without acknowledgement, to 'England' or 'England and Wales', without exploring any variations. This masks many differences – not least of which is the very different situation of Northern Ireland. Discussions of the issues surrounding race, ethnicity and crime should ideally take into account the different distribution of minority ethnic groups across Britain. Different cultural traditions may also affect the relevance of theoretical approaches – the study of violent criminal gangs, for example, may be less relevant in some cities than they are in Glasgow or the East End of London. While this book is not a comparative study of crime in Britain, it does aim to be sensitive to regional and national differences.

STRUCTURE OF THE BOOK

This book will explore how different kinds of crime are officially defined, socially constructed, researched and analysed. It will look at the relationships between crime and social inequality and apply these insights to specific patterns of crime. It aims to provide a comprehensive introduction to the study of crime and specific forms of crime and individual chapters will introduce relevant issues, theories and case studies. Detailed tables, charts and diagrams, widely available elsewhere, have been kept to the minimum necessary for illustration. The text should therefore be used along with supplementary texts, statistical material and research reports covering topics in more depth. To help readers, a short list of key reading accompanies each chapter along with a series of questions and exercises for those who wish to reflect on the issues raised.

Crime has been explored by a variety of different academic disciplines, including biology, psychology, psychiatry, economics, geography and sociology. Criminology is centred around the study of crime and criminal justice and incorporates a variety of these perspectives (see, for example, Muncie et al 1996; Maguire et al 1997). The focus of this book on crime and society has two main implications. Firstly, it emphasizes the social structural and cultural aspects of crime, mainly, though not exclusively, using sociological perspectives. Psychological and biological theories, while important, will not be covered in detail. Secondly, the book's focus is on crime rather than criminal justice policy. The two areas cannot be separated entirely as crime is legally defined and the activities of law enforcement agencies affect which crimes are subject to prosecution and conviction. Studying the actions and attitudes of criminal justice agencies is crucial for an understanding of crime, as are processes of law making and criminalization. Moreover, the study of crime is inextricably related to criminal justice policy and the significance of analyses of crime for policy will be discussed. Detailed discussions of specific policies lie beyond the scope of this text and are the subject of others (see, for example, Davies et al 1995; Newburn 1995).

The book is organized in three main parts as follows:

The main issues involved in researching and analysing crime and victimization

Chapter 2 looks at the problems and methods of researching crime and at sources of information about crime before giving a broad overview of aspects of crime in Britain. Chapters 3 and 4 are concerned with attempts to understand, explain and analyse crime. Chapter 3 deals with theoretical approaches which tried to explain crime by relating it to culture and social structure, while Chapter 4 looks at approaches which, having challenged many aspects of earlier theories, broadened the study of crime to include law enforcement, law making and social control. Chapter 5 turns to the often neglected victim of crime looking at the development of victimology, the impact of crime on victims and the fear of crime.

The relationship between crime and social inequality

Chapters 6 to 9 will examine the relationships between crime and social class, age, gender and race which were referred to earlier. Each chapter will start by looking at how these relationships have been defined, constructed and analysed before looking at the official picture in relation to offending and victimization. Different ways of approaching these relationships will then be explored, which will include asking whether figures reflect real differences or the processes of law enforcement and criminalization. The ordering of chapters does not imply that any one dimension is any more significant than others, and it will be argued that they are interrelated.

Chapter 6 looks at the long-held association between crime and social class, which has also been related to economic factors, social deprivation, poverty and, most recently, to the rise of an 'underclass'. Chapter 7 turns to the relationship between age, crime and victimization, where it will be seen that the activities of youth have been defined as a problem throughout history. It further explores the extent to which young people's structural position may make crime attractive along with increasing their vulnerability to victimization. Chapter 8 focuses on gender and crime by looking at how the lower conviction rates of women have been explained and will introduce feminist perspectives which have looked at women's crime and victimization, and at later approaches which argue that the study of crime and victimization must also involve looking at men and masculinity. Chapter 9 looks at the relationship between race, ethnicity, crime and victimization and issues raised by indications that some ethnic groups are over-represented in courts and prisons.

The role of enforcement agencies will be discussed along with arguments that some forms of crime have become criminalized by being identified with particular racial or ethnic groups who are also vulnerable to racial victimization.

Specific patterns of crime

Chapters 10 to 16 each focus on a specific form of crime, organized according to a combination of legal, commonsense and academic categorizations. Each chapter starts with a critical examination of how each category is defined and constructed, followed by a brief account of its scope and an evaluation of relevant figures on the extent of offending and victimization. Subsequent sections focus on specific issues and offences relevant to each category and on contemporary research and literature, some of which includes the accounts of offenders and victims. This is followed by an exploration of how different forms of crime have been approached by theoretical perspectives – drawing on, extending and re-evaluating approaches discussed in earlier chapters. Finally, some brief points will be made about the implications of these analyses for criminal justice and social policy.

Chapter 10 looks at violent crime and Chapter 11 at sexual offences although, as will be seen, these are difficult to separate and involve many similar considerations. Chapter 12 deals with offences which dominate the officially constructed area of property crime such as burglary, robbery and car theft, while Chapter 13 explores professional and organized crime and the changing organization of the criminal labour market. The drugs market, along with links between drug use and other forms of crime, is the subject of Chapter 14. Chapter 15 introduces the study of white collar and corporate crime, which is followed by a consideration of political and state crime in Chapter 16. Chapter 17 will attempt to draw out some of the major issues involved in the study of crime, will look at the international context within which crime in Britain must be analysed, and will discuss the significance of the study of crime and society for criminal justice policy.

Review Questions

1. Collect crime stories in newspapers over a few days. What kinds of crime are covered and how? How do they illustrate the fear and fascination of crime? How do they reflect what you understand by the social construction of crime?
2. Locate a dictionary definition of crime. How would you evaluate this in the light of the discussion of defining crime in this chapter?
3. Take one form of crime that was recently the subject of discussions about criminalization or decriminalization – for example, stalking, racially motivated crime, euthanasia, cannabis. What considerations could or should be taken into account in redefining these activities? What interests are involved?

Key Reading

Davies M, Croall H and Tyrer J (1995) *Criminal Justice: An Introduction to the Criminal Justice System in England and Wales*. London: Longman; Chapter 1

Heidensohn F (1989) *Crime and Society*. London: Macmillan; Chapter 1

Muncie J (1996) 'The Construction and Deconstruction of Crime', in Muncie J and McLaughlin E (eds) *The Problem of Crime*. London: Sage

Chapter 2

FINDING OUT ABOUT CRIME

While an enormous variety of information about crime is now available, finding out about any particular kind of crime is no easy task, and can be frustrating for both students and researchers. Official sources may not provide the kind of detail needed to investigate specific issues as much material is inevitably based on crimes which come to the attention of the authorities and crime has a large hidden figure which is difficult to penetrate. Much takes place in private, and criminals avoid making their activities public knowledge. They are not therefore readily available for research! Victims may not be aware that a crime has occurred or may fail to define incidents as crime. Criminals are dealt with behind the closed doors of the police station and in open court, and some offences and offenders are more likely than others to be officially counted.

Important questions must be asked about any information about crime. How was it collected? Why was it collected and by whom? Which kinds of offences have been counted and which not? This chapter will start by looking at the processes which produce official crimes and criminals and will then explore different ways of carrying out research into crime. This will be followed by an introduction to the main sources of data about crime and an outline of what they reveal about offences, offenders and victims. This chapter gives a broad outline and more details will be provided in relevant chapters. There are also books about criminal statistics (Bottomley and Pease 1986; Walker 1995; Coleman and Moynihan 1996), and most texts include a similar discussion (Davies et al 1995; Muncie and McLaughlin 1996; Maguire 1997).

PRODUCING CRIME AND CRIMINALS

The creation of official crime and offenders

Events do not come clearly labelled as 'crime' or as theft, assault, robbery or murder, and officially defined crimes are produced by a process in which events are defined and redefined, as illustrated in Figure 2.1. To be officially

Figure 2.1 Creating 'crimes' and 'criminals'

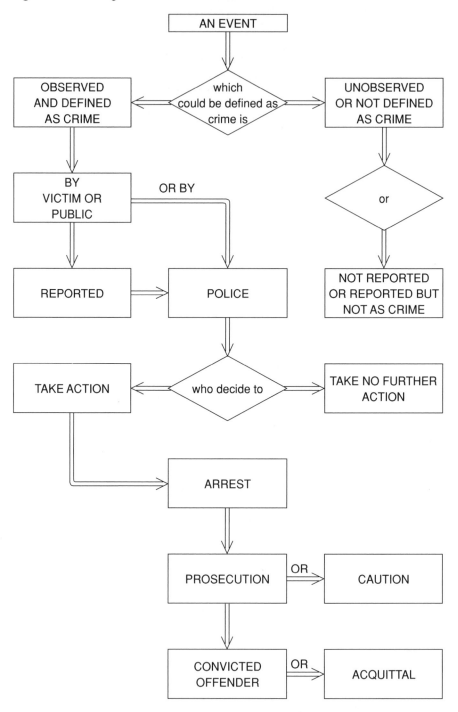

counted as crime, an event must be seen and interpreted by a member of the public, a victim or law enforcer, who must then decide to take further action. If a suspect is identified, the offence must be seen as serious enough and there must be enough evidence to justify prosecution. Only following conviction does a suspect become an official offender. The public, victims, police and other law enforcement agencies and prosecutors are therefore key definers of crime. Potential crimes and criminals disappear from this process at many stages in what has been described as a process of attrition. This section will explore these processes.

The role of the victim and the public

The role of victims and the public varies according to the offence. Some offences are relatively invisible and victims are totally unaware of any harm or of its potentially criminal nature. The sexual abuse of children, for example, usually takes place in private and children may not define the activities as crime or be in a position to report them. Other incidents may not be seen as important enough to bother with – small acts of vandalism, for example. Some activities may be culturally tolerated – how many people would report cannabis smoking at a party? Public tolerance may vary – country and town dwellers may tolerate different levels of crime or disorder. Even if the event is seen as serious enough to merit further action, criminal proceedings need not be involved. Suspicions of child abuse may be referred to social services, thefts of school property dealt with by the school itself, embezzlers may be quietly dismissed while shoddy goods or unfit food may become the subject of consumer complaints rather than police investigations.

Victim surveys, such as *The British Crime Survey* (BCS), reveal that many crimes are not reported to any official agency, which is also related to the offence. The 1996 BCS, for example, found that while 97 per cent of thefts of motor vehicles and 84 per cent of burglaries were reported, only 25 per cent of cases of vehicle vandalism, 34 per cent of common assaults and 40 per cent of thefts from the person were reported (Mirlees-Black et al 1996). Why do victims not report offences? Their reasons are summarized below using figures from the 1996 BCS for England and Wales (Mirlees-Black et al 1996):

- The incident is not seen as sufficiently serious (40%)

- The police wouldn't be able to do much about it (29%)

- The police wouldn't be interested (20%)

- The incident was not a matter for the police – better dealt with themselves (19%)

- Inconvenience (4%)

- Fear of reprisal (4%)

Assaults are more likely to involve fear of reprisals and a preference for dealing with the matter personally. Reporting rates for many property crimes, especially car theft, are higher particularly where victims are insured. Embarrassment and a fear of subsequent court appearances may deter victims of rape or domestic violence, or companies or banks who would rather conceal the frauds of their employees. On rarer occasions, victims may themselves be involved in crime – prostitutes or drugtakers may not report assault or theft as this might draw attention to their activities. Other victims may distrust or be hostile to the police.

The role of the police and law enforcement

Potential crimes come to the attention of the police and other law enforcement agencies in two main ways. They may be reported or directly encountered. Approximately 80 per cent of all recorded crimes are reported to the police by the public (Maguire 1997). Where there are no direct victims, for example with illegal drug use or prostitution, or where offences are difficult for victims to detect, such as pollution, the role of law enforcers becomes crucial. In other cases police officers on patrol encounter pub brawls, disturbances, public drunkenness or fighting. Here they have the discretion whether and how to intervene. Intervention may not lead to arrest or prosecution – they may be more concerned to calm down a situation and feel that heavy intervention might make it worse. In many situations the police act as mediators or as 'street politicians' (Brogden et al 1988). They are also, effectively, the judge, jury and sentencer as their decisions so crucially affect the subsequent process of a case.

Law enforcement decisions affect all subsequent stages. Not all complaints are recorded, creating a distinction between offences *reported* to and offences *recorded* by the police. Offences may not be recorded because they are not seen as serious enough or because they are subsequently defined as involving 'no crime' (see, for example, Coleman and Moynihan 1996). This may happen where articles reported as stolen are subsequently found, where there is insufficient evidence to proceed or because victims do not press for further action or withdraw their complaint. Incidents involving domestic disputes or pub brawls may similarly be reported as 'no crime'. This involves a vast number of incidents – around 40 per cent of crimes reported to the police do not end up in the criminal statistics (Maguire 1997). This affects the reliability of official statistics, especially as recording practices vary in different areas and may vary between England and Wales and Scotland, which has different recording procedures. Changes over time can create apparent crime waves. For example, official rates of rape increased during the 1980s as the police, responding to complaints that they did not treat women's reports of rape seriously or sympathetically, recorded a higher proportion of incidents.

Still further decisions affect the production of an official 'offender'. Not all crimes are 'cleared up' by identifying a suspect. While popular images of the police centre around their detective role, in reality, the vast majority of offences are cleared up because the informant can identify an offender, because offenders are 'caught in the act', or because their identity is obvious when the crime is discovered. In addition, in England and Wales, many crimes are cleared up because suspects admit further offences to prevent subsequent trials. Only around 26 per cent of offences recorded by the police in England and Wales are subsequently cleared up, with homicide having the highest clear-up rate at 88 per cent, followed by violence against the person and sexual offences, each at 77 per cent. Criminal damage and burglary have the lowest clear-up rates at 17 and 21 per cent respectively (Barclay 1995). In Scotland, 37 per cent of all recorded crimes are cleared up, with rates ranging from 64 per cent for non-sexual crimes of violence to 17 per cent for housebreaking (Scottish Office 1995). These variations reflect the nature of offences – where an assault is reported, the identity of the perpetrator is often obvious whereas burglars are less likely to be identified by victims.

Even where a perpetrator has been identified, they may not be prosecuted or convicted. Many complex issues underlie decisions by police and prosecution agencies to initiate criminal proceedings (see, for example, Ashworth 1994; Davies et al 1995), and procedures vary in the different legal systems of Britain. The police may decide not to proceed with a case against the sick, mentally ill, very young or very old, depending on the seriousness of the offence. They may not feel that they have enough evidence to prosecute or that the matter can be dealt in another way – by referral to the social services or for victim – offender mediation for example. They, or in Scotland the Procurator Fiscal, may decide to warn or caution offenders rather than prosecute – although in England and Wales official statistics refer to numbers of offenders cautioned and convicted.

The number of suspected or known but not convicted offenders is even higher, when the large numbers of offences not dealt with by the police but by enforcement agencies such as Consumer Protection or Environmental Health Officers are taken into account. The normal practice of many of these agencies is not to prosecute until all other avenues have been exhausted, and they have a number of options short of prosecution which may be seen as cheaper and more effective (see, for example, Croall 1992). Many other institutions, such as schools, companies, social services departments or the Inland Revenue, could refer cases to the police or prosecute themselves but do not do so – enlarging the number of 'offenders' who escape official designation.

What affects the decisions of these agencies? A vast amount of research has been carried out on this issue which has identified a number of factors including:

COST EFFECTIVENESS

Investigating and prosecuting offences is costly and, like any other public organization, law enforcers are encouraged to be 'cost effective'. There are not enough police officers to investigate *all* offences – this would be seen as a 'police state' – and activities are prioritized. Local and national pressures along with the attitudes of senior officers all affect these priorities and campaigns may be launched against particular offences such as burglary or street robbery. While the efficiency of law enforcement agencies can be measured in different ways, statistical measures of, for example, clear-up or arrest rates are often used. Police therefore tend to be sensitive about 'figures' (see, for example, Reiner 1992). Practices like 'no criming', taking no further action and clearing up crimes by taking others into consideration, have the advantage of improving these figures. Cost effectiveness may also affect decisions about prosecution – if a case is unsuccessful, law enforcers are criticized for wasting time and money and appear inefficient. It may be seen as more cost effective to settle a matter without prosecution by diverting the offender from the formal process by means of an informal settlement, warning or caution. This is particularly the case for non-police law enforcers.

OCCUPATIONAL CULTURES AND WORKING RULES

Law enforcement agents work within what sociologists describe as occupational cultures, which affect how they see their job, evaluate their performance, and develop day-to-day 'working rules' which affect how decisions are made (Leng et al 1992; Reiner 1992). Officers develop conceptions of which groups and areas are more likely to represent 'trouble' and how they can best be dealt with (Holdaway 1983). They may be subject to more attention and more use of formal processes. This can produce a 'self-fulfilling prophecy' which confirms the original definition. The culture of law enforcers also affects the kind of work that is most valued. Many studies of police officers reveal that they value 'real police work' which to them consists of, for example, the detection and prosecution of high-class 'villains' or the pursuit of suspects in high-speed car chases (Holdaway 1983; Reiner 1992). Opportunities for this kind of work are rare, and at a day-to-day level most police work involves far more mundane investigations and prosecutions, although arrests are seen as manifestations of 'real police work' and a sign of efficiency.

Other law enforcement agencies see their role differently. Regulatory enforcers such as tax inspectors, health and safety, environmental health or consumer protection officers see their main aim as being to secure high standards of compliance to better protect the public. Prosecution is only one way of achieving this. At the same time, they too have their stereotypes of rogues who merit greater attention and who are relatively easy targets. Tax inspectors, for example, target video stores and market stalls (Cook 1989), Environmental Health departments target take-aways (Croall 1989), and

Consumer Protection departments second-hand car dealers (Croall 1992). Cost and resource considerations may mean that serious frauds, which are more expensive to investigate and prosecute, may be neglected (Levi 1988).

MEDIA SENSITIVITY AND PUBLIC OPINION

In some cases police and prosecutors may respond to perceived public opinion and media sensitivity to particular issues. Recently, for example, there have been prosecutions in relation to alleged match fixing in football and assaults on football pitches which were not previously the subject of such attention. In addition, regulatory enforcers may choose to prosecute following high profile and serious incidents in response to perceived public pressure (Croall 1992).

Hidden crime and the process of attrition

Recognizing and understanding these processes has profound implications for studying crime. They underline the existence of an unknowable dark or hidden figure of crime, indeed Coleman and Moynihan call the first chapter of their book on crime figures 'Haunted by the dark figure: criminologists as ghostbusters' (Coleman and Moynihan 1996: 1). Official statistics on reported and recorded crime do not record real amounts of crime but how events are processed. Official offenders are those who have survived the process of attrition and are not representative of all who break the criminal law. The characteristics of offences and offenders may affect their chances of being detected or prosecuted. These processes also affect how crimes are classified as events are translated into offences of burglary, assault or criminal damage.

This process of attrition has been widely charted (see, for example, Barclay 1995; Davies et al 1995). Based on comparisons between BCS figures for England and Wales derived from victim reports and official records, Figure 2.2 provides a stark illustration of the net result of these processes. Out of all offences reported to the BCS by victims, in itself smaller than the true hidden figure, less than half are reported to the police. Just over a quarter are recorded, with less than 5 per cent being cleared up. The end result is that only 2 per cent of offences known to victims lead to a conviction. These figures vary for different offences, with 8 per cent of burglaries being cleared up compared to 19 per cent of woundings (Barclay 1995).

This clearly shows the danger of drawing any conclusions from figures of officially defined crimes or offenders. It can rarely be said with any certainty that any particular kind of crime is rising or falling, as apparent increases or decreases could merely represent a change in the proportion of crimes reported to or recorded by agencies. Offences which are more invisible and difficult to detect have a higher hidden figure than others. The relationship between age, gender, class and convictions may also reflect the vulnerability of different groups to detection and prosecution.

Figure 2.2 The process of attrition. Offences committed according to BCS, England and Wales

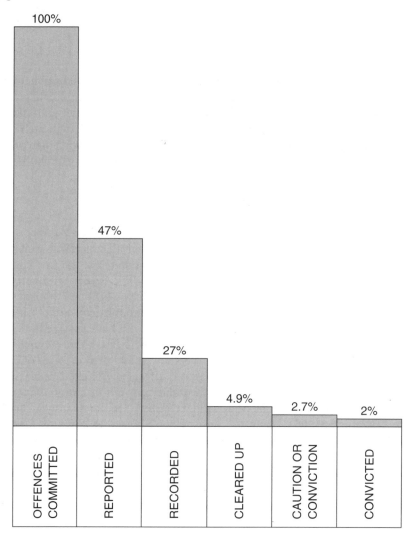

RESEARCHING CRIME

Social research

A variety of methods are used to study crime – including statistics, surveys, interviews, questionnaires, observation, case studies and biographies (see, for example, Jupp 1989). Research can be quantitative and qualitative, the former including statistics and large-scale surveys and the latter, which stresses the quality rather the quantity of information, using more detailed material obtained from offenders, victims or law enforcers. In deciding which methods to use, researchers must consider what resources are available, what questions they want to ask and how easily information can be gathered – which is particularly difficult with a topic involving crime.

Different groups of researchers are involved in researching crime. The Government sponsors research from outside agencies, and universities and academics – from senior researchers to research students – conduct research funded by the Government and a number of independent research organizations. In addition, a number of specialist research agencies and local councils, police and other criminal justice agencies, voluntary associations and special interest groups such as the Institute for the Study and Treatment of Delinquency (ISTD), the Howard League for Penal Reform and the National Association for the Care and Resettlement of Offenders (NACRO) and its Scottish and Northern Irish counterparts (SACRO and NIACRO) carry out research and compile reports into aspects of crime and the criminal justice process. Industrial organizations and special interest groups also conduct research, and while many of these reports are limited to specific interests, they can yield valuable information.

Accessing such a wide range of research can pose considerable problems. Academic research is published through books, reports or in academic journals such as the *British Journal of Criminology*, and many of these sources will be referred to throughout this text. Many libraries now have electronic and other abstracting services through which students can locate articles relevant to their own particular interests, and many reports are accompanied by good bibliographies. This section will begin by looking at the problems encountered by researchers before outlining the main forms of quantitative and qualitative research along with the major sources of information about crime such as official statistics and victim surveys.

The problems of researching crime

Accessing information

Many problems are encountered in researching crime, the first being accessing relevant material. While many official records and reports, often called secondary information, are now publicly available, they have many limitations. The researcher may therefore want to collect primary information, which means contacting public agencies who deal with crime, offenders or victims. This can pose considerable difficulties. Access to official agencies has to be negotiated and the researcher may encounter institutional barriers (Downes and Rock 1995). Agencies will inevitably want to know how the research results will be used, how widely it will be disseminated, what the purpose of the research is and who is carrying it out. They may be defensive in case their activities will be subject to scrutiny and potential criticism.

Even more problems face the researcher who wants to focus on offenders. Firstly, where can they be located? The first avenue is to approach those agencies which deal with offenders, but these offenders are inevitably unrepresentative. How can others be approached? Professional criminals, tax evaders, burglars and robbers do not advertise themselves and rarely practise their activities in public. Even if they are available, they too are likely to be highly suspicious. Researchers face other barriers. Their own backgrounds may limit access, and social class, age, ethnicity or gender may all pose problems. It may be difficult, for example, for a middle-class, middle-aged researcher to carry out qualitative research with a group of joy riders or vandals, or for a student or academic researcher to be admitted to the relatively closed world of the police or prison. To official agencies researchers may be feared as potential critics, whereas to offenders they might be seen as representatives of the criminal justice system. Care must be taken in how the research is presented, which is linked to moral and ethical problems. These difficulties also mean that a considerable amount of criminological research relies on official, government support, which limits the range of questions and issues that can be investigated.

Moral and ethical dilemmas

Research may be conducted for many reasons. It may aim to further knowledge about crime for its own sake or it may focus on a specific policy issue. It may be trying to understand and appreciate offenders and may explicitly or implicitly be critical of official agencies or government policies. Clearly, agencies are more likely to be sympathetic to researchers who appear to share their goals and whose research will be of use to them. This may compromise the objectivity of the researcher or the goals of the particular research. Similar considerations may affect research carried out with offenders or victims.

A good illustration of ethical difficulties is provided in studies where researchers have posed as members of criminal groups. This avoids the suspicion which their presence might arouse and avoids the researcher affecting the group's behaviour. Such covert research, however, involves many ethical considerations, not least of which is the dishonesty involved. In order to gain the respect of the group, researchers may be expected to participate in illegal activities and they inevitably gain information which could be of use to the police. Other questions are raised in considering how far researchers can intrude into private matters. Interviewing the victims of serious crimes involves asking them to re-live their experiences, of particular concern with sexual offences. Approaching offenders is also far from easy as they may be suspicious and, if they are in prison, may resent appearing to be guinea pigs.

Quantitative data

Statistics and large-scale surveys are often used to estimate the extent of offences, offending or victimization or to investigate trends. Surveys have also looked at the personal and social characteristics of offenders, at their social class or family backgrounds, their educational qualifications and employment records. These include:

- Official crime statistics.
- Comparisons of crime statistics with other relevant figures – for example, correlations between crime and unemployment or economic deprivation.
- Victim surveys.
- Self-report surveys which ask samples how much crime they have committed.
- Surveys measuring the personal characteristics of offenders.

Quantitative research produces extensive data but often provides few details, a typical example being a lengthy questionnaire given to sizeable samples which asks respondents to tick boxes or pre-designed responses. Such large-scale work is generally used as a basis to generate statistically valid estimates and relationships. National victim surveys, for example, have provided far more accurate estimates of the extent of some kinds of offences than official statistics as they include offences not reported to the police. Statistical work may also attempt to establish the nature of relationships between, for example, crime and unemployment or other economic indicators. Nonetheless, quantitative data suffers from many general problems and has to be interpreted with great care.

In the first place, it is often based on officially defined crimes and convicted offenders whose limitations have already been outlined. Statistics also require interpretation. How, for example, could a statistical association between intelligence and criminal convictions be interpreted? Are offenders less intelligent, or are the least intelligent offenders more likely to be caught? A correlation, however strong, is not a cause. In some cases statistics are further broken down, or disaggregated, to explore further questions. In looking at any relationship between crime and unemployment, questions have to be carefully constructed. We would not, for example, expect middle-aged redundant executives to rush out and commit street crimes and unemployment is most often associated with youth crime. Figures have therefore to be broken down to look, for example, at whether youth unemployment is related to youth crime. Even if a correlation is found, it does not tell us *why* young unemployed people might commit offences – to answer this we might do better to talk at length to young unemployed offenders. Quantitative research, therefore, often needs to be supplemented by qualitative issues. Many of these problems are illustrated in some of the main forms of quantitative data such as official statistics, victim and self-report studies explored below.

Official statistics and reports

Official statistics and reports are often used as a starting point for investigating crime or particular offences. The Home Office, along with the Scottish

Office and the Northern Ireland Office, collect a wide range of statistics which are published in bulletins and reports and the main sources are listed below.

- England and Wales: *The Criminal Statistics England and Wales; Judicial Statistics, Probation Statistics and Prison Statistics.* Scotland: *Recorded Crime in Scotland and Prison Statistics, Scotland.* Northern Ireland: *A commentary on Northern Ireland Crime Statistics.*

- The *Criminal Statistics* include information on: notifiable offences recorded and cleared up by the police; offenders found guilty or cautioned by police area, sex and age group; court proceedings; sentencing.

- Statistical bulletins are published on a variety of issues and summaries and reports of Home Office Research are available by application to relevant government departments.

- A summary of this information for England and Wales is provided in the *Criminal Justice Digest* (see, for example, Barclay 1995) which can be obtained, free of charge, from the Home Office.

- Reports of other relevant government departments: the *Annual Report of the Director General of Fair Trading*, for example, includes details about pro-secutions under Consumer Protection Legislation (Croall 1997).

While this information appears voluminous, it has all the limitations of quantitative data and some of the many questions which must be asked are indicated below.

- What do the figures include? A number of technical terms or broad cat-egories (for example, notifiable offences, personal crime or acquisitive crime) are used and their meaning must be clarified (see, for example, Davies et al 1995; Walker 1995).

- What do they leave out? Previous sections have stressed that some crimes are less likely to be observed, detected, prosecuted or convicted – how might this affect the figures? In addition, police records do not include criminal prosecutions made by other government agencies and depart-ments. They give very little information about, for example, tax evasion, many aspects of white collar crime or the activities of the British Transport Police (Walker 1995; Maguire 1997). Reports of relevant government departments must therefore be sought.

- What do they reveal about offences? Statistical information rarely gives many details about the seriousness or circumstances of offences.

- How are offences categorized? Which offences are included or omitted?

- How are they counted? Many technical factors affect how offences and offenders are 'counted' (see, for example, Walker 1995). Several offences may be committed 'in one incident' in which case only the most serious is counted. Where there is a 'continuous series of offences' such as using a stolen credit card several times, only one offence is counted (Coleman and Moynihan 1996).

- Have there been any changes in counting methods, reporting and recording methods and in the definition of offences which might affect rises and falls in the numbers of offences? This is often indicated in the small print accompanying tables.

Victim surveys

Since the 1980s, victim surveys which ask samples of the population how many crimes they, or members of their households, have experienced over a fixed period of time and whether or not these have been reported, have increasingly been used. Most often cited is *The British Crime Survey* (BCS) although this title is somewhat misleading as it most often refers to *The British Crime Survey, England and Wales* without making this clear (see, for example, Hough and Mayhew 1983; Mayhew et al 1989). Scotland was included in the 1982 and 1988 surveys with results separately published as *The British Crime Survey: Scotland* (Chambers and Tombs 1984; Kinsey and Anderson 1992; Payne 1992). A *Scottish Crime Survey* (SCS) with a broader geographical spread was carried out in 1993 (Anderson and Leitch 1994).

The victim survey has also been adopted by a large number of different agencies – local authorities and crime prevention organizations such as Crime Concern use them to explore local patterns to assist the development of policy, and special interest groups dealing with particular kinds of offences or victims also use them. Industrial, retail and other business organizations, omitted from the BCS, have also conducted their own surveys of losses from crime and there have been international victim surveys (Van Dijk and Mayhew 1993). While victim surveys will be more fully discussed in Chapter 5, their main limitations are summarized below.

- Most surveys use standard classifications of crime – reflecting the social construction of crime and missing out, for example, business crimes.

- The BCS is based on households – omitting business and institutional victims.

- Early studies interviewed only those over 16 years – omitting younger teenagers and children.

- Their results reflect respondents' definitions of events which may not be the same as legal classifications. They are also limited by respondents' memory.

- They are inevitably restricted to crimes which victims are aware of and miss out those which they cannot detect for themselves or have not defined as crime.

Self-report surveys

Self-report surveys ask groups of the population how many times they have participated in criminal activity (see, for example, Coleman and Moynihan 1996). They are often used with young people as classes of schoolchildren are relatively easy to gather together in one place. They aim to find out more about participation in crime than is revealed in official statistics and can provide more details about the class, age, sex or race of those who admit to offending. The BCS now includes a self-report study about the use of illegal drugs (Chapter 14). A growing number of surveys now combine questions about victimization, fears about and participation in crime (see, for example, Anderson et al 1994). They also have many limitations including:

- *The accuracy of responses.* Even where anonymity is assured, respondents, especially schoolchildren, fear that their answers will be seen by parents or teachers. This means that they may be reluctant to 'confess' to offences whereas others may exaggerate.

- *Their scope.* They have been largely restricted to young people and are less easy to plan for older people. It is difficult to envisage senior executives co-operating with a survey asking about tax evasion, insider dealing or fraud! Similarly difficult might be a survey asking people about how often they assault their partners.

Qualitative research

Qualitative research is more concerned with capturing the social meanings, constructions and definitions underpinning actions which cannot be 'captured' in qualitative research (Jupp 1989). It derives from interpretative sociology which argues that action cannot be understood without appreciating its meaning to those involved. Normally it involves lengthy interviewing or spending periods of time with a small number of people – usually offenders, victims or law enforcers. It explores how they perceive their experiences and actions and is often accompanied by illuminating examples of these attitudes. It is interpretative and all material has to be interpreted as objectively as possible by the researcher.

The classic way of gathering qualitative data is to carry out extensive field work with small groups, often described as participant observation or ethnography. This has a long tradition in the sociology of crime and deviance. It can be covert or overt – the latter being where the researcher openly observes and communicates with the group. In classic observation work the researcher lived with a group over a period of time, participated in their activities and attempted to appreciate their behaviour and lifestyle as fully as possible. During the 1950s and 1960s a number of these studies were carried out in many parts of Britain with juvenile delinquents, school students, on street corners or in gangs, and they will be referred to in later chapters (see, for example, Downes 1966; Patrick 1973; Parker 1974). Control agencies have also been studied in this way, illustrating how they view their role and what affects their decisions (see, for example, Cain 1973; Holdaway 1983; Hobbs 1991).

This kind of research has many limitations and the problems of access and ethical dilemmas have already been pointed out. Field work is also costly and time consuming to conduct. Researchers must remain in the field long enough to gain acceptance and fully appreciate the group. Field notes must be rigorously maintained and dangers of over-involvement avoided. Researchers must try to avoid contaminating the data with their own preconceptions and value judgements. While the covert researcher faces the ethical dilemmas of concealment, the overt researcher faces the problem that their very presence may change the group's behaviour. The material gathered can only be representative of one place and period of time and is restricted to accessible groups. There are, perhaps unsurprisingly, few ethnographic studies of crime in the stock exchange, tax evasion or political crime – as academics are generally not invited into positions to complete such studies! Serial killers, drug 'barons' and sex offenders are similarly difficult to access. Delinquent youth, drug takers and other groups whose activities are more public have been much more likely to be the subject of ethnographic research.

This kind of research is far less common than it once was. It is not, however, the only way of gathering qualitative data. In-depth interviews can be carried out with small, strategically chosen groups of offenders, victims or law enforcers which focus on similar issues. Case studies and biographies can be used where few other sources of information exist – as might be the case with historical research or research on relatively inaccessible groups of offenders such as professional criminals (Hobbs 1994). These share the limitations outlined above – they often use only small numbers who may not be representative and are inevitably based on respondents' recollections and interpretations of their behaviour. As Hobbs points out, autobiographies of notorious offenders may be written with the film in mind! (Hobbs 1994).

Research solutions

These difficulties do limit the kinds of research which can be conducted and have arguably led to an over-reliance on officially available information and the use of offenders in institutions who provide captive populations (Downes and Rock 1995). Some methods can partly overcome these problems, including those described below.

- *Snowball samples*. These aim to locate offenders who are not known to agencies. A small number of initial contacts, who may come from the researcher's own personal or professional network or are contacted through agencies, are asked to provide, in confidence, names of other offenders, who in turn provide further names. This has been used in studies of drugtaking and burglary (Parker et al 1988; Wright and Decker 1994). While this widens the scope of a sample, it may not be entirely representative as it depends on the breadth of the initial contact's network. It is also restricted to situations where groups of offenders know each other.

- *Public observation.* Some crime is carried out in relatively public areas making it easier to observe and contact participants (Downes and Rock 1995). Many classic studies were carried out with youth gangs hanging about street corners, or sitting in pubs and clubs (see, for example, Whyte 1943; Downes 1966; Foster 1990). Other forms of crime are carried out in more public, organized settings – the researcher interested in football hooliganism may start by attending matches. In a recent study of prostitution, researchers contacted prostitutes in the local red light area (McKeganey and Barnard 1996). Care has to be taken of course to avoid overtly dangerous situations – it is not advised, for example, to hang around with a violent gang! (Patrick 1973).

- *Criminal courts.* While crime and criminals are largely dealt with behind closed doors, trials in courtrooms are normally open to the public. Some useful and interesting research has been carried out by observing interactions between offenders and controllers, the behaviour, statements or 'accounts' of offenders, the treatment of different kinds of offenders, the attitude of sentencers and experiences of victims (see, for example, Carlen 1976; Eaton 1986; Croall 1988; Rock 1991).

Despite all these problems research does produce invaluable information. Methods can be used in conjunction with each other, with quantitative material being used to supplement qualitative, and quantitative techniques being used to analyse qualitative material. Another source of useful material is the mass media.

Mass and electronic media

What has been described as the 'information society' has produced a virtual explosion of material, and the news media, used with caution, can be invaluable. For some kinds of crime, particularly those not well covered in official data, investigative journalism and documentaries can provide useful descriptive detail and in-depth interviews. Newspapers also report the findings of surveys and reports, which can be followed up by applying to the source. Analysing the media by deconstructing and examining its ideological content has in itself become a major form of research into how crime is defined and socially and ideologically constructed. Popular literature on crime can also be used in this way. Using media and literary sources does have limitations. They do not claim to be representative and may not cover the issues which students wish to explore.

Statistics, reports and newspaper articles may be available via electronic media such as the internet or on CD roms. Information on the internet is extremely variable in quality, but, like newspaper articles, can be a useful starting point. Many of the organizations referred to above have websites and use these to announce the publication of reports. Some criminal statistics are also accessible through the internet and there are a number of criminological websites. Abstracts of articles and newspapers are available on CD roms which enable speedier and more accurate searches for relevant articles – although it is important to point out that almost too much information can be found in this way! As with the mass media, any research reports accessed through the internet must be very carefully checked and, where possible, 'hard copy' should be obtained.

INFORMATION ABOUT CRIME

Despite all their limitations, official statistics, victim surveys and other forms of research are essential sources. They chart amounts of officially recorded crimes along with rising and falling rates and provide details about offending and victimization. They are also used to explore international, national, regional and local variations in crime rates. While many of these will be discussed in more detail in subsequent chapters, the following section provides a broad overview of some of the major features of crime revealed by these sources.

Counting crime

Is crime rising?

Crime is popularly assumed to be rising, and recorded crime has increased enormously during the twentieth century, despite annual fluctuations. For England and Wales this can be illustrated by the following points:

- Before the 1920s fewer than 100,000 offences were recorded annually, whereas in 1994 five million notifiable offences were recorded (Barclay 1995).

- Annual figures changed little until the 1930s, rose up to and during the Second World War, and increased sharply from the mid-1950s onwards. They doubled between 1955 and 1964, doubled again up to 1974 and yet again by 1990 (Maguire 1997).

- 3.4 notifiable offences were recorded per 1,000 population in 1971, rising to 10 by 1991 (Walker 1995).

These figures may not, of course, reflect any 'real' change in crime. Maguire, for example, suggests that increasing numbers of police officers, an increase in telephones making reporting easier, increasing use of insurance and reduced levels of public tolerance to violence have all contributed. The demise of close knit communities could also make people more likely to call in the police than sort things out for themselves (Maguire 1997). In addition, new crimes have been created and there have been changes in how offences are counted and classified.

The advent of victim surveys has enabled some exploration of the extent to which rising rates reflect an increase in reporting. BCS figures suggest that while from 1981 to 1991 the police recorded 100 per cent more offences, victims reported only a 50 per cent increase (Walker 1995; Maguire 1997). This varies for different offences with 'acquisitive crime' rising at a rate closer to that suggested by police figures (Walker 1995; Maguire 1997). At least part of the increase, therefore, is accounted for by changes in reporting. Changes in police recording methods are also important, as are changes in police policy. Increases in drug trafficking in the 1980s could be explained by more aggressive policing (Maguire 1997).

The extent to which crime has really risen remains unknowable although it is likely that there has been a rise in *some* kinds of crime. The many factors involved, including increasing opportunities and the economic and social changes referred to in Chapter 1, will be explored in more depth in subsequent chapters. The importance of opportunities is indicated in the growth of crime involving motor vehicles, which now comprise 28 per cent of total recorded crime in England and Wales (Coleman and Moynihan 1996). Nonetheless, offences involving motor vehicles have risen faster than car ownership (Walker 1995). The relationship with economic and social change is complex as crime appears to have increased through very different conditions. As Coleman and Moynihan (1996: 121) point out:

> Through a world war, full employment, the swinging sixties, hyper inflation and economic decline, the crime rate has doggedly continued its skyward projection, apparently unstoppable.

Offences

Looking at specific offence groups is also important. While Chapters 10 to 16 will provide fuller details about specific forms of crime, it is useful to look at the overall pattern. Figure 2.3, based on official statistics, lists the proportions of offence types recorded by the police in England and Wales in 1994 and reveals some interesting features. While dramatic cases of murder, rape, robbery, sex and violence feature highly in popular representations of crime, the category of violent crime, which includes all these offences, forms a mere 6 per cent of the total. Property crime dominates with theft accounting for nearly one half of all recorded crimes and burglary for nearly one quarter.

Figure 2.3 Offences as a proportion of recorded crime: England and Wales 1994

Vehicle crime (including theft of and from motor cars)	26%
Burglary	24%
'Other theft' (including theft from the person, shoplifting)	23%
Other offences	21%
Violent crime (includes robbery, sexual offences and wounding)	6%
(After Barclay 1995)	

These, of course, have to be considered alongside reporting and recording variations – latest BCS figures for England and Wales indicate that burglary forms a far lower proportion of crimes reported by victims whereas far higher amounts of vandalism and common assaults are reported to the BCS than to the police (Mirlees-Black et al 1996). According to BCS estimates in 1991, only 24 per cent of all assaults are eventually recorded (Walker 1995). While the figures for assault have increased, this 'appears to be due to an increase in the reporting of the offence to the police, perhaps due to a lower tolerance of violent behaviour' (Walker 1995: 14).

Changes in crime rates reflect changes in specific offence groups. The large increase in crimes involving motor cars has already been referred to, and the highest increases in recent decades have also involved criminal damage and property offences (Maguire 1997). BCS figures, however, show slightly smaller increases in these and steeper rises in acquisitive crimes (Mirlees-Black et al 1996). Looking in more detail at specific offence categories also reveals some interesting features. Ninety per cent of the category of violent crime is made up of relatively minor woundings (Maguire 1997). Sexual offences, which constitute only 1 per cent of the total, have also increased in recent years. Rape has risen from 1,000 in 1981 to 16,000 in 1991; however, as already seen, this may be due to reporting and recording differences. These figures must also be set against the vast amounts of offences unreported to the police or victim surveys. Large amounts of theft in the workplace or in schools are not covered by victim surveys and are often not reported to the police. Large numbers of summary offences, which include minor assaults and frauds and much family violence and white collar crime, are also omitted.

Offenders

While numbers of recorded crimes have risen, numbers of convicted offenders have fallen – decreasing from 568,000 to 518,000 between 1981 and 1991 (Walker 1995). This is probably due to larger numbers of young offenders being diverted from the criminal justice process but also underlines the attrition process. Information about the characteristics of offenders comes from two main sources. The criminal statistics give details about the age and sex of offenders. Prison statistics give information about occupational status and race although these refer to the even smaller proportion of offenders who end up in prison. Some of the characteristics of offenders have already been referred to, along with the dangers of drawing any conclusions from such a small proportion. Figure 2.4 summarizes available information and confirms the characteristics outlined in Chapter 1. Young people and men predominate known offenders and ethnic minorities and offenders from lower classes are over-represented in the prison population. Thus Maguire, while acknowledging that prison figures are taken from the even smaller group of offenders who are imprisoned, argues that in comparison with the general population, the prison population contains

Figure 2.4 Characteristics of convicted offenders

Age (in 1994 in England and Wales)
- 43 per cent of known offenders were under 21

- one-quarter were aged under 18

- the peak age for offenders was 18 for males and 14 for females (Barclay 1995)

Sex (in 1994 in England and Wales)
- 81 per cent of convicted offenders were male

- 34 per cent of males and 8 per cent of females will be convicted for a standard list offence by the time they are 40 (Barclay 1995)

Ethnicity (in 1994 in England and Wales)
- 12 per cent of the male prison population were from ethnic minority communities compared with 5 per cent of the population (Barclay 1995)

Occupational status
A survey published in 1992 of prisoners in England and Wales found that:

- 18 per cent were from Registrar General's Classes I, II and III non-manual (compared with 45 per cent in the general population)

- 41 per cent were from class III manual (compared with 37 per cent in the general population)

- 41 per cent were from classes IV and V (compared with 19 per cent of the general population)

(Walmsley et al 1992, cited in Coleman and Moynihan 1996: 104)

---

many more males, young people, black people, poor people, poorly educated people and people with disturbed childhoods than one would find in a random sample.

(Maguire 1997: 174)

It has also been pointed out that these figures do not represent any real differences in offending. This can be clearly seen if we consider some of the offences which are most and least likely to be processed. We have already seen that young people's offences are more likely to be visible and more easily caught, and lower-class young men may well become more easy targets of the police. On the other hand, the gender ratio might alter significantly if participation in family violence was to be more accurately reflected. This could also change if fuller details of participation in white collar crime was known, as it is often assumed to be male dominated (Levi 1994), and would also increase the numbers of middle-class offenders.

34

Figure 2.5 Characteristics of victimization

- The risk of crime is related to a victim's age, gender and lifestyle.

- Men are more likely to be victims of violence and robbery than women.

- Men aged between 16 and 24 are most at risk from assaults.

- Women are more likely to be victims of theft from the person and from assault in the home.

- Elderly women and men have the lowest risk of assault: 26 and 65 per 100,000 of the population.

Victims

The growth of victim surveys has vastly increased knowledge about victims and victimization. Some general features are summarised in Figure 2.5, which challenge some popular images. Old people appear to have a lower risk of assault or robbery, despite the publicity given to attacks on them. Women are far more likely to be raped by acquaintances and murdered by spouses or lovers than by strangers. Young men, who feature highly among offenders, are more vulnerable to assault and robbery. This is generally assumed to reflect their lifestyles as they are more likely to go to pubs and clubs where the majority of recorded assaults take place. They are more likely than women to be murdered by a stranger and less likely to be murdered by spouses or lovers. These figures must also, of course, be considered in the context of crimes which are less likely to be counted (see Chapter 10). The elderly and the very young are vulnerable to abuse in the home and members of racial and ethnic minorities are more at risk from many kinds of crime and perceive some as being racially motivated (see Chapter 9).

THE DISTRIBUTION OF CRIME

Whether viewed in terms of offending or victimization, crime is not evenly distributed throughout the population. It also varies across Britain and by the kind of area in which people live. Some of these variations will now be explored.

National and regional patterns

Thus far figures have emphasized England and Wales, largely reflecting most discussions of official figures. There are, however, interesting variations within Britain, and between Britain and other countries. It is extremely difficult to compare recorded crime rates across countries, even within the UK, because of different offence categories, reporting and recording procedures and prosecution processes. Victim surveys enable better comparisons to be made as they can ask standard questions to samples in different countries. The publication of the most recent international crime survey caused headline news as it indicated that England and Wales were at the 'Top of the Crime League' (*Guardian* 26/5/97: 1), having the highest rate of victimization of seventeen countries. In England and Wales and the Netherlands, over 30 per cent of the population reported at least one crime in the last twelve months, compared with between 24 and 27 per cent in Scotland, the US, Canada, France and Switzerland, and under 20 per cent in Sweden, Finland, Austria and Northern Ireland with the latter having the lowest rate of all. England and Wales had the highest rates of victimization from burglary and contact crime and more people felt unsafe when going out at night (Travis 1997).

This shows considerable differences between England and Wales, Scotland and Northern Ireland which were also revealed in earlier international surveys which found England and Wales to have a comparatively high rate of victimization, Scotland a medium rate, and Northern Ireland a low rate (Van Dijk and Mayhew 1993; Barclay 1995).

Differences between Scotland and England and Wales are shown in Figure 2.6. This indicates a lower rate of victimization in Scotland, which has emerged from successive victim surveys. In the early 1980s it was assumed, on the basis of popular imagery and recorded crime figures, that Scotland had a

Figure 2.6 Victimization rates in Scotland and England and Wales per 10,000 of the population

Offence	Scotland	England and Wales
Housebreaking/Burglary	607	678
All vehicle thefts	1,188	1,891
Bicycle thefts	127	280
Theft from the person	50	108
Vandalism	1,048	1,357
Assault	380	586
Robbery	31	45
Other household thefts	746	913
Other personal thefts	272	429
Total household	**3,716**	**5,119**
Total personal	**733**	**1,168**

(After Anderson and Leitch 1994)
Figures for 1992 Scotland (reported to 1993 SCS) and 1991 England and Wales (reported to 1992 BCS)

higher crime rate. The 1982 BCS indicated that people reported more crime in Scotland, and while in England and Wales during the 1980s both the BCS and recorded crime statistics charted a rise in both victimization and reporting, in Scotland, figures showed an increase in reporting but a fall in recorded crime – household crime remained similar but personal crime fell (Kinsey and Anderson 1992). Differences widened when the 1992 BCS was compared to the 1993 SCS (Anderson and Leitch 1994). In addition, Scottish cities did not experience the scale of public disorder experienced in many English cities in the 1980s and early 1990s (Fyfe 1997). This does not mean that crime is seen as less of a problem in Scotland, with over one million crimes annually reported by victims and people in Scotland reporting increasing fears of crime (Anderson and Leitch 1994).

Local variations

There are also regional and local variations in victimization, some of which can be accounted for by differences in reporting and recording practices (Coleman and Moynihan 1996). In general terms victim surveys reveal that urban areas have higher rates than rural, and inner city areas have higher rates than suburbs (see, for example, Barclay 1995). But not all inner city areas have higher rates of crime and crime rates are related to a variety of factors including the kind of area in which people live which are not always reflected in the broad distinction between inner city and suburban areas. Geographical differences are related to social differences, which is illustrated in the way in which victimization rates are spread between different types of areas (Mayhew and Mirlees-Black 1993; Fyfe 1997). These are summarized below:

- *High-risk areas* consist of mixed inner metropolitan areas, high-status non-family areas and poorest council estates.

- *Medium-risk areas* consist of better-off council estates, older terraced housing and less well-off council estates.

- *Low-risk areas* consist of agricultural areas, better-off retirement areas, modern family housing for higher income groups, affluent suburban housing and older housing of intermediate status.

Even within these areas, local differences are found with pockets of high crime. This may be related to the lifestyle and culture of their inhabitants. Different kinds of crime exist in what geographers call micro-environments. The risk of crime differs according to age and gender which are in turn related to lifestyle. Young men are more likely to be the victims of assaults in or outside pubs and clubs while women are more vulnerable to assaults in the home. Some men and women may be more vulnerable when they are going to and from work. Home, work and the street are therefore described as sites of crime (see, for example, Fyfe 1997).

CONCLUDING COMMENTS

This chapter has looked at the processes which transform events into crimes and people into criminals. Appreciating this process is vital before any conclusions can be drawn from official crime figures. The chapter then explored the many ways of researching crime and the major sources of information about it. While all of these have limitations, from them we can gain an initial picture of officially recorded crime. This in itself corrects some misleading assumptions – although findings that violent and sexual offending are often trivial and form such a small percentage of known crime, this should not be taken to indicate that they are not serious and often under-reported problems. In addition, they illustrate the way in which crime is socially distributed – more convicted offenders are young, male and lower class, as are more victims. Again these should not be taken to indicate real differences as this pattern could change if crimes we know little about could be counted.

We can find out more about some kinds of crime than others – where there is visible harm, a direct victim and an identifiable offender, as in serious assaults taking place in public, they are more likely to be detected, reported and recorded. Many others involve less visible harm, indirect or diffuse victimization and the offender cannot be identified. Family violence and white collar crime, for example, were identified as offences we know least about. Any discussions of trends and patterns in crime or the characteristics of known offenders must take this into account. Other limitations of statistics and surveys must be recognized. In many cases they may suggest an association but cannot explain it. This is attempted by the theoretical approaches which will be explored in Chapters 3 and 4.

Review Questions

These are based on a hypothetical exercise in which you are asked to carry out research on a particular form of crime. You should choose a form of crime which particularly interests you and consider what kinds of question you want to ask and what kinds of research you might carry out. You will also wish to consider:

1. (a) What information would you like to gather?
   (b) Where would you locate it?
   (c) What problems might you encounter?
   (d) What kinds of research are most appropriate for this particular form of crime and the question you are asking?
2. (a) How is the particular form of crime defined?
   (b) How is it affected by the processes of defining and producing crime and offenders discussed in this chapter?
3. (a) What kinds of information are widely available?
   (b) What can be learnt from official statistics and victim surveys? (This should involve locating relevant statistics.)

(c) What other kinds of information are available?

(d) What are the main limitations of these sources for the particular form of crime which you are investigating?

Key Reading

Coleman C and Moynihan J (1996) *Understanding Crime Data: Haunted by the Dark Figure.* Buckingham: Open University Press

Maguire M (1997) 'Crime Statistics, Patterns and Trends: Changing Perceptions and their Implications', in Maguire M, Morgan R and Reiner R (eds) *The Oxford Handbook of Criminology*, 2nd edition. Oxford: Clarendon Press

Muncie J (1996) 'The Construction and Deconstruction of Crime', in Muncie J and McLaughlin E (eds) *The Problem of Crime.* London: Sage

Walker M (ed) (1995) *Interpreting Crime Statistics.* Oxford: Clarendon Press

Chapter 3

UNDERSTANDING CRIME: CRIME, CULTURE AND SOCIAL STRUCTURE

In the lurid headlines which accompany serious crimes, offenders are often described as beasts, animals and psychopaths, as deranged and crazed, or as mindless morons, implying that they are somehow abnormal and 'sick'. Crime itself can be described as a disease, as a cancer attacking the fabric of society which flourishes in the decaying areas of cities or in diseased or 'rotten' cultures. These popular images assume that crime is the result of a disease or 'pathology', and they echo the themes of academic disciplines which tried to find the causes of crime. The late nineteenth and early twentieth centuries saw the growth of what is often called the modernist project in which it was believed that modern scientific methods could be applied to all social phenomena, including crime. This reflected the optimism of an era in which scientific and industrial progress had fuelled the development of new, modern, societies. Crime, which was assumed to be a problem, could be systematically measured, its causes scientifically established and a cure found. The criminal statistics, themselves produced by modern statistical methods, were largely assumed to measure crime. The main question these approaches asked was, 'Why do offenders commit crime?'.

Many different fields of study were involved. Biologists argued that criminals were 'born' with a biological abnormality and psychologists examined the criminal's mind, personality or temperament and investigated the link between mental illness and crime. To sociologists, the problem was identified as social rather than individual. Some likened society to a body, with crime threatening its health, whereas to others the problem lay in cultures, or subcultures, within which crime was valued or in the problems of urban growth. A common theme in all these approaches is that crime is seen as a problem, as a sign of something wrong or absent, as a deficit or pathology.

This chapter will introduce some of these approaches. It will start by outlining individual theories which, while the focus of this text is on sociological approaches, are essential to our understanding of the development of social theories which built on their perceived limitations. Subsequent sections will introduce some of the most influential early sociological approaches which developed in the late nineteenth century. This will begin by looking at Durkheim's arguments about the normality of crime and will move on to

40

consider the anomie perspective, social disorganization and subcultural theories. Each section will outline a different approach and look at its strengths and weaknesses.

THE PATHOLOGICAL OFFENDER

A major task of early criminological research was to identify what distinguished offenders from non-offenders. An enormous range of characteristics were investigated and this section will focus on biological and psychological approaches as these most clearly illustrate the research and thinking involved. Researchers used what were seen as experimental methods, based on quantitative research, which compared samples of convicted offenders with samples of the so-called normal, non-criminal population. These aimed to isolate what made criminals 'different' and they were, in effect, trying to develop a formula which could be expressed, for example, as, *'criminal parent + aggressive personality + broken home = crime'*. As will be seen later, these methods had many problems.

Are criminals 'born' or 'made'?

Some of the earliest theories hypothesized that crime was biologically determined and could be inherited. Often quoted is the work of early criminologists such as Lombroso, who, working in the late nineteenth century, claimed that criminals were biological throwbacks to an earlier stage of evolution and were distinguished by their body type. Others explored the extent to which criminality could be inherited and criminality, like illness, has also been related to biochemical conditions. These main themes are summarized below.

Body types

From studies of offenders in custody, Lombroso concluded that they were distinguished by physical stigmata such as distinctive torsos, large hands, feet and tattoos (Lombroso 1897). Later theories linked crime to athletic body types which were associated with aggression and many studies up to the middle of the twentieth century measured physical characteristics such as height and weight (Sheldon 1949: Glueck and Glueck 1950; Williams 1994). It is difficult however to establish how these factors are related to criminality. While it might be assumed that some offences require physical strength and thereby be related to body size, many others, fraud for example, do not. In addition, physical features are related to social expectations and stereotypes – we might expect athletically built people to be aggressive.

Inherited criminality?

Others asked whether criminality could be inherited, like hair colour. One way of exploring this was to look at whether identical twins were both likely to be criminal taking account of the possible effects of their similar environment. Identical twins reared apart were investigated and while some association was found it was extremely difficult to separate biological inheritance from the environment as, even when adopted, twins may be reared in similar social and economic circumstances (Christiansen 1974 and see Williams 1994). An apparently more promising way of looking at biological inheritance emerged with the discovery of the 'criminal gene'. Inmates from an institution for offenders considered to be 'insane' were discovered to have a different pattern of chromosomes – an extra 'Y' chromosome was subsequently linked to greater height and aggression. Later studies found, however, that this affected only a small proportion of the population and was found among non-criminals (Jacobs et al 1965; Watkin et al 1977 and see Williams 1994).

Biochemistry and crime?

Other biological approaches have investigated the possible role of biochemical processes in the brain – which may not be inborn, but a result of allergies, glandular problems, diet or even the consumption of junk food which contains chemicals. Children affected by food allergies or glandular disorders may suffer from hyperactivity making them less likely to learn social skills, and more difficult to discipline (see, for example, Williams 1994).

There are many problems with these approaches and with the methods they used, which almost always relied on samples of convicted offenders. Their main problems can broadly be summarized as follows:

Can they establish the causes of crime?

In order to argue that biological factors 'cause' crime, a very strong relationship would be necessary. Yet none of the characteristics found among samples of offenders is unique to criminals as they are also found among non-offenders and so-called 'normal' people. In addition, many of these features are found in only a small number of offenders and affect only some kinds of offending.

Crime is socially constructed

A major problem with these theories is that, as seen in Chapter 1, crime is socially constructed. Its definition is dependent on cultural and social definitions and it encompasses a vast range of behaviour which is not consistently regarded as crime. How, therefore, can a tendency towards crime be biologically determined? Even if it could be assumed that a tendency to aggression could be inherited, whether or not aggression is interpreted as criminal depends on its social and cultural context. The boxer or soldier, for example, may be expected and indeed encouraged to display aggression, but this is tightly defined by rules.

Born or made?

Another major problem is illustrated in what is often referred to as the 'nature–nurture' debate – how much is inborn and how much affected by the environment? Body type, for example, can be related to diet, which is in turn related to social class and environmental factors. Children may not only inherit genetic characteristics but also learn a set of values from their parents. Thus if a child of criminal parents offends, it could be because they have learnt criminal values rather than being a result of their genetic inheritance.

The 'mad' and the 'bad'

Similar problems are encountered in exploring links between psychological traits and crime, which has been the subject of considerable research (see, for example, Hollin 1989). Crime has been linked to personality and to mental illness, in themselves difficult to define and measure. It is also debatable whether psychological dispositions can be inherited or are a product of the environment. This section will selectively focus on some major themes of this research while other psychological approaches will be encountered later.

The criminal personality?

It is often argued that some kinds of personality are related to crime – thus Eysenck related criminality to extremes of extraversion or neuroticism (Eysenck 1977). While some studies did indeed find that young offenders in institutions scored highly on these scales – this could be associated with being caught or with the experience of institutional life.

The criminal psychopath?

Serious criminals are often popularly depicted as psychopaths, although this term is difficult to define. It is often associated with an inability to form loving relationships, a lack of responsibility for actions, a failure to feel or admit guilt and aggressiveness. However studies of psychopaths have mainly been carried out with institutionalized populations and there may be many so-called normal persons with these characteristics who have committed no serious crimes. They could also be a result of incarceration. Thus one psychologist notes that psychopathy remains a problematic category and it may be a convenient label to use for those whose behaviour is particularly puzzling or problematic (Hollin 1989).

Crime and mental illness

Other forms of mental illness have been linked to crime. Schizophrenics may murder people when under the influence of delusions and depression has been linked to murder followed by suicide (West 1965). There are, however, several problems with associating crime with mental illness and other psychological traits which are summarized below.

- *The nature of the relationship.* As with biological theories, to see psychological characteristics as the 'cause' of crime would require a very strong relationship. Yet the mentally ill are no more likely to become criminal than anyone else.

- *Labelling the criminal mentally abnormal?* A circular argument may be involved as it could be assumed that because a person is criminal, they are abnormal and therefore must be mentally or psychologically disturbed. This may be part of a labelling process – if an individual's behaviour is deviant in one respect it must be in others (see Chapter 4).

- *The social construction of crime and mental illness.* Mental illness, like crime, is socially constructed and as indicated above there is no one yardstick against which mental 'normality' and 'abnormality' can be measured.

It can be seen from this brief outline that many problems surround what are generally described as individual theories. This does not mean that they are irrelevant or insignificant. Individuals turn to crime in individual circumstances and individual predispositions may affect this choice. These circumstances are also, however, affected by offenders' social environment, culture and socio-economic position and their behaviour is socially interpreted and defined. Another major problem with all individual theories is their reliance on the so-called experimental method. Research is typically based on studies of convicted offenders, who form an unrepresentative sample of 'offenders', being compared with the so-called normal population, who cannot be assumed to be made up of 'non-offenders'. Any statistical associations may therefore reflect the process of detection and conviction as much as they reflect any intrinsic characteristics of offenders.

IS CRIME PATHOLOGICAL?

The sick society?

Much early sociological work was informed by a functionalist approach which saw harmony and conformity as the norm for a healthy society. Society was likened to a physical organism with all parts paying a function in maintaining the whole, and law reflected a consensus over right and wrong. Crime was therefore dysfunctional as it threatened the stability of society and indicated a social problem. To explain crime, sociologists looked at strains in the social structure, at the development of deviant or abnormal subcultures and at the processes of social change and urban growth. Not all, however, shared the view that crime was pathological. The French sociologist, Emile Durkheim, writing in the turbulent decades at the end of the nineteenth century, related crime to the effects of rapid social and economic change and argued that a certain level of crime was normal and indeed functional. The following section will explore his ideas before turning to other sociological theories.

Crime – normal or pathological?

To Durkheim the argument that crime could be normal and healthy emerged from his concern to develop a functionalist approach and to establish sociology as a science. In one of his most famous works, *The Rules of Sociological Method*, he used concepts of 'health' and 'disease' to examine the functions of different phenomena. What was 'normal' and what was 'pathological' must, he argued, be scientifically established. If it could be established that a phenomenon was present in all known societies, it could be assumed to be normal and its function determined. Following an extensive examination of official statistics he concluded that crime existed in all known societies, and was therefore normal. He then explored how it contributed to the health of society (Durkheim 1964).

Crime and immorality are, he argued, a yardstick against which to measure conformity and moral standards. Crime is inevitable as, he argued, we cannot imagine a 'society of saints':

> Imagine a society of saints, a perfect cloister of exemplary individuals. Crimes, properly so called, will there be unknown; but faults which appear venial to the layman will create there the same scandal that the ordinary offence does in ordinary consciousness. If then, this society has the power to judge and punish, it will define these acts as criminal and will treat them as such.
>
> (Durkheim 1964, first published in 1895)

Furthermore crime integrates the community, as it serves to clarify and heighten what he called 'moral sentiments' and the 'collective conscience'. Crime brings people together and in talking about and condemning crime, rules are clarified and re-enforced. By identifying 'deviance' normality becomes clearer, and society unites in condemnation of the deviant. Durkheim likened crime to pain – while it is not desirable it is normal and useful.

Not all crime, however, is functional and he went on to argue that too much becomes pathological and can lead to disintegration. Too little crime, on the other hand, indicates that social control is too strong and can lead to stagnation. As Sumner points out, too much censure leads to inflexibility and some tolerance is needed to enable change. While those who flout or criticize the norms of society may be ostracized and branded as subversives or criminalized – social change and progress may emerge from challenges to normality (Sumner 1994).

While Durkheim's ideas appear to challenge commonsense, they also appeal to it. The media often refers to horrific crimes uniting or bringing the community or nation together in the face of grief. Some events are followed by the development of community based groups mounting appeals for victims or campaigning for action or changes in the law to prevent such occurrences happening again. Following the shooting of schoolchildren and their teacher in Dunblane in 1996, a campaign against handguns emerged. It is also difficult, as Durkheim points out, to imagine a crime-free society. His recognition that deviance and crime can be a force for social change is also an important insight taken up in later work on criminalization (Sumner 1994). Nonetheless both his methods and arguments have been questioned. Consider the following points:

- Is his argument circular as he assumes that crime is functional because it is common?

- Durkheim, like many other theorists of the time, relied on official statistics, which have been seen to be unreliable.

- Seeing crime as functional to society may neglect its severe effects on individuals, families and communities (Downes and Rock 1995).

- Who is it functional to? The community sentiments which Durkheim discusses may be whipped up in support of establishment or dominant interests or used as a diversion from other problems (Downes and Rock 1995, and see Chapter 4).

- At what point does crime cease to be normal and become pathological? Downes and Rock point out, for example, that instead of bringing people together crime may isolate them by making them stay in at night, lock their doors and avoid talking to strangers (Downes and Rock 1995). It can therefore destroy rather than integrate communities.

CRIME AND THE SOCIAL STRUCTURE

While Durkheim's ideas were influential, crime was largely seen as pathological and offenders were assumed to be drawn from lower-class, urban backgrounds which became the problem to be explained. This section will start by looking at the concept of anomie and go on to consider theories based on social disorganization and subcultures.

Anomie

The search for unattainable goals

The notion of anomie also originated in the work of Emile Durkheim. He, like many other sociologists of the time, was concerned with the effects of socio-economic change and how it threatened social cohesion (Downes and Rock 1995). Then, as now, there were concerns about declining morals, the decline of religion and community and the family and their effect on crime.

46

To Durkheim, social life in pre-industrial societies was based on small communities, and was 'mechanically' regulated by a common morality. This mechanical solidarity was a powerful form of social control, which received few challenges. The growth of industry saw what he described as a new division of labour, or organization of work. Small communities broke up as factories were located in towns. Durkheim envisaged that this would lead to a new form of organic solidarity – in which people's work and the contracts into which they freely entered would become the basis of a different kind of moral order and regulation. In the transitional period, however, the old ways of life and old moral standards were inappropriate.

This created what Durkheim described as *anomie*, a state of normlessness, in which people have few moral standards or constraints to guide them – they lack regulation (Durkheim 1970). Economic growth also heightened people's expectations – creating what he saw as boundless aspirations, which could rarely be fulfilled, leading to a situation in which they constantly searched for the unattainable. Thus,

> ... there is no restraint upon aspirations ... at the very moment when traditional rules have lost their authority, the richer prize offered these appetites stimulates them and makes them more impatient of control. The state of de-regulation of anomie is thus further heightened by passions being less disciplined, precisely when they need more discipline.
>
> (Cited in Downes and Rock 1995: 122)

In this situation the individual may be driven to crime or suicide. Again using official statistics Durkheim claimed that anomic suicide was related to economic change. While, like his work on the functions of crime, his methods were criticized, the notion that crime and other forms of deviance can be related to the frustration and hopelessness of attempting to reach unattainable goals without moral regulation is a powerful one. It has contemporary echoes in the popularly held view that the individualistic self-seeking culture of the 1980s engendered greed and a lack of respect for others which, in turn, saw a variety of crimes flourish (see, for example, Sumner 1994).

Rebels, innovators, retreatists and innovators

The concept was used and adapted by Merton, writing in the United States, where popular ideology emphasized the American 'dream' in which the United States was seen to provide equal opportunities and where status and rank were less important than achievement. This also created boundless aspirations. At the same time, the United States in the 1930s had many crime problems – many of which grew up around the prohibition of alcohol. Those familiar with gangster movies will recognize the speakeasies, gangsters and mobs which characterized this era, and juvenile delinquency appeared commonplace in many cities. Merton drew on Durkheim's notion of anomie, arguing that there was a disjunction, or strain, between the culture which

Figure 3.1 Adaptations to anomie

Adaptations	Goals	Means
Conformist	+	+
Innovator	+	−
Retreatist	−	−
Ritualist	−	+
Rebel	±	±
+ signifies acceptance; − signifies rejection		

promised equal opportunities, and the social structure, which could not produce prosperity for all (Merton 1938). Mass production and consumption and advertising created wants and dissatisfactions. Materialism and wealth became universal goals but their pursuit was constrained by social values and the law. Hard work, educational achievement and honest business were legitimate means of achieving the goals. Many found, however, that these did not lead to achievement, which created a strain experienced more acutely by those in the lower class – whose opportunities to achieve the goals were blocked. Individuals could adapt to this structurally induced strain in a variety of ways summarized in Figure 3.1.

Most people are not aware of any contradiction and continue to conform – aspiring to the goals and attempting to achieve them through work, promotion or education. Others adopt deviant adaptations. The innovator uses illegitimate means to achieve the goals. Thieves, robbers, fraudsters or organized criminals may turn to crime to obtain material goods and money. Others retreat from the struggle by rejecting both the goals and the means. This may take the form of alcoholism, drug taking or suicide or adopting an alternative lifestyle. Ritualists carry on with their day-to-day existence, having abandoned all hope of fulfilment or achievement – the means become the end. Yet others reject the goals and the means and additionally attempt to substitute their own by taking a political or rebellious stance.

Evaluation

This concept has become one of the most influential in the sociology of crime. Its basic argument is very simple as it sees crime arising from a failure to achieve the goals which are seen as desirable in society. Before exploring its influence, however, some of the main questions raised in its evaluation must be considered. These include:

- Are the adaptations clearly distinct? Where, for example, does conformity end and ritualism begin? Many may simply fall into a rut of conformity but have abandoned any hope of success. Is this a deviant adaptation? (See, for example, Downes and Rock 1995.)

- Why might people become innovators, retreatists, rebels or ritualists?

- Is anomie restricted to the lower social classes? Might it not also be related to the crime of those higher up the social hierarchy who might similarly be frustrated at not reaching the height of their aspirations?

- How can the theory be tested? People do not always consciously plan or perceive their actions as motivated by frustrated ambitions.

- It may become a circular argument – anomie is inferred from high crime rates which in turn reinforce the theory.

- Are there universally accepted goals? Different groups may pursue different goals. Not all members of the lower class may expect to achieve, and women might have different goals from men – Merton's model assumes primarily male goals (see Chapter 8).

- How relevant is it to societies in which, unlike the United States, there is no culture of equal opportunities? In Britain, for example, when Merton was writing, not all would expect to succeed.

- How does the situation come about in the first place? Why can only some achieve? Laurie Taylor, for example, likens Merton's model to the analysis of a fruit machine whose payouts are rigged, but which most players delude themselves is fair. According to Downes and Rock:

> The deviants are those who try to rig the machine to *their* advantage (innovators); who play it blindly and obsessively (ritualists); who ignore its existence (retreatists); or who smash it up and seek a better model (rebels). Nowhere however . . . does Merton tell us who is taking the profits, and who put the machine there in the first place.
>
> (Taylor 1971, cited in Downes and Rock 1995: 130)

Despite these powerful criticisms, anomie remains an influential concept and formed the basis of many subsequent theories. It is implied in popular explanations which link crime to the search for consumer items or wealth. It provides a persuasive explanation of the often hypothesized relationship between crime and social disadvantage, and can also explain the apparent paradox of why crime rates appear to rise along with rising prosperity (Downes and Rock 1995, and see Chapter 6). Durkheim's ideas also recognize the search for ever greater fulfilment in a society where there are fewer constraints on individualism and where temptations are aroused by media and advertising images. To Sumner it recognizes the contradiction between the relentless search for profit and other forms of fulfilment and the need for moral regulation (Sumner 1994). Moreover, argue Downes and Rock, the many criticisms do not invalidate the model. While there may be few universal goals, different goals, if not achievable, may also produce anomie. The deviant responses of schoolchildren who vandalize schools, or truant, could be related to their failure to achieve the school's official goals of high academic success. A similar strain between goals and legitimate means may exist

49

in the workplace which can be related to many kinds of crime among employees (see Chapter 15).

Social disorganization and the Chicago School

Popular theories also link crime to urban growth or decay, and this was echoed in the work of the Chicago School, the writings of a group of sociologists working in the University of Chicago, based on their extensive research into different aspects of life in that city in the 1920s and 1930s. Chicago was characterized by a colourful world of street gangs, speakeasies, hustlers, rackets, criminal gangs, prostitutes and drug takers and was the home of Al Capone, the notorious gangster (see, for example, Sumner 1994). The concentration of such a wide variety of deviant lifestyles in the inner city indicated what they saw as social disorganization which, to them, was brought about by a natural process of city growth.

To some writers in this school, cities grew according to a natural law, like a tree or plant, and some areas flourished while others decayed. As cities grow, different groups settle in different areas – a process repeated in patterns of resettlement (see, for example, Park and Burgess 1925). In many cities, early, wealthy residents deserted the crowded and dirty inner cities for the more spacious suburbs. As cities grow, immigrants settle and develop their own communities. Each area is therefore subject to a process of invasion, dominance and succession as new groups move in and become dominant. As cities tend to grow outwards, the inner zone becomes the target of newly arrived immigrants and those at the margins of the legitimate economy who have to find the cheapest forms of housing. This creates a zone of transition which was seen as lacking stability and a dominant culture. Thus the *area* was seen as pathological – an inevitable result of the natural development of the city.

The Chicago School is also associated with field work based on qualitative, observational research which produced a variety of studies of different cultures, of street life and the world of the delinquent gang (see, for example, Thrasher 1927; Shaw 1930; Shaw and McKay 1942; Whyte 1943). Many of these became classic examples of participant observation and remain fascinating insights into aspects of life in the inner city. By looking in detail at delinquent and adult gangs and a host of deviant lifestyles from the perspective of their participants, these studies challenged the perception that crime was the product of pathological individuals. They rather drew a picture of the normality, attraction and fun of crime and delinquency – delinquents were seen not as sad, pathological individuals but as individuals behaving normally within their own environment.

There is much appeal in the work of the Chicago School, particularly its focus on inner city urban areas, long associated with crime. Many cities have 'dangerous areas' – signs of which are often dilapidated housing and other obvious neglect (Graham and Clarke 1996). Ghettos, slums, or twilight zones have for long been associated with the so-called dangerous classes. But are these areas inevitably caused by city growth as suggested by the Chicago school? Are they disorganized? Why are their inhabitants viewed as dangerous? A number of questions must be asked in evaluating these theories.

Is there a natural law of city growth?

It is now generally recognized that the development of cities is far from 'natural' but is affected by socio-economic factors and housing policy. Housing policy in many British cities sought to destroy what were seen as slums and create new communities, often on the outskirts, or periphery of cities (Graham and Clarke 1996). Immigrant groups arriving in a British city are unlikely to obtain council housing as they do not have the requisite 'points'. They may face discrimination when seeking both public and private housing, forcing them into particular kinds of housing – often cheap and substandard and in unpopular areas. This may also happen with other groups who lack the means to obtain a mortgage or gain access to a declining stock of public housing. City growth and the character of areas is therefore affected by a variety of factors which may take a different form in different cities.

Disorganization, difference and diversity

To some observers, areas characterized by ethnic and cultural diversity, or associated with high crime, gangs, prostitution or drugs may well appear to be disorganized and to lack any sense of community. This may, however, overlook the organized nature of these activities. In charting the world of the delinquent gang and many other deviant lifestyles, the Chicago School sociologists revealed many different forms of social organization. While the notion of social disorganization implies disapproval and pathology, the words difference and diversity need not. Disorganization could be interpreted therefore as indicating a different form of organization rather than pathological disorganization. A circular argument can also be involved – because the area was characterized by high crime it was assumed to be disorganized, which in turn explained the crime (see, for example, Matza 1969; Sumner 1994; Downes and Rock 1995).

Pathological cultures?

The assumed pathological nature of disorganization gives rise to another problem. By describing different cultures as deviant, crime was in effect being blamed on the inhabitants' cultures, particularly immigrant cultures. Researchers were looking at these cultures from their own cultural viewpoint, using what some call a middle-class gaze. This could amount to scapegoating different cultures by seeing them as responsible for crime (Sumner 1994). It can also divert attention away from the wider social, economic and political policies which may affect the processes described.

51

Despite these criticisms the Chicago School influenced much later work. It provided rich, detailed descriptions of deviant lifestyles and its qualitative methods remain outstanding examples of sociological field work. It drew attention to the geographical distribution of crime and to the importance of looking at crime in its local and cultural context.

Criminal subcultures?

The work of the Chicago sociologists emphasized the normality of delinquent, criminal and other deviant activities within groups. This indicated the existence of subcultures, a term which implies a departure, among a minority, from an assumed majority culture. Within subcultures an alternative value system is found in which deviant and delinquent activities are valued. Subcultures are also characterized by a distinctive language in which words, places, symbols or concepts take on a different meaning recognized and shared by participants. Dress, hairstyles, music, lifestyles, language or speech can be used to distinguish subcultures. As will be seen in subsequent chapters, car thieves use a whole host of words such as 'hot rodding' to describe their activities (see Chapters 6 and 12).

Subcultural theories detail the activities and experiences of participants and interpret the meaning, to those participants, of the subculture along with exploring why they emerge. There have been many different versions of this approach, which also originated in the United States, with later versions developing in Britain. While based in different cultures and following a number of different theoretical traditions, a number of common themes in subcultural theory can be identified and are summarized below:

- Crime and delinquency is seen to be committed by groups within which the activities are seen as normal and attractive – members' commitment is expressed in and inferred from their language and values.

- Their main focus has been on lower-class male subcultures.

- The subculture is seen as a collective response, or solution to a shared problem, often construed as a failure to achieve cultural goals.

Theories differ in how they account for the emergence and persistence of subcultures and in how they analyse the relationship between subcultures and so-called majority culture. To some, following the Mertonian tradition, subcultures are an adaptation to a strain between cultural goals and approved means; to others they signify opposition to or rebellion against the culture of dominant groups in society – young criminals are seen as rebels, albeit unconscious ones, against a system which denies them the opportunity to achieve. The following sections will look at a selection of the most influential subcultural approaches – starting with earlier American work followed by some British work. Contemporary examples will be referred to in subsequent chapters. Finally, a number of questions will be raised in order to evaluate the perspective.

American subcultural theories

American subcultural theory was strongly influenced by the empirical work of the Chicago School and by Merton's model of anomie. It has been pointed out that this left open many questions. What, for example, is the mechanism through which anomie leads to crime? What adaptation might be adopted and why?

In one influential work, Cloward and Ohlin addressed the issue of how and why the potential delinquent should adopt one kind of response rather than another (Cloward and Ohlin 1960). They followed Edwin Sutherland, who argued that those exposed to more criminal than non-criminal values were more likely to adopt criminal values (Sutherland 1947). Different groups were exposed to different sets of values with criminal values being learnt through a process of differential association. Cloward and Ohlin argued that youth will be exposed to different kinds of criminal values depending on their local area and culture. They identified three main kinds of criminal and delinquent subculture:

- The *conflict* subculture was found in areas with a history and tradition of fighting, violence and 'gang warfare'.

- The *criminal* subculture was found in areas with a pre-existing criminal culture and adult organized crime. This also provides an illegitimate market to sell the proceeds of property crime.

- The *retreatist* subculture consisted of drop outs such as drug takers, winos, hobos, vagrants and bohemians.

The history and traditions of an area provide a pre-existing set of cultural values and what they describe as a structure of illegitimate opportunities. Delinquents aspiring to property crime need a supportive economic structure to convert the proceeds of property crime into money, and must also learn how to steal cars or break into houses. Those wishing to consume illegal drugs require a source of supply. The cultural values of an area and its structure of illegitimate opportunities therefore affect the kind of adaptation. While the accuracy of Cloward and Ohlin's typology could be criticized, it will be seen in subsequent chapters that the notion of the illegitimate opportunity structure continues to affect analyses of crime.

A different argument was provided by Albert Cohen in *Delinquent Boys* (Cohen 1955). He disagreed with Merton that delinquency was necessarily directed towards achieving goals – vandalism or violence, he argued, were 'negativistic' rather than 'goal directed'. These responses could arise from a rejection of and opposition to mainstream goals. To Cohen, youth were subjected to a series of middle-class goals in the mass media and schools which provided a 'middle-class measuring rod' against which failure or success could be assessed. Feelings of failure experienced by lower-class youth led to a reaction out of which an oppositional value system rejecting middle-class values emerged.

These are only two out of many versions of classic subcultural theory which was enormously influential and has an immediate commonsense appeal. They appear to provide a convincing explanation of why lower-class youth might be attracted to crime as a means of achieving status or material goods or as a rejection of the value system under which they are seen as failures. Delinquency thus provides a solution. Nonetheless there were many problems with these theories, and many alternatives were offered, which are summarized below.

Were there delinquent subcultures?

Subcultural theories assume a male delinquent gang committed to and organized around delinquent activity. Later studies found, however, that these gangs were far from widespread and that their members showed a much lower commitment than suggested. In New York, for example, Yablonsky found that gangs were more typically made up of a few hard core 'nutters', and a larger periphery of followers whose commitment was sporadic and who were less attached to delinquent values (Yablonsky 1962).

Culture and subculture

Many theories, like anomie, assumed the existence of a majority culture from which the subculture deviated. Others argued that there were a plurality of cultures, in some of which forms of crime and delinquency were tolerated. An early critic of subcultural theory, Walter Miller, argued that within what he called lower-class culture, 'focal concerns' centred around toughness, masculinity, and a tolerance of many forms of theft. Delinquent values were not therefore so much opposed to mainstream culture as a part of lower-class culture (Miller 1958).

Too much delinquency?

In providing such a convincing account of why lower-class youth might become delinquent subcultural theory was accused of over-predicting delinquency by explaining too much. Accepting the official statistics, they looked mainly at lower-class life (see, for example, Matza 1964). Furthermore, delinquent values were not necessarily oppositional. With Sykes, Matza found that delinquents regularly use what they called 'techniques of neutralization' to account for their actions, which echoed conventional values. Thus delinquents were likely to use one of the following strategies (Sykes and Matza 1957):

- A denial of the victim – *'They had it coming'*.

- A denial of injury – *'Didn't do any harm'*.

- A denial of responsibility – *'I was led into it'*.

- Condemning the condemners – *'Everyone's picking on me'*.

- An appeal to higher loyalties – *'I didn't do it for myself'*.

Rather than being committed to delinquency, Matza argued, delinquents drifted between conformity and deviance, directing attention to the attractions of delinquency and to its transitory nature (Matza 1964, 1969).

Application to Britain?

The subcultural approaches looked at so far were developed in America and did not always appear relevant to Britain where violent or criminal gangs were rarer and where there was no well-developed culture of equal opportunities. In Glasgow, where there was a tradition of violent gangs, Patrick, like Yablonsky, found a group of hard core leaders and less committed followers (Patrick 1973). There was a generally recognized working-class culture and Miller's work was probably more influential than Cohen's or Cloward and Ohlin's. The development of subcultural theory in Britain will be explored below.

British subcultural theories

The critiques of American subcultural theory influenced British work. In an influential study of delinquent youth in Stepney and Poplar in London, Downes found that youth did not conform to the image suggested by Cohen or Cloward and Ohlin. Delinquent activities were seen largely as 'fun' and the boys, primarily low educational achievers, did not display any frustration at their lack of success, having never expected to succeed. Rather than being opposed to mainstream values they were 'dissociated' from middle-class and school values. Their delinquency could, however, be related to 'leisure goals' of youth culture. Compared to middle-class youth they could not afford to own cars or participate in expensive leisure pursuits but they had more time for leisure, being less involved in educational pursuits. Searching for kicks and fun made delinquent activities an attractive solution to a leisure problem (Downes 1966).

Against the image of the rebellious, oppositional delinquent, there emerged a picture of the bored delinquent, drifting between conformity and delinquency. Delinquency was seen as no big deal, as something which simply happened in some circumstances. Arguably, however, Matza's model underpredicted delinquency (Downes and Rock 1995), and British work on subcultures developed further with the emergence of a host of youth and cultural styles in the 1960s and 1970s, including teddy boys, mods, rockers, hippies and the growth of illegal drug use. These alarmed the older generation and appeared to challenge conventional values. Many of these were studied by researchers based in the Birmingham Centre for Contemporary Cultural Studies, who approached subcultures from a different intellectual tradition, Marxism, which will be discussed more fully in Chapter 4 (Hall and Jefferson 1976; Muncie 1984; Brake 1985).

This approach was highly critical of earlier subcultural approaches based on the anomie tradition, with its emphasis on culturally shared, consensual goals. While they recognized the existence of dominant cultural goals, these were seen to be encouraged and disseminated by dominant groups through the mass media and school and were imposed rather than emerging from a consensus. They also argue that there are many different cultures, including a working-class culture which is itself an adaptation to the dominant culture. Cultures are not static and are affected by local, national and international influences through films and television. Youth may ape the cultures they are exposed to by the media, thus youth in Britain may aspire to the styles displayed in Australian soaps or Hollywood blockbusters while at the same time being affected by their local culture. Thus cultures reflect a combination or *pastiche* of different cultural influences. Each new generation faces a new set of problems in the light of local economic conditions. Success goals may derive from the dominant culture or from the culture of their parents, often called their parent culture. In areas with declining industries youth may face the double failure of not being able to achieve the goals of their parent culture or the dominant culture.

Subcultural styles were interpreted as representing a solution to these problems by expressing alternative status values. The skinhead style, for example, with its emphasis on hard, masculine forms of dress and behaviour reflected a parent culture and adapted to modern conditions. Subcultures provided cultural 'space'. To Cohen, for example, working-class youth subcultures in the 1960s developed out of changes in housing and employment which affected the working class as a whole (Cohen 1972). Communities became fragmented, and youth were faced by the contradictory ideologies of increasing affluence and traditional working-class ideology. Many of the traditional jobs which were valued were disappearing. Thus he argues: '(the) latent function of subculture is to express and resolve, albeit magically, the contradictions hidden or unresolved in the parent culture' (Cohen 1972).

Evaluation: the delinquent rebel?

While these theories emerged from a very different theoretical starting point, they make similar points to anomie. Subcultures represent a form of resistance to mainstream or parent cultures whose goals are unachievable. These arguments also have considerable appeal. The social and economic changes of recent decades have meant that some young people may in effect be excluded from mainstream society and crime – as will be seen in later chapters looking at youth, property and organized crime – may become an attractive way to obtain success symbols or provide a sense of achievement. In general, subcultural theories, by pointing to the attractions of crime and delinquency, provide an invaluable corrective to work which sees the delinquent as an abnormal or disturbed individual. Yet they too have many problems, summarized below.

Why the delinquent solution?

As we have seen, one of the problems with early subcultural theory was that it could over-predict delinquency. While many theories recognized that not all lower-class youth adopted the 'delinquent solution', many could not sufficiently explain why the majority did not (Downes and Rock 1995).

Interpreting subcultures

Subcultural theory tries to explain why subcultures emerge and to analyse their content, or style, all of which is highly interpretative. The complex processes described cannot be directly tested. Interpreting the meaning of a subculture raises further problems (Cohen 1979). How can it be established that a particular subcultural style such as the skinheads do indeed reflect a desire to re-create the imagery of a long-forgotten industrial past? The interpreter is drawing on signs and symbols which appear to link the past to the present but may not always recognize the original style or the influence of contemporary consumerism. Thus Hobbs, commenting on work suggesting such a link, points out that workers in East London would not have had their hair cropped or worn US army surplus flight jackets. Indeed, he argues, the perception of some youth that the community was under threat by immigrants would require a 'style of aggressive masculinity with a more visually intimidating image than the donkey-jacket, monkey boots (not Doc Martens) and sandwich box' (Hobbs 1988: 131–2).

The romantic rebel?

Subcultural theory can also present a somewhat idealized picture of the delinquent as a rebel – resisting and opposing an oppressive culture. This image may be far from accurate. Cohen's account, for example, stresses the 'imaginary' nature of such a response – the delinquent's resistance is not conscious, nor is it successful. Crime does not provide real jobs or real achievement and more rebellion may produce a harsher response. Interpreting delinquency in such a way may also neglect its other features. In an argument which will be developed in Chapter 4, Young argues that these theories may romanticize the delinquent – portraying them as anti-heroes, when many of their activities have a devastating effect on victims and do not reflect any real resistance (Young 1986). Skinheads, for example, target youth from ethnic minorities and much property crime is directed not at the wealthy who might be seen to 'deserve it' but to the poor and powerless (Young 1975; Lea and Young 1993). Hobbs also criticizes the tendency to glamorize and romanticize working-class children, who are, he argues, portrayed as noble savages (Hobbs 1988).

Lower-class delinquent boys?

A major problem with much subcultural theory is that it accepted the assumption that crime was overwhelmingly a problem of young male lower-class adolescents. This not only meant that it neglected to explore the potentially delinquent behaviour of middle- or upper-class youth, but it also neglected the maleness of the participants. Many theories assumed that the members of subcultures were boys without analysing why this was significant. Were girls absent from these subcultures? Or was their presence merely ignored by largely male researchers? Did girls have their own subcultures (McRobbie and Garber 1976)? Gender was recognized without being analysed. In many subcultural accounts what is effectively being argued is that young *men* need to find alternative ways of being a man. Feminist theories argue that subcultural theories have to recognize and analyse the development of *both* masculine and feminine forms of subcultural activity (see Chapter 8).

CONCLUDING COMMENTS

This chapter has provided an introduction to different theoretical perspectives and readers are advised to look at some of the work cited, preferably in its original form, and consider for themselves many of the issues raised above. Many of these attempts to explain crime or to look for its causes were fundamentally flawed. They assumed that crime was pathological, they took its definition for granted, and based much of their research on convicted offenders. They assumed that crime was more prevalent in the lower classes and did not explore processes of criminalization and social control. They failed to identify the causes of crime which many now see as a fruitless task. Crime cannot be reduced to simple cause–effect relationships and asking why offenders commit crime is only one of the many relevant questions.

Given all these failings, it could be asked whether these theories have any relevance to contemporary Britain. Some of this relevance has been referred to and, as will be seen, they have had an enormous influence on later theories which will be discussed in Chapter 4. It will also be seen later in this book that many of the concepts and arguments developed in these early theories remain important and influential. Durkheim's argument that crime can be functional has influenced later writing and challenges the commonsense view that crime is pathological. Anomie theory, with all its weaknesses, nonetheless points to the possibility that crime is related to inequalities in the social structure and to the failure of some to achieve the goals. It, along with subcultural theory, also indicates that crime can be seen as a normal, rational and attractive option for those who may be excluded from these legitimate forms of achievement.

Review Questions

1. Outline, in your own words, Durkheim's argument that crime is functional to society. Do you think that this has any contemporary relevance?
2. Summarize the main points of anomie, subcultural, and social disorganization theories. What do they have in common? What kinds of criticisms can be made of their assumptions about crime?
3. Identify an example of a youth subculture which is associated with crime. Describe the main characteristics of this subculture – for example, its associated forms of speech, dress and 'style'. How might its emergence be explained by subcultural approaches?

Key Reading

Downes D and Rock P (1995) *Understanding Deviance: A Guide to the Sociology of Crime and Rule Breaking*, revised 2nd edition. Oxford: Clarendon Press

Muncie J, McLaughlin E and Langan M (eds) (1996) *Criminological Perspectives*. London: Sage

Rock P (1997) 'Sociological Theories of Crime', in Maguire M, Morgan R and Reiner R (eds) *The Oxford Handbook of Criminology*, 2nd edition. Oxford: Clarendon Press

Walklate S (1998) *Understanding Criminology*. Buckingham: Open University Press

CHAPTER 4

UNDERSTANDING CRIME: CRIME AND CONTROL

Criticisms of the theories outlined in Chapter 3 centred on their assumptions that the causes of crime could be established and lay in the deficits or pathologies of individual offenders, society or culture. This neglected other, equally important, questions. Why and how are some activities defined as crime? What effect does social control have on offenders and on crime itself? Are the activities of some groups more likely to be subjected to criminal definitions and social control? Later work, drawing on different intellectual traditions, developed these questions and emerged in a different historical and socio-economic context. Some originated from what was seen as a break with traditional theories during the 1960s, often seen as a period of liberalization. Earlier work was criticized for its acceptance of what was seen as an establishment agenda which looked for solutions to the crime problem. Later approaches introduced an offender's perspective, providing a 'view from below'. Others explored how definitions of crime and the organization of social control reflected the interests of the powerful. They were overtly critical of government agendas and were often generally described as critical, new or radical criminology.

Writers from different traditions were also aware of the limitations of earlier work, as it came to be recognized that the modernist project had failed. The causes of crime had not been established, and policies which were associated with it, such as rehabilitation, had little effect in reducing crime or changing offenders. Crime rates continued to rise despite increasing affluence, contradicting the thrust of sociological perspectives. This created what Young calls an aetiological crisis – a crisis in the way in which crime was explained (Young 1997). It also created problems for policy makers. If the causes of crime could not be established and policies were ineffective – what strategies could be adopted? Could crime be reduced without establishing its causes?

This chapter will introduce these different ideas. It will start by exploring the arguments and influence of the labelling perspective before briefly looking at the contribution of phenomenology and outlining the main ideas of critical criminology. It will then turn to control theories and the increasing emphasis on crime prevention and finally the main arguments of realist criminology will be outlined. Many of these perspectives are widely used and their analyses will be further developed in subsequent chapters. The analysis of crime has also been affected by feminist perspectives, which will be dealt with in more depth in Chapter 8.

THE LABELLING PERSPECTIVE

The labelling perspective emerged from the well-established interactionist tradition in sociology, which stresses the importance of exploring the meanings involved in social interactions in order to make sense of behaviour. People behave according to how they define any given situation, a definition which is affected by everyday signs and symbols. A row of desks, for example, indicates a classroom, and those in that classroom behave according to well-established shared meanings. In everyday interaction we present ourselves to the world and express our identity by our speech, mannerisms, dress or body language. In turn we respond to others' cues. These everyday features of social interaction are often taken for granted and unconscious and may need negotiation in new situations (Plummer 1979). The normality of everyday interaction is often revealed by deviance which causes embarrassment, and we react to the deviant with a mixture of feelings such as suspicion, avoidance or disapproval. Exploring these complex meanings requires qualitative research methods, and offenders and law enforcers were studied to explore how they perceived their activities. Some of their ideas are outlined below.

Creating outsiders

As seen in Chapter 1, actions are socially interpreted and, in a much reproduced quotation, Howard Becker (1963: 8–9) argues:

> Social groups create deviance by making the rules whose infraction constitutes deviance and by applying those rules to particular people and labelling them as outsiders. From this point of view, deviance is not a quality of the act the person commits, but rather a consequence of the application by others of rules and sanctions to an 'offender'. The deviant is one to whom that label has successfully been applied; deviant behaviour is behaviour that people so label.

A distinction can be made between acts which could be defined as deviant and those which have been labelled – between what Edwin Lemert called primary deviance, the initial act, and secondary deviance, which occurs after the deviant label has been applied (Lemert 1951). Being labelled deviant affects a person's subsequent behaviour, often producing further, secondary deviance. People are labelled in many different situations but not all labels have such a profound effect as a deviant label. This is because deviance is a 'master status' which overshadows other aspects of identity. People who are considered deviant in one respect are often assumed to be deviant in other respects. Physically impaired or blind people, for example, are often assumed to be hard of hearing and often complain that people shout at them or are protective and condescending. As seen in Chapter 3, it is often assumed that convicted offenders are mentally disturbed. Deviants experience stigma – people avoid them, are embarrassed, and behave differently towards them. Ex-prisoners may find it difficult to obtain a job because of their previous convictions. Being labelled deviant therefore creates 'outsiders' and deviants may be excluded from normal activities (Becker 1963). In turn, those labelled must cope with or 'manage' this new identity.

The deviant identity

Being labelled deviant therefore affects a person's identity. They may pursue a deviant 'career' by moving from the initial label to a changed lifestyle which confirms their deviant status. The child labelled by a teacher as troublesome may seek the company of other troublesome children. A homosexual may go through a process of adjusting to a new sexual identity, eventually 'coming out' and emerging with a new public and private identity. Becoming deviant may involve 'rites of passage', which confirm deviant identities. The drug taker may be part of a subculture where injecting heroin is an important part of being an addict. These careers may involve learning from other deviants in a subculture, which places the deviant further outside normal society. Sub-cultures resolve the problems of stigma and provide an alternative set of values in which negative evaluations are neutralized or resisted. The subcul-ture of prostitutes, for example, was traditionally seen an essential support for the new prostitute – it provided support and assistance, advice about the tricks of the trade and a set of values which neutralized the stigma. Some groups may resist the deviant label, and homosexual groups, for example, successfully changed their designation from 'queer' to 'gay' and campaigned to change the law.

Agencies of social control develop strategies for managing deviants. Creat-ing categories of deviance makes sense of behaviour which may be puzzling, confusing and threatening. If a person is behaving 'oddly', defining them as mentally ill helps to make sense of their behaviour. Agencies expect those who have been labelled to behave in specific ways. Scheff, for example, argues that those defined as mentally ill are expected to adapt their behaviour and non-conformity – which might include resisting the label and denying the problem – may be interpreted as a further sign of illness (Scheff 1966). Once in an institution, prisoners or the mentally ill go through a 'rite of passage' in which aspects of their former identity are systematically removed. Clothes are often replaced by a uniform, and they become an inmate with a number. This may be experienced as a form of degradation – as one's iden-tity is being challenged. Institutions reward conformity – reassertions of indi-viduality can be regarded as a further sign of deviance. Inmates of such institutions often form an inmate culture, attempting to re-establish choice and identity (Goffman 1968).

Figure 4.1 A deviancy amplification spiral

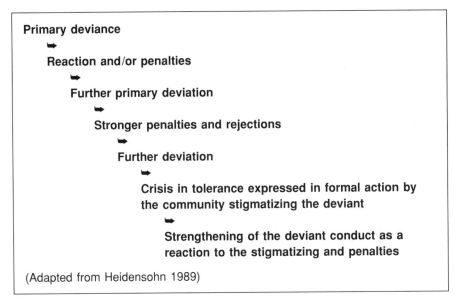

Primary deviance

→

    Reaction and/or penalties

    →

        Further primary deviation

        →

            Stronger penalties and rejections

            →

                Further deviation

                →

                    Crisis in tolerance expressed in formal action by the community stigmatizing the deviant

                    →

                    Strengthening of the deviant conduct as a reaction to the stigmatizing and penalties

(Adapted from Heidensohn 1989)

Deviancy amplification

This suggests that labelling and social control can set in train a spiral of ever-increasing deviance – creating a self-fulfilling prophecy. A possible sequence is sketched out in Figure 4.1 adapted from Heidensohn (1989). This is well illustrated in Stanley Cohen's now classic work, *Folk Devils and Moral Panics* in which he analysed the reaction to fights between rival groups in the South of England in the early 1960s (Cohen 1972). What were in effect routine incidents involving youths became interpreted as confrontations between groups identified as mods and rockers. Press reaction was intense and they became what he described as folk devils, whose activities were seen as symptomatic of the problems of the younger generation. Subsequent reports of routine crimes described defendants as 'mods' or 'rockers' further associating these groups with criminal activity. The incident took place on a May Bank Holiday and there was subsequent press speculation, fuelled by interviews with self-styled mods and rockers that it would be repeated. On the next holiday weekend, the police, media and observers, who had all arrived in strength, were expecting trouble and shops were closed. Eventually a small fracas broke out which rapidly escalated. Cohen's analysis suggests that the expectations of trouble played no small part in creating the disturbance.

Such amplification may occur in other situations where trouble is expected. Police and demonstrators, for example, each fired up with anticipation, may 'have a go' at each other (Jefferson 1990), and interactions between police and football hooligans or joy riders may also lead to an escalation. This may happen particularly in situations where, for example, relations between police and minority ethnic groups have been characterized by hostility (see Chapter 9).

Evaluation

The labelling perspective suggests therefore that social control may exacerbate deviance or crime. Labelling, categorizing and stigmatizing offenders may confirm a deviant identity and produce secondary deviance. This suggests that social control agents should keep their intervention to a minimum. These ideas have been extremely influential, not only in the analysis and treatment of crime but also in the fields of education, medicine and psychiatry. Braithwaite argues in his work that any form of control or punishment must seek to avoid creating outsiders and oppositional cultures (Braithwaite 1989). Despite its enormous appeal a number of critical points have been raised. Many of these do not invalidate the approach as some are based on a misconception of what labelling perspectives set out to achieve (Plummer 1979; Downes and Rock 1995). These questions are summarized below.

A perspective or a theory of crime?

To those concerned with the causes of crime, the labelling approach was limited. Its focus on secondary deviance neglected the question of why primary deviance occurred in the first place. Plummer argues that this was never the intention – the primary focus was on the impact of labels (Plummer 1979). Many prefer however to describe the labelling approach as a perspective rather than a theory – it does not seek to fully analyse crime but focuses on how crime and criminals are processed. It can also be combined with other theories (Plummer 1979; Heidensohn 1989; Downes and Rock 1995).

Is it too deterministic?

To some critics it appears as if, once labelled, the deviant automatically responds with more deviance and it is therefore too determinist and assumes little choice. As pointed out above however, deviants may resist labels and, while much work does imply a deviant career, can withdraw from the process at any stage (Plummer 1979). This has been likened to proceeding down a long corridor with doors off to the side – some follow the corridor to deviance, others exit at different points.

The deviant's perspective

To others, the approach was too sympathetic to offenders. Many studies looked at forms of crime such as drug taking or delinquency where an appreciative stance was easier, with few looking at violent or sexual offenders. It was also overtly critical of official policy and was often linked with arguments for liberalizing laws. Offenders were portrayed as victims of harsh social control, presenting a somewhat romantic view of deviants and offenders (see, for example, Young 1986). This criticism does not invalidate its main arguments as it can be used with other groups and has been used with the police and other law enforcement agencies.

Who has the power to define deviance?

To yet others, it neglected to explore the power involved in defining crime and the political nature of deviant labels. While it was recognized that definitions of deviance could be resisted, labelling theorists did not explore the wider structure of political power. As we shall see, these were questions taken up by critical and Marxist scholars.

MAKING SENSE OF THE PHENOMENON

The meaning of actions to participants and the categorization of behaviour was taken even further by phenomenologists who asked how these meanings could be established. To them, the researcher must interpret data and the meanings of events or situations may be very difficult to capture. Phenomenology argued that the meaning of any phenomenon could not be taken for granted and that the researcher also attributes meaning. To Downes and Rock, phenomenology attempts to address the problems posed by the difficulty of knowing about things as they 'really' are, as opposed to how they seem (Downes and Rock 1995). This challenges how much we can 'know' about any phenomenon. While it lies beyond the scope of this book to discuss fully the issues raised, it is useful to explore how phenomenologists approach the task of interpreting meanings and how their deliberations have influenced thinking on crime (see, for example, Hester and Eglin 1992).

Phenomenologists advocate the use of ethnomethodology, which should not be confused with ethnography and which can be described as the 'study of members' methods of making sense . . . that is their methods of producing and recognizing "sensible" social actions and settings' (Hester and Eglin 1992: 14).

Phenomenologists argue that in everyday life people 'produce' their own local social order attributing a whole range of meanings to everyday circumstances. This is difficult to interpret – the researcher must reflect on what words or phrases mean and how they are used and interpreted by participants, described as being reflexive. Everyday objects, words or phrases have different meanings and can be interpreted differently according to key signs. A street sign for example is a piece of metal, which indicates the name of a street. To local people it may have other connotations (Hester and Eglin 1992). Ethnomethodologists are concerned to unpack these unstated and taken for granted meanings which may only emerge if deviated from. Words and phrases must be carefully explored – in Chapter 2, for example, the tendency of the police to talk about 'real' police work was referred to. This often used word encapsulates a whole host of meanings about the role and function of the police (see, for example, Holdaway 1983 and Chapter 2). Many readers may also have a concept of 'real' or 'good' work which could be similarly explored. Ethnomethodologists use the technique of conversational analysis to uncover these kinds of background assumption.

Using some of these techniques, Hester and Eglin illustrate how we read meaning into words. As an example they cite a news headline: '*Mother Charged in Death of Child*'. On its own this says little. On the basis of commonsense knowledge we would however take this to mean that a mother has been charged with killing her own child. The word charge is assigned a legal rather than a financial meaning and the association of charge and death leads to the assumption that it involves the police, a murder and a mother–child relationship (Hester and Eglin 1992).

The most influential phenomenological work of relevance to crime has dealt with official statistics and the work of court officials. Kitsuse and Cicourel explored how the police categorize complex events into legal categories such as assault or burglary. Official reports are inevitably 'truncated' versions of what happened and are affected by the local context in which events and people are defined (Kitsuse and Cicourel 1963). This may be affected by what Sudnow saw as the taken for granted assumptions of criminal justice agents about what kinds of offences and offenders are 'normal' (Sudnow 1965). Agents' use of phrases such as 'normal burglaries' incorporated assumptions about offenders, victims and the areas concerned. This was only evident to the observer when 'abnormal' crimes occurred – for example, when a middle-class youth was found committing a crime normally associated with lower-class youth. Normal crimes were routinely processed – cases of burglary, for example, would be reduced to larceny following a plea bargain. This 'bargain' was not spelt out as each participant – police, prosecutor and defender – worked with shared assumptions of what would happen.

While these kinds of studies reveal much about the often unstated processes underlying the categorization of offences, phenomenology had a limited influence (Downes and Rock 1995). In one sense it appears to deny all advances of knowledge – if all research is contaminated by the observer, how can we trust the phenomenologist's interpretation? Many would prefer to believe that there is some 'reality' (Downes and Rock 1995). While their work was often meticulously detailed it was generally based on very small-scale and local observations and led to few generalizations. Focusing in such depth on the minutiae of taken for granted assumptions, revealed, according to Sumner, a lot of trivia, which neglected the structural context within which norms develop – he likens it to:

describing the flow of fluids in an engine . . . without telling us about the vehicle, its normal functions and the direction it travels in – or about the driver and what he or she has in mind for the passengers.

(Sumner 1994: 241)

CRITICAL CRIMINOLOGY

Many criticisms of these and earlier theories originated from the perspective known as critical criminology, which developed out of radical criminology and is also associated with strands of feminist and critical race theories. The word critical implies criticism – and indeed critical criminology is critical of many theoretical approaches and criminal justice policies. It is also critical in the sense that it seeks to expose the ideological nature of dominant ideas about crime. Its main focus is on the structural, political and ideological factors underlying the definition of crime, the criminal law and its enforcement. While the labelling perspective recognizes the power of social controllers to define crime, critical criminologists place this within a broader context – the former focuses on the daily routine of agency, while the latter aims to expose structural relations which involve the economy, the state and ideology (Scraton and Chadwick 1991). Critical criminology is a constantly evolving area and encompasses many different strands. This section will introduce some of its main ideas which will be further developed in subsequent chapters. It will start by looking at the issue of conflict and consensus in relation to law making, introduce Marxist perspectives and look at how it has broadened the questions asked about crime to incorporate the process of criminalization.

Law, crime and conflict

To critical criminologists a crucial question is 'whose definitions of crime are dominant?' and they take a very different view to the functionalist theories looked at in Chapter 3. Whereas to Durkheim, criminal law reflected the moral sentiments of the 'collective conscience' and to other functionalists law and morality reflect consensus, many argue that law emerges out of conflict. Chapter 1 argued that legal definitions of crime are politically contested and that their criminal status can be challenged. Rather than seeing this as reflecting a changing societal consensus, conflict theories argue that they are the outcome of conflict. In addition, social order, rather than being maintained by consensus, is maintained through a constant process of accommodation between different interest groups.

Different theoretical positions analyse this conflict in different ways. Pluralists argue that a variety, or plurality, of different interest groups come into conflict with each other. The success of any particular campaign will depend on the balance of power between opposing parties. Groups campaigning to have the criminal status of an action changed will have to secure the support of others to be successful. Some groups may have more power than others, affecting their likely success, but no one group holds a monopoly. Thus campaigns by homosexuals and women's groups to secure legal changes have been partially successful, which demonstrates that the law can be changed. This pluralist model is rejected by Marxist theories who argue that, despite the appearance of plurality, the interests of the ruling class tend to be consistently reflected. To appreciate this position some of the main ideas of Marxist theory must be briefly outlined.

Marxist perspectives

Marxist theories developed out of the work of Karl Marx whose nineteenth-century writings covered a broad span of economics, philosophy, sociology and politics. He was concerned to analyse how changes in society were related to the economic and class structure of society. His ideas influenced academic writers and political movements and are often associated with the growth of communism, although Marx himself rejected the way in which his work had been used. Later writers developed many of his ideas and applied them to contemporary society. They are generally known as Marxist, a term which encompasses many different perspectives drawing on Marx's original ideas. This section will introduce some of their main themes.

To most Marxists, laws and popular belief systems, ideologies, reflect ruling-class power as, to Marx, the ruling ideas of any society were those of the ruling class. Law supports the economic base in which the owners of the means of production extract the surplus value of their employee's labour by paying them a wage and retaining the profit. Employment law codifies this contractual relationship. Class is based on the economic relationships of capitalism and there are therefore two main classes – owners and labourers. Marx and many later Marxists believed that eventually the main subject class, the proletariat, would become aware, or conscious, of its subject position and act as a class to overthrow the ruling class. That they did not in most Western countries may have indicated the ability of the ruling classes to prevent the development of class consciousness by securing the consent of the lower classes. The contradictions of capitalist society, the subjection and exploitation of the subject classes, become more evident at certain periods, described as crises, such as economic recession and high unemployment, when the subject class may develop class consciousness by realizing their disadvantaged position.

The application of Marxist thought to crime developed out of the many criticisms of traditional and functionalist theories which were themselves seen as ideological. A full theory of crime or deviance, it was argued, must explore how crime is defined and controlled and relate these to state power (Taylor et al 1973). Marxist thinkers approached crime in different ways. To some, crime was interpreted as an indication of class consciousness and represented a rebellion against class rule. There were many problems with this. Marx himself had not seen crime in this way as, to him, criminals were part of what he called the lumpenproletariat, a parasite class which did not contribute to the means of production. Crime was therefore unimportant in the class struggle, and some argued that Marxism could not be applied to crime (Hirst 1972). Marx's collaborator, Engels, did suggest a link between crime, poverty and social change, attributing crime to the demoralizing effects of exploitation and seeing it as a nascent revolt. This, however, accepts that there are higher rates of crime among the lower class, an assumption which critical criminologists rejected. How, under this approach, could white collar crime be explained? Moreover as Young argued, this notion of crime invoked a false 'Robin Hood' image of the poor stealing from the rich whereas the poor largely steal from the poor and crime could hardly be seen as a successful revolt (Young 1975).

To other Marxist writers, a more interesting question was to identify the processes in which ruling-class interests came to be reflected in legal and ideological conceptions of crime and social control. To them this was illustrated by the contrasting treatment of the crimes of the powerful and the powerless. Thus the criminal law was used to control the activities of lower-class offenders such as theft or burglary, which damaged the interests of capitalism, whereas some business or commercial activities, which were equally harmful but not a threat to the interests of capitalism, were not defined as crime. Lower-class activities which posed a threat to social order, such as demonstrations, were also subject to public order legislation. The criminal law therefore served ruling-class interests by criminalizing the activities of the powerless (see, for example, Pearce 1976). One problem with this argument is that the activities of business are subject to the criminal law. This was explained by arguing that these laws performed a symbolic function, while they were technically criminal they were not subjected to the same kinds of policing and social control (see, for example, Croall 1992 and Chapter 15).

The police, courts and prisons were therefore seen to operate in the interests of the ruling class. In times of crisis, when the ruling class perceived a threat, these agencies could be used to control and contain it. While the formal ideology of the police emphasizes its service role in detecting and prosecuting criminals, their real function, argued critical criminologists, was to maintain law and order. Thus the police, along with courts and prisons, were used against working-class protests, illustrated in the rise of an increasingly tough control culture emerging in the 1970s in which the criminal law and the police were used against industrial and political protests (Sim et al 1987). Increasingly heavy or paramilitary tactics were used by the police, many imported to mainland Britain from Northern Ireland and originally used in colonial territories such as Hong Kong.

Many of these ideas will be developed in later chapters. While there are many different strands within critical criminology, some versions of Marxist approaches were criticized in important respects. They could be somewhat simplistic and circular. The assumption that all laws reflected ruling-class interests was difficult to refute, particularly as any examples of laws which appeared to contradict this were seen as symbolic. It was also difficult to establish how the ruling class secured such a situation, particularly given the plethora of interest groups involved in creating any particular criminal law. Who were the ruling class and how did they rule? Marxist thought was criticized for suggesting a rather mechanical conspiracy theory which could not be empirically substantiated.

Later versions were influenced by the ideas of the Italian writer Gramsci, which moved away from a narrow conception of the ruling class. To Gramsci, the ruling class maintain power by securing the consensus of the ruled. This is achieved by the maintenance of a hegemonic culture in which ruling-class power is legitimated and the ruled in effect consent to be ruled by accepting, for example, that governments have the 'right' to rule. This consent means that action need only be taken when threats to this cultural domination emerge. Behind the 'velvet glove' of consensus, therefore, lay the 'iron fist' of class power, which becomes visible when law and social control become tougher. A major work in this tradition was Stuart Hall and his colleagues' analysis of the moral panic surrounding mugging in the 1970s (Hall et al 1978). This began when a case of robbery was described by a senior police officer as a 'mugging gone wrong'. Previously mugging was not seen as a crime common in Britain and the term was rarely used. This comment set in train a moral panic about the significance of an assumed rise in mugging. The researchers found no evidence that there was such an increase and accordingly asked how the reaction could be explained.

To them, mugging, which was associated with a growing problem in the inner cities and with black youth, assumed a symbolic significance. The moral panic reflected the orchestration of consensus through which dominant definitions and interpretations were disseminated. The media quoted the police, who in turn quoted the media – politicians used both and were quoted by the media. The media therefore acts as an 'ideological state apparatus' as it reflects, reinforces and disseminates ideas, values and beliefs. Mugging was perceived as a threat to key values associated with 'Englishness' – the family, the need for discipline, respectability and decency. The black mugger was subtly portrayed as an outsider, an alien, and thereby a folk devil – a scapegoat for economic and social decline. The moral panic was related to a crisis in hegemony, the maintenance of consent, brought about by a deterioration in economic conditions. The state needed to 'define away the crisis' – to see it in terms other than class relations. The black mugger was therefore a suitable folk devil.

From crime to criminalization

This amounted to what has been described as the criminalization of black youth – which will be discussed in more depth in Chapter 9. It also suggests that the process of criminalization includes a process in which the law, agencies of social control and the media associate crime with particular groups who are identified as a threat. To Scraton and Chadwick, it involves the 'application of the criminal label to an identifiable social category' (Scraton and Chadwick 1991: 172). This in turn is used to divert attention from economic and social conditions, particularly in times of economic change which could produce political unrest. Overtly political protests are also criminalized, as seen in the description of political terrorists as 'common criminals', which neutralizes the political nature of their actions. This helps, argues Hillyard, to attract popular support for anti-terrorist measures as it is easier to mobilize state intervention against criminal acts than for the repression of what might be seen as a just political cause (Hillyard 1987, and see Chapter 16).

Criminalization can therefore be used to justify harsher social control measures often taken against economically and politically marginal groups. These groups may have few means of resisting such moves due to their economic and political situation. It will be seen in Chapter 6, for example, that the major economic changes of recent decades have altered the situation of many in the lower class. Immigration, rising unemployment and the casualization of employment have created a surplus labour population which is required in times of growth but disposable during a recession. This fragments the lower class and has created what some describe as a one-thirds–two-thirds society in which two-thirds work and participate, while one-third become marginalized, on or below the poverty line. These groups have for long been seen as the 'dangerous classes'. By criminalizing their activities their situation can be attributed to their own weaknesses, thus justifying harsher control measures. These ideas refer not only to class domination but also, as will be seen in later chapters, to patriarchal, generational and racial domination (Scraton and Chadwick 1991).

Critical criminologists ask a number of important questions. They attempt to strip away or deconstruct dominant perceptions of crime and criminals seeing crime not as a problem of individual offenders or strains in society but as a process related to wider economic and political structures of power. This is enormously useful in exploring why and how the activities of some groups are subjected to the criminal law. They also question the way in which social control operates and is used. Their ideas, like any others have however raised a number of criticisms which are outlined below.

The ruling class conspiracy?

Reference has already been made to the problems of directly relating law and social control to the direct intervention of the state or ruling class. Young argues that it provides a mirror image of functionalism as all evidence can be interpreted as fitting the model (Young 1986).

71

Establishing the relationship

It is also difficult to empirically test many arguments. Downes and Rock, criticizing Hall and his colleagues' work, argue that while they demonstrate how the moral panic develops they cannot establish its precise relationship to the assumed crisis (Downes and Rock 1995). Analyses of the discourses of the media and politicians is interpretative and can be selective as quotations may be taken out of context.

Attitude to criminal justice policy

Critical criminology has also been criticized for its apparent lack of interest in policy – Young, for example, sees it as left idealism which makes few policy suggestions (Young 1997). On the other hand, being critical of the way in which policies are formulated is in itself a contribution. If the crime problem is constructed on false premises, policies will be limited. Some strands of critical criminology have also been associated with an abolitionist stance which argues that the formal processes of police and prisons which criminalize some groups and exacerbate their problems should be abolished or greatly reduced and more informal means of conflict resolution should be adopted.

CONTROL THEORIES AND CONSERVATIVE CRIMINOLOGIES

From explaining to controlling crime

The limitations of traditional approaches were also recognized by policy makers and there was a general disillusionment with what were described as dispositional theories, which related crime to the dispositions of offenders, be they individually or socially determined. There was, therefore, a need for new theories and policies, in which control played a major part. Control theories argued that crime was more likely in the absence of controls and other writers stressed that offenders freely choose to offend, a choice which was affected by the likelihood of being caught and punished. Crime, it was argued, could be reduced by increasing the chances of being caught. This also implied that, contrary to earlier models, crime could be prevented without understanding its causes. Controlling rather than explaining crime therefore became the focus of attention. These ideas have been associated with what has been described as administrative or conservative criminology as they were linked to the concerns of administrators and allied with the policies of the 'new right' conservative governments in both Britain and America. This section will start by outlining aspects of control theories and illustrating their links with conservative thinking before outlining some of their limitations.

72

Crime and lack of control

Control theories are based on the commonsense notion that crime is more likely to be committed where offenders have insufficient controls to constrain them (Downes and Rock 1995). They reverse the question asked by earlier theories – instead of asking *'why do people commit crime?'* they ask *'why do people not commit crime?'*. Most people, they argue, do not commit crime; they think it is wrong or they fear disapproval and punishment – thus attachment to conventional morality and lifestyles are a form of control. This attachment is learnt through the process of socialization within the family, the community and the school, often described as informal agencies of social control. To Hirschi, an influential control theorist,

> a common property of control theories at their simplest level is their assumption that delinquent acts result when an individual's bond to society is weak or broken.
> (Hirschi 1969, cited in Downes and Rock 1995: 221)

To Hirschi the social bond consists of four elements. Attachment to conventional values means that people care about other people's opinions, which constrains their behaviour. They become committed to conventional behaviour by investing time and energy in obtaining material goods and achieving a certain status. Involvement in a conventional lifestyle leaves them less time or motivation to deviate. Finally, they believe that this is right. The delinquent is freer from these controls, has few attachments, is uncommitted to a conventional lifestyle and does not believe in the need to obey rules. In his research Hirschi found that delinquency was more common among boys who reported fewer bonds with their family based on measurements of, for example, parental supervision and intimacy of communication (Hirschi 1969). In Britain, Wilson found in a deprived area that non-delinquents were distinguished by what she describes as 'chaperonage' which included fetching children from school, rules for coming in at night and restrictions on their freedom to be in the street. Lax discipline was related to the stress of unemployment, disability or poverty (Wilson 1980).

Rationally choosing crime

In Britain, control theory influenced the development of theories and policies of crime prevention in the work of the former Home Office Research Unit. From the early 1980s a succession of publications argued that much offending, rather than being predisposed, was opportunist. Some situations provided the opportunity for committing crime without being observed or detected. Crime could be prevented by reducing these situational opportunities. Thus Clarke argued that crime prevention was possible without understanding the causes of crime by reducing opportunities and making offences more difficult to commit (Clarke 1980; Clarke and Mayhew 1980). Crime, he argued, resulted from a rational choice on the part of the offender who assessed the risks of any particular situation. This argument has an obvious appeal as reducing the opportunities for committing crime may be a much more cost-effective way to prevent it. An enormous amount of research therefore directed attention to the immediate circumstances surrounding offences and how opportunities could be reduced – a strategy often described as situational crime prevention.

These strategies included 'target hardening' – making the target of a crime harder to remove or vandalize. More effective security devices, better street and security lighting, identity marking and increased surveillance were all explored. Research sought to establish how criminals identify targets and what areas and situations were most crime prone (see, for example, Bennett and Wright 1984 and Chapter 12). Surveillance was particularly important as the chances of being observed, and therefore caught, were crucial features of the immediate situation in which offences occur. Some of this was based on the work of Oscar Newman, who argued that if space 'belonged' to someone it was defensible. For example, where houses overlook a communal area, vandals or thieves are more likely to be seen, identified as intruders and stopped. This suggested that crime could be 'designed out' of buildings and urban space by increasing informal surveillance. While Newman's work had many criticisms, it does point to the significance of informal social control and raises important questions about 'features which enhance the social sense of belonging to a neighbourhood and make for a feeling of involvement rather than indifference' (Downes and Rock 1995: 233, and see Young 1997).

Conservative criminologies

Control and rational choice theories had an enormous influence and had much popular and commonsense appeal which must be seen in its wider context. They were associated with what came to be called 'new right' or conservative criminology which emerged in the 1980s and 1990s. Successive Conservative governments were also committed to the development of free market economic policies, an emphasis on individualism, and to keep state intervention – which was seen as undesirable – to a minimum. Theories attributing crime to the rational choice of individuals or to a lack of control or discipline placed the responsibility for crime on individual offenders and their families, whereas attributing crime to social conditions or individual predispositions could be seen as being 'soft' on or excusing crime. Conservative politicians tended to blame crime on the permissive attitudes of parents and schools and on wickedness, and dismissed arguments that crime was related to economic conditions such as unemployment. Families were exhorted to take their responsibilities seriously and some blamed crime on single-parent families (Brake and Hale 1992; Loveday 1992). This deflects attention away from the social inequalities which, argued Brake and Hale, Conservative policies had produced.

Control theories could therefore be used to justify technological crime prevention, harsher policing and tougher punishment. In addition to placing the responsibility for offending on individuals it also placed a responsibility on individual citizens to prevent it by securing their houses or participating in neighbourhood watch schemes. This, along with the contribution of business and community groups, reduced the government's role in crime prevention.

Evaluation

Whatever their ideological basis, control theories, like many others, have much appeal as they directed attention to the sources of conformity and to the significance of informal social controls. Research on crime prevention has provided many useful ideas to reduce the risks of victimization. Nonetheless they also have many shortcomings, some of which are outlined below.

The neglect of motivation

A major limitation is their neglect of offenders' motivations. While they focus on the immediate situation in which crime occurs they do not ask why offenders are in that situation, why they choose to avail themselves of opportunities or why they choose any particular form of crime (see, for example, Downes and Rock 1995). They cannot therefore explain social patterns of crime and do not address its definition. Moreover, argue Downes and Rock, they imply that everyone could be delinquent when the 'lid is off' (Downes and Rock 1995).

Displacing crime

A major limitation of crime prevention is that offenders, deterred from one situation, may move on to another – crime may be displaced. If offenders are predisposed, they will actively seek different situations. This will be explored in later chapters.

Crime prevention and the quality of life

Others fear the oppressive nature of crime prevention strategies which involve locks, bolts and electronic surveillance. This affects the quality of life and can produce an oppositional response – offenders may take pride in circumventing them. Young argues that 'locks and bolts alienate ... and ... serve to feed sources of discontent rather than eliminate them' and furthermore 'condemn many old people ... to virtual imprisonment in "safe houses", free from crime but with a vista of iron bars and a barrier of answer phones' (Young 1994: 116–17).

The neglect of social conditions

Others argue that control theories deflect attention from the social conditions which may underlie crime and from the links between crime and social deprivation. In some respects they could be said to be dealing with the symptoms of crime rather than its causes. Young, for example, argues for social crime prevention by attacking unemployment and housing deprivation (Young 1997).

REALIST CRIMINOLOGY

Rising crime rates and concerns with the impact of crime on victims also influenced the development of what has been called 'realist' criminology. This was critical of the dispositional, pathological or deficit theories already outlined and of the thrust of labelling theory and critical criminology which, by focusing on social control and the definition of crime, appeared to deny that crime was a 'real' problem. In addition, no earlier approaches had produced 'realistic' ways of dealing with crime. Approaches based on intervention with individual offenders had failed to reduce crime and the non-interventionist strategies of the labelling approach, and the abolitionist strategies of critical theorists, were seen as impracticable or idealistic. Young criticized the left idealism of critical criminologists for failing to develop practical strategies, for denying the reality of crime and being over-concerned with the crimes of the powerful (Young 1986). Policies, they argued, should be based on what could be achieved, accepting that crime is a real problem. In the United States, realism became associated with crime prevention and new right policies, in Britain with the development of 'left realism' – so called to distinguish it from 'right realism'. This was associated with the work of writers and researchers at Middlesex University who, in several publications, have outlined the basic ideas of left realism, summarized below (see, for example, Matthews and Young 1992; Young and Matthews 1992; Lea and Young 1993).

Left realism

Crime really *is a problem*

A basic assumption of left realists is the 'lived reality' of crime. These can be explored by naturalistic methods and realism advocated the use of radical victim surveys which aimed to explore the impact of crime on victims and communities (see, for example, Jones et al 1986 and Chapter 5).

The square of crime

Crucial to their approach is the notion of a square of crime. This, illustrated in Figure 4.2, emphasizes that in order to fully understand crime, all of its

Figure 4.2 The square of crime

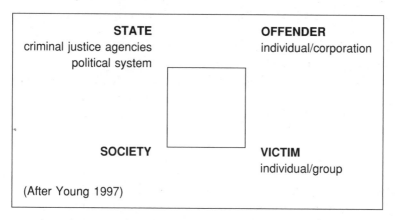

STATE
criminal justice agencies
political system

OFFENDER
individual/corporation

SOCIETY

VICTIM
individual/group

(After Young 1997)

dimensions – offenders, victims, the public and the state and its agencies, and the interrelationships between them – must be fully explored. Earlier theories focused on only one point of the square – on offenders, social control or the state and most neglected the victim. The interrelationships between all points must be explored, thus research should investigate the causes of offending, factors which make victims vulnerable, social conditions which affect public levels of control and tolerance and social forces which propel formal agencies.

Multiple aetiology

Young uses this phrase to describe the attempt to determine the causes of crime. Earlier attempts to identify single causes have however failed and the multiple causes of crime must be recognized.

Specificity

These causes may be different for different offences, thus generalizations about 'crime' should be avoided. They would, for example, reject any argument that unemployment leads to crime as it leads to some kinds of crime in some circumstances.

Minimal intervention

In general, accepting many of the points made by labelling approaches, realists argue for minimal intervention by the criminal justice system, but recognize the need for police and prisons and to reduce crime. Intervention should be focused on each point of the square. They accept that crime arises from social structural conditions and therefore that structural intervention such as improving employment opportunities is most likely to be effective.

Nonetheless, schemes aimed at reducing victimization are necessary – but should not be seen as sufficient.

Rational democratic input and output

Intervention should be based on democratic input and output. This means that the impact of crime should be recognized and those affected should be consulted about policy. They advocate the use of radical victim surveys based on local areas to assist targeting resources on those whose need is greatest.

Relative deprivation

While single causes of crime are rejected they argue that much is brought about by relative deprivation. This does not mean that deprivation in itself produces crime as there is no clear evidence to substantiate this argument and such an argument neglects white collar crime (Lea and Young 1993, and see Chapter 6). It was seen in Chapter 3 that one of the problems with anomie theory is that not all have the same expectations and will not therefore experience the same frustrations. Deprivation can, therefore, be relative. People have different expectations which are related to what they feel they deserve. They may compare their situation with others whom they would expect to equal – to a reference group. If these expectations are not met they may feel deprived – not absolutely but relatively. Unemployed youth may feel relatively deprived compared with employed youth and feel frustrated because they feel their unemployment is not their fault. Young members of ethnic minorities may experience deprivation in comparison to white youth if they have experienced discrimination. Members of some occupational groups feel deprived in comparison to others whose jobs they feel are of equal value. The executive may feel relatively deprived if denied the chance of promotion. Not all these feelings will lead to crime – there are legitimate avenues to pursue many grievances. They may lead to crime if legitimate avenues are not open and if the group is socially or politically marginalized – such as the young unemployed or members of minority ethnic groups.

Evaluation

The left realist approach is difficult to evaluate as it is, as Young argues, an evolving approach. Like many other approaches it has some appeal. By recognizing the importance of looking at all points of the square it aims to provide a broader view of crime than many others. It recognizes the victim, often neglected by other approaches (see Chapter 5). It attempts to provide realistic options for policy while at the same time recognizing the socially constructed nature of crime. The concept of relative deprivation brings back a concern with social inequality. These strengths, however, are associated with weaknesses and it has been criticized from the viewpoint of other perspectives as follows:

Can it be tested?

Like all structural approaches it is difficult to test empirically and, as we have seen, many 'right realist' and other criminologists have abandoned the search for the causes of crime and reject links with inequality.

Criticizing realism?

It is distinguished from critical approaches by its assertion that crime should be taken seriously and that policies can make a difference. Critical criminologists accuse realists of accepting the ideological construction of crime as a problem, accepting the establishment agenda, and failing to fully account for the class-based nature of law and structures of domination (Sim et al 1987).

Is it a distinct approach?

Its attempt to synthesize the contributions of different approaches attracts criticism that it is not a distinctive approach and that it selectively chooses theories which fit its model.

CONCLUDING COMMENTS

Taken together with the theories looked at in Chapter 3, readers might feel somewhat confused by the range of theories and the evident disagreement between them. How is crime to be analysed? Has all this theoretical work advanced our knowledge about crime? Which theories are more useful? There are no simple answers to these questions. Theories start with different aims and assumptions which affect how they approach crime. Some, taking for granted that crime is a problem, aim to find its causes and to develop policies which reduce it by targeting individual offenders or wider social problems. Later policies have increasingly placed a higher priority on the control of crime rather than its explanation. Others argue that the 'crime problem' is constructed and that social control exacerbates crime and criminalizes some groups, often the most powerless, at the expense of others. Taking all the different approaches together indicates that to understand crime comprehensively a number of different questions have to be asked. These include exploring how crime is defined and constructed, why offenders find it attractive, why some groups are more likely to be criminalized, and why some are more likely to turn to crime.

It will be seen in subsequent chapters that all the theoretical approaches outlined above have affected contemporary work, often in combination. To them must be added the insights of feminist perspectives which will be explored in Chapter 8. The theories looked at in this chapter have broadened the questions which have been asked about crime. They have moved away from the narrow focus of earlier work to include a recognition of the importance of revealing the way in which crime is constructed and the necessity of looking at social control as well as at crime. More recent approaches have also included the victim of crime, and these concerns will be explored in subsequent chapters.

Review Questions

1. Taking an example of deviance from your own experience, draw up a deviancy amplification chart to illustrate the ideas of the labelling perspective.
2. Identify a recent example of a moral panic. How would it be analysed by the labelling and Marxist approaches reviewed in this chapter? Does it involve criminalizing any particular group?
3. Why have control theories been criticized for their neglect of motivation?
4. Why is the phrase 'crime *really* is a problem' so significant for left realists?
5. Describe situations in which crime could be attributed to absolute deprivation and contrast these with situations in which it could be attributed to relative deprivation.

Key Reading

Downes D and Rock P (1995) *Understanding Deviance: A Guide to the Sociology of Crime and Rule Breaking*, revised 2nd edition. Oxford: Clarendon Press
Lea J and Young J (1993) *What is to be Done about Law and Order?*, 2nd edition. London: Pluto Press
Sim J, Scraton P and Gordon P (1987) 'Crime the State and Critical Analysis: An Introduction', in P Scraton (ed) *Law, Order and the Authoritarian State*. Milton Keynes: Open University Press
Sumner C (1994) *The Sociology of Deviance: An Obituary*. Buckingham: Open University Press

CHAPTER 5
THE VICTIMS OF CRIME

The offender, rather than the victim, was the main focus of early theories of crime and of criminal justice policy. More recently, however, considerable attention has been paid to the victim and early approaches were criticized for their neglect. To realists, the 'reality' of victimization underlined the argument that crime really is a problem. To administrative criminologists, the victim plays a role in the situations in which crime takes place, has a major role to play in crime prevention and criminal justice policy is also more sensitive towards victims. Women's groups played a major part in drawing attention to the victimization of women and children in the home, and critical criminologists to victimization from corporate, state and racially motivated crime.

This chapter will start by exploring how victimization is socially constructed before outlining the development of victimology and the so-called rediscovery of the victim. It will discuss the role and significance of the victim survey, which as seen in Chapter 2 has become a major source of information about crime. It will then explore aspects of the impact of crime on individual victims and the general public who are often said to have an exaggerated fear of crime. Further aspects of victimization, such as its social distribution and fuller details of the findings of victim surveys as they relate to specific offences will form part of later chapters.

CONSTRUCTING THE VICTIM

The concept of the victim is intricately related to the social construction of crime. Victims, for example, may feel less victimized if they feel that they are partly to blame for offences. This echoes an often made distinction between the innocent victim who deserves sympathy and the undeserving victim who is considered to have provoked offences. The words 'innocent victim' imply a more serious offence with archetypical innocent victims being the old lady who has been mugged or a child murder victim (Walklate 1989). On the other hand, the drunken victim of an assault resulting from a fight, the woman whose dress or behaviour is said to be 'provocative', the householder

81

who leaves a window open, or the car owner who fails to lock the car might all be said to have 'asked for' an attack or theft.

This distinction is deeply rooted in commonsense understandings of victimization and is reflected in law and policy. The techniques of neutralization described in Chapter 3 use the notion of the undeserving victim by suggesting that victims 'had it coming to them'. In a criminal trial, victims' credibility may become an issue as offenders attempt to justify their actions. Insurance companies encourage householders to install security devices. Victim compensation schemes exclude victims who have contributed to their victimization and sentences may be higher or lower depending on the harm done to the victim. Defrauding a 'vulnerable' pensioner, for example, may be seen as more serious than defrauding a company or the state (Levi 1989). This raises a number of questions. Is a burglary any less serious or the burglar less blameworthy because a window is left open? Is leaving a car radio or briefcase visible in a car inviting theft? Is rape less serious because a woman has invited a man into her home? Is an attack in a street the victim's fault for being in that street? The victim is, however, often blamed.

Victimization is also associated with notions of passivity and helplessness, and the examples of archetypal victims reflect conceptions of powerlessness and vulnerability. The elderly and children are assumed to require protection and to be relatively helpless in the face of an attacker. Other victims are expected to 'fight back' and protect themselves. Women are expected to resist sexual assault before yielding to the assumed superior strength of the male attacker. A common question asked about victims of domestic violence is why they stay with violent partners, again assuming a passive victim. Indeed, some feminists suggest using the term 'survivor' which implies a more active response than the term victim (Kelly 1988, and see Chapter 10). Men, on the other hand, are less 'ideal' victims as they are assumed to be able to protect themselves. This may mean that they have more difficulty coping with and accepting victimization (see Chapter 8).

BLAMING THE VICTIM: THE DEVELOPMENT OF VICTIMOLOGY

This tendency to blame the victim was a prominent theme in the development of victimology, and victims, like offenders, were seen as different. Early victimologists, echoing the concerns of criminology with the causes of crime, explored the extent to which the victim could be a 'cause' of crime by precipitating it and asked whether victims possessed any distinctive characteristics which made their victimization more likely (Walklate 1989; Davies et al 1996). It was thus hypothesized that some people were more prone to become victims, that victims precipitated offences and that different lifestyles carried a higher risk of victimization. These arguments are summarized below.

Victim proneness

To von Hentig (1948), some groups were more prone to becoming victims. These included young people, women, the elderly, the mentally defective and immigrants and he also referred to the wanton and the fighting victim. This was largely based on theoretical speculation rather than empirical study (Walklate 1989). The idea of victim proneness also featured in the work of Mendelsohn (1947) who saw some victims as culpable because they contributed to the crime. To him, victims ranged from the most innocent, such as children, to the most guilty, such as the person who attacks someone and is killed in retaliation.

Victim precipitation

Other studies attempted to establish the extent to which victims, especially victims of violence, directly precipitated an offence. In a study of police records, Wolfgang estimated that victim actions precipitated 26 per cent of homicides (Wolfgang 1958). In a similar study of rape, Amir (1971) estimated that 19 per cent were victim precipitated, where women had agreed to sex but later retracted or had not resisted strongly enough. This latter study attracted criticism on the grounds that it implied that women were inviting rape, and some queried how strongly women should have to resist. Victim blaming was therefore a major problem with the idea of victim precipitation. Another difficulty with these kinds of study was their reliance on official reports, which include the interpretations of investigators, and are not accurate and unbiased accounts of events (Walklate 1989; Zedner 1997).

Lifestyles and victimization

People's lifestyles are strongly associated with victimization as, quite simply, those who never go out are unlikely to be attacked in the street while many people live, work or spend their leisure time in places where crime is more likely. Hindelang and his colleagues argued that there was a strong link between routine daily activities and exposure to high-risk victim situations (Hindelang et al 1978). Role expectations and structural characteristics such as class, age or gender were also important as they affected lifestyles and victimization was, for example, related to the amount of time spent in public places. As victims and offenders must both be present in the same place at the same time, they often share similar lifestyles. This can partly explain some findings that victims and offenders tend to be of the same age group, come from the same area or from the same social class. Thus, the victims and the perpetrators of assaults taking place in public tend to be young males who go out drinking. This approach can be empirically tested by looking at victims' experiences, rather than relying solely on official records (Walklate 1989). It can also be a useful guide to policy, in that identifying high-risk lifestyles can lead to prevention.

These approaches, often described as conventional or conservative victimology, have many common problems. They looked largely at public or street crimes and are limited to crimes with identifiable victims thereby neglecting many forms of crime (Davies et al 1996). The concepts of victim precipitation and victim proneness quite clearly involve victim blaming and writers uncritically accepted stereotypical assumptions in relation, for example, to gender. Many assumed, as in Amir's work, that the woman who does not struggle enough has precipitated an assault (Zedner 1997). Lifestyle approaches can involve victim blaming by implying that some have more risky lifestyles and can avoid victimization, which may not be possible for those who cannot avoid dangerous areas. They therefore tend to neglect the structural dimensions of victimization and victim–offender relationships; while they describe groups and lifestyles with high risks, they do not explore the reasons why these groups face such high risks (Walklate 1989). Despite these limitations, conventional victimology echoes widely held views about victims and affected both criminal justice policy and subsequent work on victims (Davies et al 1996).

Other approaches to victimology include radical, feminist and critical approaches. While later criticized for its neglect of the victim, radical criminology was concerned to expose the 'human misery' created by the crimes of the powerful. Thus Box (1983), detailing cases of deaths occurring as a result of breaches of safety regulations, argued persuasively that corporate crime 'kills' and has real victims. A major part of the development of left realism, outlined in Chapter 4, was the development of what Young (1986) described as radical victimology. This would focus on the structural basis of victimization and it was argued that large-scale victim surveys neglected the greater victimization of the poor and inhabitants of inner city areas. Left realists argued for more locally based victim surveys designed to be more qualitative, to better measure the impact of crime in local areas and to use a broader definition of crime which attempted to tap hidden crimes of sexual violence and harassment (Jones et al 1986). Radical victimologists also aimed to work with local groups and local authorities as the victim survey provided a form of democratic input into the framing of criminal justice policy (Davies et al 1996).

Feminist approaches were highly critical of the stereotypical assumptions and victim blaming of conventional victimology, particularly as it related to female victims of rape which re-enforced the construction of the passive and powerless female victim (Walklate 1996). They also criticized the focus on offences taking place in public which neglected violence in the home. A large amount of feminist research and writing sought to expose the victimization of women in the home and to improve the treatment of female survivors of violent relationships and rape by the police and criminal justice process. On the other hand, feminist approaches have been criticized for their emphasis on women's victimization and a neglect of male victimization (see Chapters 8 and 10).

Some argue for the development of a critical victimology to build on the criticisms of other approaches. Thus Mawby and Walklate (1994) call for a deeper understanding of the meaning of victimization and what is meant by words like 'lived reality' used by realists. In addition, they contest that the resurgence of interest in the victim must be critically examined by asking whether it serves victims' interests or those of the state. Research on victims, they argue, must be contextualized. Why, for example, do some victim movements succeed at certain points in time? Whose interests are served by the success or otherwise of victim movements? Which victims are neglected and why? The concept of the victim, as with crime itself, is seen to be related to wider issues of state power and domination (Mawby and Walklate 1994).

REDISCOVERING THE VICTIM

Until the 1960s, the victim was regarded as a 'forgotten actor' and was largely neglected by offender-centred theories of crime and criminal justice policy. Since then the victim has emerged as a 'key player' in both research and in criminal justice policy (Zedner 1997). This has often been attributed to a victim 'movement', although concern with the victim of crime emerged from diverse sources which did not form a concerted campaign or coherent set of theories or policies (Newburn 1995; Davies et al 1996; Zedner 1997). A number of initiatives sought to provide victims with compensation, and women's groups campaigned on behalf of the victims of sexual and physical abuse. Victims received little emotional or practical help and also felt marginalized by the criminal justice process. These developments will be briefly outlined to illustrate the so-called 're-discovery' of the victim.

Compensating victims

Victims, particularly those of violent offences, were seen to be inadequately recompensed. While national insurance and health schemes protect people from the effects of unemployment or ill health, crime victims have no such state protection. In addition, it had for long been argued that the sentencing of offenders should include some form of reparation to victims. This could serve as a deterrent by imposing an additional financial penalty, or a rehabilitative one, by emphasizing the harm done by offending. There are therefore two main ways of compensating victims: through financial awards funded by the state, or through the criminal justice system.

A Criminal Injuries Compensation Scheme was introduced in 1964. It has been highly selective in distributing awards, and selection reflects the distinction between deserving and undeserving victims. Victims who failed to report crimes to the police, were related to offenders or who were considered to have provoked offences were excluded from its inception. The Home Office White Paper introducing the scheme illustrates the rationale for this:

The Government does not accept that the State is liable for injuries caused to people by the acts of others. The public does, however, feel a sense of responsibility for and sympathy with the *innocent* victim and it is right that this feeling should find practical expression in the provision of compensation on behalf of the community.
(Home Office White Paper 1964, cited in Newburn 1995: 150)

This measure emerged largely as a penal reform measure rather than from any campaigning on the part of victims, indeed there was no consultation with any victim group (Rock 1990; Newburn 1995).

Compensation for victims through the court largely involves the imposition of a compensation order added to a sentence, and courts' powers to grant compensation orders were increased in successive legislation. Schemes to encourage mediation between offenders and victims have also been introduced. Like the introduction of state-funded schemes, however, these measures, argues Newburn, were more influenced by the need to fill a gap in penal policy than from any clear concern with victims. Thus he argues 'although it involved victims it was, strictly speaking, in many ways not really about victims' (Newburn 1995: 154).

The role of the women's movement

Reference has already been made to the significant role of the women's movement from the 1970s (Dobash and Dobash 1992, and see Chapters 8 and 10). This challenged the conventional construction of crime and victimization which focused almost entirely on property crimes and public violence. The compensation scheme, for example, excluded victims of domestic violence. It was also argued that female victims became further victimized in the criminal justice process as the police often took little action against 'domestics' and often failed to take complaints of rape seriously. In court, the rape trial could in effect become a trial of the victim. Women's groups, in addition to exposing these problems, set up refuges for women in violent homes and support groups for the victims of rape. These began on a largely voluntary basis and led to some improvements in the way in which the police handled rape victims although financial and state support was often lacking (Dobash and Dobash 1992; Newburn 1995; Zedner 1997).

Supporting victims

The voluntary sector was also concerned with the plight of victims, who often felt that their victimization was compounded by an absence of support in coping with the effects of crime and neglect by the police and courts. Victims complained that while they provided the police with essential information they were ignored after making an initial report. They were not informed adequately about the progress of investigations or whether they would be required in court. If called as a witness, they were ill prepared for the often hostile cross questioning of defence lawyers and faced re-living painful experiences and encountering offenders in court (Rock 1990, 1991).

A network of voluntary victim support schemes under the umbrella of the National Association of Victim Support Schemes (NAVSS) developed from 1974, and aimed to provide emotional support and help for victims. They also attempted to improve the treatment of victims in court by providing support for witnesses (Rock 1991). Early schemes tended to focus on largely conventional crimes although their scope was subsequently extended to include cases of rape and sexual assault.

Taken together these developments led to far greater attention to the victim. They were, however, limited and many argue that despite many changes and the publication in 1990 of a Victim's Charter, the criminal justice system remains offender centred (Newburn 1995; Davies 1996). It can also be argued that the re-emphasis on the victim functioned as a means of diverting attention from the inability of the criminal justice system to develop credible alternatives for dealing with offenders. Emphasizing the harm suffered by victims was also associated with the more punitive stance of conservative criminology which stressed the responsibility of individual offenders for their offences and for the harm done to victims. This formed the context in which greater attention was paid to the victim, an important part of which was the development of the victim survey.

SURVEYING VICTIMS

The importance of victim surveys as a source of information about crime and some of their findings were outlined in Chapter 2 and this section will focus in more detail on the context within which they developed and on some of their strengths and limitations. Following a growth in the use of victim surveys in the United States and some exploratory investigations in Britain, the first BCS was carried out in 1981. Each sweep, as the samples are called, interviews one adult from randomly selected households asking about experiences of victimization in the year preceding the survey and about how worried they are about crime. The range of topics has increased in successive sweeps to include questions about current policy concerns such as contacts with the police, attitudes to crime in local neighbourhoods, membership of Neighbourhood Watch, experiences of witnessing crime, self-reported offending and cannabis use, attitudes to drugs and experiences of racial and sexual harassment (Mayhew 1996). The BCS has several aims, which Mayhew (1996) summarizes as follows:

- to provide an alternative count of crime to statistics based on police records

- to measure trends in crime

- to provide more information about the nature of crime and victims' experiences

- to assess the risk of crime among different social groups

- to look at other crime related issues.

These aims are inevitably policy oriented and they do provide an invaluable source of information for policy makers, serving, as Coleman and Moynihan (1996) point out, the needs of administrative criminology.

Early surveys attracted many criticisms. As seen above, realists argued that as they were based on large national samples they did not reflect the concentration of victimization among specific groups. They are largely based on conventional constructions of crime and early surveys did not cover domestic violence or racially motivated crime. As seen above, radical victim surveys aimed to look at smaller, local areas and included a wider range of incidents and offences. The prototype of these was the *Islington Crime Survey* whose results indicated higher levels of victimization in inner city areas along with higher levels of sexual and racially motivated offences (Jones et al 1986). Many other local crime surveys were carried out, including those in Edinburgh and Merseyside (Kinsey 1984; Anderson et al 1990). Other studies focused on specific problems that were not well covered by large-scale studies, such as child abuse or sexual assault, and, as mentioned in Chapter 2, many industrial organizations now sponsor surveys to cover the institutional victims not dealt with in household-based studies.

While victim surveys have produced an enormous amount of information they have their own dark figure (Coleman and Moynihan 1996). Some use different methods and definitions which makes their results difficult to compare and many offences are omitted. Respondents may not always remember incidents clearly. They must therefore be interpreted with caution and some of the main considerations to be taken into account are outlined below.

The definition of offences and victimization

Victim surveys inevitably omit many offences. Clearly they can only ask about crimes which victims are aware of and they therefore omit offences like fraud or pollution. The focus of the BCS on individual households limits their scope to largely personal offences such as assault and property offences affecting individual household members. While initially criticized for neglecting domestic violence and racially motivated offences, later BCS sweeps have used specially designed questions to include domestic violence and have taken 'booster' samples of minority ethnic groups (Mayhew 1996). The BCS also omits crimes against institutional victims such as schools or shops – shoplifting, for example, is not covered. Professional and organized crime, white collar crimes and state crime are also omitted.

Surveys also vary in how offences are defined and victims' accounts do not always fit readily into legal offence categories. As the BCS aims to compare victim reports with police records, it uses legal criteria to determine whether or not an incident is a crime and how it can be legally classified. Other surveys use different criteria and often include incidents such as bullying or harassment which are not technically crimes. This makes surveys difficult to compare and produces different results.

Choosing samples

Any victim survey must choose as representative a sample of the relevant population as possible. The BCS was originally based on the electoral register which inevitably excluded those who did not register, among whom might have been particularly vulnerable groups such as those without permanent housing, recent immigrants or those who chose not to register. Since 1992, the sample has been taken from post code address files (PAF) which is said to have increased its representativeness (Coleman and Moynihan 1996; Mayhew 1996). Another problem with large-scale surveys was, as seen above, that they found it difficult to take account of the experiences of smaller groups at local levels. The booster samples taken in the last three sweeps of the BCS have attempted to take this into account and the 1992 survey also included a sample of children aged between 12 and 15, who were excluded from earlier surveys (Mayhew 1996).

The accuracy of victims' reports

Victim surveys inevitably rely on people's memory. Victims may however exaggerate incidents or fail to remember them at all. In addition, they cover a fixed time period which creates the problem of telescoping where victims may remember an incident but move it forwards or backwards in time. While these problems may cancel each other out, some research indicates that more trivial incidents tend to be forgotten or telescoped backwards, whereas more serious ones are remembered and telescoped forwards. This may lead to an overestimation of serious incidents (Coleman and Moynihan 1996). In addition, victims may not wish to reveal particularly sensitive experiences, and while there have been attempts to overcome this by the use of special questions, it is still generally accepted that surveys underestimate much violence and sexual abuse in the home (Coleman and Moynihan 1996; Mirlees-Black et al 1996).

Interpreting victim surveys

All these limitations must be borne in mind when interpreting the findings of victim surveys, which often deal with broad statistical aggregates. Much criticism, for example, surrounded the conclusions of the first BCS that the average person could expect a robbery once every five centuries; an assault resulting in an injury once every century; a car to be stolen once every sixty years and a burglary every forty years (Hough and Mayhew 1983). This gave a somewhat reassuring picture of people's risk of crime, leading to the conclusion that people's fear of crime was exaggerated. But, it could be asked, who was the average person? Local surveys, such as the *Islington* survey produced far higher figures, suggesting that people's fears were far from unrealistic (Jones et al 1986). It must also be reiterated that victim surveys only provide information about some kinds of crime.

THE IMPACT OF CRIME

One of the main strengths of victim surveys is that they provide much fuller information about the impact of crime on victims and on the general public. Exploring this involves more than assessing the direct effect of individual offences on individual victims. Offences may lead not only to material losses or physical injury but to emotional effects to victims and others less directly affected. For some, crime may be a recurring experience and, for others, the threat of crime may be as worrying as an actual offence. Perceptions that crime is rising may lead to a more widespread fear of crime and can affect the quality of life. This section will explore some of these different effects.

Dimensions of victimization

The objective and subjective impact of crime

A distinction is often made between the objective and subjective impact of offences (Walklate 1989). The objective impact includes the immediate financial or physical effect; however, many offences have additional costs. Stolen items have to be replaced, damage to property must be repaired and, even if the victim is insured, claiming from insurance policies involves paperwork, time and trouble. This contributes to the 'nuisance value' of offences which also includes the time taken to report offences, give statements to the police and possibly attend court. Some offences also have a subjective, psychological impact. Many victims report a mixture of emotions such as shock and anger and some offences may lead to sleeplessness, avoidance of particular places, recurrent memories of the event and, with serious crimes, post-traumatic stress syndrome and other psychological problems (see, for example, Zedner 1997).

Victim surveys explore these different aspects of victimization. The BCS for example asks whether victims were affected a lot, quite a lot or a little and looks at what offences upset people most and what the most upsetting features are. Some general points from these questions are summarized below:

- The majority of victims are not greatly affected by offences. In the 1984 BCS only 11 per cent said that crime affected them very much and 17 per cent 'quite a lot'. In the 1988 BCS: Scotland, more than half of the reported incidents involved losses of under £25 and only 8 per cent of victims reported emotional reactions lasting more than a month (Kinsey and Anderson 1992).

- More severe effects are found among victims of robbery, wounding, burglary, threats and major vandalism. The 1988 BCS found that victims were most affected by more serious personal crimes, and least by less serious household crimes (Mayhew et al 1989).

- Burglary has the most severe effect of household crimes, particularly where premises have been entered. While some find the inconvenience and nuisance most upsetting, the invasion of privacy emerges as a major feature upsetting many victims (Mirlees-Black et al 1996). The Scottish crime survey found that this was mentioned more frequently as the single worst thing about a burglary and some victims also reported sleeplessness and tearfulness – this latter being more common among women (Kinsey and Anderson 1992).

- Perhaps unsurprisingly, personal attacks create the strongest reactions. For men, mugging is the most upsetting experience and, for women, domestic violence (Mirlees-Black et al 1996).

The direct and indirect effects of victimization

Some crimes affect more people than those directly victimized, while others have no direct victim but have a diffuse effect on residents and communities. Some examples of these indirect effects of crime are outlined below.

EFFECTS ON FAMILIES AND RELATIVES

Victims' relatives, particularly in cases of serious crime, can also be adversely affected. This is seen most vividly in the case of murder where relatives have to cope with the trauma and grief of losing family members. They require counselling and support and, in some cases – particularly where large numbers are killed in one incident – have formed support groups to exert pressure on investigations, inquiries and legal changes to prevent similar occurrences. Victims' children can also be affected – children of burglary victims may suffer from insomnia, nightmares and increased bed wetting and they are also affected by living in homes with violent parents (Morgan and Zedner 1992).

WITNESSING CRIME

Witnesses to crime may also suffer shock, heightened fear and may feel threatened. In some offences witnesses may be directly threatened as, for example, in an armed robbery or other violent incident. They may fear intimidation if they give evidence to the police. They may also suffer the nuisance and inconvenience of having to give statements, and, like victims, may face hostile questioning in court (Rock 1991). In some neighbourhoods witnessing crime forms part of an overall experience of crime which may particularly affect young people's attitudes to crime and the police (Anderson et al 1994, and see Chapter 7).

THE DIFFUSE EFFECT OF CRIME

Many crimes have no direct victims while others have only a small effect on individual victims. Their impact may be more diffuse. Prostitution and illegal drug use, which have no direct victims, may nonetheless damage the reputation and quality of life in an area, and local residents may face harassment and violence by those seeking the services of a prostitute or drug dealer. Many frauds and white collar crimes have only a small effect on individual victims. A classic situation in these offences is where an employee or company charges a small amount extra for goods or takes a small amount from, for example, a bank account. These individual losses may be negligible but the net profits are considerable. Consumers may have to pay more to compensate for losses from shoplifting and employee theft, and tax payers may have to pay more to compensate for losses from tax evasion. If fraud and corruption is seen to be commonplace, trust in business or government declines (see Chapter 16).

THE THREAT OF CRIME

Even if an incident is trivial or no offence has actually occurred, the threat of crime can have an adverse impact. Seemingly trivial incidents of harassment, name calling, bullying or insults can have severe effects if repeated or persistent. This is particularly the case with domestic and racially motivated offences. It will be seen in later chapters that survivors of violent relationships and members of minority ethnic groups are particularly affected by living under a constant threat of crime and violence.

Repeat victimization

This indicates the significance of repeat or multiple victimization. While the majority of victims suffer only one crime, 24 to 38 per cent of property crime and 48 to 59 per cent of personal crime in the 1992 BCS was reported by victims who had experienced five or more offences (Ellingworth et al 1995). Expressed differently this means that:

> 63 per cent of all property crime was suffered by people who had already suffered a property crime during the period and 77 per cent of all personal crimes were suffered by people who had already suffered a personal crime during the same period.
>
> (Ellingworth et al 1995: 363)

It has also been estimated that the BCS underestimates repeat victimization due to its limited time period (Pease 1997).

Many kinds of crime involve repeat victimization. Embezzlement and employee theft are often repeated, as are cheque and credit card frauds. Domestic violence and the sexual abuse of children also involves the same participants over long periods of time (Pease 1997). Racially motivated harassment and vandalism can involve persistent, repeated attacks on the same target as can shoplifting or commercial burglary. Repeat victimization can vastly increase the impact of crime, compounding its cost and nuisance value along with increasing the emotional effects leading, in severe cases, to physical and mental ill health. Establishing some of the factors which produce repeat victimization could therefore prevent some of the most adverse effects of crime and, if this led to more successful prevention, could have a dramatic effect on the crime rate (Pease 1997).

Why does repeat victimization occur? In many ways it makes sense from a rational choice perspective. If an offence has been carried out successfully in one situation it is easier and less risky to commit an identical offence (Farrell et al 1995). Burglars have learnt how to break into a house successfully and know their way around. In addition, they may assume that stolen property has been replaced, or that other items are available for stealing (see, for example, Wright and Decker 1994). Similarly, shoplifters, having been successful once, may re-visit familiar territory. It may also be more likely where there is an absence of a guardian, someone who will see a crime and protect the victim (Farrell et al 1995). This could account for the recurrence of, for example, domestic violence which is also exacerbated by the proximity of the victim and offender.

Worrying about crime

Victim surveys also ask respondents about what is generally described as the 'fear of crime'. In Britain, and in most Western societies, many people see crime as a major social issue and, particularly in inner city areas, report feelings of being unsafe in the streets (Mawby and Walklate 1994). It has been argued that people's worry about crime far exceeds their risk of crime, leading to suggestions that the fear of crime is in itself a problem and that people's fears are irrational (see, for example, Zedner 1997). Moreover, those most at risk of assault, i.e. young men, express less worry about it, whereas those least at risk, i.e. the elderly, worry most (Zedner 1997). In the latest BCS for England and Wales, nearly a third felt that they were certain, very likely or fairly likely to be burgled in the next year, whereas only around 6 per cent of households were burgled in 1995. One in six felt that they were certain, very likely or fairly likely to be mugged, whereas the statistical risk is less than 1 per 100 (Mirlees-Black et al 1996). Yet are people's fears really so irrational? What are people really expressing when they say are they worried about crime and how likely they are to be victims? Would we expect worries to be related to risks? Kinsey and Anderson (1992), for example, point out that, while people worry about car accidents and take precautionary measures, this could be seen as sensible rather than irrational.

Are fears and worries about crime irrational?

The BCS asks respondents whether they are very worried, fairly worried or not worried at all about specific kinds of crime. In the latest sweep, more people worried about burglary than about other forms of crime. Women were generally more worried than men about all offences and rape caused the highest feelings of worry among women (Mirlees-Black et al 1996). In the

Scottish crime survey, over half female respondents were very or fairly worried about rape, and just over half the sample were very or fairly worried about housebreaking (Kinsey and Anderson 1992). Respondents are also asked how safe they feel walking on the streets after dark and answers to this question reveal much higher rates of fear among the elderly and women.

To what extent are these fears irrational? Realists, in their criticisms of early victim surveys, argued that surveys did not relate these fears to respondents' experiences. If people lived in high-crime areas their fears were more related to their perceived risk. In addition, women's worries about rape appear far more rational when the extent of unreported rape is taken into account (Zedner 1997). For those sections of the population most at risk, therefore, high levels of fear may be realistic. Recent crime surveys have also shown that fear of crime is highest among low-income groups, which parallels their higher risk (Kinsey and Anderson 1992; Mirlees-Black et al 1996). The higher fears of the elderly and the poor may also reflect the more severe impact of crime on these groups. The elderly may worry more about violence because of their physical frailty and because they would take longer to recover from any attack. Those with low incomes are less likely to be insured and can least afford to replace stolen goods. They may also be most affected by the nuisance value, losing income and time in making repairs or going to court. Indeed, as Kinsey and Anderson (1992) point out, these groups report more severe financial and longer lasting emotional effects. Again, therefore, worries cannot be dismissed as irrational.

It can also be asked: 'What do answers to these questions indicate?' Seeing fears as irrational implies that we should only be worried in proportion to our risk – yet we may be worried about unemployment as a social problem without fearing imminent redundancy (Kinsey and Anderson 1992). People may be worried about crime in general, the risk to their family or their worries may be related to personal experience (Kinsey and Anderson 1992). Concern about crime may reflect more general concerns about, for example, moral decline, the decline of a neighbourhood, public drunkenness or general feelings of insecurity (Zedner 1997). They may not therefore be related to an assessment of immediate risk.

One way of looking at this is to explore the extent to which worry about crime affects people's routine activities. This is difficult to extract from general questions on feelings about safety. Old people may avoid walking on the streets at night, but this may be because they are afraid of falling in the dark or because they are physically infirm rather than through worry about crime. Others may not go out because they have child care commitments, no car, nowhere they want to go or no money for leisure (Mirlees-Black et al 1996). Only 3 per cent of the women sampled in the 1996 BCS gave crime-related reasons for staying at home at night although this rose to 9 per cent among the elderly and was higher in inner cities (Mirlees-Black et al 1996). In the Scottish crime survey, only 1 in 10 men compared to 1 in 3 women gave crime as reason for not going out on foot. Women were also more likely to take a car rather than walk and go out with someone else and avoid certain streets (Kinsey and Anderson 1992). Crime does therefore affect people's behaviour, but so does fear of other misfortunes.

While worry about crime as measured in victim surveys is generally described as fear of crime, this word can be misleading. It was pointed out above that worries may express many different feelings and crime itself provokes a mixture of reactions which do not always include fear. Thus many victims report shock and anger rather than fear; many complain of the nuisance value of offences; and many are affected very little (Kinsey and Anderson 1992). Seeing fear of crime as a major problem may therefore be somewhat exaggerated. Kinsey and Anderson argue that rather than promoting fear, crime has an impact on everyday life.

THE SOCIAL DISTRIBUTION OF VICTIMIZATION

Chapter 2 illustrated that victimization is unevenly distributed among the population and this chapter has also referred to the higher risks and impact of crime faced by some groups. While this will be discussed at length in later chapters, this section will outline some general considerations about the impact of crime on different groups. In general terms, area of residence, class, gender, race and age are all related to victimization and vulnerability to crime which, to Mawby and Walklate (1994), consists of a combination of fear and risk. These factors work in combination with each other. Thus, area of residence is closely related to income and lifestyles which are, in turn, related to gender, age and race. One form of vulnerability may be compounded by another, meaning that some groups are disadvantaged on several counts. Members of racial and minority ethnic groups for example may be disproportionately represented among low-income groups and, through discrimination in the housing market, be over-represented in high-crime areas. They may additionally face racially motivated harassment, vandalism and violence (see Chapter 9). Other offences may specifically target women, the young or the elderly because of their status. Thus some murders are specifically directed against women and children, and all of these groups may be the target of fraudsters because of their assumed lack of financial or technical knowledge (see Chapter 15). Many of these relationships will be explored in later chapters.

The limitations of victim surveys must also be borne in mind when looking at statistical measures of risk and fear in relation to these factors. Lower-class young men, for example, emerge as the group most at risk from violent offences, but crime surveys measure greater proportions of public violence than other forms (see Chapter 10). Against this can be placed the apparently greater vulnerability of women and children to violence and sexual abuse in the home, although this can also affect men. This also affects the elderly with elder abuse being even more hidden than other forms of domestic violence (see Chapter 10). Different patterns might also be found if the full picture of victimization from fraud, corporate or state crime were to be included. These include older victims and may show different patterns of gender, income group and race.

Moreover, as seen above, statistical assessments of the risk of crime do not adequately reflect the differential impact of crime. It has been seen that lower income groups, inner city residents, the elderly and women report more severe effects and worry about crime more, although it has been argued that men may be more reluctant to admit to being affected or being worried about crime. It has also been argued that this is related to the more severe impact of crime on groups who have fewer means to protect themselves or remedy the losses. Thus vulnerability must be seen in a wider social context. The more affluent can choose not to live in high-crime areas, and can afford to protect themselves (Lea and Young 1993). It has also been pointed out that lifestyle theories, which contain elements of victim blaming, may overlook the difficulties which some face in avoiding 'risky' lifestyles (Mawby and Walklate 1994). Other victims are especially powerless. The elderly or young children, for example, can do little to protect themselves from the crimes of other family members on whom they may be dependent – a situation which may also affect those who may be tied to violent partners by economic dependency. It will be seen in later chapters that inequalities of class, gender, race and age, gender and generation are all involved in crime and victimization.

CONCLUDING COMMENTS

This chapter has explored many aspects of victimization and illustrated how it has emerged as a major element in analysing crime. Indeed, as Zedner points out, 'far from being simply a compartmentalized topic, victim research has impacted upon every aspect of criminological thinking and profoundly altered our picture of crime' (Zedner 1997: 607). The victim survey is used not only to measure crime but to explore many different aspects of people's experiences of, attitudes towards and worries about crime. Looking at the experiences of victims has also enhanced our understanding of crime itself, the situations in which it occurs, and relationships between victims and offenders. The victim has also become a more significant aspect of criminal justice policy and crime prevention.

Despite all this, however, many aspects of victimization remain underexplored, and some commentators remain sceptical about the extent to which victims' interests have been fully recognized. Like crime, victimization is socially constructed, and this construction affects policy and research. Victim surveys omit many forms of crime and, while violence in the home is now more widely recognized, this resulted from the vigorous campaigns of women's groups, indicating a political dimension in the construction of crime and victimization. Less attention has been paid to the victims of professional and organized, corporate, white collar and state crime which, as will be seen in later chapters, have a direct as well as a diffuse effect. Elements of victim blaming, so evident in early victimology, continue to affect how victims are perceived and dealt with. To critical victimologists, crime surveys gloss over the structural basis of victims' vulnerability which may be related to wider inequalities of class, age, race or gender (see, for example, Mawby and Walklate 1994). In addition, as has been seen, many reforms which have taken the victim into consideration in criminal justice have been initiated to meet the need for new directions in policy rather than being motivated solely by the needs of victims. Many of these issues will be taken up in subsequent chapters.

Review Questions

1. Locate one of the British or Scottish crime surveys and construct a short questionnaire based on questions about experiences of and worries about crime. Administer this to some selected respondents and consider the following questions.
   (a) How accurately do people respond?
   (b) How are offences defined?
   (c) Which offences are omitted?
   (d) What do you think respondents mean when they say they are worried about crime and specific crimes?
   (e) Are their fears out of proportion to their risk of victimization?
   (This exercise can be done in groups.)
2. From media or other sources find examples illustrating the social construction of victimization in respect of 'victim blaming' and contrasts between deserving and undeserving victims.

Key Reading

Davies P, Francis P and Jupp V (eds) (1996) *Understanding Victimisation.* Northumbria Social Science Press

Mawby R and Walklate S (1994) *Critical Victimology: The Victim in International Perspective.* London: Sage

Walklate S (1989) *Victimology: The Victim and the Criminal Justice Process.* London: Unwin Hyman

Zedner L (1997) 'Victims', in Maguire M, Morgan R and Reiner R (eds) *The Oxford Handbook of Criminology*, 2nd edition. Oxford: Clarendon Press

CHAPTER 6

CRIME, CLASS AND THE ECONOMY

Relationships between social class, crime and the economy have been a prominent theme in many analyses of crime. Early approaches tried to explain the higher rates of conviction of the lower classes, whereas later ones argued that the criminalization of lower class activities was the main problem to be explained. Recent economic restructuring and rising unemployment have revived a concern with inequality and crime. These have produced communities in which many have little hope of stable employment and all that goes with it – financial independence, marriage and family life or participation in the consumer society. This has been linked to the growth of an 'underclass' characterized by, among other features, high rates of crime. Many questions about class, crime and the economy are worthy of exploration. What kinds of relationships can be established? What kinds of crime are involved? Are poverty, deprivation or unemployment related to crime? Are they related to criminalization? What is the impact of recent economic change on crime?

This chapter will start by exploring how the relationship between class and crime has been conceptualized. It will then look at links between crime and economic factors such as recession and unemployment before going on to explore how crime has been associated with the development of an 'underclass' and to wider social and economic policies. Finally, it will look at different ways of analysing this relationship, drawing on the theoretical approaches introduced in Chapters 3 and 4. It will focus largely on lower-class crime although it will stress the significance of white collar and corporate crime which will be explored in Chapter 15. It is also difficult to separate issues of class and crime from gender, age and race – and themes will be introduced in this chapter which will be taken up in subsequent chapters focusing on these interrelated forms of inequality.

SOCIAL CLASS AND CRIME

Before looking at the association between social class and crime, the concept of social class must be briefly outlined. Class is not an easy concept to define, and the many controversies surrounding its definition and measurement lie beyond the scope of this text. It is generally related to economic differences although few strictly follow the Marxist approach outlined in Chapter 4 in which it is seen to derive from ownership of the means of production – producing two main classes. Income, employment status and wealth are also important and most talk about lower, middle and upper classes. These differences are also related to a host of more subjective differences such as status, lifestyle, culture or patterns of consumption – commonly used phrases like 'working-class culture' or 'middle-class lifestyle' incorporate many different dimensions. People's identification of themselves as working, middle or upper class also reflects a combination of characteristics.

Class involves other features. The class structure and relationships between classes may change along with economic conditions – thus recent economic changes are said to have produced an 'underclass'. Marx predicted that differences between classes would polarize and that the exploited class would become more aware, or conscious, of its position and more politically active. Consciousness of a common identity is therefore important. The notion of class also involves notions of reproduction or closure – classes reproduce themselves by controlling entry. Wealth, in the shape of property and capital, enables the accumulation of more wealth which is passed on to children. Sociologists also talk of cultural capital – where the culture of a class is passed on to children through, for example, education. This enables them to be socially mobile or retain their superior class position. It will be seen below that all these aspects are important in analysing the relationships between class and crime.

Social class and offending

While the lower-class status of offenders is generally assumed, the class of offenders or victims is not routinely recorded. Other indicators, such as samples of known offenders, tend to confirm the assumption that the majority of convicted offenders come from lower-class backgrounds (Coleman and Moynihan 1996). A recent study of persistent young offenders found that only 8 per cent came from non-manual backgrounds (Hagell and Newburn 1994). Other studies have found that offenders tend to live in the most economically deprived areas and self-report studies, while originally finding a weaker association, also confirm the general pattern (Coleman and Moynihan 1996). It has also been pointed out that risks from burglary are highest in poor housing estates which implies the lower-class status of offenders – unless, comment Coleman and Moynihan, it can be supposed that 'middle class burglars are travelling to poor areas hoping to find something worth stealing' which, they argue, is unlikely! (Coleman and Moynihan 1996: 108).

These figures refer only to known and convicted offenders. To what extent are they produced by the different treatment of offenders with different class backgrounds? This could happen in two ways. Lower-class suspects may be treated differently as the police make judgements about the character of those they encounter based on dress, speech or deference – all more likely to favour middle-class offenders (see, for example, Piliavin and Briar 1964). The stereotypes and self-fulfilling prophecies pointed to by labelling theorists are all relevant. The police may associate some, mainly lower-class, areas with high rates of offending and perceive their residents as potential offenders. Middle-class offenders may have a better chance of being cautioned as this often involves considerations of, for example, the quality of the home, parental occupation and the likelihood of re-offending (see, for example, Landau and Nathan 1983).

Individuals from different classes rarely, however, commit the same kinds of crime. Middle-class youth have less need to steal a car to go joyriding as they may take their parents' car. Reference has already been made to the lower rate of detection, prosecution and conviction characteristic of white collar crime which is assumed to involve middle- and upper-class offenders. Simple contrasts are inappropriate as not all white collar offenders are of such high status as often assumed and class may not be the main or only factor affecting their treatment (Croall 1992, and see Chapter 15). Nonetheless it is the case that crimes such as burglary, robbery or theft, which are largely associated with lower-class offenders, are more likely to be prosecuted than crimes such as tax evasion or breaches of health, safety or consumer legislation, which are associated with middle-classes offenders (Croall 1992).

This suggests a far more complex relationship between class and crime. Different kinds of crime are associated with offenders from different social class backgrounds. This may be related to a host of factors including different opportunities – the unemployed burglar is rarely in a position to commit a financial fraud and the senior executive is unlikely to resort to burglary in favour of fraud or embezzlement. Discussions of the relationship between class and crime must therefore recognize the different offending patterns of different classes. This indicates that concerns about the class–crime relationship are themselves socially constructed – it is the greater criminality of the lower classes which is defined as *the* problem.

Class and victimization

Chapters 2 and 5 also drew attention to the uneven distribution of victimization and indicated that the risks of many kinds of crime are higher in lower-class urban areas. The most recent BCS found that the risk of burglary was highest for those in inner cities, council accommodation and with low income (Mirlees-Black et al 1996). Victimization from domestic violence and homicide has also been related to class (Coleman and Moynihan 1996; Levi 1997). Victimization from other offences is more widely dispersed – after all, high-income groups have more worth stealing and can be targeted by burglars or robbers (see Chapter 12). Nonetheless, as seen in Chapter 5, it may have a particularly severe impact on the poorest who are also subject to repeat and multiple victimization.

While crime is often portrayed as an inter-class phenomenon – with the poor stealing from the rich – the picture emerging is that it is largely intra-class and that offenders and victims are drawn largely from the same social groups (Lea and Young 1993; Coleman and Moynihan 1996). While some burglars do target the homes of the wealthy, and car thieves prefer high-status cars, by and large, property and personal crime takes place within a local context. Burglars generally do not travel far from their own area; violence in the family is also intra-group as are assaults in pubs and clubs.

The relationships between social class, crime and victimization are therefore complex. A further problem is the extent to which social class is the key factor and how it is related to other aspects of inequality, such as economic deprivation and disadvantage, unemployment, family life, housing, area and the economic context in which these inequalities are generated and maintained. These may also be associated with the treatment of suspects within the criminal justice process. In addition, class inequalities cannot be separated from those of gender, age or race – the problem is not only constructed as one of lower-class crime, but, as will be seen, as a problem of lower-class youth.

EXPLORING CLASS AND CRIME: THE DANGEROUS CLASS?

Social and economic change

It was seen in Chapter 3 that early approaches linked crime to social and economic change. Durkheim's analyses were written at the end of the nineteenth century following major social and economic upheaval, and Merton's around the time of the great economic recession. As the end of the twentieth century approaches, major economic changes continue to be relevant. While sociologists dispute the precise nature and effects of what is often called economic restructuring, most agree that major changes have had an enormous impact on local communities. Technological change has brought about what is often described as globalization – industries, finance, retailing, telecommunications and the mass media operate on a global scale. Many large industries moved production to less-developed countries which provided a cheap supply of labour. This, along with technological change, led to a decline in traditional manufacturing industries – a process often called de-industrialization.

This has been accompanied by changes in industrial organization and employment. The development of computer and other technologies made many traditional crafts and skills redundant, producing a smaller skilled labour force and a larger number of unskilled workers who could be hired or fired according to immediate needs. This produced what is often described as a dual labour market, consisting of a smaller number of core, skilled workers who can expect security of employment, career progression and higher salaries and a larger, peripheral group of unskilled workers who have little security of employment or opportunities for career progression. This surplus labour force contains disproportionate numbers of women, minority ethnic groups and immigrants. Industrial restructuring has therefore been accompanied by deskilling and casualization and the need for a flexible labour market – a process often described as Post-Fordism to indicate a move away from the mass production systems characteristic of the car industry, known as Fordism. At the same time, the power and influence of trade unions has declined. Rising unemployment is most marked in those areas most affected by de-industrialization, industrial restructuring and downsizing which were previously dependent on major manufacturing industries such as mining, cotton, steel or shipbuilding.

There have also been significant changes in housing and the geographical distribution of socio-economic groups. From the 1950s onwards residents of older 'slums' were rehoused in new estates, often on the periphery of cities. The consequent break up of working-class communities accompanied early signs of the polarization of jobs and the decline of traditional industries (Taylor 1997). To Taylor, it is more than a coincidence that this was also a period of rapidly rising crime (Taylor 1997). These changes, however, according to Taylor, shrank into insignificance compared to the changes of the 1980s, when the recession led to steep increases in the number of jobless and long-term unemployment.

The net effect of all this on individual communities can be described as devastating (Taylor 1997). Long-term unemployment affects the economic life of an area, threatening the viability of shops and businesses. Some talk of a lost generation of youth consisting of those who reached employment age in the early 1980s and have not been able to enter the job market. Valued crafts and skills have declined and young men can no longer aspire to the jobs or responsibilities of their fathers – a situation which affects traditional gender and family relationships. These areas are recognized popularly as 'estates' or neighbourhoods from 'hell', the modern equivalent of the 'dangerous areas' of the nineteenth century, which now include peripheral estates as well as the inner city. In the 1980s and early 1990s a series of disturbances erupted in many English cities, the later ones drawing attention to peripheral estates (Campbell 1993; Graham and Clarke 1996). There has been considerable research and discussion about how these features of contemporary Britain are associated with crime.

Crime, unemployment and economic cycles

The difficulties of establishing relationships between unemployment and crime have produced contradictory conclusions. A number of assumptions are involved in asking how the two can be linked which affects how any data can be interpreted. In addition, the effects of unemployment are difficult to distinguish from labour market changes and the effects of cycles of recession and growth. This section will explore some of these issues.

The social construction of unemployment and crime

Economists and social commentators have for long recognized the different ways in which crime can be related to economic conditions. To the economist Adam Smith, crime was related to economic dependency which could corrupt, and to independency which increased honesty – the growth of commerce and manufacture, he argued, increased independency and prevented crime (Pyle and Deadman 1994: 340). Economic cycles of growth and recession produce changes in employment and consumption. In a recession, consumption declines and unemployment rises – often seen as the trigger for increasing crime. Expansion, which leads to higher incomes and consumption, can also lead to crime. One nineteenth-century commentator, noting an increase in convictions in the 1850s following the 'hungry 1840s', attributed this to the 'intemperance which high wages encourage among the ignorant and the sensual' (cited in Taylor 1997: 267). Unemployment was also popularly related to crime through assumptions that 'good work habits' encouraged discipline and responsibility. The unemployed were often portrayed as 'idle' and their situation blamed on their 'workshy' nature. Increases in unemployment were perceived as a threat to law and order (Crow et al 1989).

Social and welfare policy reflected a distinction between the deserving and undeserving poor. The former were seen as being poor through no fault of their own, and deserved assistance. Others were seen as unwilling to work and therefore undeserving. Means tests and later requirements that those applying for benefit should be actively seeking work reflect the notion that only the deserving should receive state benefits. The undeserving poor were also associated with weak morals and a propensity to crime and drug abuse. This was echoed in the often made division between the rough and the respectable elements of the labouring classes with the former constituting the 'dangerous class'.

Other features of unemployment have been popularly linked to crime. The unemployed are assumed to have more time and opportunity to commit crime – 'the devil makes mischief for idle hands'. As control theories might suggest, they are seen to have fewer constraints by having less to lose, thus work can be seen as a form of social control. There are many problems with these notions. It has already been pointed out that the employed also commit crime and not all who do not work are assumed to be criminal. No such imagery surrounds the retired, the 'idle rich' or the redundant executive for example (Lea and Young 1993). Worklessness in itself is not assumed to lead to crime. The problem is also therefore constructed around the activities of lower-class young men – involving elements of class, gender and age, and often race. This also directs attention to the social meaning of unemployment to different groups (Lea and Young 1993).

Measuring the unemployment–crime relationship

Statistically establishing any relationship between crime, unemployment and economic cycles poses many methodological problems. Extremely complex statistical and econometric measures are necessary which will not be fully detailed here, but the main problems will be outlined before looking at the conclusions of these kinds of investigations.

THE RELIABILITY OF STATISTICAL INDICATORS

The many limitations of criminal statistics have already been rehearsed. Victim surveys, while also limited, do provide a more accurate indicator of rising crime. Measurements of statistical trends before the advent of victim surveys are therefore less reliable. Unemployment statistics are also 'constructed' and difficult to interpret – unemployment is subject to many different and changing definitions and figures are widely recognized as underestimates.

THE 'TIME LAG'

Explorations of trends and associations must account for the time taken for economic changes to have an impact. Economic recession takes time to produce higher unemployment which, in turn, takes time to lead to changes in behaviour.

THE DIFFERENT EFFECTS OF ECONOMIC CYCLES ON CRIME

It was pointed out above that economic cycles may have different and conflicting effects on crime. Economists refer to two alternative theories:

- *Opportunity theory* suggests that in a period of growth crime will rise. Incomes rise and there are more goods in circulation which creates more opportunities for crime.

- *Motivational theory* suggests that during a recession the unemployed turn to crime as their legitimate income decreases, implying increased motivation.

If these theories are both correct they would have different effects on crime rates, making the figures even more difficult to interpret (Pyle and Deadman 1994).

It is hardly surprising, therefore, that statistical evidence linking crime and unemployment has been inconsistent and that economists are cautious in stating any firm conclusions (Pyle and Deadman 1994). In a thorough review of research, Box (1987) found a slight but inconsistent relationship between rates of unemployment and recorded crime. This tends to be stronger for youth crime and unemployment, with recent work finding higher rates for burglary among men under 25 during periods of unemployment and lower rates during periods of recovery, although there is an overall upwards trend (Wells 1995). The relationship is stronger for men, suggesting that unemployment may have a different impact on males and females (Naffine and Gale 1989).

In a major study carried out for the Home Office, Field looked at different kinds of crime, concluding that unemployment did not have a separate effect on crime rates which were more strongly related to personal consumption (Field 1990). Personal consumption per capita, the amount that each person spends during the year, is inversely related to property crime – the more people have to spend, the lower the crime rate. As personal consumption falls, crime rises. This is only a short-term effect and is related to both motivation and opportunity theories. In the short run, he argues, recession has an inflated effect on a small group who move between criminal and legitimate economic activities. A sharp fall in consumption growth 'may trigger frustration as economic expectations are lowered' and undermine social controls (Field 1996: 117). When the economy recovers, this group move back into legitimate occupations, producing an immediate fall in crime rates. As the economy continues to recover, economic growth increases the opportunities for crime, producing higher rates (Field 1990; Pyle and Deadman 1994).

A different relationship is found with personal crime. When consumption grows slowly, so too does personal crime, but it increases more rapidly when consumption grows rapidly. Personal crime, he argues, is not directly affected by goods but by patterns of routine activities. It has already been seen that people who go out more often are more likely to be the victims of personal crime, and more time is spent outside the home when people have more disposable income, thereby increasing personal crime. These trends were particularly strong in England and Wales during the 1980s, where recorded property crime grew very rapidly at the beginning of the decade, whereas personal crime grew very little. Later years showed a reverse pattern with personal crime growing rapidly in 1987 and 1988, whereas property crime rose slowly. His conclusions have been broadly accepted as confirming a relationship between property crime and the business cycle (Pyle and Deadman 1994).

The role of unemployment is less clear. A greater time lag is involved as employers take some time to recognize the significance of economic indicators and to increase or reduce labour (Pyle and Deadman 1994; Wells 1995). They may also use overtime or short-time working which are also significant (Wells 1995). While Field argues that unemployment is not a major factor, Wells argues that his analyses illustrate its effect as surges in consumption first affect those whose position in the labour market is weak or marginal. Additionally, argues Wells, police statistics confirm a strong association between property crime and unemployment as areas with highest unemployment in England and Wales (Cleveland, Merseyside, Northumbria, Greater Manchester, South Yorkshire, West Midlands, Greater London and South Wales) are also areas with the highest crime rates (Wells 1995).

These statistical correlations may establish relationships but cannot explain them and can in some ways be seen as superficial. Any association between changes in the labour market and different kinds of crime must be interpreted by exploring how people are affected by changes. It has already been pointed out that unemployment does not in itself lead to crime as it is experienced in different ways by different groups. Long-term unemployment or short periods of casual work may have a more severe impact than temporary unemployment. They mean that individuals have no stable income, which adversely affects their chances of obtaining a mortgage or better housing and undertaking long-term financial or other commitments. It is these effects of long-term unemployment which may affect crime (Crow et al 1989). These kinds of relationship are more difficult to explore statistically but are linked to arguments that the class structure is changing and that there is a growing 'underclass'.

The criminal 'underclass'?

The term 'underclass' has been used in different ways. In the United States it was used in connection with areas in cities like Los Angeles and the 'frostbelt' of de-industrialized northern cities with high rates of gang warfare, drug offences, violence and property crime. This has been linked by right wing commentators such as Charles Murray to permissive welfare policies and a culture of dependency which is passed on through generations (Murray 1990; 1996). To others the 'underclass', consisting of the most disadvantaged, emerges from the processes of de-industrialization and a reduction in the value of welfare benefits (see, for example, Wilson 1987). It is, like Marx's 'lumpenproletariat', typically seen as a class below the rest of society, consisting of those trapped by unemployment, low incomes or poor housing. Its inhabitants are socially and geographically isolated and excluded from the benefits of other citizens (Bagguley and Mann 1992; Taylor 1997). This section will look critically at notions of the 'underclass' and its links to crime and family life.

Is there an 'underclass'?

On the basis of research in Britain, Murray (1996: 123) argues that,

> Britain has a growing population of working-aged healthy people who live an a different world from other Britons, who are raising their children to live in it, and whose values are now contaminating the life of entire neighbourhoods.

He identifies three key features of the 'underclass' – illegitimacy, violent crime and drop out from the labour force – and goes on to explore how these affect individual communities as follows.

106

- Illegitimacy, while found across all classes, is most prevalent in lower-class communities, in some of which it predominates. To Murray, 'communities need families' and 'fathers', as an absence of fathers provides young men with few role models and they become aggressive and run wild (Murray 1996: 124).

- Increasing crime devastates communities, fragmenting them and leading young men to look up to criminal role models.

- In Britain and in America, many young, healthy, low-income males choose not to take jobs and fail to see work as a source of respect. They do not obtain work habits and responsibilities. This affects whole communities as they cannot support families and find other ways to 'prove that they are men, which tend to take various destructive forms' (Murray 1996: 133).

- The British 'underclass', like its American counterpart, is a result of liberal social welfare policies, which by providing public housing and social security enable young women to have children without the support of a father, and young men to choose not to work. Reducing state benefits would prevent this.

Many aspects of his arguments have been criticised and some major questions are summarized below:

IS THERE AN 'UNDERCLASS'?

The term 'underclass' is often used very loosely (Bagguley and Mann 1992). It was pointed out above that to sociologists the term class implies a coherent grouping capable of reproducing itself and from which outward mobility is difficult. The term 'underclass' was previously used to characterize the situation of racial minorities, excluded by processes of racism and discrimination but many minority ethnic groups can and do improve their situation. Others use the term to describe the situation of the very poor or the reserve army of labour (Bagguley and Mann 1992). There is little evidence however that it is a cohesive group or that its membership passes through generations (Bagguley and Mann 1992).

DO THE ARGUMENTS HAVE ANY EMPIRICAL SUPPORT?

There is little empirical support for Murray's arguments, particularly those asserting links between illegitimacy, single-parent families, attitudes to work and crime. Bagguley and Mann argue that these do not specify precise relationships or how one affects any others. Any empirical evidence which is advanced is often highly selective. Bagguley and Mann (1992) ask if there is any evidence at all to show that women find social security benefits so attractive that they have children to obtain them? An account of Easterhouse, an estate on the outskirts of Glasgow, mentioned specifically by Murray, challenges many points. Holman confirms that unemployment is high, incomes are low and furthermore argues that there is a link between poverty and crime. This does not, however, indicate the presence of an 'underclass'. As he argues

> Young people may be unemployed but not from choice; most want desperately to work and even compete to deliver newspapers or cut grass. Most children live with two parents. Most residents, including lone parents, care deeply about family and community life . . . Easterhouse is not being overrun by an 'underclass'. That is a myth. The reality is of a majority of ordinary and decent citizens who yet find themselves in the midst of crime and vandalism.
>
> (Holman 1994: 12)

Rather he argues, social deprivation generates feelings of futility which makes some steal and others take drugs. It gives rise to a sense of grievance against inequalities which justifies property crime.

BLAMING THE POOR?

The 'underclass' notion in effect blames the poor for their situation and it can therefore be used ideologically to divert attention from structural problems. It was pointed out above that the notion of a dangerous class lacking 'respectable' morals has long echoes in history. Descriptions are often written as if describing foreign populations on excursions into unknown territory (Graham and Clarke 1996). To Campbell, it draws on a 'long tradition of class contempt for poor people' (Campbell 1994: 19). Bagguley and Mann illustrate aspects of this – the paupers of the 1830s were described as 'feckless idlers who had been cushioned by the allowance systems', and the poor of fifty years later were seen as a 'residuum whose behaviour was conditioned by their genes'. By the 1920s they had become a class of 'unemployables' who had lost the will to work (Bagguley and Mann 1992: 124). The notion of the 'underclass' is an ideology of the upper and middle classes. Rarely, they argue, do we hear of

> the Wall Street 'underclass' demoralized by their junk bond dependency culture! The divorces, white collar crime, drug taking, drinking, the phenomenal benefits of state welfare dependency (£7 billion in tax relief on mortgage interest alone in 1989), and the casual sex of the middle classes does not of course demoralise them.
>
> (Bagguley and Mann 1992: 123)

To them it is ideological in that believing in it sustains relations of domination involving class, patriarchy and race. They do not deny that there are real divisions but argue that the 'underclass' theory obscures rather than illuminates an understanding of the real problems of poverty and the processes which produce it. To critical criminologists, attributing crime to the poor denies any governmental responsibility for the economic and social policies which produce these conditions (see, for example, Brake and Hale 1992).

THE TRULY DISADVANTAGED?

Other models of the 'underclass' attempt to avoid so overtly blaming the poor. Wilson describes the combined effects of racial segregation brought about by housing discrimination, structural economic transformation, black male joblessness, and the migration of the employed from areas of maximum deprivation (Wilson 1987; Sampson and Wilson 1995). This concentrates urban black poverty and family disruption in specific areas, producing social isolation and disorganization. Residents are deprived of resources and conventional role models, and of cultural learning from mainstream social networks. Social isolation rather than race is related to subcultural development. In the United States, race is seen as a crucial feature of the 'underclass', while in Britain class and area are seen as more significant, with the 'underclass' often being associated with traditional lower-class areas such as the north east and north west of England and parts of Scotland – it may indeed have a Celtic connotation (Bagguley and Mann 1992; Taylor 1997). Wilson's work can nonetheless be criticized for its focus on culture – as Bagguley and Mann (1992: 117) argue, 'whichever way you look at it, the poor remain poor because they've got an attitude problem'.

The term 'underclass' must therefore be looked at very critically. Many critics would accept that some groups face severe problems which may be related to crime. Few would dispute that there are areas of towns and cities characterized by a constellation of social problems including crime. Taylor argues that Murray and others point to the real problems of the 'absolutely destructive effects' of structural unemployment which have been magnified by the pursuit of free market economic policies with no real care for their human consequences. To him, older industrial cities of the north of England and lowlands of Scotland are:

> plagued by what would previously have been quite unknown levels of theft and burglary, car stealing, interpersonal violence and also by a crippling sense of fear and insecurity, which cuts thousands of their residents off from the pleasures of the broader consumer society and the compensations of friendship and neighbourhood.
>
> (Taylor 1997: 285)

Pearson also describes clusters of crime, drug misuse, high levels of unemployment and poverty, wretched housing and poor access to public services – arguing that these produce subcultures organized around fighting, thieving, drug misuse and graffiti writing. Thus,

> if the poor and disadvantaged are largely passive victims in these processes of exclusion which manufacture ghettos of despair, the active human spirit will also strive to create alternative systems of status, achievement and social meaning.
>
> (Pearson 1994b: 4)

The family, crime and the 'underclass'

A prominent theme in contemporary versions of the 'underclass' is the assumed breakdown of the family. This in itself involves assumptions about the ideal or normal family seen to be under threat by increasing divorce and single parenthood. Murray and other commentators conjure up an imagery of lone mothers producing the next generation of 'feckless mothers to be and uncontrolled males' (Graham and Clarke 1996: 168). The family has been blamed in many ways for crime. It has been seen to pass on pathologies or criminal values, to fail to control and discipline children and to affect them adversely by divorce or conflict. This is also seen as a class problem. Divorce and single parenthood are increasingly common in all social classes, yet only assumed to produce crime in the lower class. In addition, a whole series of studies of family characteristics and delinquency have found it difficult to separate the family from its social and economic context.

Summarizing a long series of studies, Farrington lists poor parental supervision, erratic or harsh discipline, parental disharmony, rejection of children, low parental involvement with children, large family size and the presence of criminal parents and siblings as being associated with delinquency (Farrington 1994). These are, however, strongly related to socio-economic factors and strong relationships have also been found between delinquency and low income, large families and residence in run-down housing estates (West and Farrington 1973, 1977).

The role of the mother has often been construed as the problem. During the 1950s a popular theory associated delinquency to maternal deprivation (Bowlby 1953). This was based on slender evidence, but did point to the quality of the relationship between the child and their main carer (Utting et al 1993). This is also the case with theories linking delinquency to working mothers who were responsible for producing 'latch key' children who came home alone from school and were left unsupervised to roam the streets. Again research failed to substantiate this argument. West and Farrington found that children whose mothers worked full time were less likely to be delinquent as the mothers were able to provide more for their children by supplementing the family income (West and Farrington 1973, 1977). Again this emphasizes the quality of child care. Feminists have been extremely critical of many of these theories as they are based on a highly stereotypical view of the mother – as Utting et al (1993) point out, why was the role of the father not explored?

Another popular argument related delinquency to family breakdown and, while some studies did find a relationship, the key factor was found to be conflict which had an adverse effect whether the parents lived together or separately (West and Farrington 1973, 1977). The current emphasis is on single-parent families and, following Murray, on families who have never had a father. Research has, however, found few clear links between delinquency and one-parent families whose situation could indeed be contrasted favourably to two-parent families characterized by abuse and conflict (Utting et al 1993).

While few dispute that the family is important, its effects are clearly related to socio-economic circumstances, although it should not be assumed that all

110

children from poor families are at risk of becoming delinquent or that all children from better off families conform. Like the 'underclass' argument, linking the family and crime can scapegoat families by blaming them for their children's delinquency. Campbell for example argues that some talk as if the turbulence of family life belongs only to the poor. They also invoke stereotypical notions of gender. Mothers' morals, she argues, are blamed for their sons' bad behaviour, while less attention is paid to the macho, militaristic cultures which exhaust and frighten neighbourhoods (Campbell 1994). Notions of the 'underclass' perpetuate a stereotypical notion of the male provider and dependent mother. Even had such families existed, conditions have changed. Women are in a changing labour market position, and men can no longer aspire to the lifetime employment on which such notions were based (Bagguley and Mann 1992).

The effects of free market policies

A major theme running through all of these discussions is the effect of industrial restructuring. This has an air of determinism and it can too easily be assumed that these effects are inevitable. Taylor, for example, argues that crime is not inevitably related to de-industrialization and economic change, but to the free market policies of governments during the 1980s (Taylor 1991, 1997). It was seen in Chapter 4 that conservative policies were associated with individualism and a reduction in state intervention and they also involved an attack on welfare benefits. Elliot Currie has linked these policies to crime by a series of propositions which, while he talks mainly of the United States, are also relevant to Britain. They are summarized below.

- *Market society promotes crime by increasing inequality and concentrated economic deprivation.* The polarization of work, which has resulted in the increase in unstable, part-time and low paid jobs is, he argues, a result of deliberate economic and social policy. At the same time the real value of low wages has declined as this was seen as essential for profitability.

- *'Market society promotes crime by weakening the capacity of local communities for "informal" support, mutual provision and socialization and supervision of the young'* (Currie 1996: 345). As communities suffer from the long-term loss of stable incomes, they can no longer provide social support: 'If you're having tough times you can't lean on your neighbours . . . because they're having tough times too' (Currie 1996: 346).

- *'Market society promotes crime by stressing and fragmenting the family'* (Currie 1996: 346). The pool of 'marriageable men' who can support a family is reduced, leading to the proliferation of single-parent families. To survive economically some families must take on two or even three jobs – reducing their leisure time and time to spend with their children.

111

- 'Market society promotes crime by withdrawing public provision of basic services for those it has already stripped of livelihoods, economic security and "informal" communal support' (Currie 1996: 347). In America welfare benefits have been reduced and many public services in Britain are short of resources.

- 'Market society promotes crime by magnifying a culture of Darwinian competition for status and dwindling resources and by urging a level of consumption that it cannot fulfil for everyone through legitimate channels' (Currie 1996: 347). This echoes the classic theories of anomie. Currie paints a chilling picture of violent street crime, illustrating how it can be related to the pursuit of consumer goods or status. 'Some of our delinquents will cheerfully acknowledge that they blew someone away for their running shoes or because they made the mistake of looking at them disrespectfully on the street' (Currie 1996: 348).

Critical criminologists such as Brake and Hale also associate rising crime with government policy, arguing that:

Conservative criminology is part of the ideological background of economic liberalism. A moral climate has been created in which collective responsibility has become unfashionable. Instead, we have the enterprise society where profit at any cost has become the holy grail. Ironically, with its determined attempt to restructure the British economy at the expense of the working class, and by taking such a hard line on scroungers and loungers, the Conservative government has created the very social conditions which have led to the intensification of the very crime wave it was elected to end.

(Brake and Hale 1992: 171)

These policies affect not only lower class but all kinds of crime. It will be seen in later chapters that the encouragement of individualism and the aggressive pursuit of profits can be associated with law breaking among managers or executives and with an increase in financial frauds (see Chapter 15). Economic and industrial change have also affected organized crime which can become an alternative labour market (see Chapter 13). The following section will attempt to draw together some of the arguments outlined above and relate them to earlier approaches.

CLASS, CRIME AND CRIMINALIZATION

It has been seen above that there are many different ways of approaching links between social class and crime. Earlier theories related lower-class crime to social and economic change – a theme which remains prevalent. At the same time critical approaches point to the way in which issues of class and crime are constructed around the assumed lawlessness of lower-class areas while ignoring the criminality of other classes. This section will begin by summarizing how crime can be related to class and economic conditions and will move on to discuss issues of criminalization.

Class, crime and deprivation

The classic themes of anomie and strain theory remain relevant in discussions of economic disadvantage and crime. Box, for example, argues that periods of high unemployment and recession are accompanied by more 'thwarted ambitions' which affect different groups in different ways (Box 1987). While older workers may accept unemployment, the young are more likely to be frustrated than the old, and men may experience different problems to women. It was also seen in Chapter 4 that relative rather than absolute deprivation may be a significant factor. Box found a strong association between widening income levels and crime, and it has been seen above that labour market restructuring has produced a growing gap, or polarization, between the situation of the higher paid, whose relative income has risen, and those who are unemployed or partly employed. The existence of visible affluence alongside poverty increases feelings of relative deprivation, fuelled by advertising and a consumer culture. As seen in Chapter 4, relative deprivation is related to what people feel they deserve. Those in employment may try to improve their conditions; however, recent decades have also seen a decline in the power of trade unions and the loss of job security. The young unemployed, particularly those who feel particularly discriminated against, such as residents of peripheral estates or minority ethnic groups, are particularly marginalized and they may be more likely to resort to crime (Box 1987; Lea and Young 1993).

Other theoretical perspectives are also relevant. It has been seen that work can be a means of social control, and, if nothing else, means that for large periods of time workers are occupied in work. Control theory may also therefore be relevant (Box 1987). Box argues for example that unemployment can weaken bonds in families and affects the legitimacy of institutions like schools which prepare people for jobs. The social exclusion which 'underclass' theories imply means that some groups feel that they have little stake in society – which may loosen constraints against committing crime.

The relevance of these approaches is not restricted to the crimes committed by lower-class offenders. Employee and corporate crime may also be affected by the same social and economic changes. During a recession, for example, a strain between the need to maximize a firm's profitability and survival may lead to the neglect of quality or safety regulations which produces greater amounts of corporate crime (Box 1987; Croall 1992). Times of economic growth may heighten aspirations and a culture of individualism can create a moral climate in which financial crimes appear legitimate. Workers at all levels of the hierarchy may feel relatively deprived if they feel they have been unjustly denied promotion or pay increases – justifying embezzlement or theft from employers (see, for example, Croall 1992). Moreover some of these crimes may be enabled by a reduction in regulation brought about by free market policies (Taylor 1997).

The above discussions also suggest the importance of cultural and subcultural approaches. Murray's approach to the 'underclass' in effect blames the

113

culture of the poor and Sampson and Wilson talk of the disorganization in areas increasingly isolated from participation in dominant cultural pursuits. These share many of the problems of theories which identify cultural sources of crime. Nonetheless, it was also indicated above that subcultures adapting to new economic situations may emerge as an active response to exclusion and isolation. It will be seen in later chapters that some forms of crime can be construed as an alternative means of employment and of participating in the consumer society.

Any attempts to explain relationships between crime and deprivation must at the same time recognize the way in which this relationship has been constructed which can amount to the criminalization of lower-class activities. Many of these approaches accept the dominant construction of crime and take for granted the greater criminality of the lower classes. Thus 'underclass' theories can be criticized as ideological and as diverting attention away from the policies which may produce the situation. To critical criminologists, therefore, explaining why unemployment is related to crime is not the major issue as to them the unemployed and economically disadvantaged are victims not only of crime but of criminalization.

Class, crime and criminalization

Fears of the threat to law and order posed by growing numbers of unemployed have for long been associated with increasing social control. Vagrancy acts were used in the nineteenth century to regulate the movements of the 'indigent' and, as seen in Chapter 4, critical criminologists have associated the development of a control 'culture' with such fears. Economic restructuring was accompanied by industrial disputes and protests, from the miner's strike of 1984 to the poll tax protests of the early 1990s. These were interpreted, not as justifiable protests, but as instances of lawlessness by picketing miners or rioters. This, together with the use of aggressive police tactics served to criminalize lower-class protests and have also, argue critical criminologists, been used to justify harsher control measures. Box and Hale for example found a strong relationship between unemployment and imprisonment (Box and Hale 1986; Box 1987). While this could be expected – if crime is rising, so too will prison rates – they argue that unemployment has a separate effect which is consistent over several years and is also found in different countries. How can it be explained?

A variety of factors could be involved. The police may target the unemployed who are more likely to be on the streets, and they may perceive the young unemployed as likely offenders. Areas characterized by high unemployment may also be seen as 'problem' areas, particularly those with high black populations, and subjected to more intensive policing. The employment status of a defendant may also affect decisions taken in the criminal justice process. The police may be more likely to divert an employed offender from prosecution seeing them as less likely to continue their offending and, similarly, courts may be deterred from sending an employed person to prison (Crow et al 1989). To Box and Hale (1986) it can also result from increased state coercion produced by the perceived threat of rising unemployment.

Critics argue that this amounts to a conspiracy theory which is impossible to prove and that courts are not consciously punitive towards the unemployed. They may be more likely to be sent to prison because there are fewer alternatives – they cannot pay fines and courts may be deterred from sending the employed person to prison (Crow et al 1989). Box argued, however, that no conscious bias need be established. Police and magistrates do not deliberately discriminate against the unemployed but act according to their own 'logic' or commonsense – they assume that an unemployed person is more likely to repeat offences and they may share the popular conception of the unemployed as an implicit threat to law and order.

CONCLUDING COMMENTS

This chapter has explored many dimensions of the relationship between social class and crime. It has challenged the assumption that lower-class status is necessarily linked to crime, pointing to the way in which the problem is constructed and that the activities of the lower classes are more subject to criminalization. Different kinds of crime may be associated with different social classes and this in turn may be related to economic and social change and the inequalities which this produces. Recent decades have seen an increasing polarization between those in secure, well-paid jobs and those in casual, poorly paid jobs or who have no jobs at all. The economically disadvantaged have become increasingly excluded from society and geographically and socially isolated. This may well be related not only to property crime but also to other offences such as personal crime or drugtaking. This does not imply that lower-class people are more likely to perpetrate crime as it was also pointed out that the same changes affect the more invisible crimes of other classes.

Finally, it must be asked how significant social class is. It has been seen that crime can be related to class through its associated inequalities such as economic disadvantage and relative deprivation. The significance of other forms of social inequalities have also been indicated. Popular constructions of lower class crime are also associated with age and gender – it is lower-class young men, not lower-class middle-aged women, who are associated with crime. In some areas this also takes on a racial connotation. Subsequent chapters will explore these other dimensions critically, starting with the next chapter which will look at age and its relationship to crime.

Review Questions

1. Unemployment is often said to lead to crime. Draw up a list of arguments which support this and a list of arguments which contradict it. What

evidence can be used to support each argument? How can these apparently contradictory arguments be resolved?

2. On what basis can it be argued that the notion of the 'criminal underclass' is ideological?

Key Reading

Box S (1987) *Recession, Crime and Punishment.* London: Macmillan

Muncie J, McLaughlin E and Langan M (eds) (1996) *Criminological Perspectives.* London: Sage – see readings by Murray, Currie and Field

Taylor I (1997) 'The Political Economy of Crime', in Maguire M, Morgan R and Reiner R (eds) *The Oxford Handbook of Criminology*, 2nd edition. Oxford: Clarendon Press

CHAPTER 7

AGE AND CRIME

Crime is so strongly associated with young people's activities that many theories deal almost exclusively with juvenile delinquency. Successive moral panics have surrounded young people's activities, with many folk devils, from the mods and rockers of the 1960s, through the punks, skinheads, football hooligans, joyriders, muggers, protestors and rioters of the 1970s and 1980s to the yob culture, knife-carrying gangs, ravers, one-boy crime waves, teenage rapists and girl gangs of the 1990s. But is the association between age and crime as strong as is often assumed? As with class, the association is based on official statistics and convicted offenders. It could reasonably be assumed, however, that professional and white collar offenders might be older and that, as with class, different age groups commit different crimes. Young people do, however, commit crime and, as will be seen, they are among its major victims. To young people, especially those most adversely affected by the social and economic changes outlined in Chapter 6, crime is thrilling, provides a chance to acquire the icons of the consumer society and can even become an alternative form of employment. At the same time moral panics about youth crime are associated with tougher policing and tougher laws and young people may be 'demonized'.

This chapter will start by critically exploring the relationship between age and recorded crime and victimization. It will consider age and youth as socially constructed categories and will look at how 'juvenile delinquency' emerged as a 'problem'. This will be followed by an account of some contemporary work on young people's experiences of crime, focusing on a sample of youth in Edinburgh and a study of persistent young offenders. Other aspects of youth crime such as joyriding, illegal drug use and property crime will be looked at in later chapters. Finally, contemporary analyses of youth crime will be related to the theoretical perspectives already introduced. The main focus of the chapter is on youth crime as there is very little material on 'elder' or 'middle' aged crime, which in itself reflects how the age and crime relationship has been constructed.

AGE AND CRIME

Age is formally associated with different roles and responsibilities. As far as crime is concerned, the law distinguishes between different age groups on the grounds of their assumed responsibility for their actions. Thus far reference has been made to juvenile delinquency which, while not a legal category, is often used to refer to crimes committed by those aged under 21. In law, children are assumed to be incapable of telling right from wrong and cannot be convicted of a crime, although there is little agreement about the age of criminal responsibility, which is 10 in England and Wales, but 8 in Scotland (Davies et al 1995). In England and Wales a child is legally defined as someone under 14, and those between 14 and 18 are legally termed 'young persons'. The term 'young offender' is currently used for those between 15 and 20, and those aged between 18 and 20 are sometimes described as 'young adults' (Davies et al 1995). The law also makes some activities which are legal for adults illegal for young people – so-called status offences make it illegal for youth to engage in activities such as driving, buying cigarettes and alcohol or engaging in sexual activity (Pearson 1994a).

Age and Offending

The high proportions of young people among convicted offenders was indicated in Chapter 2, with 43 per cent of offenders convicted for indictable offences in England and Wales in 1994 being under 21 and only a very small proportion being over 30 (Barclay 1995). The peak age for offending changed slightly between 1984 and 1994, with the number of known offenders per head of population aged 10–17 falling by 21 per cent, the number of those aged 18–20 rising by 15 per cent, and for adults over 21 rising by 5 per cent (Barclay 1995). Despite the general perception that youth crime is rising, official figures show different trends. While the number of offenders aged between 14 and 17 increased by almost 150 per cent from 1959 to 1977, they fell by 37 per cent from 1980 to 1990 (Newburn 1995). This may be related to changes in criminal justice policy. The increases could be attributed to the so-called 'net widening' effect of a rise in cautions which brought more young offenders into the criminal justice process, and later decreases to the rise of diversionary strategies and informal warnings. Young people commit a wide range of offences. Only 10 per cent of offences involving juveniles in 1990 involved violence, with the majority involving theft, handling stolen goods and burglary (Newburn 1995). The often repeated assumption that crime is overwhelmingly a young person's activity requires some careful questioning, however. Taking account of the already well-rehearsed limitations of official figures, the following points should be considered.

118

Public and private offences

Young people's lifestyles make their offences more visible, as they more often take place in the streets or other public places. They are also more likely to be detected as they carry out their offences in groups, unlike older offenders who more often work alone and in a less public arena (Coleman and Moynihan 1996). Young people's preference for hanging around street corners can be seen as threatening and attracts public complaint (Anderson et al 1994). While we know little about the age of offenders involved in less visible crimes, it could be assumed that those involved in family violence, white collar and professional and organized crime have a higher peak age (Pearson 1994a; Steffensmeier and Allan 1995; Coleman and Moynihan 1996).

Age, experience and crime

Young people lack the skills and experience needed for some kinds of crime. They are less likely to be in a position to evade taxes or commit corporate or financial frauds or to be employed in the world of serious crime. Lack of technological expertise and experience may also make them less competent criminals and more likely to be caught than older, more experienced offenders (Pearson 1994a). As Steffensmeier and Allan (1995: 107) argue:

> Advancement into higher-ranking criminal occupations such as 'con man' or 'racketeer' depends upon age-related factors such as skill, experience, financial success, and the ability to avoid imprisonment.

Different patterns of age and offending

Some confirmation of this can be found when the age curves for different crimes are compared. In the United States, Steffensmeier and Allan compared burglary, fraud and gambling. For burglary, described as a 'high risk' but less lucrative crime, the peak was around 15 years while for fraud and gambling, described as low risk and more lucrative, there was a more even spread between ages (Steffensmeier and Allan 1995). Con men and racketeers showed a peak in the 50–59 age group, and press reports suggest that white collar offenders are older. In Britain, offences like tax evasion are less likely to involve young people and there is some evidence that elderly shoplifters are less likely to be reported (Coleman and Moynihan 1996). It has also been found that, whereas participation in offences such as theft of a vehicle decline with age, theft from work increases with age (Coleman and Moynihan 1996). Thus, conclude Coleman and Moynihan (1996: 94): '. . . if we were to turn our energies to those offences with the largest dark figures, then age becomes less relevant as a variable.'

Criminal careers

Crime can become a career and it is generally assumed that, while most young offenders stop committing crime somewhere around their late teens, a minority go on criminal careers. They may graduate from less serious, high-risk offences to more serious offences with a lower risk of being caught and are perhaps less physically demanding! Joyriders may become car thieves, burglars may become involved in organized crime or football hooligans may turn to the rave scene (Hobbs 1995). Steffensmeier and Allan (1995: 110) liken this to the careers of athletes:

> Eventually, professional criminals – like professional athletes – reach a point in their lives when they seek less arduous careers. . . . Just as athletes eventually move on to less demanding activities and often seek opportunities in related fields such as sports broadcasting, so too a talented thief with appropriate resources and connec- tions may seek a related career in fencing stolen property.

This criminal career, like a legitimate one, may be affected by their experience and by family and local neighbourhood connections.

Age and victimization

Chapters 2 and 5 indicated a strong relationship between age and victimiza- tion with the elderly emerging as less at risk from both violent crime and burglary and young men emerging as the group most at risk from assault. As with offending, this picture – derived from victim surveys such as BCS – has to be critically explored by exploring the potential effect of more hidden offences. In respect of age, the following points must be taken into account.

Children's victimization

There has been a growing recognition of children's victimization, from phys- ical abuse and neglect to sexual abuse – offences which are difficult to invest- igate in victim surveys (see Chapters 10 and 11). Children may not be aware of their victimization until a much later age and, even if questioned, may be afraid to talk about being physically or sexually abused. Their claims may also be dismissed as fanciful (Walklate 1989). Research suggests that child abuse is far more prevalent than hitherto assumed – with some studies indicating that as many as one in four girls and one in ten boys are likely to experience some form of child sexual abuse before the age of 16 (Walklate 1989, and see Chap- ter 11). There have also been recent revelations about both physical and sexual assault in residential establishments and, as seen in Chapter 5, children are indirectly victimized by crimes in the home (Morgan and Zedner 1992).

The victimization of teenagers

Teenagers may be victimized by crimes within the home or residential insti- tution and also by a variety of crimes and incivilities in school and on the streets. This includes bullying which, while not in itself criminal, involves many elements of crime such as threatening behaviour, assault and actual bodily harm (Morgan and Zedner 1992). Much of this is also hidden and unreported to adults or the police. Other forms of victimization, such as the theft of bags or fights at school, may appear trivial but may be persistent. Studies of schoolchildren reveal the often considerable extent of these incidents. In a study of schoolchildren in Edinburgh, Anderson found that half the children reported having been victims of assault, threatening behaviour or theft from person (Anderson et al 1994). One in seven boys and nearly one-third of 14- and 15-year-old girls reported importuning or flashing. Around one in three children report bullying, which may also be related to racial or sexual harassment (Morgan and Zedner 1992; Hartless et al 1995).

The victimization of the elderly

There has also been a growing recognition of the victimization of the elderly within the family and in residential care (see Chapter 10). They, too, may be subject to physical and sexual abuse and additionally to financial frauds which may be within the family, in residential homes or through the activities of financial fraudsters or high-pressure sales tactics playing on their need to enhance their incomes or increase their safety (Croall 1997). Again this victimization is often hidden with some elderly victims, particularly sufferers of dementia, being unaware of offences and unable to report them (see Chapter 10).

Both offending and victimization are therefore related to age. In part this can be related to different lifestyles. It will be seen below that young people's activities may involve them in both crime and victimization. Old people, on the other hand, tend to go out less making them less vulnerable to public crime, but more vulnerable to crime in the home. These lifestyles are in turn related to the social expectations surrounding age and its associated roles and responsibilities and to the structural position of different age groups. The elderly and children may be especially vulnerable to offences committed within families and the relative powerlessness of youth may affect both offending and victimization. Some of these factors will be explored in the following section.

EXPLORING THE AGE AND CRIME RELATIONSHIP

The relationship between age and crime is, therefore, far more complex than often assumed. While young people have for long been associated with crime it appears that, as is the case with social class, different age groups commit different kinds of crime and that these patterns are associated with the different social expectations surrounding age such as experience and responsibility. This directs attention to the way in which age is socially constructed, and to the issue of why youth crime is so often identified with the crime problem. This section will explore these issues before going on to look at the different ways in which young people can be involved in crime.

The social construction of age and youth

Categorizations and perceptions of youth and childhood are not fixed by biological characteristics but have changed over time (Pearson 1994a). Childhood is today associated with innocence and children are assumed to need protection, being vulnerable, weak and not fully responsible for their own actions. Children and youth were accorded a very different status in earlier eras (Muncie 1984; McLaughlin and Muncie 1993; Anderson et al 1994; Pearson 1994a). They were expected to assume adult responsibilities and work as soon as they were physically capable, without any protracted period of adolescence. Aries' work on the discovery of childhood illustrates how conceptions of 'childhood' developed with the decline of child mortality (Ariès 1962). Parents, who had hitherto placed little emotional investment in children, came to see them as needing nurture, affection and protection. This was particularly the case among the landed gentry and middle-class parents, who, in the nineteenth century, kept their children separate from lower-class children by schooling. Children were gradually seen to require discipline and an introduction to adulthood – creating the status of 'youth' (Anderson et al 1994; Muncie 1984). While this was originally restricted to the middle and upper classes it spread to working-class children with the development of state education. By the twentieth century the concept of childhood was universalized and applied to all classes although, as will be seen below, lower-class children were the ones who became 'delinquents'.

The rise of the juvenile delinquent

The activities of young people have long been the subject of public concern (Pearson 1983). These concerns have been consistently linked to fears about social change, the break up of the traditional family and community, the dwindling power of authority figures such as parents, teachers, magistrates and police and the pernicious effects of popular entertainment (Pearson 1983, 1994a). As early as 1603, a group of youth known as the London apprentices were banned from playing football, playing music or drinking in taverns and were also ordered not to 'weare their haire long nor locks at their eares like ruffians' (Pearson 1994a: 1116). More modern themes emerged with the industrial revolution when youth crime was attributed to the decline of discipline and religion, heredity and the breakdown of the family. They were also said to be imitating the popular dramas of theatres and music halls (Pearson 1983, 1994a). The early twentieth century saw the emergence of 'hooligans' who wore bell bottom trousers, ornamental leather belts, neck scarves, peaked caps and short cropped hair. Pearson (1994a: 1168) comments:

Whereas we think of 'youth cultures' as a novel development deeply characteristic of the post war years in Britain, they have been observable for a century or more . . . youth cultures and youth crime assume the appearance of ever-increasing outrage and perpetual novelty.

Rising rates of juvenile crime attracted particular concern towards the end of the nineteenth century when the term juvenile delinquency became widely used (McLaughlin and Muncie 1993). It was seen as product of lower-class homes and associated with parental irresponsibility, genetic factors and individual pathology. Delinquents were seen as saveable and in what has been described as the 'child saving movement', largely middle-class reformers advocated policies which would save delinquents, who were seen as not responsible for their actions, from a continued life of poverty and crime. Juvenile justice was separated from adult justice, young offenders were sent to 'reformatories' or put in the charge of Police Court missionaries – the forerunners of the Probation Service (Muncie 1984; McLaughlin and Muncie 1993).

Delinquency was thus firmly associated with conditions of working-class family life and also, argue McLaughlin and Muncie, departed from notions of Englishness. The dangerous classes were often described as a 'class apart' and slum children as 'street Arabs' and 'savages' (Graham and Clarke 1996). Pearson notes that the 'hooligans' were seen as an 'un-British' phenomenon – 'indeed we must allow that it was most ingenious of late Victorian England to disown the British Hooligan by giving him an "Irish" name' (Pearson 1983: 75). While cruelty to children was recognized, most concerns were about young people's offending rather than their victimization (Morgan and Zedner 1992).

Concerns with successive waves of what was seen as youthful lawlessness continued throughout the century. It was seen in Chapter 3 that a number of subcultures emerged from the late 1950s. The media tend to focus on the most dramatic and expressive subcultures which may be far from typical, and many subcultures do not involve serious criminal activity, if indeed they involve any at all. They are, however, seen as potentially disruptive, and young people as a whole often complain that they are stopped by the police or complained about for no other reason than that they are hanging around in groups. This, according to Pearson (1994a: 1188), reflects and re-enforces the popular link between youth and crime – thus:

in a cultural context where it sometimes appeared that to be young in itself constituted a reason for being regarded as one of the 'usual suspects', the youth-crime connection is cemented in both social imagery and official statistics.

This may, argues Pearson, reflect deep-seated fears about the rapid progress of social change – of modernity (Pearson 1994a). Older generations experience loss and regret in the face of massive social change. They may feel that their world is falling apart and recall former times with nostalgia. These memories may not be accurate and they may interpret 'folk memory' by recalling an altogether more peaceful time. Young people, on the other hand, welcome the new and unfamiliar, and become a symbol of social change and breakdown. This may account for part of the hysteria which young people's activities may attract and for their 'demonization' (Pearson 1994a).

Young people's experiences of crime

However misplaced fears about rising rates of youth crime may be, as realists would argue, young people do commit crime. Exploring young people's experiences of crime whether as victims, witnesses or participants is also important as it can help to establish the different ways in which youth are involved in crime and how they are attracted to it. It was pointed out above that youth crime may take many different forms. Some may be little more than part of a process of growing up (Anderson et al 1994). Many young people experiment with forms of petty crime, whereas others become involved in more serious or persistent offending. For many, involvement in crime may be transitory, for others it may be the start of a criminal career. To some it is exciting, for others it has a more financial motivation. The following sections will summarize studies focusing on contrasting experiences. The first looks at the everyday experiences of crime among schoolchildren in Edinburgh (Anderson et al 1994), while the second focuses on a recent study of persistent young offenders (Hagell and Newburn 1994).

The interrelationships between young people's victimization and participation in crime, and the meaning of crime to a group of young teenagers, is illustrated in the work of Anderson and his colleagues (1994). They studied a sample of young people aged between 11 and 15 in Edinburgh, drawn from different areas including peripheral estates and middle-class suburbs. Based on self-report and interview data, the study explored how the groups' experiences of crime were related to where they lived and how they perceived different areas. Their perception of the dangers posed by inhabitants of specific areas were associated with deeply ingrained perceptions of the class structure, culture and development of Edinburgh where, following the destruction of inner city slums, the urban poor were relocated on peripheral estates or hidden suburban areas, hiding brutal poverty from the public gaze. While, contrary to what might have been expected, young people across the city had similar experiences of crime, they had different views of different areas. Those from central Edinburgh told exaggerated stories about the 'schemes', and those from the 'schemes' complained of discrimination because of where they lived. Some main points of the study are summarized below (Anderson et al 1994).

Being a victim of crime

Reference has already been made to the high levels of victimization experienced by teenagers. In all areas, half of the respondents had been the victim of either theft, assault or threats in public places in the nine months preceding the study. Boys were more likely to be both the victims and the perpetrators of assaults and threats, with as many as half the boys compared with under a quarter of the girls reporting some form of direct assault, nearly half from strangers and many from older boys. Two-thirds of the sample had experienced some form of name calling or harassment, with nearly half reporting having been frightened by someone 'shouting' or 'staring' at them. The pattern across schools was broadly similar, with harassment by adults, which girls experienced more than boys, causing most fear.

Witnessing crime

As seen in Chapter 5, fears of crime can be heightened by witnessing it. The sample had witnessed considerable amounts of rowdiness, fighting, shoplifting, use of offensive weapons and vandalism – all of which they saw as not very serious. Over half had witnessed at least one crime involving violence, drugs or dishonesty, nearly a third had witnessed a serious crime of violence, and 40 per cent had seen people buying, selling or taking drugs. These experiences were higher in housing estates and similar for boys and girls, although fewer girls had witnessed violence. Young people, they argue, see more crime than adults as they spend more time in public places thus:

> streets are contradictory places for young people. On the one hand, they are places where young people can generate their own fun, in relative freedom from adult supervision; on the other they can be dangerous places where young people come into contact with crime as both victims and witnesses.
>
> (Anderson et al 1994: 65)

Double trouble

Many of these experiences were not reported to parents, teachers or the police. This was partly due to loyalty to people they knew or to fear of reprisals. It was also related to what they describe as 'double trouble'. They feared that if they told the police or parents they would not be believed and, if they were, would be told not to hang about the streets.

Coping with crime – safety in numbers and cautionary tales

They developed what the authors describe as strategies for self-protection which included 'cautionary tales' about dangerous places, people and situations. These took the form of myths or exaggerated stories about events in places such as underpasses or lifts in high-rise buildings and about the activities of gangs. Another response was to adopt the strategy of safety in numbers by hanging around in large groups. This, however, attracted adverse attention from local residents, the police and other groups, which made them appear as perpetrators rather than as victims and could also lead to petty acts of delinquency and fighting. Thus victimization, living with crime on the streets, and participation in crime were all interrelated. This is illustrated in the following comments:

A: 'Well you feel safer with a gang cos you never ken who's goin to jump oot on ya.'

B: 'When I'm oot with a couple of lassies I'm still scared. But when I'm oot really late with loads of laddies and lassies I feel safer.'

(ibid: 85)

Another commented: 'That's why you hang about in groups. So if someone beats you up, you've got someone else to beat them up . . .' (ibid).

Participating in crime

Many of the young people reported participating in crime. Seven out of ten reported committing an offence on one or more occasion, although this included 49 per cent who reported being involved in rowdiness in the street. Under one-third had committed what were seen as serious offences. Just over one-third reported shoplifting, 18 per cent drugs, 15 per cent assault and 14 per cent car vandalism. At the more serious end, one-tenth reported buying and selling drugs, 5 per cent car theft, 3 per cent housebreaking and 2 per cent mugging. Similar rates for less serious offences were found across all areas, indicating that rule breaking and petty crime 'were very much a normal feature of young people's lives, wherever they come from and whichever school they go to' (ibid: 90–1), although serious offending was found more in the peripheral estate of Wester Hailes. Boys reported more serious offending than girls, and serious property offending tended to advance with age.

Gangs and violence

To these young people, violence was an accepted part of life, arising from fights between rival groups of 'casuals'. These groups received exaggerated press coverage and were seen as a problem by the police. Young people themselves were affected by these reports and described 'heavies', 'heavies in the elite', an 'elite nappy crew' and 'baby crew'. This, argue the authors, represented a mixture of myth and reality as the groups appeared to have little, if any, formal organization. They were, they felt, loose networks based on school or area rather than highly organized gangs. Some young people did display signs of membership by their dress and some girls were described as 'casualettes'. Some feared the gangs while others saw them as providing security, and yet others were excited by them. Fights were described but appeared more as ritual or seasonal events, characterized by symbolic rather than actual violence. In general terms vandalism and rowdiness in the street were seen as a source of fun and creativity. Thus they argue,

126

while it is important to recognise the real damage that can be done both by and to young people by crime, it is equally important to remember that crime can be fun for the young.

(ibid: 122)

Property crime

A small number did participate in relatively serious property crime and organized shoplifting, and circulation of stolen goods did play a major part in the local economy. This was rooted in economic inequality and social divisions and those in poorer areas showed an awareness of poverty and social injustice. The authors argue that different approaches must be applied to different kinds of crime – economic crime can be related to economic deprivation, but much petty crime is an extension of play and learning about formal and informal rules through which young people learn the boundaries of what is and is not permissible.

Persistent young offenders

A recent folk devil has been the persistent young offender, with stories of young teenage boys committing massive numbers of offences and being responsible for a large proportion of offences in local areas. Tough action was called for against this group. A Home Affairs Committee on juvenile crime concluded, on the basis of consultations with the Association of Chief Police Officers (ACPO), that there was a 'small hard core who have absolutely no fears whatsoever of the criminal justice system' (Home Affairs Committee 1993 para 15, cited in Newburn 1995: 144). While the size of this group was difficult to assess it was agreed to be small – Probation Officers estimated that there might be around ten in Hampshire and between twelve and twenty in Newcastle, but the Committee concluded that they caused a 'disproportionate amount of the crime attributed to young people' (cited in Newburn 1995: 145). Hagell and Newburn obtained information about and interviewed a sample of 531 offenders in London and the Midlands. They were all between 10 and 16 and were known to have committed three or more offences in the space of one year by the beginning of 1992. As they were all known to the police they could, acknowledge the authors, be unrepresentative of persistent offenders. Some of their main findings are summarized below (Hagell and Newburn 1994).

Who are persistent offenders?

It was, they argued, difficult to identify a distinct group of persistent offenders. What number of offences distinguishes the persistent from other offenders? Over what period of time must the offences have been carried out? There were also many research difficulties – any one offender may have committed more offences than those officially recorded and may have committed crimes in other areas.

The offenders

Of the sample, one-third were unemployed and a further 16 per cent were non-employed, with only 5.4 per cent working full time. Approximately half lived in households with non-working or unemployed heads, which 'reinforced the general picture of disadvantage that appeared to characterise the lives of these young reoffenders' (ibid: 44). The majority had been arrested on three, four or five occasions, with only around one-fifth having been arrested six to ten times and only 5 per cent having been arrested more – which did not indicate a substantial group of very frequent offenders. Nor, while a small group had committed a large amount of offences, did they account for a very large proportion of offences. The thirty most persistent offenders accounted for less than a quarter of all juvenile offences in the areas studied. While there were fewer girls in the sample, they had committed a similar number of offences.

Offences

Offenders had committed a range of different offence types, most commonly theft and driving offences. In interviews some also reported drug offences.

Reasons for offending

Many claimed to have offended because they were bored, for the fun of it, and for financial gain – including the desire to buy drugs. The excitement and 'buzz' associated with car theft and burglary was evident from accounts: '*I get a buzz out of twoccing*' or '*when I find money in a house it's a big buzz*' (ibid: 89). Many had learnt the skills involved from friends, with some having learnt about 'twoccing' in children's homes. When asked what would make them stop committing crime, they cited a fear of the consequences, mainly prison.

Chaotic lives

Offenders did not conform to any specific 'type'. They did, however, appear to have more chaotic lives than other adolescents, having experienced a high frequency of dramatic events such as admissions for accidents, crashes and stabbings. And, while wary of drawing conclusions from such a small group, they found some evidence of 'disruption and loss in their lives' and truancy. In general they reported good relationships with parents, although a quarter had no relationship with their fathers and reported some family discord. They also reported higher use of drugs than representative samples suggest

– three-quarters had tried cannabis and a third had taken amphetamines. Half had been referred for counselling or psychological help for drugs, fighting, anger, depression, offending and school exclusions – often a result of action by mothers or schools. All of this, suggest the authors, makes them 'far from typical of adolescents as a whole' (ibid: 93).

The most persistent offenders

There were few indications that a small group of most persistent offenders were any different from the sample as a whole, although they had slightly more chaotic lives and higher rates of contact with social services. They were no more likely to be male, older, or to show different offence patterns. Less than 1 per cent had committed very serious offences and their offences were typical of juvenile crime generally. Thus, argue the authors (ibid: 120):

> it is important . . . not to confuse persistence with seriousness. The fact that the vast majority . . . commit the same types of offence as the bulk of young offenders, and that they are generally distinguishable only by the fact that they commit them more often, is something that is often lost sight of when discussing possible sentencing practice in relation to this group.

YOUTH, CRIME AND CRIMINALIZATION

Chapters 3 and 4 outlined many approaches, especially subcultural theory, which have been used to analyse youth crime. This section will explore how these theories can be applied to contemporary youth, who face very different economic and social conditions to their predecessors. These include the problems of long-term unemployment outlined in Chapter 6, which has arguably produced an 'extended adolescence'. Young people's activities may also be subject to criminalization, as their activities produce such a strong reaction.

Subcultural theories and contemporary youth

Recent studies point to the dangers of generalizing about such a varied phenomenon as youth crime. The studies cited above, and others, indicate the diversity of young people's involvement in criminal or quasi-criminal activities. For some it is transitory, for others a commitment; for some it is prompted by 'buzz' and excitement while others have financial motivations – thus no one subcultural style emerges. The local area is a significant part of young people's experience and, as the Edinburgh study illustrates, perceptions of crime and the meaning of their activities must be understood in the context of local culture and local histories. As suggested by the Chicago School, local traditions, cultures and experiences, along with local illegitimate opportunity structures, affect young people's experiences of different forms of crime. Marlow and Pitts (1997: 13) point out that youth riots on the Blackbird Leys estate in Oxford, inter-racial gang fighting in East London and shop-lifting in Hartlepool are plainly not of a piece. They have different origins, different meanings and different social consequences.

To Ruggiero and South (1995: 203) the 'static image that the idea of "subculture" implies seems increasingly less applicable and relevant to youth trends in late- or post-modern society'. There is no one subculture and not all are based on economic deprivation, with polydrug use, commercialization and depoliticization all being important elements.

As well as tending to generalize about subcultural styles and youth crime, both the media and academic theories tend to exaggerate the threat posed by youth subcultures. As seen in Chapter 4, Matza argued that subcultural theories overemphasized the commitment to delinquency. The study of youth in Edinburgh clearly indicates that involvement in crime can be a normal part of young people's lives. This exaggeration also contributes to the criminalization of young people. Pearson (1994a: 1185) points out that:

> The single-minded preoccupation in the mass media and elsewhere with spectacular youth cultures is one means by which youth as a generation can be defined as 'deviant'. Unwittingly, perhaps subcultural criminology sometimes risked doing the same.

Bearing in mind the dangers of generalization, some themes can be drawn from studies of contemporary youth crime. It was seen in Chapter 4, for example, that delinquency, rather than being a sign of commitment to a delinquent culture, could be a result of boredom. It can also, as recent work indicates, be intrinsically attractive and exciting and can be placed in the context of a global consumer culture in which clothes and style are significant features of young people's identity. Economic factors remain important; as Downes (1997) has recently pointed out, earlier approaches in effect signalled problems if young people could not participate in the employment market and grow out of crime.

The excitement of crime

Recent writers have pointed to the inherent attractiveness and seductiveness of crime (see, for example, Katz 1988). The Edinburgh study draws attention to the fun involved in many delinquent acts – vandalism can be seen as a form of creative art work, and gang fights, whether real or imagined, occasion excitement and thrill. This is also illustrated in studies of joyriders, many of whose accounts stress the intrinsic excitement of performance driving or chases with the police (see Chapter 12). Many forms of property crime also give rise to a 'buzz' or thrill, as does drug taking (see Chapter 12). In a study of drug takers and property offenders, Collison (1996) argues that it is also related to young people's desire to take risks. Young men want to 'push it to the edge' and predatory street crime and a heady mix of crime and excessive drug use exemplify life 'on the edge'. Drug taking enhances these feelings. According to one offender 'trips make you want to go out and do cars' (ibid: 434). One offender encapsulates several different themes (ibid: 435):

> like what I really want to do like to occupy my time, I'd like to go jump out of planes . . . that's exciting to me, I couldn't afford things like that . . . so I just pinch cars, get chases, do burglaries and enjoy myself.

Crime can therefore be more than a response to boredom, argues Collison, by providing a more exciting alternative to school and work.

Crime and consumption

The expansion of consumerism was a major theme running through earlier theories of crime, from Durkheim's notions of boundless aspirations to Merton's emphasis on the growth of the consumer culture and advertising, and the historical and cultural significance of youth cultural styles were also explored by the subcultural theories of the Birmingham school (see Chapter 4). In contemporary society, as any parent or schoolteacher will confirm, young people from all social backgrounds 'need' to conform to certain styles and to wear designer clothes, often from a very early age. Offenders often talk of the need to possess goods like trainers – not any trainers, but named brands. To Collison, young people increasingly speak of relations to one another through a language of consumption which includes judgements of self-identity. Clothes, drugs, music and style are all important. The young offenders in his sample wanted to be super consumers – they drew from, embellished, parodied and fragmented the subcultural traditions of New York, Los Angeles and Milan. One young man comments, 'I'd see me mates walking around with all these fashionable clothes . . . if you haven't got them you're a tramp' (Collison 1996: 430). Anderson and his colleagues (1994) also comment that young people from the most deprived areas were clothed in contemporary styles and that these goods featured in the informal economy.

Youth, crime and the economy – extended adolescence?

As suggested by subcultural theorists, lower-class youth have fewer legitimate opportunities to participate in attractive pursuits and consumer culture and they may, therefore, be more likely to turn to crime for financial reasons. As seen above, Anderson and his colleagues point to feelings of injustice and deprivation and other studies also point to the financial motivation for many forms of property crime (see Chapter 12). Collison points out that low or no wages can and do feature in offenders' explanations for crime – one offender is quoted as saying that it was 'not worth working all week for £30 when I could go out and make that in about ten minutes' (Collison 1996: 438). A female interviewee in Parker's sample of drug takers expresses similar sentiments:

I get £56 per fortnight but by Saturday tea-time I haven't got any left. The social just isn't enough. You're paying out too much. Gas £12, electric £15, food so that's more than half your giro. You also need clothes . . . a pair of trainers £60, haircut nearly £20, jeans £20, toiletries, cleaning stuff, bus fares . . . You have to go out nicking. I've been to the job centre and applied for loads of jobs and got fuck all. There's nowt.

(Parker 1996: 292)

Later chapters will also illustrate that involvement in the irregular economy of crime, and especially the drugs economy, may provide an alternative form of work and income (Ruggiero and South 1995, and see Chapters 13 and 14).

As the above quote indicates, property crime may be seen as necessary to supplement inadequate benefits, or for survival where young people are homeless, having left or been excluded from families or care institutions (see Carlen 1996). One of Parker's sample blames crime on 'the government stopping benefits for 16–18 year olds . . . they need money from somewhere so they do crimes' (Parker 1996: 292). Carlen draws attention to the plight of a particularly deprived group, the young homeless, whom she sees as socially excluded – in attempts to survive, often without benefits, homeless young people resort to begging, busking, prostitution, drug taking, drug dealing, more systematic and serious crime and bouts of public drunkenness (Carlen 1996, 1997).

While linking crime to deprivation is not new, the situation of contemporary youth may be different to previous generations, who could look forward to some form of engagement with the legitimate economy. To Pitts, 'enforced adolescence means that young people on the social and economic margins are, quite literally, prevented from growing up' (Pitts 1996: 281). The effect of this may be different for boys than for girls, which will be explored in Chapter 8.

Lawless young men? The demonization of youth

It has also been argued that young people's activities may be more subject to criminalization as there is no inevitable link between youthfulness and crime and many styles of youth subcultures, which often so alarm the older generation, may appear novel and rebellious but are not in themselves criminal. Many so-called delinquent activities are relatively trivial, are part of a normal process of growing up and involve youth from all social classes. Nonetheless youth and, in particular, young men from the lower classes continue to arouse concern and, as seen above, youthful activities and young men can be demonized (Pearson 1994a).

The insights of labelling perspectives and critical criminology are relevant in exploring this issue. In general, young people's activities are more likely to be labelled as troublesome and groups of young men hanging around the streets or making a noise are likely to attract complaints from older residents. Anderson and his colleagues, for example, point out that while to young people a certain amount of vandalism may represent no more than fun or high spirits, persistent vandalism is likely to be taken seriously by older residents, who may call for tougher policing (Anderson et al 1994). The police may be more likely to act against youth who are seen as troublesome, particularly those who are suspected of gang membership or violence, which they, like the media, often exaggerate. Areas acquire reputations, and all young people from these areas may be labelled as potentially troublesome. Anderson et al (1994) found that youth from one of the 'schemes' complained of not getting jobs because of where they lived. This may also affect how they are dealt with by the police and other criminal justice agencies.

Other factors are also involved. Chapters 4 and 6 illustrated how critical criminologists relate criminalization to wider structures of economic and political power and to the perceived threat posed by different groups in times of economic crises. Young people may be particularly vulnerable to this process and there have been many signs of increasingly stringent controls on their lifestyles. Throughout the 1980s, for example, different policies sought to control the perceived threat of young people leaving home, avoiding work and developing alternative lifestyles. Reference was made above to the plight of the young homeless and to the perception that government policies towards young people were responsible for crime. Many argue that the withdrawal of benefits to young people who did not participate in the labour market or live with their families effectively excluded them from a legitimate income. Crime or begging therefore became major means of survival (Carlen 1997). Many young people become homeless, she argues, because of the need to leave violent homes and to avoid abuse. A vicious circle then ensues in which they are denied benefits and cannot get jobs because they have no address – they are effectively excluded from the benefits of citizenship. New age travelling and squatting emerged as creative responses to this exclusion (see, for example, Carlen 1996). These in turn were controlled through the 1994 Criminal Justice and Public Order Act and young people's protests were interpreted as yet further signs of their incipient lawlessness. Their situation is blamed on their own inadequacies and refusal to conform – diverting attention away from the economic and social policies which excluded them. There have been other examples of the increasing criminalization of young people, and particularly young men. Styles of leisure such as rave parties were also subject to tougher controls and successive moral panics about joyriders, rioters and persistent young offenders prompted calls for much heavier sentencing of young offenders, including young people's prisons and boot camps and electronic tagging. More recently, parents and the police in many areas are being encouraged to prevent youth being on the streets after a certain hour, popularly known as 'curfews'.

Young people are particularly vulnerable to criminalization. Their youth makes them relatively powerless to resist the labelling or demonization of their activities. It may also make them more vulnerable to victimization. Within the family, children are victimized by the older generation who supposedly protect them. This power enables their complaints to be dismissed – their powerlessness and dependency denies them the status of victim (Walklate 1989). On a broader scale they are, being politically marginal, equally unable to resist the demonization of their activities, thus indicating the significance of generational power.

CONCLUDING COMMENTS

This chapter has explored many dimensions of the long-held association between age and crime. It has questioned this association, arguing that if the crimes of older people were fully counted, young people's apparent share of crime would diminish. It has also shown that young people engage in a wide variety of criminal or quasi-criminal pursuits, but that their involvement in crime, as Matza suggested, is often trivial and transitory (Matza 1964). At the same time they emerge as often hidden victims of crime. Despite this, concerns about youth crime continue to dominate discussions of the crime problem, and the activities of young people are being subjected to ever greater surveillance. These may be related to general fears about rapid social change and about the effects of the exclusion of some young people from participation in employment and consumerism. Many of these themes will be returned to in later chapters.

Analysing the relationship between age and crime also illustrates how age is related to other inequalities. While all young people are relatively power-less and may experiment with crime, the most disadvantaged youth may be more likely to be in a situation where crime is an attractive option and be more vulnerable to criminalization. This may also be related to race as in some areas black youth have been criminalized and are also vulnerable to racial harassment and racially motivated crime (see Chapter 9). It has also been suggested that gender, the subject of the next chapter, is a significant part of both involvement in crime and victimization.

Review Questions

1. Can you, by looking at official statistics and reports of crime in the media, provide any evidence to question the widespread view that young people commit more crime?
2. Explore how and why young people's activities are 'demonized'. You might wish to consider:
   (a) Are there any recent examples of this in recent press coverage of crime and criminal justice policy?
   (b) Was youth crime an issue in the moral panic you identified in Chapter 3?
   Focus on your local area and experiences:
   (c) Is youth crime an issue in your local area?
   (d) What kind of youth are associated with 'trouble'?

(e)   How are they perceived in school and by local schoolchildren?
(f)   Where do they live?
(g)   Are the young residents of any particular area near you identified with 'trouble' and 'crime'?
(h)   How are they described?
(i)   Are specific places perceived as 'dangerous'?
(j)   Do you 'know' if they are really involved in crime?
3.   How can crime be seen as attractive to contemporary youth?

Key Reading

Anderson S, Kinsey R, Loader I and Smith C (1994) *Cautionary Tales: Young People, Crime and Policing in Edinburgh*. Aldershot: Avebury

Campbell B (1993) *Goliath: Britain's Dangerous Places*. London: Virago

Hagell A and Newburn T (1994) *Persistent Young Offenders*. London: Policy Studies Institute

Newburn T (1997) 'Youth Crime and Justice', in Maguire M, Morgan R and Reiner R (eds) *The Oxford Handbook of Criminology*, 2nd edition. Oxford: Clarendon Press

CHAPTER 8

GENDER AND CRIME

It has for long been assumed, on the basis of conviction rates, that men commit more crime than women. Indeed, one criminologist once commented that 'if men behaved like women, the courts would be idle and the prisons empty' (Wooton 1959: 32, cited in Walklate 1995: 20). While early theoretical approaches took for granted that offenders were male, often referring to the criminal as 'he', this characteristic of offenders was rarely discussed. Previous chapters suggest, however, that a number of questions should be asked. Do women really commit less crime and men more? How can this be explained? As was so often assumed, are women 'naturally' less criminal and men 'naturally' more so? Alternatively, are men more subject to criminalization? It has also been seen that victimization is related to gender and that women's victimization in the home for long remained a hidden form of crime. Feminists criticized sociological and criminological approaches for their neglect of both women's crime and victimization and sought to make women more visible. The gendered nature of both crime and victimization turns attention to the maleness of crime and to asking how crime can be related to masculinity.

This chapter will address many of these questions. It will look in more detail at the official picture of male and female offending and victimization before considering how the relationships between gender and crime have been constructed. It will then explore how criminologists have explained differences in male and female involvement in crime and how feminists criticized these approaches. The development of feminist perspectives will be outlined and some of the issues raised above will be considered by looking at women's involvement in crime, gender and victimization and masculinity and crime.

THE GENDER GAP: MALE AND FEMALE INVOLVEMENT IN CRIME

Gender and offending

The different conviction rates of men and women can be expressed in many ways, all of which reflect the so-called gender gap. In 1991, 82 per cent

Figure 8.1 Ratio of male:female offenders found guilty or cautioned for selected offence groupings

Over 20 : 1	Sexual offences	75 : 1
	Taking and driving away motor vehicles	33 : 1
	Burglary	23 : 1
	Motoring offences (indictable)	20.6 : 1
5–20 : 1	Offences under the Public Order Act 1986	17 : 1
	Criminal damage (summary/less than £2,000)	16.5 : 1
	Drunkenness	16.5 : 1
	Robbery	13.5 : 1
	Criminal damage (indictable/over £2,000)	9.4 : 1
	Drug Offences	9.4 : 1
	Common assault (summary)	7.0 : 1
	Violence against the person (indictable)	5.7 : 1
	Assault on constable	5.5 : 1
Under 5 : 1	Theft and handling stolen goods	2.8 : 1
	Fraud and forgery	2.8 : 1
Under 1 : 1	TV licence evasion	0.5 : 1
(women form majority)	Offence by prostitute	0.01 : 1

(After Coleman and Moynihan 1996: 95–6)

of known offenders were male and around one-third of men are likely to be convicted for at least one standard list offence before the age of 35, compared with only 8 per cent of women (Barclay 1993). The ratio of male to female offenders is currently 4.5 to 1 for indictable offences (Coleman and Moynihan 1996). It can therefore be argued that criminal convictions are relatively 'normal' for males but very unusual for females (Heidensohn 1997).

Men and women are convicted for different kinds of offences, with women having even lower rates for murder, serious violence and professional crime. Figure 8.1, which incorporates both summary and indictable offences, illustrates how the sex ratio varies for different offences. It also shows that while women are found in all offence groups, they form a majority in only two – prostitution and failing to pay a TV licence. Prostitution is primarily defined as a female offence whereas sexual offences which include offences of rape and indecent assault are primarily defined as male (Coleman and Moynihan 1996). The higher figure for not paying a TV licence is partly due to women being more likely to answer the door to enforcers and thus being prosecuted (Hedderman 1995; Coleman and Moynihan 1996). Men form a majority of every other offence category, with taking and driving away motor vehicles being the second most male-dominated offence, and violence falling closer to the average ratio. When women are convicted it is more likely to be for offences involving theft and handling stolen goods and fraud and forgery, with the former accounting for over 70 per cent of women cautioned or convicted in 1992 (Walklate 1995).

In general terms women are convicted of less serious offences. The ratio for summary offences, generally assumed to be less serious, is 2.4 to 1 (Coleman and Moynihan 1996). Within offence categories, men tend to be convicted of more serious offences, with women committing more serious crimes far less often than men (Walklate 1995). A slight narrowing of the gap for overall convictions has been noted, from 7.1 during the 1950s and 1960s to around 5.1 in 1991 (Walklate 1995). These figures of course reflect convictions and are not necessarily an indicator of 'crime' and their interpretation will be discussed below.

Gender and victimization

Chapters 2 and 5 illustrated that men and women have different experiences of victimization. In respect of violent crime, for example, it has been seen from victim surveys that while men are more likely to be victimized in public spaces, women are more likely to victimized at home. Within the home, surveys also indicate that women are more likely to be assaulted by their partners and men by other household members or relatives (Mirlees-Black et al 1996, and see Chapter 10). Women are also the major victims of reported sexual assault, although men are raped and boys are the victims of sexual abuse (see Chapter 11).

Less is known about victimization from other kinds of crime. Figures for burglary relate to households although, as seen in Chapter 5, women report more severe effects. Other forms of crime may target specific groups and women may be particularly vulnerable to some forms of fraud and white collar crime with popular depictions of fraud conjuring up images of 'little old ladies' being defrauded by charming con men (Croall 1995). As is the case with age, women may be targeted because they are assumed to be less financially or technically competent, making them more vulnerable to, for example, financial frauds or frauds by garages (Croall 1992). They may also be the victims of dangerous and inadequately tested cosmetics, perfumes or drugs (Croall 1995; Szockyj and Fox 1996, and see Chapter 15). At the same time men, who are more likely to be employed in what are seen as 'dangerous' jobs on oil rigs or in building sites, may be endangered by non-compliance with health and safety regulations. Many of these kinds of victimization are gendered in that women or men are victimized because of their gender, drawing attention to the wider context of gendered relationships within which they occur. This will be discussed later in this chapter.

EXPLORING GENDER AND CRIME

As with class and age, it has to be asked to what extent these figures reflect real differences in participation in crime and victimization and how these can be explained. Discussions of this have tended to see 'the problem' as being women's apparently lower involvement in crime. Accordingly it has been asked whether there is a larger hidden figure of female crime and, if not, why women might commit less crime. As the problem was constructed around women's assumed conformity, a related problem was how to approach those women who did commit crime and were often seen as more 'abnormal' or pathological than male criminals. Before discussing these issues, the social construction of gender must briefly be explored.

Why gender?

The word gender is often used in preference to sex, reflecting a distinction between sex, which is biologically determined, and gender, which refers to the way in which biological differences between the sexes are socially constructed. To sociologists, differences in the social roles, expectations and identities which can be encapsulated in constructions of 'masculinity' and 'femininity' transcend biologically determined characteristics. These are learnt during socialization where cultural norms of what it means, for example, to be a 'man' or a 'woman', 'husband', 'father', 'wife' or 'mother' are transmitted. These differences are often assumed to be 'natural' and taken for granted; however, closer exploration, as will be seen below in relation to crime, reveals that they are socially constructed.

Women's lower involvement in crime was not generally questioned because crime was associated with 'masculine' traits such as aggressiveness, physical strength and also to men's greater participation in the public sphere. Crime, quite simply, was 'unfeminine' and women's roles as wives and mothers, which kept them in the private sphere, were assumed to be associated with conformity. To many, therefore, differences in rates of convictions were a simple matter of 'strength, skill and opportunity'. When women did commit crime, however, they were seen as 'unfeminine', which made them doubly deviant as they were not only 'criminal' but 'abnormal' women. A question rarely asked was that if crime was 'unnatural' for women, was it therefore 'natural' for men and, if so, why?

Is there a gender gap?

Before turning to these issues, it has to be asked whether women really do commit less crime than men. Popular and academic discussions often imply a 'chivalry' hypothesis in which it is assumed that women's crime might be less likely to be reported by victims and that suspected female offenders are treated more sympathetically by the police (see, for example, Heidensohn 1996, 1997). Some ways of exploring this are outlined below.

Masked crime

To Pollak, women's crime was masked and convicted offenders represented only the tip of a very large iceberg (Pollak 1961). He argued that women's domestic roles as mothers, wives and servants provided many opportunities for committing and concealing crime, as they could, for example, conceal poison in the food which they prepared. He saw women as innately deceitful, accustomed to deceptions like concealing pregnancy or faking sexual pleasure. Moreover, men who were attacked or defrauded by women would be too embarrassed to reveal their victimization, a classic instance being men whose money is stolen by a prostitute. While based on largely stereotypical assumptions and difficult to establish empirically, his ideas nonetheless reflected pervasive notions about gender roles.

Victims' reports

Victim surveys provide little support for arguments that women's crimes are reported less, although many victims do not know and do not report the sex of offenders. Where they do, they appear to report male assailants in comparable proportions to conviction figures (Walklate 1995). There could nonetheless be some under-reporting of some kinds of crime. As women tend to commit less serious offences than men, and victims tend to report more serious offences, some women's offences might be unreported. Male victims of domestic violence, for example, may be particularly reluctant to come forward. And, as seen in Chapter 7, shopkeepers may be less likely to report the offences of elderly and heavily pregnant women. Nonetheless, many male crimes are also unreported and this alone would do little to narrow the enormous gender gap (Coleman and Moynihan 1996).

Police chivalry?

There is little evidence to support arguments that the police deal with women more leniently. Women are cautioned more often but this can be explained by the less serious nature of their offences (Eaton 1986; Heidensohn 1997). They are less likely to be stopped and searched than men but only a small number of stops result in arrests. While the police may treat women differently this does not imply leniency and there has been some evidence that in some circumstances girls and women are more likely to be referred to court. When dealing with young girls, for example, the police may be more protective and more concerned about their moral welfare. This can justify more intervention and referral to court (Gelsthorpe 1989). Girls' delinquency may also be 'sexualized', by assuming that they are involved with, for example, gangs, as a result of sexual involvement with boys, which also justifies intervention (Shacklady-Smith 1978). Some groups of women have complained about uncaring and callous treatment by the police, thus prostitutes have complained about being treated discourteously and women involved in public protests such as the peace camp at Greenham common faced physical confrontations with the police (Heidensohn 1997).

Self-report studies

Self-report studies have explored gender differences and, while American and British studies have found that girls report more offending than conviction rates would suggest, it tends to be less serious (Heidensohn 1996). One study found that girls were more likely to report truanting, whereas boys were more likely to report offences (Mawby 1980, cited in Heidensohn 1996). In general, while some recent studies do suggest some narrowing of the gap, boys continue to report far higher levels of involvement in more serious activities (Coleman and Moynihan 1996).

Hidden male and female crime

While much female crime is hidden, so too is much male crime. Although there is little evidence about those offences which official figures do not cover, they could reasonably be assumed to involve men as well as women. While female domestic violence may be even more hidden than male, surveys still reveal an enormous gap, with male violence towards women and children far exceeding women's (Heidensohn 1997, and see Chapter 10). Other offence groups involve hidden male crime as well as female. Although women are involved in organized crime, it has traditionally been male dominated (see Chapter 13). While there is little systematic data on white collar crime, it also appears to be male dominated, if for no other reason than that women are less likely to be in a position to commit the most serious forms of fraud or corporate crime (Box 1983; Levi 1994). Ultimately, the real amounts of male and female crime are unknowable, and on the basis of existing evidence, most would agree that women really do commit less crime, even though the exact proportions cannot be determined.

Explaining the gender gap

The weaker sex: biological and psychological approaches

The assumption that women were 'naturally' less criminal than men was related to biological differences and women's hormones, and their reproductive functions were related to weakness and lack of aggression. Lombroso and Ferrero, to whom criminal men were biologically less evolved, saw women as being less evolved than men and closer to primitive types and argued that natural selection had bred out their criminal tendencies. The female criminal was therefore more abnormal and more 'evil' (Walklate 1995; Heidensohn 1996). Thus, they argued, 'women are big children . . . their moral sense is deficient', and the female criminal was masculine and virile, showing 'an inversion of all the qualities which specially distinguish the normal woman; namely reserve, docility and sexual apathy' (Lombroso and Ferrero 1895: 153, cited in Heidensohn 1996: 114).

Other theories also saw female crime as pathological. To Thomas, delinquency among 'unadjusted' girls was a sign of sexual delinquency. They were unadjusted to social change and, for the deprived, crime was related to a desire for 'costly and luxurious articles of women's wear' which disorganized the lives of many 'who crave these pretty things' (Thomas 1923: 71, cited in Heidensohn 1996: 117). Female crime among girls and women has also been related to biological abnormalities and to girls being more 'masculine'. Cowie and his colleagues argued that women's chromosome pattern was different to men's and related female delinquency to biological and masculine traits. Delinquent girls were described as 'oversized, lumpish, uncouth and graceless' (Cowie et al 1968: 167, cited in Heidensohn 1996: 123). Many other problems and pathologies have been associated with women's crime including mental illness and 'women's problems' such as pre-menstrual tension and the menopause. Women are more likely to be referred for medical and psychiatric reports in court which reflects these assumptions (Edwards 1981).

The arguments against biological and other pathological theories rehearsed in earlier chapters also apply to gender. It has been argued that gender differences cannot be reduced to a biological differences alone, and women cannot be said to be innately less disposed to crime as many women do commit crime. Such an argument would also imply that men are 'naturally' criminal, but not all men commit crime. Moreover, as will be seen below, women's involvement in crime cannot be attributed to pathologies.

If the gender gap is not biologically determined, is it therefore related to the different social roles of men and women? Sex role theory suggested that crime is more consistent with male roles. Boys are brought up to be tough, to be able to look after themselves in a fight, to be protective of women and to be 'breadwinners' and a certain amount of violence is tolerated and indeed encouraged among boys. Girls, on the other hand, are socialized into the more caring roles of wives and mothers and fighting and non-conformity are seen as unfeminine. Early versions of sex role theory however, based on functionalist approaches, rarely questioned the 'naturalness' of these role distinctions or the gender relationships which they reflected. They too, therefore, saw criminal women as 'abnormal' (Heidensohn 1996).

The invisible sex

To other sociological approaches, including most of those already outlined, issues of class, social deprivation and age were more significant than gender. While it was recognized that offenders were male, and the focus was on delinquent 'boys', this was not seen as a feature worthy of exploration. Women, whether as offenders, victims or conformists, were largely invisible. Thus the so-called 'causes' of crime were in effect the causes of male crime. Some feminist criticisms of these theories were referred to in Chapter 3. The anomie paradigm discussed goals as if they were universal and did not question whether women had the same goals. Taking this into account would have entailed asking different kinds of questions. If, for example, women's goals were different and centred round the home and family rather than material success, could this explain their lesser criminality? Alternatively, it could be asked whether failure on the part of women to achieve their goals could be related to women's deviance.

Subcultural theory similarly neglected gender, even though it focused clearly on the male-based culture of the 'lads'. As seen in Chapter 3, major questions surrounded the invisibility of girls (McRobbie and Garber 1976). Were the strains of adolescence different for girls, suggesting a different 'solution'? McRobbie and Garber, for example, argued that girls' culture was centred around the private space of the 'bedroom', and that girls experienced a strain between preparing for their future role by being available to boys without at the same time being seen as 'sluts'. Teeny bopper and fan culture, for example, could resolve this problem by idolizing the male 'star' with little risk to a girl's reputation (McRobbie and Garber 1976). Yet girls are involved in delinquency and do get involved in gangs, although, as seen above, this was liable to be 'sexualized'.

While later theories, as seen in Chapter 4, were critical of many aspects of these approaches, gender did not form a part of these criticisms and it has often been pointed out that Taylor, Walton and Young's *The New Criminology* makes no reference to gender (Heidensohn 1996). While labelling theory looked at the how stereotypes affected the production of deviant categories, gender did not feature significantly in their studies. Critical and radical approaches, with their focus on class, control, criminalization and the crimes of the powerful were also criticized for being gender blind. While they focused on power relations in their work on the criminal law, the relationship between gender and power involved in, for example, laws on rape, prostitution, family and sexual violence were not systematically explored, although these have now, as a result of feminist work, been incorporated into many critical approaches.

Control theories did have the potential to explore gender, as girls and women may be subject to greater control. Girls are more likely to be 'chaperoned' by parents and subject to more restrictions in their use of free time and discouraged from hanging about on the streets. As adults, family roles also control women in that they are expected to be caring for children and looking after the home rather than engaging in the more public pursuits associated with crime. The family itself can therefore be seen as a means of controlling women. While this appears a convincing argument, it is difficult to substantiate empirically and it also rather unquestioningly accepts stereotypical notions about gender (Heidensohn 1997). Women and girls may resist gendered stereotypes and may resent the different treatment they receive in comparison to boys.

Feminist perspectives

The failure to look at gender issues and the 'maleness' of offenders has been described as 'gender blindness', and formed a major part of the critique developed by feminist writers, influenced by the growth of 'second wave' feminism and the women's movement. This spanned a range of disciplines which similarly rendered women invisible and used biological arguments and stereotypical assumptions to analyse gender differences. Feminists challenged what they saw as the subordination of women throughout society, seen most clearly in education, employment and the family. While it lies beyond the scope of this book to fully discuss these developments, some of the central ideas of feminism will be outlined to illustrate the broader context within which feminist approaches to crime developed. This section will introduce the concept of patriarchy before going on to look at the main arguments developed by feminist criminologists.

Feminism and the concept of patriarchy

While feminism is often referred to as a single perspective, the term encompasses many different approaches which are related to other theoretical traditions. A distinction between liberal, socialist and radical feminism is often made which, while it does not fully reflect the many different strands of feminist thought, illustrate broadly different perspectives. Liberal feminism is associated with exposing inequalities of opportunity and discrimination on the grounds of sex, with the aim of securing equal opportunities. To others the roots of this discrimination lie not in the actions of agencies, but in the structure of power in society. To radical and socialist feminists women's subordination derives from a patriarchal state. Socialist feminism, as its title implies, is linked to socialist and Marxist ideas and it relates gender inequalities to those of class, whereas to radical feminists, gender is seen as the main form of inequality. The nature of patriarchy, and its links to other forms of structural inequality, is therefore contested, although it can broadly be defined as 'a system of social structures and practices in which men dominate, oppress and exploit women' (Walby 1989: 214).

According to Walby, patriarchy is made up of six structures which involve social relationships and practices (Walby 1989, 1990). These are:

- A patriarchal *mode of production* in which women's labour is expropriated by husbands within marriage and the household. While many individual women choose to be 'housewives', the domestic division of labour disadvantages women as a whole.

- Patriarchal relations in *work* where women are often excluded from paid work or segregated within the labour market.

- A patriarchal *state* which excludes women who have less representation in government or branches of the executive such as the judiciary, police and

144

legal system. While there have been struggles over women's right to vote and for equal rights at work, other laws affecting gender relationships are determined by men – for example, divorce, prostitution, marriage, sexuality, pornography and fertility.

- The maintenance of patriarchy through *male violence* over women. Women are subject to the threat of violence at home, in public, or at work, from sexual harassment, flashing, sexual assault and abuse. In some states this is widely tolerated whereas in others these activities are treated less seriously than other forms of crime.

- Patriarchal relations are also seen in the *regulation of sexuality*. Laws promote the norm of the nuclear family and heterosexual relations by criminalizing homosexuality and prostitution.

- Patriarchal *culture* is reflected in institutionally rooted notions of masculinity and femininity and disseminated through institutions of cultural production such as the media and education.

Feminism and crime

Just as there are many different strands to feminism, there is no one coherent set of arguments which can be described as 'feminist criminology' (Gelsthorpe and Morris 1988, 1990; Heidensohn 1995; Walklate 1995; Gelsthorpe 1997). Despite this, a number of core elements of feminist thinking can be identified which are broadly summarized below (Gelsthorpe and Morris 1988; Heidensohn 1995).

- To feminists, the question of women is central.

- Feminist approaches are critical of the stereotypical images of women which dominated earlier theories.

- To advance a feminist argument means accepting the view that women experience subordination on the basis of their sex and working towards the elimination of that subordination.

- Criticizing earlier theories or simply 'adding on' studies of women to studies of men is not sufficient. Gender must become a central feature of analysis. This can be described as re-thinking the sociology of crime and criminology by 'engendering' it and exploring it with a gendered 'lens' (Rafter and Heidensohn 1995; Walklate 1995).

- Theories of crime must be able to take account of both men's and women's criminal behaviour and victimization. If, for example, crime is related to unemployment, its different effect on men and women and its relationship to their different patterns of crime should be explored.

Feminist approaches were first used to provide a critique of criminological theory as it existed up to the 1970s (Smart 1977). Feminists aimed to do more than simply criticize other theories for their neglect of women. To some, exploring women's involvement in crime made women more 'visible'. This was overshadowed by the focus on women's victimization which, as seen in Chapter 5, emerged from a political campaign for better treatment for the victims of rape and domestic violence. At the same time many feminist researchers turned their attention to the way in which women were treated in the criminal justice process (see, for example, Eaton 1986; Worrall 1990). Others argued, as outlined above, that gender should become a major area of criminological analysis by re-thinking theoretical approaches rather than 'tacking on' women as if as an afterthought. To some, however, this was an impossible and fruitless task. Debates also occurred over how far women should be the central concern and how far feminists should broaden their analyses to include gender and male crime and victimization (see, for example, Gelsthorpe and Morris 1990; Heidensohn 1995; Gelsthorpe 1997). There have also, as will be seen below, been discussions about how gender can be related to other inequalities (Carlen 1992; Gelsthorpe 1997). Many aspects of feminist approaches will be developed in later chapters on specific patterns of crime while others, such as their work on the criminal justice process, lie beyond the scope of this text. The following sections will focus on how they approach the study of women's involvement in crime and their analyses of gender and victimization.

Women's involvement in crime

The pathological female offender?

An initial focus of feminist work on female offending was to challenge the pathological view of the female offender. Thus, they argued, women are involved in as wide a range of offences as men, albeit in different proportions. Not all of this could be attributed to pathologies, and women's crime, like men's, could be economically motivated. On the basis of an ethnographic study, Carlen argued that women made conscious decisions to engage in crime, and to the women in her study crime was a positive response, could be enjoyable and exciting and, for some, represented an escape from poverty (Carlen 1985). In court, however, women's crime was 'medicalized' by the use of psychiatric reports and the assumption that women offenders were abnormal. The double deviance attributed to women could also lead to more women being sent to prison at an earlier stage in their criminal careers than men (Carlen 1983; Carlen and Worrall 1987; Worrall 1990). This served to neutralize the economic and social circumstances of women which, to Carlen, are major factors underlying female offending (Carlen 1988).

The liberated female offender?

As women became apparently more 'liberated', it was argued that they would also become more criminal. The so-called 'liberation hypothesis' argued that a 'new female criminal' was developing; thus, the American author, Adler, argued that:

Women are no longer indentured to the kitchens, baby carriages or bedrooms of America . . . in the same way that women are demanding equal opportunity in fields of legitimate endeavour, a similar number of determined women are forcing their way into the world of major crimes.

(Adler 1975, cited in Heidensohn 1996: 155)

While Adler claimed that this could be statistically established, others pointed to the dangers of exaggerating increases in the already small female crime rate, and to the difficulties of relating crime rates to 'emancipation' (Smart 1979). In a detailed examination Box and Hale found no evidence that any increase in women's crime was associated with measures of emancipation. While there had been an increase in violent crime committed by females, it had not grown much in comparison to male rates, and while women's share of property offences had increased this was more likely to be due to economic marginality than to 'liberation' (Box and Hale 1983). There are other problems in relating so-called emancipation to crime. Like convicted male offenders, female offenders are overwhelmingly drawn from the lower classes whereas liberation and equality have most affected middle-class women. Indeed, following Box and Hale, many would argue that any increase in female participation in crime is due, not to emancipation, but to greater poverty.

Poverty and the female offender

The social and economic changes outlined in Chapter 6 have reduced the career and employment prospects of women as well as men. Whereas marriage and family have often been seen as alternative goals for women, the growth of young male unemployment has reduced their chances of providing for a family. As the number of single-parent families, many headed by women, has increased, women have become poorer and indeed some writers talk of the feminization of poverty (Carlen 1988). A survey carried out by Breadline Britain revealed that over 50 per cent of one-parent households lived in poverty, with those headed by women being twice as likely to be in poverty than those headed by men (Pantazis and Gordon 1997). This may explain the increase in the numbers of women being imprisoned for failing to pay their TV licences. Pantazis and Gordon argue that, as so many are living in poverty, they are less able to afford a TV licence and, when fined, cannot afford the fine. Paying a fine has to have a lower priority than paying for basic necessities such as food, rent and heating (Pantazis and Gordon 1997).

It has also been seen that the majority of women who do offend are convicted of property crime, suggesting that women offenders commit crimes for largely economic reasons, quite literally argue some, to put food on the table (Walklate 1995). Studies of women in prison have found that many offences are motivated by need rather than greed, to supplement meagre state benefits, and to provide children with clothes, toys or food (Carlen 1988). Trying to get more from the 'social' or not paying TV licences or heating bills may in effect become crimes of necessity for poor women (Carlen 1988). Prostitution is also generally motivated not, as is often popularly imagined, by pathological sex drives, but for economic reasons (McLeod 1982; McKeganey and Barnard 1996, and see Chapter 11). Young women may see little future and Worrall argues that crime among girls, rather than being a sign of trying to be equal with boys,

> . . . has far more to do with certain impoverished young women seeing no future for themselves other than lone parenthood, state dependency and social stigma and saying 'anything must be better than that'.
>
> (Worrall 1995: 6)

The attractions of crime and girl gangs

Poverty may explain why some women resort to crime, but cannot be applied to all female crime. Not all poor women commit crime, and not all women who commit crime are poor. For women as well as men, a drugs habit can lead to involvement in shoplifting and particularly to prostitution (Walklate 1995, and see Chapter 13). The peak age for offending for girls is 15, which for most women precedes motherhood or entry into the job market (Heidensohn 1997). Crime can be attractive for girls as well as boys and it can, as seen in Chapter 7, be exciting. Like boys, girls commit crime to obtain the clothes and accessories which are seen as essential to express their identity. Another way in which girls have recently been associated with crime has been through involvement in so-called 'girl gangs'.

There have been recurrent 'moral panics' about growing rates of female violence, manifested in the apparent emergence of gangs of girls who have been associated with muggings and cases of bullying and even murder. This has led to speculation that girls are increasingly becoming involved in violence, which has also been associated with growing equality and feminism (Worrall 1995). Despite this, however, criminologists remain cautious. While there has been a recent increase in convictions for violent crime among girls and the second most common crime for young women is violence, in 1993, as Worrall (1995) points out, only 190 girls compared with 546 boys in England and Wales were placed on supervision for offences of violence. Worrall (1995: 6) further argues that:

> . . . our criminal courts are not filled with over-educated, ambitious young women. When girls raise their sights, broaden their horizons, increase their aspirations and self-esteem, they are *less* likely, not *more* likely to behave deviantly.

While under-researched in Britain, girl gangs have been studied in the United States (Campbell 1984; Messerschmidt 1995). These studies indicate a complex relationship between gender and gang violence. Like boys, girls from impoverished and marginalized backgrounds join gangs from a need for belonging and to protect their territory. While some girl gangs are seen as subsidiary to boy gangs, girls also construct a form of 'bad girl' femininity (Messerschmidt 1995). Male and female gangs engage in gender appropriate crime and, in some, the girls perform gendered roles such as cooking and child care, but they may also commit the same kinds of crime. While girl gangs are often seen as a sign of changing gender roles, it can be argued that the girls are not trying to be like boys. While their behaviour may depart from accepted notions of femininity, outside the gang girls behave according to these expectations (Messerschmidt 1995).

MEN, WOMEN, CRIME AND VICTIMIZATION

A central feature of feminist perspectives was their approach to women's victimization, many aspects of which were outlined in Chapter 5. Indeed to some, mainly radical, feminists this issue was central as it was so clearly related to patriarchy and women's subordination. To them, therefore, 'the problem' was male violence against women. This approach was in turn criticized for neglecting the victimization of men, which could also reflect gendered relationships. In addition, as seen above, some feminists also argued that a gendered analysis of crime should look not only at female crime but also at how male crime was related to masculinity. These issues will be explored before turning to an assessment of feminist perspectives.

Men, women and victimization

Violence against women

To many feminists, male violence against women reflects male power, and the way in which it is conceptualized and dealt with reflects the operation of the patriarchal state and patriarchal culture. It was seen above that violence against women is one of the structures of patriarchy described by Walby and to many feminists the threat of male violence is a major means of oppressing and controlling women. Rape and other forms of sexual and physical assaults are expressions of male domination and reflect men's assumed 'right' to women's bodies and sexual relationships. This is reflected in law; for example, until recently, rape within marriage was not regarded as crime, as women were assumed to have 'consented' to sexual activity through the marriage contract. Male power in the patriarchal family is also reflected in the assumption that a man, husband or father has a right to discipline his wife or children – they become in effect his 'property'. Male violence and power are exercised not only in the family as women face the threat of sexual violence at work or in public places. Sexual harassment and the assumption of many men that they have a right to touch and fondle women are also expressions of male power, and to some writers women's lives are constrained by recurring and pervasive fears of male violence (Stanko 1990a, 1994). They are afraid to go out at night because they are afraid of being attacked (by men) and have to adjust their dress and behaviour to avoid being seen as provoking male sexual advances and attacks. Women, therefore, live in a climate of 'unsafety' as a result of male violence (Stanko 1994). Male violence can therefore be conceptualized as a continuum ranging from rape through other forms of physical and sexual violence to sexual harassment (Kelly 1988, and see Chapter 10).

The way in which sexual violence is constructed and dealt with by police and courts amounts to its effective condonation by the patriarchal state. To many feminists, police reluctance to intervene in so-called 'domestics', their denial of credibility to rape victims and the treatment of rape victims in court all reflect the operation of a patriarchal criminal justice system, as does the treatment of female offenders as 'pathological'. The mythology which surrounds rape, sexual assault and domestic violence 'blames the victim' by assuming that women and even children have provoked attacks (see Chapters 10 and 11). This mythology is widely accepted by women as well as men and by victims themselves, indicating the pervasiveness of patriarchal culture. This could also, argue some, be seen in the way in which high profile cases of alleged child abuse gave rise to complaints of excessive intervention into the sanctity of the family (Walklate 1989). Many of these arguments, dealt with in outline here, will be developed in Chapters 10 and 11 and these will also provide illustrations of the kind of work which feminist researchers have carried out to substantiate them. A major difficulty, particularly with analyses which see women's victimization and male violence as the central problem, is that they may find it difficult to analyse women's violence and that they neglect men's victimization.

Men's victimization

However much women's victimization may be under-represented in official figures, men are also major victims of violence, often at the hands of other men (Stanko and Hobdell 1993; Newburn and Stanko 1994). Boys as well as girls suffer from physical and sexual assaults in the home and adult men are victims of domestic violence, in both hetero- and homosexual households. Recent evidence also suggests that male rape is a largely hidden problem (see Chapter 11). Men may be victimized because they are seen as deviant or 'abnormal' men – thus homosexuals are the victims of homophobic attacks. Many so-called male on male assaults involve contests of honour and reputation where fights arise over assumed insults to 'manhood' (Polk 1994, and see Chapter 10). Men from minority ethnic groups are also the victims of racist attacks and murders.

Gender therefore features in male victimization as well as women's. It may affect how men experience victimization as they may be more reluctant to seek help or express their feelings. The notions of weakness and passivity involved the construction of victimization, outlined in Chapter 5, run counter to images of masculinity as men are expected to be tough and 'handle' situations. Yet men are emotionally affected by crime and it often has long-lasting effects (Stanko and Hobdell 1993). They view their victimization, however, through a male frame which sees victimization as 'weak and helpless' (Stanko and Hobdell 1993).

Men, Masculinity and crime

Masculinity has also emerged as an important element in exploring involvement in crime. It was argued above that to feminist perspectives, the importance of the maleness of offenders was largely ignored in theories of crime although a theme running through subcultural theories was the importance of toughness, holding one's own in a fight and delinquent activities within male lower-class subcultures (see, for example, Miller 1958). And Willis, referred to in Chapter 3, discussed the sexism in the culture of the 'lads' (Willis 1977). At one level, the relationship between crime and masculinity is straightforward – men are more likely to be criminal therefore crime must be related to masculinity. This is, however, over-simplistic as not all men commit crime or are violent, and while crime may seen as more normal for men it is still 'abnormal' as most men do not obtain a criminal conviction. Expressing masculinity need not involve crime, violence or aggression.

This can be approached by using the concept of hegemonic masculinity developed by Connell (Connell 1987). In this conception a normative model of masculinity provides a set of cultural expectations emphasizing toughness, aggression, power and control and pervades all aspects of public and private life (Walklate 1995). Walklate points, for example, to similarities between the 'yob' culture of young urban lower-class males, and the 'yobbish' behaviour of male politicians in Parliament although it is the former who are seen as a problem. Men's need to 'win' need not, however, involve violence or crime. As Walklate argues, all men can call on the cultural resource of masculinity but violence or crime does not have to be a part of this and is only one way of expressing masculinity. Some men will use physical violence to assert control, whereas others will call on mental resources.

Many aspects of crime involve expressions of masculinity. Earlier chapters have illustrated that the growth of unemployment can be seen as amounting to a 'crisis' in masculinity where young men cannot look forward to living up to expectations of being the male provider. Joyriding, theft or burglary may provide alternative means of expressing masculinity, of taking risks and of providing for families (Campbell 1993). Campbell argues that while their fathers or grandfathers spent their lives in the male spaces of work and the pub as well as the home, unemployed young men live their lives in the space of the home and street. Within the home they have no clearly identifiable role as this is still seen as women's space. The world of cars represents an alternative masculine space and car crime becomes a major arena for young men to express themselves as men (Campbell 1993).

Similarly, being involved in 'business', whether of a legitimate or illegitimate nature, can be seen as a quintessentially masculine concern. With the decline in legitimate work, involvement in the 'business' of drugs or organized crime can be similarly related to elements of masculinity, as can the culture of football hooligans (Williams and Taylor 1994; Hobbs 1995, and see Chapter 12). In the business world, male aggression may be related to white collar crime – in takeovers the predator company is often depicted as male and the target is female and the language of war and competition are used (Punch 1996, and see Chapter 15). While financial frauds do not involve violence, they may nonetheless reflect the value placed on aggressive business tactics and provide another expression of masculinity (Levi 1994). Many of these themes will be developed in later chapters.

Feminism, gender and crime

While the feminist approach has succeeded in placing gender firmly on the agenda of the sociology of crime and criminology it has not been without its critics and there are many debates within feminist circles. Major issues include the central focus on gender and on women's victimization. Downes and Rock, for example, argue that their criticisms of earlier theoretical approaches are misplaced. To them, sociology and criminology have been 'crime led', focusing on male crime because it is statistically most prevalent. Gender is not the only neglected variable as race and white collar crime have been similarly under-explored. Moreover, theories developed for male criminals can be and have been applied to women. The labelling perspective is not intrinsically difficult to apply to women and both anomie and subcultural theories can be used. Later subcultural writers did discuss the sexism and racism of subcultures and the approach can also be applied to female subcultures (Downes and Rock 1995).

Others are sceptical of what feminism has to offer. Carlen, for example, argues that apart from patriarchy there is little to distinguish feminist approaches from others, although she does not deny their contribution. She also criticizes the central role of gender which, she argues, may divert attention from inequalities such as class or race which are important for women. As seen above, she argues that women commit crime mainly as a result of poverty, and a realist approach, combined with feminist insights, can better analyse these problems (Carlen 1992). In addition, black women have argued that feminist perspectives neglected the dimension of race (Mama 1989). The focus on female victims and male violence provides a further limitation in that it may find it difficult to incorporate women who abuse their children or who engage in violent crime. At the same time, however, as feminist approaches continue to develop, many of these issues are being taken account of (Kelly 1996; Gelsthorpe 1997).

CONCLUDING COMMENTS

This chapter has outlined many elements of the relationship between gender and crime, which will be further developed in later chapters. Many questions about gender and crime remain unanswered. The real size of the gender gap is possibly unknowable as there are few ways of assessing how much male or female crime is hidden. While it is argued that domestic violence is under-estimated, it is not known how much of this is perpetrated by men or women. Questions about women's involvement in white collar, professional or organized crime remain. In addition, while there may be little evidence to support arguments that women are becoming more criminal as a result of liberation, relatively little is known about the attitudes to and involvement in crime among contemporary girls.

It is clear, however, that gender plays a major role in patterns of both offending and victimization. Women may be victims for no other reason than that they are women, and men because they are considered to be 'deviant' men. Social and economic change may have a differential effect on men and women leading some women to resort to crimes of survival. Crime can also be related to masculinity and to male expectations. In conversations with children on a peripheral estate, Campbell asked what they wanted to be. One girl replied that she wanted to be 'a mam', whereas a boy replied, 'I don't want to be a dad . . . want to be a robber' (Campbell 1993, cited in Walklate 1995). Simple equations between gender and crime are, however, too simplistic. Women do commit crime, they commit violent and sexual offences and there has been a slight narrowing of the gender gap. In addition, gender operates alongside other structural inequalities such as class, age and race. As Walklate (1995: 192) argues:

> Gender may hold some of the clues to the 'crime problem', but it would be misguided to think that it holds all of the answers. A gendered lens certainly helps us see some features of the crime problem more clearly perhaps; but how and under what circumstances is that clarity made brighter by gender or distorted by it?

Review Questions

1. Using a 'gendered lens':
   (a) Look at popular representations of crime in televised crime dramas and/or the press. How do these reflect gendered images of victimization and offending?
   (b) Look at an example of the work of early anomie, subcultural, or critical criminologists, possibly one looked at in Chapter 3. How does it reflect what feminists describe as 'gender blindness'?
2. What evidence would you look at to assess whether women's greater equality is likely to lead to their committing more crime?
3. How can the concept of patriarchy be related to crime?
4. How would you assess the argument that forms of crime are related to forms of masculinity?

Key Reading

Gelsthorpe L (1997) 'Feminism and Criminology', in Maguire M, Morgan R and Reiner R (eds) *The Oxford Handbook of Criminology*, 2nd edition. Oxford: Clarendon Press

Gelsthorpe L and Morris A (eds) (1990) *Feminist Perspectives in Criminology*. Milton Keynes: Open University Press

Heidensohn F (1996) *Women and Crime*, 2nd edition. London: Macmillan

Walklate S (1995) *Gender and Crime: An Introduction*. London: Prentice Hall/ Harvester Wheatsheaf

CHAPTER 9

RACE, ETHNICITY AND CRIME

Throughout history crime has been popularly linked to race and ethnicity as well as to class, age and gender. In nineteenth-century Britain, the Irish were portrayed as part of the 'dangerous classes' and to social disorganization theorists, crime was related to immigrant cultures – a theme which has recurred in conceptions of the 'underclass'. The urban disturbances in England and Wales in the 1980s and 1990s were attributed to racial tension and it has been seen that race is also a feature of victimization. Many questions have been asked about race and crime. Can involvement in crime be related to race and ethnicity? How could any such association be explained? Does discrimination in the criminal justice process 'produce' different rates of conviction? Are some minority ethnic groups subject to criminalization? Are some kinds of crime and victimization racialized? How are any relationships between race and crime related to wider structures of discrimination and disadvantage?

As with earlier chapters this chapter will begin by critically exploring what can be learnt from official statistics and surveys, after briefly discussing the problems of using such information in relation to race and ethnicity. It will then look at how race and ethnicity are constructed before considering the issues raised in what has been called the race and crime debate. The role of the police, so often seen as significant will be investigated and experiences of racial victimization will be analysed. The final section will explore the significance of race in relation to crime and criminalization.

RACE AND CRIME

Methodological problems and issues

Official statistics, often the starting point for analysis, do not record the race or ethnic identity of offenders. There are therefore, no equivalent figures to those for age or sex in relation to conviction rates. Information comes from a variety of sources which have many limitations. Prison statistics are often used; however, as such a small proportion of offenders end up in prison, they cannot be read as indicating conviction rates. On the basis of locally based samples, some studies have investigated the proportions of different groups at successive stages in the criminal justice process. These are limited by the size of samples and by their use of different definitions of race and ethnicity. Other figures have been obtained from police records and surveys which are not available on a systematic or national basis. Their definition of race and ethnicity may be reliant on visual identification by police officers which further restricts their reliability (Fitzgerald 1995).

A major problem is how race and ethnicity can be defined for the purposes of research. As will be seen below, these are highly contested terms and there is no simple way of categorizing people into racial or ethnic groups. Country of origin, often used in the past, is misleading as in contemporary Britain many black or Asian people are not immigrants but were born in Britain. Should they therefore be described as British, 'black', 'British black' or Afro-Caribbean? Early studies tended to compare 'black' and 'white', terms which encompass very different groups. The 'black' category included Asians and Afro-Caribbeans, each of which include many different groups, and the 'white' category, still used, contains people who may define themselves as Irish, Scottish, Welsh, English, Australian or American or as belonging to any other European country. More recently, the census asks people about their ethnic identity, which provides more reliable breakdowns, although many studies continue to make broad comparisons based on different combinatons of groups (Fitzgerald 1993).

Interpreting figures based on these comparisons is also very difficult. In the first place, any differences between groups must be related to their proportion in the population of any given area. It has also been seen that crime rates can be related to age, area of residence, gender, employment and many other socio-economic factors, making it difficult to establish if race has any separate effect. It will be seen below that any differences between racial groups could be affected by differences in the age structure of minority ethnic populations and by patterns of employment, income or residence (Fitzgerald 1995; Coleman and Moynihan 1996). The different distribution of minority ethnic groups throughout Britain has also to be taken into account. Most research relates to England and Wales but Scotland and Northern Ireland have lower minority ethnic populations.

Race, ethnicity and offending

Given these limitations, what does research indicate? Figure 9.1 summarizes information about the involvement of racial and ethnic groups at different stages of the criminal justice process. In general terms, the majority of studies indicate that black people are over-represented throughout the criminal justice process, with proportionately more being stopped and arrested by the police and being sentenced to prison. Asians, on the other hand, tend to be under-represented, although proportions vary for different Asian groups. Further aspects of these figures are outlined below.

Figure 9.1 Race, ethnicity and criminal justice: some selected figures

---

The Prison Population (Smith 1997)

In 1994, in England and Wales:

- Black men (of West Indian, Guyanese and African origin) formed 11.1 per cent of the male prison population compared with 2.3 per cent of the male population aged 15–39.

- Black women formed 20.4 per cent of the female prison population compared with 2.3 per cent of the female population aged 15–39.

- South Asian men (of Indian, Pakistani and Bangladeshi origin) formed 2.2 per cent of the male prison population compared with 3.8 per cent of the male population aged 15–39.

- For British nationals, black people's imprisonment rate was six times higher than white people's and for South Asians it was half that of white people. Among Pakistani men it was equivalent to white people and lower among Bangladeshi and Indian men.

Police Activity

- *Police stops*: In the 1988 BCS, 15 per cent of white, 20 per cent of Afro-Caribbean and 14 per cent of South Asian young men reported being stopped by the police in the preceding fourteen months. These differences remained significant when other factors such as age, income and sex were taken into account (Smith 1997).

- *Arrests*: In 1987, 18 per cent of those arrested in London were black (compared to 5 per cent of the population), with little variation by offence other than higher figures for robbery and other violent theft (54 per cent), and for non-violent thefts from the person (51 per cent) (Smith 1997).

- *Caution and Prosecution*: Available evidence suggests that black young men are more likely to be cautioned (Smith 1997).

Self-Report Studies

- In a Home Office self-report study of young people aged 14–25 carried out in 1992/3, there were no differences between black and white respondents and self-reported offending was lower among all South Asian groups (Graham and Bowling 1996).

Prison statistics

Prison statistics consistently indicate an over-representation of black men and women. The high figures for women are largely explained by the number of African women imprisoned for drug importation offences (Smith 1997; Fitzgerald 1995). Among Asians, more recent figures indicate higher than expected proportions for Pakistani men, who, along with Bangladeshis, are more economically disadvantaged than Indians (Fitzgerald 1995). The differences are greater for some offences than others, with relatively more Afro-Caribbeans being imprisoned for offences involving drugs, rape and robbery. Smaller differences are recorded for burglary and other sexual offences. South Asians have higher rates of imprisonment for drug offences than whites, but very low rates for burglary (Smith 1997). Prison statistics must be interpreted with caution as any over-representation could be the result of differences in earlier stages.

Police activity

Since the 1970s, successive studies have reported that black people are more likely than white to be stopped by the police and are also likely to be stopped more often (Stevens and Willis 1979; Smith and Gray 1985; Jefferson and Walker 1992). These figures also have to be interpreted with caution. They may reflect the social composition of the area in which they are carried out. Ethnic groups tend to be concentrated in specific areas of towns and cities and figures based on a large area may not reflect local differences which can be revealed by looking at smaller areas (Walker 1987). In a study based in Leeds, Jefferson and Walker found that, for Leeds as a whole, black youth were stopped more often than white; but black youth were stopped more often in areas where the majority of residents were white, and white youth were stopped more often in areas dominated by black people and Asians. These variations could be a feature of the local context of policing. The police could, for example, regard a black person in a white area with greater suspicion, or be more careful about stopping black people in a black area. Alternatively, minority populations in any area may be more transient, more likely to live in temporary accommodation and therefore be seen as more worthy of police attention (Jefferson and Walker 1992; Holdaway 1996).

The criminal justice process

There is very little systematic information about later stages, especially about rates of arrest. Figure 9.1 indicates that in some areas black youth have disproportionate arrest rates for some kinds of crime (Walker 1987; Smith 1997). Once arrested, black youth appear more likely to be taken to court rather than cautioned, although again, information is sparse and often based on studies carried out in the 1980s (Landau and Nathan 1983; Smith 1997). In the Leeds study cited above, black youth were more likely to be taken to court, and Asians had the highest cautioning rates (Jefferson et al 1992). These differences may in part be related to more black youth refusing to plead guilty, which is necessary to obtain a caution (Jefferson et al 1992; Smith 1997). Studies have also looked at proportions remanded in custody, given bail, tried, convicted and given particular sentences. In general, there are some indications that black youth are more likely to be remanded in custody, tried in Crown as opposed to magistrates' courts and more heavily sentenced. This may be related to offence patterns as black youth tend to be over-represented in offences such as robbery, which are considered to be more serious. Moreover, there are some indications that black youth plead not guilty more often – thus depriving themselves of the guilty plea discount (Walker 1989; Davies et al 1995).

All of these variations can be attributed to many factors and they cannot be taken to indicate differences in participation in crime. They are more often used to explore the extent of any discrimination against minority groups in the criminal justice process. This has produced conflicting results and the limitations of this kind of research will be discussed below.

Race, ethnicity and victimization

Race and ethnicity are related to victimization in two main ways. Minority ethnic groups are more at risk from some of the offences measured by the BCS, and some crimes such as vandalism, assault or robbery may be racially motivated. Some recent figures indicating racial and ethnic differences are summarized in Figure 9.2. This shows that in the booster samples taken by the BCS, Afro-Caribbeans and Asians reported higher levels of both household and personal crime (Holdaway 1996; Smith 1997). As with other statistics, teasing out a race factor is complicated by the interrelationship between race and area of residence, age or income, and when these are accounted for,

Figure 9.2 Race, ethnicity and victimization: some selected figures

- *For crimes measured by the BCS in 1988 and 1992*: Asians reported significantly higher rates than whites for household vandalism, burglary with loss, vehicle vandalism, threats and robbery and theft from the person. Afro-Caribbeans reported significantly higher rates than whites for burglary with loss, all thefts, bicycle theft, assaults and robbery and theft from the person (Fitzgerald and Hale 1996).

- *In the BCS 1988 and 1992*: 24 per cent of offences reported by South Asians and 14 per cent by Afro-Caribbeans were perceived by victims to have been racially motivated (Fitzgerald and Hale 1996).

- A Policy Studies Institute Survey in 1994 found that 1 per cent of a combined sample of Caribbeans, South Asians and Chinese had been racially attacked, 2 per cent reported racially motivated damage to their property and 12 per cent had been racially insulted (Virdee 1997).

- This also found that three-fifths of those subject to racial harassment in the last year had been subject to more than one incident and just over one-fifth had experienced five or more incidents. In two-thirds of cases more than one offender was involved (Virdee 1997).

these differences tend to be reduced (Smith 1997). This kind of information gives little indication of the extent of racially motivated offences, although the BCS has also found that Asians are more at risk of assault by white people whom they did not know, and by groups of perpetrators, suggesting racially motivated attacks (Holdaway 1996; Zedner 1997). Moreover, Asians were three times more likely than whites to report criminal damage to buildings, suggesting racially motivated vandalism (Holdaway 1996). Figure 9.2 also indicates that many felt that offences were racially motivated. For Asians this was more pronounced for assaults, threats and acts of vandalism, and for Afro-Caribbeans it was more pronounced for incidents in pubs and at work. These differences also reflect different cultural patterns as Asians frequent pubs less often than other groups (Holdaway 1996).

Estimating the extent of racially motivated offences is particularly difficult as any racial element is not always recorded and the time frame of surveys such as the BCS may not reflect persistent incidents (Bowling 1993; Holdaway 1996). Difficulties also arise in how racial motivation is defined and counted. The police have been criticized for not taking account of the racial motivation in offences and it is recognized that police figures are particularly unreliable (Holdaway 1996). On the other hand, it has been argued that victims' perceptions of racial motivation is subjective. It is therefore difficult to compare surveys based on victims' perceptions with those based on police reports (Smith 1997). In addition, some surveys include harassment, which is not technically a crime, whereas others measure only officially defined offences. Police records indicate that the number of racially motivated incidents rose from 1,945 in 1985 to 3,373 in 1991, although this may reflect a greater willingness to record the racial element in offences (Smith 1997). Local surveys produce higher figures. One study in Newham in 1986 found that one-quarter of blacks reported incidents of racial harassment and another in Plaistow in 1989 reported that over a fifth of Afro-Caribbeans and Asians reported harassment. It can be concluded therefore that some racial and minority ethnic groups are more at risk from some kinds of crime and are additionally victimized by racially motivated crime.

EXPLORING RACE, ETHNICITY AND CRIME

The kinds of figures summarized above can be read in contrasting ways. On the one hand, they could indicate different rates of involvement in crime. Alternatively, they could reflect discrimination on the part of the police and courts, or they could arise from a combination of these two elements. In what is often called the 'race and crime debate' the meaning of these figures is strongly contested and the role of the police is particularly significant. To administrative criminologists the problem to be investigated is the extent of bias or discrimination. To realists, the figures represent a combination of patterns of crime and interactions with the police. These arguments are contested by critical race theorists to whom they represent a process in which black youth are criminalized. Before looking at these issues, the definition and social construction of race and ethnicity will be outlined.

The definition and construction of race and ethnicity

The terms race and ethnicity are used to categorize groups on the basis of a number of assumed differences. While race is often seen as biologically determined, scientific research has failed to establish any distinct biological differences between so-called races and it is now widely acknowledged that race is a socially constructed category (Miles 1989; Mason 1995; Holdaway 1997). Historically the concept has reflected relationships of inferiority and superiority. During periods of colonial expansion, indigenous or 'native' populations, often distinguished by their 'darker' skin, were seen as inferior to 'civilized' white Europeans and described as 'savages' or 'barbarians' (Miles 1989). Race was associated with colonial domination, with slavery being the most extreme form of racial domination. Skin colour has not been the only means of differentiating races, and the worst form of racism this century was the Nazi persecution of Jews.

Defining race in terms of difference is therefore a social process and race can be seen as a social and ideological construct rather than being based on fixed, biological characteristics. Social relationships become racialized when racial differences are assumed to be significant (Miles 1989). Perceiving or describing an individual or group as 'black' or 'Asian' implies a racialized relationship if this is seen as 'the' significant distinguishing feature. As the term race is so often linked to difference, domination and oppression, some have argued that it should be abandoned. Most writers continue to use the term, which is often placed in inverted commas, 'race', to indicate its problematic nature. To others this is seen as an unnecessary, stylistic fashion (Holdaway 1997).

Ethnicity is a broader term than race but also implies difference. It does not carry implications of biological difference, but is based on a variety of characteristics such as culture, religion, country of origin or language. While race is often seen to be a fixed category, ethnicity is associated with perceptions of identity. As such it need not imply superiority or inferiority, although it is often used in conjunction with the word minority which implies a deviation from a 'majority'. The word ethnic is often used to imply difference and 'foreigners', thus the word ethnic when used to describe food or crafts implies difference and foreignness. Rarely is the 'majority' described as 'ethnic', thus some prefer to use the phrase minority ethnic group and stress the importance of diversity rather than difference which so often implies deviation from, and inferiority to, the 'majority' (Mason 1995). Like race, ethnicity can become the basis for atrocities, seen most vividly in the 'ethnic cleansing' of religious groups in the former Yugoslavia. Both race and ethnicity are associated with prejudice, discrimination and racism and these terms will now be briefly outlined.

161

Prejudice and discrimination

Prejudice implies a *belief* that any category of people, often defined in terms of race, ethnicity, religion, culture or nationality, possess common character-istics, often inferior. It is most often expressed by stating confidently that 'they . . .' are different in some respect, opinions which are so fixed that any evidence to the contrary is rejected. Discrimination, on the other hand, occurs where *actions* treat people differently solely on the grounds of race or any other ascribed characteristic. Thus if a black person is stopped by the police for no other reason than their blackness, or a white applicant is given a job instead of an equally qualified Asian because of their colour, this would constitute discrimination. Prejudice need not necessarily lead to discrimina-tion, although it often does.

Institutional discrimination

In the above examples, the discrimination is direct, and the agent is con-scious of making a discriminatory decision. Discrimination can also be the result, not of a conscious decision, but of policies and practices which pro-duce unequal outcomes. For example, for many years the English police had a height requirement which excluded many Asian recruits. While it applied to all applicants, Asians, because they tend to be smaller, were unfairly dis-advantaged, as were women (Holdaway 1996). This is an example of what is described as institutional discrimination where the policies of an institution lead to an unequal outcome even if no conscious discrimination is involved.

Racism

While the term racism was originally used to describe a belief that any group, racially defined, was different and inferior it is now used more broadly to include actions which treat groups differently on a racial basis whether or not they are based on beliefs, thus incorporating prejudice, direct and institu-tional discrimination. It is also used in connection with any form of unequal outcome irrespective of the processes leading to that outcome. Some would argue, for example, that the disproportionate numbers of black people in prison in itself signifies a racist criminal justice process. To others, using the concept of racism so widely precludes a full understanding of the social processes involved (Miles 1989).

New racism

While the belief that some races were biologically inferior has now been largely discredited, there have been arguments that a new form of racism, based on cultural rather than biological differences, has emerged in Britain, drawing on the legacy of colonialism and fuelled by the wave of immigration in the post-war period (see, for example, Gilroy 1987a). 'New racism' emerged in fears that the country would be 'swamped' by coloured immigrants and by the continued existence of racial and ethnic stereotypes. 'Multi-cultural communities' are often seen as 'problem communities' thereby associating race with problems such as inner city decay and crime. It was further argued that discourses of patriotism, nationalism, 'Englishness' and 'Britishness' make no mention of and exclude minority ethnic groups, thus 'there ain't no black in the Union Jack' (Gilroy 1987a). Despite being born in Britain, black youth were seen as 'immigrants', as outsiders whose lawlessness posed a threat to 'British culture' and the 'British way of life'.

The race and crime debate

As seen above, relationships between race, crime and victimization can be approached in different ways. As biological approaches to race are now largely discredited, few argue that any one group is biologically predisposed to crime, although there have been implications that black cultures and family patterns are weak and lack discipline – to Gilroy a sign of new racism. In Britain, until the 1970s, criminological perspectives were largely 'colour blind' and race was rarely discussed. Many early approaches are, however, relevant as anomie and subcultural theory relate crime to the social structure and social disadvantage, and racial and minority ethnic groups have been found to be especially disadvantaged in terms of education, housing, employment and income. If deprivation is a factor in crime it could therefore be argued that minority ethnic groups would show higher levels of crime (Lea and Young 1993). In addition, the labelling perspective can be used to explore the significance of race and ethnicity in the activities of the police and other control agencies. The so-called race and crime debate largely involves the different approaches taken by administrative criminology, left realism and critical race theory (Hudson 1993).

Administrative criminology and the 'race factor'

Administrative criminology, with its concern for policy, has tended to focus on investigating the extent of discrimination in the criminal justice system through the kind of studies outlined above. These use the statistical technique known as regression analysis to assess whether race has a separate or independent effect over and above any other factors such as age, class or area of residence (Holdaway 1997). Direct rather than indirect discrimination is the main focus, and studies are primarily quantitative rather than qualitative (Hudson 1993). Research is designed to establish whether race is a factor in decision making, but this is approached statistically rather than through qualitative work based on the decision makers themselves or on the subjective experiences of groups as they encounter the different stages of criminal justice (Holdaway 1997; Smith 1997). This has produced inconclusive results about the possible extent of discrimination. This may well be a consequence of their methodology in which race is seen as a separate quantifiable feature rather than as a social process. As will be seen below, race cannot be separated from the wider context in which individual police decisions are made (Holdaway 1996, 1997).

Left realists: race, crime, deprivation and the police

To left realists, the higher involvement of black people in the criminal justice process is a product of both racism on the part of criminal justice agencies and the structural position of minority ethnic groups in society (Lea and Young 1993). Against the view that higher rates of black imprisonment are a product of racism they argue that:

- Such an argument implies that all groups should be convicted in equal proportions and are equally involved in crime. This denies the cultural and social basis of crime and also implies that Asians are under-represented as a result of police partiality. Yet Asians have complained about the police attitude to racial attacks, and studies of police culture reveal that Asians as well as blacks are the subject of racial taunts and stereotypes.
- The involvement of black people in crime was not defined as a problem by the police until the 1970s, before which time black people had lower crime rates (see also Holdaway 1996). Have the police only become racist since that time?
- Suggesting that police racism alone is responsible for the over-representation of black people denies any link between deprivation and crime as the disadvantaged situation of minority ethnic groups in itself could be expected to produce higher crime rates.

To realists, arguments that racism produces higher rates of black convictions denies the 'reality' of black involvement in crime and its relationship to the structural position of minority ethnic groups. First-generation immigrants, they argue, were less likely to be involved in crime as their migration was largely motivated by the desire for employment and an improved standard of living. Having achieved this, they have little motivation for crime. The second generation internalize the expectations of the majority and expect equal opportunities which are denied through discrimination and the economic recession. This produces a situation in which minority ethnic youth are relatively disadvantaged in comparison to white youth and they are also more politically marginalized. Crime among minority ethnic youth is therefore related to relative deprivation and can be explained in the same way as all lower-class youth crime, with race providing an additional dimension of disadvantage.

This does not imply that police actions are not important and, to Lea and Young, relationships between the police and the black community can be analysed as a form of deviancy amplification. The police react strongly to crime among the black community which in turn produces hostility to the police. In many communities, they argue, the police rely on information and co-operation from older residents who are upset by high levels of crime and blame the young. Older black residents, perceiving the police to be hostile to black people as a whole, withdraw any co-operation. The police then have to resort to 'harder' policing tactics involving stopping and searching suspects as opposed to acting on information and to more intensive surveillance and saturation policies (Lea and Young 1993). As more black youth are stopped this produces increased hostility leading to 'flashpoints' like the urban disturbances of the 1980s, which were often described as race riots.

Critical race theory: criminalization and the mythology of black crime

This analysis has been strongly criticized by critical race theorists like Gilroy who argue that it underplays the significance of race and the structural processes of racism (Gilroy 1987b). It accepts the 'myth', which is part of new racism, that black crime is a problem (Gilroy 1987b). Relating race to class and the problems of lower-class youth as a whole underplays the role of race and the process of criminalization. To critical race theorists, the conflict between police and black youth is about race and not crime, and accepting the 'reality' of black crime is associated with conservative and new right 'racist' views that black culture is pathological. They argue instead that popular imagery, which associates crime with race, implies a racialization of crime in which black youth are scapegoated for rising rates of crime and lawlessness. They tend to use the term race to encompass all groups who suffer from racism, and the term black is often used to encompass a wide range of groups.

These arguments draw on the analysis of mugging, outlined in Chapter 4, which placed the moral panic about mugging in the context of the deepening crisis and in which the crimes of black youth were seen as a threat to traditional English values (Hall et al 1978). This moral panic was followed by urban disturbances in many areas of England throughout the 1980s and early 1990s, many of which were attributed to racial problems. In April 1981, confrontation between police and black people occurred in Bristol, followed by Brixton in London and later in Toxteth in Liverpool, Moss Side in Manchester and Handsworth in Birmingham. Confrontations between the police and black youth were followed by looting and burning of property. Concerns about race, crime and urban deprivation converged, with 'multi-ethnic' or 'multi-cultural' communities being associated with a variety of problems. Thus the police talked about the problems of policing a 'multi-cultural' society and 'police community' relations were constructed around racial and ethnic 'problems' (Keith 1993). A succession of images linked Afro-Caribbean youth to crime – thus:

> ... from the pimp of the 1950s, to the Black Power activist of the 1960s, to the mugger of the 1970s, to the rioter of the 1980s and quite possibly to the ultimate folk devil – the underworld Yardie of the 1990s.

> (Keith 1993: 245)

Reactions to these events – as expressed in cultural sources including the speeches of politicians, the statements of official personnel and images in the mass media – reflect new racism. These expressions are all interrelated. For example, following the publication of police statistics based on victims' descriptions of assailants which claimed that a high proportion of muggings were carried out by black people, one Judge, sentencing five West Indians following a street robbery commented that:

> These attacks have become a monotonous feature in the suburbs of Brixton and Clapham, areas which within memory were peaceful, safe and agreeable places to live in. But immigration resettlement which has occurred over the past 25 years has radically transformed that environment.
>
> (Solomos 1993: 125)

While there have been many accounts of the urban disturbances, there is little agreement about what 'caused' them, or about the significance of race (Scarman 1981; Keith 1993; Holdaway 1996). While often associated with race, not all participants were black and statistics of arrests in Brixton indicate that white youth were also involved (Keith 1993; Holdaway 1996). In Southall, in West London, Asian youth had reacted against right wing political activity. As Holdaway points out, these did not involve 'race riots' of black against white (Holdaway 1996). In Lea and Young's analysis, they represented the culmination of the spiral of mutual hostility and resentment exacerbated by the adoption by the police of an aggressive policy of stop and search in Brixton, known as SWAMP 81, to deal with rising rates of street crime (Lea and Young 1993). The official inquiry conducted under the supervision of Lord Scarman blamed the incidents on a deterioration of relationships between the police and the community but also referred to the wider context of unemployment and disadvantage experienced by black youth (Scarman 1981). To others the riots signified a rebellion on the part of black youth. Popular reactions, such as that of the then Prime Minister, Margaret Thatcher, saw them as examples of mindless hooliganism and a 'spree of naked greed' (Solomos and Rackett 1991). Emphasizing the criminal element rejected any link with unemployment or deprivation, thereby criminalizing racial issues (Solomos and Rackett 1991).

This was also seen in the aftermath of the 1985 disturbances on Broadwater Farm estate in London in which a police officer was beaten to death. The media invoked notions of 'ghettos' and 'black bombers' and downplayed the immediate cause of the riot which was the shooting of a black woman during a police search of her home. The suggested involvement of drug barons further criminalized what to many was a racial issue (Solomos 1993). These responses further cemented the association between race, crime and disorder which, Keith argues, became a symbol of the 1980s (Keith 1993: 247):

> At a simple symbolic level British Black communities are, for white society, associated with racist stereotypical notions of law and disorder, powerfully connoted by

the images of burning buildings and angry crowds so frequently seen on the screens of British television sets in the 1980s.

The processes of racialization and criminalization are also related to the social and economic restructuring described in Chapter 6. The situation of minority ethnic groups is affected by the history of immigration which, in Britain, was related to colonialism and to the need, in the post-war period, to fill vacant positions in the labour market. Immigrants form a major part of the 'reserve labour army' which is essential to capitalism. Following industrial restructuring, as seen in Chapter 6, this army was no longer required and some minority groups face particularly high rates of unemployment. They therefore became, to critical race theorists, convenient scapegoats for the apparent increase in lawlessness and crime. This process is further enabled by the deeply embedded racism in British culture. Before evaluating this and other approaches to the race and crime debate, the role of the police will be explored.

The role of the police

The role of the police is significant to all the approaches outlined above. Administrative criminologists have attempted to investigate the extent of police discrimination while realists are concerned with their role in the build up of hostility between them and minority ethnic communities. To critical race theorists police racism is a crucial element in the criminalization of black people. This draws attention to the significance of race in police work and organization, which may take different forms. Reiner argues that police racism can be individual, cultural or structural (Reiner 1989). Thus individual officers may discriminate, officers' actions may be affected by the police culture in which black people are seen as more troublesome and suspicious, and the higher numbers of black suspects may be related to wider structures of disadvantage, which bring the police and youth together in situations of conflict. These different aspects will be explored below.

Police discrimination

While many studies of police practices, such as those outlined earlier in this chapter, have attempted to assess the extent of direct racial discrimination, they have produced conflicting estimates of any direct discrimination. It is extremely difficult, if not impossible, to argue on the basis of existing research that individual discrimination plays a substantial role in producing higher numbers of black defendants, although it cannot be ruled out entirely (Reiner 1989). While, as will be seen below, police culture contains elements of racial stereotyping and prejudice, one major study found little evidence of discrimination 'on the street' (Smith and Gray 1985). Studies of prejudice among individual police officers have also failed to connect this clearly to discrimination. Thus Holdaway (1996: 80) concludes:

There may be a small number of officers who hold consistently extreme attitudes of racial prejudice but there is no clear evidence that an explanation in terms of their personality characteristics is sufficient.

The difficulties of establishing direct discrimination lie partly in the statistical methodology outlined above. As will be seen below, in everyday policing, race is only one among many factors which may affect a police officer's decision to stop or arrest a suspect. The police are in effect expected to discriminate, in that they are expected to judge, in any given circumstance, when an individual's behaviour is 'suspicious'. In reaching this assessment they rely on a number of cues such as dress, behaviour or whether a person 'fits' in a particular situation. This relies on their local knowledge of an area and its inhabitants and race may or may not be one of these cues. If a black youth, clutching a holdall, is observed running out of a shop, is it 'blackness' or their behaviour in that particular context which leads to their being stopped? In any individual decision, therefore, race cannot be separated from the situational context.

Police culture

A large number of studies have revealed considerable amounts of prejudice within police culture (Holdaway 1983; Smith and Gray 1985; Graef 1990). The Policy Studies Institute research, carried out in the early 1980s, in which researchers accompanied police officers on the street and in the more relaxed environment of the police canteen, described a 'canteen culture' in which the police described black and Asian people in stereotypical and derogatory terms. Police culture has also been portrayed as an ethnocentric, white, male-dominated culture (see, for example, Reiner 1992). Holdaway found similar attitudes that officers characterized 'blacks' as disliking the police, as disorderly, as being predisposed to crime and violence and as untrustworthy (Holdaway 1983, 1996). These, quite clearly prejudiced attitudes, not only reveal racial stereotypes. The Irish may also be seen as potentially dangerous, disorderly, or as potential terrorists (Hillyard 1993). Sexist stereotypes are also prevalent with women, including women officers, being seen stereotypically as 'whores' or as 'butch' (Heidensohn 1992; Reiner 1992). In general, police culture reflects the male, lower-class culture from which the police are largely drawn, and which forms the context in which racial attitudes must be interpreted (Reiner 1992).

The extent to which these views affect everyday policing on the street is difficult to establish. The police see their job as a 'mission' to protect society from crime and disorder by pursuing those guilty of crime and those who are suspected of being 'troublesome'. All potential suspects and the groups from which they are drawn may therefore be regarded with disdain. The police world is made up of those who represent 'trouble' who are likely to contain larger proportions of the young, the unemployed, vagrants, and many other groups (Holdaway 1983). Race forms one dimension of this broader context. Thus Holdaway (1996: 83) argues:

> race mingles with other characteristics of incidents officers identify as signs and symbols that some kind of intervention is required. Race will sometimes be at the forefront of an officer's mind when a black or Asian person is stopped. Values and related ideas and actions found in the occupational culture will, however, also be relevant and probably in the ascendant.

The structural context of police activity

Police behaviour and attitudes must also be placed in a wider structural context. Their priorities reflect and reinforce the association of the crime problem with particular groups and areas. If an area is defined as a high-crime area, it will be targeted for greater attention. As these areas are often characterized by deprivation, and may also contain large proportions of minority ethnic groups, the police and inhabitants of these areas encounter each other in a climate of hostility and suspicion. Young black lower-class men may become the targets of police suspicion largely because they are on the streets and do not appear to be legitimately employed. They may become what some have described as 'police property' (Reiner 1989). To black youth, this provides a further experience of racism, producing a hostile reaction, which may set in train the spiral of declining relationships. As with institutional discrimination it is therefore the way in which police work is organized, rather than conscious discrimination, which produces the seemingly unequal outcome of higher numbers of black people in the criminal justice process.

Racial victimization

The victimization of racial and ethnic groups is also part of the overall pattern of disadvantage. Like sexual violence, racial violence can be seen as a continuum ranging from racially motivated taunts and harassment to assaults or murder, and some forms may be persistent and have a cumulative effect. The police have often been criticized for failing to react to racially motivated crime or recognize its racial nature, underlined in the recent case where the London teenager Stephen Lawrence was killed by a group of white youths, yet no prosecution was undertaken. Crime can therefore become another aspect of the racialized experiences of minority ethnic groups.

The cumulative effects of persistent harassment was starkly revealed in one survey in an East London local authority housing estate which found that in six months thirty Bengali families had experienced on average four and a half attacks (Sampson and Phillips 1992). One family reported a sequence of incidents involving stone throwing, chasing, being threatened and prevented from entering their flat, being punched and verbally abused and armed robbery. Another family reported being pushed by youths, having their front door kicked, having eggs thrown at their window, common assault, having a lit cigarette and newspaper shoved through their letter box and verbal racial abuse. The continual threat of harassment and violence meant that most of the women were afraid to go out and many children were not allowed to play outside.

It has also been seen that, irrespective of racially motivated crime, minority ethnic groups are more at risk from some offences. This is because they are more likely to be concentrated in high-crime areas, a concentration which reflects racialized processes of discrimination in the housing market and the economic situation of minority ethnic groups. Crime therefore forms another aspect of deprivation. However measured and counted, argues Holdaway, the perception of minority ethnic groups that offences are 'racially' motivated illustrates that crime is experienced within the broader framework of race and racialized experiences (Holdaway 1996). Whether or not incidents are racially motivated, victims' experiences of racism lead to their perception that they are – as Holdaway (1996: 43) argues: 'the experience of victimisation amongst black and Asian people is a thread running through other social contexts within which race is articulated.'

Gender is also related to racial victimization. The feminist approaches discussed in Chapter 8 were criticized by black feminists for ignoring the experiences of black women, for whom sexual harassment and violence has an added, racial, component. Images of black women's sexuality are racialized and expressed in verbal abuse. Pakistani women, for example, are taunted with being Paki 'whores'. Minority ethnic men face the added threat of racial violence, largely at the hands of white men. In Asian communities this may lead to the development of informal, vigilante style protective groups, giving the impression of inter-racial violence (Webster 1997). In addition, as will be seen in Chapter 10, violence within minority ethnic families is affected by its cultural context and may be exacerbated by the socially disadvantaged situation of households (Mama 1989).

RACE, CRIME, CRIMINALIZATION AND RACIALIZATION

Assessing the significance of race as a factor in crime and victimization therefore raises many different questions. One major question is the extent to which some groups have been subject to criminalization and whether this is primarily determined by race or is related to other features of social inequality. In addition, generalizing about race or minority ethnic groups may inadequately reflect the different experiences of different groups. This section will explore some of these issues.

As seen above, to critical race theories, race and criminalization are intricately linked. There are, however, many problems with their analyses and their reliance on published sources, on the speeches of politicians, senior police officers and judges. This work is highly interpretative and, as they aim to reveal 'hidden' elements of racist discourse, they often infer racism from speeches and sources which do not directly refer to race (Holdaway 1996). While their analyses do indicate the pervasive nature of racism, their sources can be seen as highly selective and politicians' speeches and opinions may not reflect those of the wider population. As Holdaway (1996: 103) argues:

> There is also a significant gap between the apparent meanings contained in speeches, and other formal discourses analysed, and the everyday, common-sense discourse of various publics. We cannot assume that because a leading politician of influence articulates ideas of racial differentiation in the guise of nationalism they are some-how directly routed into the consciousness of newspaper readers, television viewers, or through rumour, mundane conversations or any other form of communication.

The relationship between race and class is also problematic. To critical race theorists, race is the major dimension of differentiation and race is generalized to include many different minority groups. This poses a number of problems. While the notion of the 'underclass' outlined in Chapter 6 can contain elements of race, in Britain, it also includes white unemployed groups and can have a 'northern' or 'Celtic' connotation (Bagguley and Mann 1992). In areas of the north of England and Scotland, often identified with the underclass, there are lower levels of minority ethnic and particularly black groups. While the concept of the 'underclass' was associated with the use of minority ethnic groups as surplus or reserve labour, this was criticized as not all members of these groups are equally disadvantaged and there are growing differences in the social and economic situation of specific minority ethnic groups. There is a growing black middle class, and some Asian groups are less disadvantaged than some white groups.

The dangers of generalizing about minority ethnic groups can be illustrated by an exploration of the experiences of diverse groups. The often noted lower involvement in the criminal justice process among Asians has, for example, often been attributed to cultural factors. The Asian community is depicted as conformist and law abiding and the role of the extended family and religion is also seen to operate against involvement in crime. This 'idealized' version of the Asian family is contrasted negatively with the assumed weakness of the Afro-Caribbean family (Webster 1997). There are signs, however, that Asian youth are involved in gangs and violent incidents which are often attributed to the effects of youth unemployment and a rebellion against the culture of the older generation. The proportion of young people in some Asian communities is also rising and this combination has led some to argue that Asian crime may become a new moral panic (Coleman and Moynihan 1996).

These kinds of arguments, however, see Asians as an undifferentiated group. They also associate young Asian men with general lawlessness whereas in some areas Asian 'gangs' were formed in response to the threat of racial harassment and right wing political activity, as was the case in Southall in

171

West London (Webster 1997). This essentially protective involvement has been perceived, in some areas, as an attempt by Asian youth to dominate territory and has led to localized instances of fighting between rival groups of white and black and Asian youth to a point where white young people see themselves as being racially victimized (Webster 1997). Webster also stresses that it is important not to generalize about 'Asian' youth as youth in different Asian communities adopt very different responses. Many remain conformist while others experiment with cultural styles which rebel against their parent culture. Older youths, led by 'toughies' – physically strong and 'hard' Pakistani youth – engage in vigilante activities. In conclusion, he argues that Asian young people become criminal for very much the same reasons as their white counterparts, which includes youth unemployment and relative deprivation (Webster 1997).

Other groups, less often seen as races, can also be criminalized. The Irish have effectively become, argues Hillyard, a 'suspect community' through the operation of Prevention Against Terrorism legislation (Hillyard 1993). Historically the Irish were portrayed as an inferior race, being seen as violent, drunken and dishonest. Yet the Irish experience of policing has rarely been discussed. As a consequence of the PTA he argues, anyone with an Irish background is seen as someone who can legitimately be stopped. To the extent that this legislation is directed at the Irish, he argues, it is an example of institutionalized racism. It has criminalized the Irish in Britain who are subject to police investigation simply because of their status and irrespective of their behaviour.

These examples illustrate the difficulties of using broad categories such as race in relation to processes or racialization and criminalization. While some forms of crime have been racialized and some groups, in some areas, criminalized, this varies for different groups and may differ across the country in relation to patterns of minority ethnic settlement. In some areas black young men may be seen as a major problem, in others groups of white and Asian youth, and in still others the residents of peripheral or inner city estates. In yet other areas of Britain sectarianism and religious conflict may affect crime. One recent controversial case in Glasgow, for example, involved a particularly brutal sectarian murder where a young teenage Celtic supporter was killed by a Protestant youth.

CONCLUDING COMMENTS

This chapter has illustrated how race and ethnicity are involved in crime and victimization, although their significance has been hotly contested. It is clear that different ethnic and racial groups are involved in the criminal justice process as offenders in different proportions. It is also clear that this may be partly due to processes of criminalization and that, in some areas, some kinds of crime have been racialized. While the police have been accused of racism, race is only one among many factors which affect police decisions and the significance of race has to be seen in the wider context of structural inequalities which affect crime and policing along with victimization.

The relationship between race and other inequalities reviewed earlier, such as age, class and gender, is clearly complex. Race can and does form a separate dimension of victimization, and experiences of victimization are a further feature of racial and ethnic disadvantage. At the same time race is closely related to these other forms of inequality. Lower-class young people in all groups face the problems of unemployment, disadvantage and social exclusion although this may be exacerbated by racial discrimination. These experiences are also mediated by culture, race and ethnicity, which produce different responses. For some, they may lead to increasing involvement in crime, in some cases as a response to the threat of racial attack. Further aspects of the interrelationship between different forms of inequality will be seen when exploring the specific patterns of crime, which will be the subject of subsequent chapters.

Review Questions

1. Using local newspaper reports along with your own perceptions and those of your friends and neighbours, consider the extent to which crime has been racialized in your own local area.
   (a) Are some kinds of crime attributed to particular racial or minority ethnic groups?
   (b) Are particular areas associated with racial or ethnic 'problems'?
   (c) How are these constructed?
   (d) How can experiences in your local area be related to discussions of the significance of race as a factor in crime and victimization?
   (e) How do they relate to other dimensions of inequality such as age, class or gender? (This may be related to your answers to the questions in Chapter 7.)
2. Why is it so difficult to assess the extent of police racism or discrimination?
3. Compare and contrast the arguments involved in the 'race and crime' debate. If working in a group, this can be structured as a debate.

Key Reading

Cook D and Hudson B (eds) (1993) *Racism and Criminology*. London: Sage
Holdaway S (1996) *The Racialization of British Policing*. London: Macmillan
Keith M (1993) *Race, Riots and Policing*. London: UCL Press
Smith D J (1997) 'Race, Crime and Criminal Justice', in Maguire M, Morgan R and Reiner R (eds) *The Oxford Handbook of Criminology*, 2nd edition. Oxford: Clarendon Press

CHAPTER 10

VIOLENT CRIME

Violent crime is the most threatening form of crime and often arouses emotional reactions. Despite this, official figures, as seen in Chapter 5, suggest that it forms a very small proportion of reported and recorded crime. These figures, however, reflect the way in which 'violent crime' is constructed and it will be seen that, when the many forms of violence which are not counted as violent crime are taken into account, violence is far more widespread. It is very difficult to generalize about such a vast category as 'violent crime' which ranges from trivial assaults to mass murder and can take place in public, in the home, in the workplace, on the football pitch, in pubs, clubs, schools and on the road where 'road rage' has recently become yet another manifestation of the assumed spread of violence. It can be approached from many different perspectives. Offenders are often portrayed as abnormal, as 'crazed', 'psychos' or 'thugs' and indeed violent crime, as will be seen below, has been 'medicalized'. On the other hand, many manifestations of violence are a feature of everyday life and to feminists, as seen in Chapter 8, the threat of male violence pervades women's everyday lives. It can be thrilling, fascinating and is often glorified in popular entertainment. It may be part of subcultures and, as seen in Chapter 8, can be linked to masculinity. It can be gendered and can also, as seen in earlier chapters, involve power relationships of race, class or age.

This chapter will focus on those forms of violent crime which are included in official categories, while recognizing that these omit many other forms of violent crime. The first sections will explore how violent crime is socially constructed and counted. As no single chapter can cover all aspects of violent crime in depth, three main forms, not included in later chapters, will be examined in more depth. The most serious form of violent crime – murder – will be explored and the following sections will look at two further forms of violent crime. Violence at work, often neglected, has attracted more recent attention, and violence in the home has, as seen in Chapters 5 and 8, been subject to considerable attention by feminist researchers. Finally, contrasting approaches to violent crime will be outlined. Other aspects of violent crime will be discussed in subsequent chapters. It is often argued for example that sexual crime, the subject of Chapter 11, is also violent crime and, as will be seen, official constructions of violent crime also omit institutional and state violence which will be explored in Chapters 15 and 16.

WHAT IS VIOLENT CRIME?

Official categories of violent crime include offences of homicide, grievous bodily harm, wounding or actual bodily harm, with figures for England and Wales normally excluding summary offences of 'common assault'. Some figures include sexual offences, such as rape and sexual assault, and robbery as violent, personal or contact crime. These categories sometimes distinguish between instrumental and expressive violence. In the former, violence is used to further financial gain, whereas in the latter it is the main feature of the offence. Broadly speaking, official categories of violent crime emphasize its interpersonal and confrontational nature along with the deliberate infliction of physical injury, reflected in the phrases actual or grievous bodily harm. Many questions can be asked about this official construction of violence.

Forms of violence

Instrumental violence

It is difficult in practice to separate instrumental from expressive violence. The robber may experience an added thrill or buzz from using or threatening violence and choose robbery because of this while other offenders avoid any risk of violence (Stanko 1994, and see Chapter 12). Violence is also an important element in organized crime and the drugs market (Hobbs 1995, and see Chapters 13 and 14).

The threat of violence

Earlier chapters have illustrated that the threat of violence can be as damaging as actual violence, particularly where, as with racial or sexual violence, it may be persistent. It has also been seen that violence can be seen as a continuum ranging from harassment and bullying to serious assault and murder. The focus on physical injury may therefore minimize the amount and impact of violence – cruelty can be mental as well as physical.

Individual and institutional violence

The focus on interpersonal violence perpetrated by individual offenders also neglects what some describe as institutional or corporate violence, where death or injury result from the neglect of quality or safety regulations (Wells 1993; Levi 1997, and see Chapter 15). These do not fit the social construction of violence in that they do not involve a specific intent to harm individual

175

victims. Intent, however, is not always crucial for convictions for other forms of violence – recklessness about the consequences of actions can lead to conviction and an individual's role may not always be clear in, for example, a gang fight (Levi 1997).

State violence

What can be described as state-sponsored or sanctioned violence is also omitted from official categorizations (Stanko 1994; McLaughlin 1996). Yet the most extreme forms of violence often take place during wars. Genocide, 'ethnic cleansing', mass rape and other forms of brutality are examples of 'war crimes' which are segregated from the category of violent crime (see Chapter 16). A very fine line also divides the legitimate use of 'force' from illegitimate violence, particularly in relation to the activities of, for example, police and army officers (McLaughlin 1996, and see Chapter 16).

Violence and abuse

Previous chapters have also illustrated that many forms of violence in the home were formerly regarded, not as 'violent crime' but as 'abuse' which placed them in a separate category which implies that they are less serious.

Official categories of violent crime therefore reflect a social construction which emphasizes a rather narrow range of violence. They tend to overemphasize public manifestations of violence and underemphasize violence in the home, the violence of official agencies and the dangerous practices of institutions (Stanko 1994; Kelly and Radford 1996). In so doing they also focus on, and in effect criminalize, the activities of primarily lower-class individuals and minimize the 'real' amount and impact of violent crime. Some argue for a much wider definition of violence. For example, Stanko (1994: 38) argues that 'broadly speaking, violence involves the infliction of emotional, psychological, sexual, physical and/or material damage'.

THE SCOPE OF VIOLENT CRIME

Research problems

Many of the problems of researching and assessing the extent of violent crime have already been referred to. It could be assumed that, because violence threatens or causes injury, it is more likely to be reported to the police, but this not the case. Many incidents involving injury are not reported and even where medical attention is required they may be dealt with as accidents. Some of the reasons for this were outlined in Chapter 2. Embarrassment, fear of reprisal or feelings that the incident is too trivial are important, as are victims' feelings that they themselves provoked an attack. The limitations of victim surveys were outlined in Chapter 5. The BCS is acknowledged to under-represent violence in the home and other surveys also have limitations. Many are based on small and possibly unrepresentative samples and they use different definitions. Some include threats and harassment, some incorporate sexual violence, some include psychological abuse, and some give composite figures which can be misleading (Walklate 1989). They may use different time periods with some covering one year and others covering respondents' lifetimes. This makes their results very difficult to compare (Walklate 1989). Moreover, all of these kinds of measurements exclude corporate and state violence. Official measurements also reveal little about the nature of the violence involved. Assault occasioning actual bodily harm, for example, could be sexually or racially motivated and could take place at home, at work, in the pub, at a football match or in the street – all of which represent very different kinds of offences.

Officially recorded violent crime

Some of the main features of official statistics on violent crime, summarized in Figure 10.1, have also been encountered in previous chapters. This indicates

Figure 10.1 Some features of violent crime

- *Violent crime forms a small proportion of officially recorded crime*
  In 1995, 6 per cent of offences reported to the BCS were woundings and robberies, and another 15 per cent were common assaults.

- *Serious injury is rare*

- *Officially recorded violence rose during the 1980s*
  Recorded victimization rose by 40 per cent for males and 90 per cent for females between 1984 and 1989. Domestic violence showed the largest rise, followed by acquaintance violence. Stranger violence showed the smallest increase. This is assumed to reflect an increased awareness of and willing-ness to report domestic violence.

- *Acquaintance violence is most prevalent*
  In the 1996 BCS, 1.7 million incidents of acquaintance violence were reported compared with one million incidents of domestic violence and a similar figure for stranger violence.

- *Alcohol or drugs were said to have been involved in nearly half of all violent incidents*
  Alcohol was associated with over half of the incidents involving stranger violence, under a half involving acquaintance violence and a third involving domestic violence. Drugs were said to have been involved in around one-fifth of cases of acquaintance violence and less for other kinds.

continued overleaf

- *Men are at more risk from reported violence*
  6.7 per cent of male and 3.8 per cent of female BCS respondents reported contact crime in 1995.

- *The young are more at risk from violent incidents*
  13.2 per cent of victims were aged between 16 and 29 compared with only 1 per cent of those over 60.

- *Those living in privately rented accommodation are most at risk*

- *Women are more at risk from domestic violence and men from stranger and acquaintance violence*
  Over 3 per cent of women aged between 16 and 29 reported domestic violence compared with 1.7 per cent of men; 6.5 per cent of men aged between 16 and 29 reported stranger violence compared with 2.1 per cent of women; 9 per cent of men in this age group reported acquaintance violence compared with 3 per cent of women.

- *Offenders are more likely to be male*
  Women were more vulnerable to domestic violence from current or former partners. Male offenders were reported as responsible for nine-tenths of stranger attacks against men and just under two-thirds of those against women. Four-fifths of offenders in acquaintance violence were male – 'although "women on women" incidents were more common in acquaintance violence than in any other type' (Mirlees-Black et al 1996: 35).

(All figures taken from Mirlees-Black et al 1996)

that even when victim surveys are taken into account violent crime forms a small proportion of reported crime, and that officially reported violence most typically involves fights between young men who know each other in and around pubs and clubs. Women are more at risk in the home – and when they commit violence it is also more likely to be in the home (Mirlees-Black et al 1996). While violent crime appears to be rising, this is generally assumed to be a result of people being more prepared to report violence (Barclay 1993). They say little, however, about the more everyday forms of violence as harassment and threats are not generally counted, nor do they fully indicate socio-economic differences although they indicate that risks are higher in poorer areas. Subsequent sections will look at different kinds of violence in more depth.

DIMENSIONS OF VIOLENT CRIME

The following sections will look at contrasting forms of violent crime. Homicide, while statistically rare, attracts enormous attention and, like violent crime itself, is socially constructed and includes many different kinds of killings.

While, as seen above, the public manifestations of violence are most often reported and recorded, far less is known about the violence which people suffer as a consequence of their work and this will be briefly explored. The significance of violence within the family has been referred to at several points in this book and it will receive more detailed attention below.

Homicide

Of all crimes, homicide probably attracts the greatest fascination and it is a prominent theme in both classical and popular literature and drama. A variety of different social relationships are implied in terms used to describe different kinds of homicide. Thus matricide, infanticide, patricide or fratricide imply family relationships, femicide implies a gendered relationship, assassination a political motive, and manslaughter a less deliberate killing. Some murders have financial, political, racial, sexual or religious motivations, while others appear motiveless. People can be killed for their possessions – from wealth, property or power to fashion clothing. As the fictional detective Adam Dalgliesh in PD James' novels often reiterates, it is motivated by love, loathing, lust and loot. While murder is generally seen as a matter of individual responsibility, the growing recognition that companies and employers can be responsible for corporate manslaughter questions this social construction (Wells 1988, 1993). This is also called into question by offences such as causing death by dangerous or drunken driving – not hitherto seen as homicide.

Defining and counting homicide

Officially, homicide includes murder, manslaughter and infanticide (White 1995). Although legal categories appear clear cut, a very fine line divides 'murder' from 'accident', 'licensed killings' by law enforcers or euthanasia. While it is often assumed that most murders are officially counted because of identifiable bodies, this is not the case. Some deaths, particularly of the terminally ill, may be cases of euthanasia where the cause of death is difficult to detect (Levi 1997). More gruesomely, not all bodies are discovered – some 'missing persons' may be murder victims, revealed most dramatically in the case involving the West family where many victims were listed as missing. While clear up rates are high, many offences are initially counted as murder but later defined as accidents or subject to reduced charges, and attempts and threats to kill can amount to six times the figures for homicide (White 1995). Official figures also exclude causing death by dangerous and reckless driving (Levi 1997). While it is often assumed that homicide, like violence, is increasing, fewer people are murdered in twentieth-century Britain than was the case in previous centuries (Levi 1997). There was an overall decline in the murder rate from the Second World War to around 1959 since when the rate has steadily increased, albeit more slowly than that for other violent crimes (White 1995).

179

Figure 10.2 Who murders whom?

- Children less than one year old are the most likely victims of homicide – around 10 per cent of homicides are of children by parents.

- Those aged between 5 and 15 are least likely to be victims; those aged between 16 and 49 are most likely to be victims.

- Most convicted offenders are male.

- Men are more likely to be victims than women – in 1994 there were 407 male victims compared to 270 females.

- Most victims are killed by people they know – only one in five is killed by a stranger.

- In 1994, 37 per cent of female victims were killed by their present or former spouse or partner, 22 per cent by other family members and 18 per cent by friends or associates.

- In 1994, 8 per cent of male victims were killed by their present or former spouse or partner, 12 per cent by other family members and 35 per cent by a friend or other associate.

- In 1994, 36 per cent of male victims were killed by strangers compared to 12 per cent of female victims.

- Seven per cent of homicides are carried out in furtherance of theft or gain, which are the main recorded motives for 4 per cent of acquaintance and 11 per cent of stranger homicides; 55 per cent of homicides are the result of quarrels, revenge or temper.

(Figures from Barclay 1995; White 1995; Levi 1997)

Figure 10.2 summarizes aspects of the relationship between offenders and victims, and dispels some commonly held myths. Many are now familiar with the statistic that the majority of homicides involve people known to each other, and members of families are often 'prime suspects'. The more publicized murders of children give the impression that young children are particularly vulnerable to killing by strangers – yet they emerge as least at risk. In a study of 250 murder cases from 1978 to 1982, Mitchell found that over half were committed by men aged less than 30, and 14 per cent by men under 17 years of age (Mitchell 1990). He also found that where homicides involved younger people they were more likely to involve gang fights or financial motivation, whereas most spouses or cohabitants were killed by people aged between 30 and 50. Those convicted were mainly from lower-level occupations or were unemployed (Mitchell 1990). Homicide, therefore, involves many different relationships and takes place in many different situations. Multiple homicides arouse enormous interest whereas 'confrontational homicides' among men are more typical. Femicide, or the killing of women, draws attention to the often gendered nature of homicide. These contrasting forms will be briefly explored below.

Multiple murder

Recently, Gresswell and Hollin (1994) reviewed the literature on multiple murder, defined as murders involving three or more victims. Firstly, they looked at official figures for England and Wales which showed no significant increase. Between 1982 and 1989, 52 incidents were recorded which involved 58 perpetrators and 196 victims, who constituted 3 per cent of homicide victims. Almost 90 per cent of offenders were male, as were over half of the victims. Half of the victims were family members, 15 per cent were acquaintances or friends and a high proportion of the perpetrators killed themselves. Three main forms of multiple murder were identified in the literature they reviewed:

- *Mass murder* most typically involves a lone assassin killing several people in the same area in a short time. Typical offenders are described as 'pseudo commandos', i.e. young men obsessed with fire arms, 'set and run' killers who plan a lethal episode and escape, 'psychotic killers' including leaders of cults who initiate mass suicides of 'disciples' and depressed men who kill their family before committing suicide.

- *Spree murder* most typically involves killing several victims over a period of hours or days in different locations. Perpetrators are most often male and they are impulsive and frenzied, make little effort to evade detection and often kill themselves or are killed by the police.

- *Serial murder* most typically involves repeated killing over a long time with no direct connection between killers and victims. Victims may come from an identifiable group such as prostitutes. Killers are often motivated by fantasies, seeing themselves as visionaries or missionaries.

Gresswell and Hollin point out that these categories are not exhaustive and they miss out contract killers or 'hit men'. While constituting a varied group, some characteristics of offenders have been identified. The majority are male, aged under 35, and are commonly described as 'inadequately socialized'. They usually have a complex rationale for their actions and are described as distant from everyday life, which enables them to legitimate and normalize violence and sadism (Gresswell and Hollin 1994).

Confrontational homicide

Far more typical, according to statistics, are homicides which result from fights and quarrels in public leisure arenas such as pubs and clubs. These, which often involve seemingly routine or trivial incidents, have been described as confrontational homicide and have been studied in the United States (Daly and Wilson 1988) and in Australia (Polk 1994). Polk found that such confrontational homicides constituted 22.1 per cent of homicides in Victoria, Australia, and he studied 84 cases. Typically, they involved 'contests of honour and lethal violence' brought about by men's willingness to challenge the honour of other men and to engage in physical violence to protect that honour. Seemingly petty disputes become life threatening when routine insults such as apparent invasions of a person's space are interpreted as a disparagement of manhood and become an 'affair of honour' (Daly and Wilson 1988). Alcohol, which is often involved, may lead to these interactions being misread provoking the violent reaction. Some insults involve sexual prowess or the protection of women, others involve ethnicity or group membership. They involve maintaining 'face' or 'reputation' and, to Polk, are 'quintessential masculine matters' (Polk 1994: 183).

Femicide

Femicide has been a feature of patriarchal societies across the world and includes killing female babies and killings which may be racially and sexually motivated (Radford 1992). Femicide is distinct because, argues Radford, men are rarely killed because they are men whereas women are. Nonetheless women are often blamed, as killing prostitutes may be seen as less serious because they are assumed to have provoked violence. 'Dominant mothers' can be also be blamed for their own death or for their sons' behaviour. Trials of spousal homicides are typically, argues Lees, surrounded by a mythology of woman blaming with a wife's apparent neglect of her 'duties', or her 'nagging' or adultery being accepted as mitigations (Bland 1992; Lees 1992, 1997).

In a study of trials of spousal homicide, Lees found that husbands' and partners' accounts of their motives for murder reveal assumptions of ownership – most typically centring around the theme 'If I can't have her, no one can'. Killings often followed accusations of adultery or desertion and are popularly attributed to 'jealousy'. Men have been able to reduce charges of murder to manslaughter or to claim a temporary loss of control because they were 'provoked' (Lees 1992, 1997). 'Provocation' can include nagging, women not fulfilling household duties or committing adultery – situations in which it is assumed that the 'reasonable' man might lose control. In one case, an alleged affair on the part of the wife was accepted as grounds for provocation. The husband had stabbed his wife 23 times with a kitchen knife – but was described as a gentle and good man. Lees (1997: 173) comments that

> For a judge to describe a man who has murdered his wife for whatever reason as good is surely symptomatic of patriarchal justice. It would be inconceivable for a woman who had killed her husband to be described as good.

She argues that there are double standards – women who have killed husbands following years of violence have had considerable difficulty having provocation accepted, and murder reduced to manslaughter (Lees 1997).

Violence at work

Much violence takes place at work and people's jobs present different risks of violence. Some are more at risk – such as the police, social workers or prison officers – because they work with violent people. Eight police and prison officers were killed on duty in England and Wales in 1986–90 (Levi 1997). Others are vulnerable by dealing directly with the public and still others face journeys to work at times and in areas carrying a higher risk of violence. While this section will focus on interpersonal violence, workers also suffer ill health and injury as a result of dangerous working conditions, which will be explored in Chapter 15 (Levi 1997; Wells 1993).

Job-related violence, including assault and robbery, constitutes a significant proportion of violent incidents. The 1988 BCS found that people who worked blamed their jobs for nearly a quarter of violent incidents and more than a third of threats. Three-quarters of these involved members of the public. They affected more men than women and women reported fewer serious incidents. From a small sample, they found more than three times the average risk among welfare workers, nurses, production and site managers, office managers, entertainment managers (bouncers) and security workers. When threats and verbal abuse were included, teachers joined this high-risk group. Shop and retail workers also face considerable risks from potential thieves and members of the public (Beck et al 1994). More incidents involved adult perpetrators, while women were more at risk from young people. One-tenth of the incidents involved drunks and, for non-whites, 60 per cent of incidents involved racial abuse (Mayhew et al 1989).

Despite this, there have been few studies of violence at work (Painter 1991a). Studies of National Health Service workers suggest that one in 200 staff suffer a major injury each year, one in 21 are threatened with a weapon or implement and more than one in six are threatened verbally (Brundson and May 1992). It has also been suggested that this kind of violence has risen disproportionately. Care in the community workers are seen as particularly vulnerable, in part as a result of the move away from treating the mentally ill in institutions, leaving more difficult cases in 'the community' (Brundson and May 1992). The casualty department of Edinburgh Royal Infirmary recently installed a police station to deal with increasing levels of violence against staff who reported an average of two incidents requiring police action every day. Most attacks are said to be drink or drugs related with up to 1,000 each year ending with an arrest (Alba 1996). One study of retail staff reports that one in nine had been attacked, one-third of whom had been physically injured (Beck et al 1994). Violence at work is often under-reported. Some workers may not report incidents because they blame themselves for not having handled the situation better, while others fear that disclosing these problems might threaten their career (Painter 1991a; Brundson and May 1992; Beck et al 1994).

Persistent sexual or racial harassment also takes place at work, as do threats of or actual sexual assault and what has been described as exploitative rape where male managers abuse their organizational power (Box 1983). The Islington Crime Survey found that 13.5 per cent of sexual assaults took place in the workplace (Jones et al 1986). Sexual harassment and a perceived threat of violence can cause anxiety, fear and a loss of confidence in work, sometimes leading to employees resigning (Stanko 1990a; Kelly and Radford 1996). In Kelly and Radford's study (1996: 26), a nurse reported regular harassment by male patients, and an office worker recounts being 'pissed off' and exhausted at the end of a day facing half-joking propositions from male colleagues. For black women these experiences are exacerbated by racial harassment (Kelly and Radford 1996).

Violence in the home

It is now widely recognized that the home, conventionally regarded as a re-fuge, is a major site of violence with all family members being potential victims (Saraga 1996). Many different terms are used to describe violence in the home. It has been seen that terms such as 'abuse' or 'domestic' or 'family' violence have been criticized for segregating these forms of violence. They can also lead to blaming the family, particularly women, who are blamed for not fulfilling their role as mothers or wives. To feminists, they can also downplay gender – seeing the family, rather than men, as the problem (Saraga 1993, 1996). Others criticize the separation of sexual from other forms of violence as this underemphasizes the violent nature of sexual offences.

Exploring a hidden problem

While often seen as a 'new' problem, violence in the home was recognized in the nineteenth century when cruelty to children and wife battering were seen as largely lower-class problems (Saraga 1996). Cruelty to children, however, attracted lower sentences than other forms of violence, and the Royal Society for the Protection of Cruelty to Children was formed after the equivalent society for animals (Morgan and Zedner 1992; Saraga 1996). The home was seen as a private domain and the sanctity of marriage highly regarded. Judges considered that men could legally chastise their wives for adultery or not fulfilling their allotted role (Dobash and Dobash 1992). Incest was seen as unnatural rather than as an abuse of parental power (Saraga 1996). As seen in Chapter 7, concerns about children focused on their delinquency, and child abuse was largely seen as a social welfare problem (Morgan and Zedner 1992; Parton 1985). This continued until well after the Second World War, a period which idealized the nuclear family and parent and motherhood

(Saraga 1996). Few dispute that there was violence in the home throughout this period, although vastly under-reported. From the 1960s onwards it became far more widely recognized following high-profile cases and the establishment of refuges for battered women and self-help groups for victims of both physical and sexual attacks. This led to a growing amount of research exposing and analysing different forms of family violence (Dobash and Dobash 1992; Saraga 1996; Zedner 1997).

The nature and extent of violence in the home

While violence in the home is now widely acknowledged, the many problems of establishing its extent have been seen. Some of its characteristics are indicated in Figure 10.1 and other research has produced a variety of different estimates. One study carried out in 1993 in North London found that a third of women reported some form of violence ranging from mental cruelty to actual violence and/or rape in their lifetime. One in ten reported a similar experience within the previous twelve months (cited in Walklate 1995). Often cited is a study in which a third of women reported being hit by their husbands (Painter 1991b, cited in Saraga 1996). It has been estimated that around 95 per cent of physical assaults are perpetrated by men, but women do physically assault family members, some would argue in greater numbers than previously assumed (Kelly 1996). Men are also victims – the latest BCS indicates that nearly half of these were perpetrated by partners or ex-partners with a quarter each by other family members and relatives (Mirlees-Black et al 1996).

The mythology of violence against wives – why does she stay?

Many studies of violence against wives reveal the potency of myths which typically blame women for their victimization. Women are assumed to provoke violence by not fulfilling their wifely duties or are said to enjoy violence. A typical response to violence against wives is 'Why does she stay?' (Kelly 1988; Walklate 1989, 1995). To Walklate, it is illuminating to rephrase this question as 'Why doesn't she leave?'. Answering this question illustrates much about gendered power relationships and women's lives. It involves economic considerations – women may have no financial resources and may be afraid of losing their children. They may have nowhere else to go. They are often socially isolated by their partner's activities, and believe they can change him. Moreover, domestic violence often involves partners undermining women's self confidence and threatening them with losing their children – threats which women take seriously (Walklate 1995: 91).

Survivors' experiences

Women's accounts illustrate the effect of threatened and actual violence which is often accompanied by forced sexual activity (Kelly 1988). Some of the women interviewed by Kelly reveal the fear and tension involved. An atmosphere of violence and verbal abuse, even without physical violence, can undermine women's self-confidence. Violence often erupts in situations where men assert control and it was often triggered by women's performance of domestic duties or work or education outside the home. Many women subject to repeated violence came to believe it was their fault. One survivor expresses this well:

> He definitely sapped my confidence over the years. It's like a drip on your head . . . and I got to believe by the end that I was hopeless at everything, that everything he said about me was actually true. Which is another reason why I didn't leave, because if I was that hopeless how on earth was I going to exist on my own without him?
>
> (Kelly 1988: 131)

Women often minimized the threat of violence, feeling that physical violence was more serious. This is revealed in the often made comment that 'nothing really happened' (Kelly and Radford 1996). Another survivor (ibid: 29) comments:

> quite a lot of the time he wasn't physically violent, but there was just this threat all the time you see . . . you don't see it as serious at the time, it's only when you get out that you realise how much it affected you.

For many, increasing levels of physical violence led to their eventual departure. One woman comments: 'He used to bang my head against the wall or the floor. I finally left him when I thought he was trying to kill me' (Kelly 1988: 130).

These experiences have severe effects. Many women became scared of men, and report long-term effects on their strength, autonomy and sense of self. Some had breakdowns, and far from being passive victims, many women develop coping strategies, carry on with work and child care and attempt to resist their violent partners (Kelly 1988). Thus Kelly sees them as 'survivors' rather than as victims, which implies a more passive role.

Black women's experiences

Feminist perspectives were initially criticized for not taking account of black women's experiences and Mama (1989) points out that men of all cultures beat women but in a culturally specific context. In her study of black female victims she encountered similar experiences to those above and points also to the significance of social and economic factors. Housing was a major factor in black women's experiences. Black women with children have a higher chance of being allocated housing, whereas black men were more often homeless. When women tried to evict violent men, they could refuse to leave and, even when they did, threatened violence from vindictiveness and what she describes as socio-economic jealousy. For black women in a racist culture, speaking out could be seen as a sign of disloyalty. Violence often had a culturally specific content – Muslim and Rastafarian men used religion to assert their patriarchal authority, and some women were criticized for being too Western. While, argues Mama, arranged marriages are not related to violence, Asian women who had refused an arranged marriage faced little family support and a strongly patriarchal culture in which women do not leave husbands. For other women, migration could lead to isolation from family and community support. An additional problem for immigrant women was that if they left their husband they faced possible deportation.

Child victims

Children are also victims of physical violence. Child abuse is generally taken to include sexual and physical violence along with neglect, which can be likened to physical injury (Saraga 1996). Physical abuse and neglect came to public attention through high-profile cases, which led to the development of 'at risk' registers, following which the number of children registered and reported incidents of abuse increased – although this probably reflects a greater awareness of the problem (Saraga 1996). While, as we have seen, men are more likely to be offenders, and are the main offenders in dual parent households, women have been found to be involved in physical abuse and neglect. This reflects their different circumstances. Saraga argues that they are more likely to be held responsible as they are seen to be the parent most responsible for child care. Physical violence and neglect are also more common in working-class homes. However, this could reflect the fact that more lower-class families are likely to come into contact with social services and be considered 'at risk' (Saraga 1996). Child sexual abuse will be explored in Chapter 11.

Elder abuse

Elder abuse is even more hidden, although professionals have recognized it for some time (Aitken and Griffin 1996). Few cases end up in a criminal prosecution and it is particularly difficult to identify. Media 'scares' about 'granny dumping' (leaving old people in a hospital), violence in geriatric wards and 'granny battering' have led to the stereotype of the elderly woman being abused by a stressed daughter or carer – reflecting the assumption that women are the main carers (Aitken and Griffin 1996). Elderly women are more likely to be victims than men as they live longer and are often poorer and more dependent. The stereotype is inaccurate in other respects, however. Both sons and daughters abuse both mothers and fathers and elderly couples may abuse each other. While women are more likely to be abused, the abusers are most frequently men. Physical abuse is more likely to happen where family members cohabitate, and it has also been found that those suffering from dementia (who may themselves appear to be violent) are among those most victimized. Women do abuse, particularly in institutions where the majority of care workers are women. This must, however, be viewed within the context of institutions in which 'policing' confused elderly patients may assume priority over 'caring' (Aitken and Griffin 1996). More victims are from lower-class backgrounds; however, as with other forms of violence in the family, this could be due to the reliance of studies on professional agencies who tend to deal more with lower-class clients (Aitken and Griffin 1996; Saraga 1996).

UNDERSTANDING VIOLENT CRIME

Many different approaches have attempted to explain and understand violent crime. Despite a vast amount of research, however, there is little agreement about its roots. This is possibly because, as Levi points out, there are many different kinds of violent crime and little agreement over what is to be explained (Levi 1997). Violent offenders are often portrayed as 'psychos', as aberrant and abnormal, and the pathological approaches outlined in Chapter 3 have been applied in the study of individual offenders. These clinical approaches have in effect 'medicalized' violence, and pathological approaches have also been applied to families and to victims. It has been seen, however, that many forms of violence are more commonplace suggesting a cultural basis for violence. Some feminists, as seen in Chapter 8, construct the problem of violence as one of male violence and patriarchal power, and the relationship between violence and masculinity has also been explored. This section will focus on these approaches, drawing on some of the material outlined above.

The medicalization of violence

There have been many attempts to relate violence to biological characteristics and mental illness. Violence has, for example, been related to excess levels of testosterone in men; however, there is little evidence to support this or other biological theories which relate violence to men's inability to control their 'natural aggression' (Stanko 1994). They also suffer from the problems of many biological approaches in that they cannot explain why only some men are violent or why some women are. Links between violence and mental illness have also failed to produce a comprehensive explanation. While few dispute that mental illness and other psychiatric and psychological problems do play a role in violent crime – particularly in serious cases of, for example, serial homicide – they form a minority. It should also be pointed out that not all mentally ill people are violent.

Violence has also been linked to alcohol which is a factor in many violent incidents. Alcohol can affect a person's ability to interpret behavioural cues – which can make the seemingly inappropriate response of violence more understandable where a simple comment may be interpreted as an insult. While this may affect some violent incidents, alcohol does not make all drinkers violent and its effects must be seen in a situational context. It is likely that violent people have other problems which underlie both drinking and violence. Some offenders use alcohol to assist offending as it gives an added buzz, whereas property and violent offenders may desist from alcohol before offending to give them a clear head (Parker 1996). Alcohol-related violence, like other forms of violence, must therefore be placed in its social context, which involves exploring cultural and structural factors.

Cycles of violence and the dysfunctional family

Other pathological approaches have related violence, particularly violence in the home, to the family and the victim. Some pointed, for example, to the 'battered wife syndrome' which was related to an addiction to violence, masochism and 'learned helplessness'. Battered wives were seen as unable to cope, withdrawn, dowdy and either nagging or submissive (Dobash and Dobash 1992; Saraga 1993). The phrase 'battered wife', which was originally used to emphasize women's suffering, was later rejected by feminists on the grounds that by medicalizing the problem it blamed the victim and diverted attention from the abuser (Dobash and Dobash 1992). At the same time some men were seen to be 'clinically' prone to abuse and not in control of themselves. The battered baby syndrome was also medicalized, with parental abusers being characterized as immature and unable to control their aggression.

Violence in the home has also been attributed to dysfunctional families, although this is a somewhat circular argument as the violence is taken as a sign of the dysfunctional family (Saraga 1996). This is related to approaches which stress the importance of looking at the whole family and with theories that some families are characterized by cycles of abuse. This again turns attention from the violent person to family relationships, often to the mother. Mothers can be blamed not only for violence against themselves but for not protecting their children by stopping physical abuse. 'Cycles of abuse' theories developed from findings that many violent offenders suffered violence in their childhood – although this has not been subsequently borne out (Saraga 1996). There is some appeal in these theories – the experience of abuse can lead to lack of confidence and a wish to control in future relationships. It also suggests that people can learn violent responses – a point made by Toch who argued that offenders learnt violent scripts (Toch 1969, cited in Levi 1997). However, as not all who have been abused subsequently abuse, and not all who are violent have been child victims, it can therefore only provide a partial answer (Levi 1997). In addition, Saraga (1993) argues that it fails to take account of the social, cultural and material context of abuse.

Subcultural theories and the thrill of violence

This directs attention towards culture and subcultural theory has also been applied to violence, with lower-class subcultures being characterized as violent

(Wolfgang and Ferracuti 1967). In poor neighbourhoods where people suffer from low self-esteem, violence is often seen as crucial to maintaining a man's reputation. While it may appear irrational, it may be a form of gaining respect within the subculture (Levi 1997). Toughness and aggression, as seen in Chapter 8, have been related to male lower-class subcultures manifested in both professional crime and football violence (Williams 1994; Hobbs 1995). It can also be related to violence in prisons where both officers and male prisoners share the lower-class hegemonic culture of masculinity (Sim 1994).

Violence can also provide excitement and buzz. It can become a way of seeking gratification, as the seemingly irrational and bizarre accounts of violent offenders, particularly serial killers, demonstrate (Katz 1988; Stanko 1994). Katz criticizes the pathological view by pointing out that violence can be valued for itself and be a chosen option: it gives a 'high', offenders can claim a 'righteous rage' and it can provide a source of pleasure. Focusing on these aspects alone, however, can exclude the social situations and gendered nature of much violence (Polk 1994).

It is lower-class subcultures that are characterized as violent and this, suggests Levi (1997), could be linked to the low esteem which pathological approaches have associated with violence. Additionally, he argues, the increased tension in personal relationships and the strain placed on families through poverty and unemployment can also provoke violence. As seen above, violence in the home can arise out of the frustration and stress brought about by unemployment, bad housing and poverty, exacerbated for black women by racial factors (Mama 1989). It can, as Polk's work indicates, also be a means of protecting honour and masculine status which may be significant in the absence of employment opportunities and a culture in which being a 'man' can be expressed by fighting and violence (Levi 1997). Levi also suggests that while the 'spirit of enterprise' is not in itself related to violence (violence against competitors is not, he argues, advocated!), the devaluation of the 'social' may make excusing violence easier. The superior economic resources of middle-class men may enable them to express masculinity without violence. Business tactics or 'macho management' suggest a different form of aggressive masculinity which does not require physical violence (see Chapter 15 and Levi 1997). As Daly and Wilson (1988: 287) point out: 'Poor young men with dismal prospects for the future have good reason to escalate their tactics of social competition and become violent.' This does not, however, explain violence in middle-class homes, nor does it explain why most families in such conditions do not abuse (Saraga 1996; Mama 1989).

Violent men: gender, violence and masculinity

Many of these arguments reflect the growing tendency to relate male violence to masculinity outlined in Chapter 8. It was also seen in that chapter that to some feminist approaches 'the problem' of violence is violent men, and that male violence is related to the structures of patriarchy. The examples of feminist research used to explore femicide and violence in the home illustrate how male violence can be related to male proprietorial rights. The mitigations used by men to account for killing their wives can be linked to patriarchal domination in which women are seen as men's sexual or reproductive property (Daly and Wilson 1988). Adultery or a failure to carry out domestic chores are routinely used to justify violence, and the example of confrontational violence also shows that insults about manhood or women can trigger violence. In Kelly's and Mama's work, women's failure to carry out domestic duties or their efforts to gain independence by education, work or participation in the culture outside the home, also attracted violence from partners.

The way in which violence has been medicalized also illustrates, to feminists, the pervasiveness of the patriarchal culture and reflects deeply rooted notions of blaming the victim seen most clearly in the mythology surrounding family violence. Thus 'battered women' were portrayed as being addicted to, provoking and enjoying violence. Women's acceptance of the social construction of violence is also seen in their accounts which frequently echo the theme that 'nothing really happened'. This further underlines the point that, to feminists, male violence is not abnormal but is an everyday occurrence which forms part of women's routine experiences (Stanko 1990a, 1994).

It was also seen in Chapter 8 that constructing the problem of violence around male violence and power faces the problem that not all men are violent and some women are. Is it being suggested that all men are potentially violent? Yet, as seen above, there is no biological basis for violence. It can therefore over-predict male violence in the same way as earlier subcultural theories over-predicted lower-class crime (Levi 1997). Others have argued that the continuum of violence, by including trivial incidents, exaggerates the problem of violence against women and children. Kelly (1996) argues, however, that the continuum does not see all forms of violence as the same, and it does draw attention to the damaging effects of persistent threats and harassment. Women's violence remains a problem as women are violent within the family, in institutions and in the street, and this can less easily be incorporated in the feminist perspective. Kelly has acknowledged this problem, initially suggesting that women's violence may be defensive and therefore related to male power (Kelly 1996). Women may also, like men, learn to solve problems with violence and, as seen above, women's violence towards their children may also be related to adverse social and economic situations (Saraga 1996). This remains, however, an under-explored area. A final problem with the feminist and other approaches which have focused more on the victims of violence is that they divert attention away from looking at the offenders – it is, as Levi (1997) points out, easier to carry out research with and empathize with victims than with offenders.

CONCLUDING COMMENTS

This chapter has outlined a variety of perspectives on violent crime and illustrated how conceptions of violent crime are socially constructed. Violent offenders are often seen as pathological, whereas to feminists, male violence is structurally and culturally constructed and its roots lie in male power. Violent crime is, however, a vast area and this chapter has been selective. Much more could be said about studies of violent offenders and about the controversial role of the media which, in disseminating images of violence, has been accused of triggering copy-cat violence or of re-enforcing the culture of male violence.

The different approaches to violence suggest very different policies. How to deal with violent offenders often excites emotional responses and there have been recurrent suggestions that 'dangerous' offenders should be given particularly heavy sentences. A major problem with this has always been that it is very difficult to determine at what point a violent offender should be defined as 'dangerous' or how many convictions for violence should be the defining point. There is, however, some evidence suggesting that, as a result of so-called bifurcation in which more 'serious' property and violent offenders are given heavier sentences, more violent offenders are ending up in prison (Levi 1997). Medicalizing violence, on the other hand, suggests intervention with individuals and families which is undoubtedly valuable and has had some success (Levi 1997). This can, however, attract criticism from those who wish to see retributive sentences – and there have been adverse reactions to sentencing violent offenders to 'anger management' courses.

These kinds of programme, which are undoubtedly of benefit to individual offenders, do little to tackle the cultural sources of violence. This is far from easy, although the campaigns of women's groups which have aimed, for example, at 'Zero Tolerance' have had some impact. There have also, as seen in earlier chapters, been major changes in the way in which violence in the home is dealt with and many police organizations now have special units to deal with it. Organizations such as Childline have enabled children's complaints to be dealt with more sympathetically and seriously. Exposing violence in the home also challenges crime prevention strategies which focus on 'stranger danger' (Stanko 1990b). These issues also emerge in relation to sexual violence which, along with sexual offences, will be the subject of the next chapter.

Review Questions

1. Illustrate the way in which violent crime is portrayed in films, television or in newspapers. This could include looking at characters in popular soaps such as the Mitchell brothers in *EastEnders* or the Jordache family in *Brookside*, along with popular films from 'Rambo' to 'Sleeping with the Enemy'.

    (a)   How does this portrayal of violence reflect the social construction of violence?

    (b)   How is it related to masculinity?

    (c)   Are there examples of female violence?

    (d)   How is this portrayed?

2. Is violent crime better approached as pathological or normal?

3. Outline what you understand by a feminist approach to violent crime. How can this be evaluated?

Key Reading

Hester M, Kelly L and Radford J (eds) (1996) *Women, Violence and Male Power*. Buckingham: Open University Press

Levi M (1997) 'Violent Crime', in Maguire M, Morgan R and Reiner R (eds) *The Oxford Handbook of Criminology*, 2nd edition. Oxford: Clarendon Press

Newburn T and Stanko E (eds) (1994) *Just Boys Doing Business?* London: Routledge

Saraga E (1996) 'Dangerous Places: The Family as a Site of Crime', in Muncie J and McLaughlin E (eds) *The Problem of Crime*. London: Sage

CHAPTER 11
SEXUAL OFFENCES

Sexual offences share many of the characteristics of violent crime. 'Sex crime' is associated with lurid headlines, a high fear of crime and moral panics about sex fiends, serial rapists and child molesters. It prompts calls for punitive sentences and offenders are often described as beasts, animals, perverts and outcasts. It is often seen as abnormal, but, like violent crime, can be related to cultural aspects of sexual activity and sexual relationships. It can involve elements of 'victim blaming', with women and even children being seen to have provoked offences, and is surrounded by a pervasive mythology. A similar range of approaches has been used in its analysis, and gender, race, class and age are also important elements.

The first part of this chapter will look at how sexual offences are officially categorized, followed by an exploration of the nature and extent of sexual offending and victimization. Aspects of rape, considered to be at the extreme end of the continuum of sexual violence, and child sexual abuse will be outlined before turning to prostitution which represents a different kind of sexual offence involving no direct victim, except in cases where, for example, a child prostitute may be seen as a victim. Finally, the main theoretical perspectives used to understand sexual offending will be outlined, drawing on the discussion in Chapter 10.

WHAT ARE SEXUAL OFFENCES?

Official categories of sexual offences include buggery, indecent assault on a male, indecency between males, rape, indecent assault on a female, unlawful sexual intercourse with girls less than 13 and 16, incest, procuration, abduction, bigamy and gross indecency with a child (Sampson 1994: 2). These reflect the different ways in which the law seeks to regulate sexual activity. Some, such as rape or child sexual abuse, involve forcing sexual activity on a victim without their consent. Consent is affected by age, with sexual activity with those under a certain age being regulated. Other laws deal with what are considered to be 'indecent' forms of sexual activity and with 'public indecency'. Some forms of homosexual activity and prostitution are legal in private but not in public. A number of questions arise when these categories are considered.

The sexual component?

Distinguishing sexual from other offences is not as easy as might be assumed. It has already been seen that they are difficult to separate from violent offences as many of these are sexually motivated and forced sexual activity is violent. Other offences can also have a sexual component as rape or sexual assault may be involved in burglaries or robberies (Sampson 1994). Some classifications incorporate both violent and sexual crime as personal or contact crime. The feminist conception of the continuum of violence includes threats and harassment much of which has a sexual connotation, and race may also be a factor. Sexual crime therefore extends further than legal classifications.

Consent

Consent, crucial in defining sexual offences, raises many problems, not least of which is establishing that the victim did not consent. Age, as seen above, affects consent, but there is wide variation between countries over the 'age of consent', which is also an issue in relation to homosexuality, which at present carries a higher age of consent (Sampson 1994). Chapter 8 referred to the exclusion, until recently, of rape within marriage as marriage implies consent. So-called 'date rape' is often distinguished from 'real rape' as women's behaviour may be interpreted as implying consent. It will be seen below that the mythology of rape typically involves notions of women having implicitly consented to sexual activity.

The social construction of 'normal sex'

Laws regulating sexual activity reflect perceptions of 'normal' and 'natural' sexual activity which can be challenged and changed. While most would probably agree that sexual activity between adults and children represents 'deviant' activity, it is justified by paedophiles as natural and normal (Morgan and Zedner 1992; Sampson 1994). The legal status of both homosexuality and prostitution changed in the 1960s with laws reflecting a distinction between private and public acts of 'indecency'. To feminists the regulation of sexual activity is related to the maintenance of the patriarchal family and its reproductive role. 'Normal' sexual activity is directed towards reproduction and takes place within the family, whereas homosexuality is seen as abnormal. Sexual activity for financial gain is also seen as abnormal and while prostitution involves both men and women it is the female prostitute rather than the male client who is criminalized. Within the home, men's sexual activity is less regulated, as illustrated by the law on rape, and in child sexual abuse cases social workers are frequently criticized for intervening in the sphere of the family (Morgan and Zedner 1992).

THE SCOPE OF SEXUAL OFFENDING

Research problems

Estimating the extent of sexual offences is particularly difficult. Many of the problems of under-reporting, particularly by children, were outlined in Chapters 5 and 10, along with the problems of carrying out victim surveys on such sensitive topics. With prostitution, there are no direct victims to report offences; police action is the only means of recording offences and not all known cases are prosecuted. Sexual offences are also particularly affected by the process of attrition. There are often no visible injuries and no witnesses, and in trials the victim's version of events is pitted against the defendant's. This is the case in many trials but is a particular problem in cases involving sexual offences. Rape trials, for example, often become a test of the victim's credibility which deters many women from reporting and taking cases to court as their sexual history and behaviour become key issues in the trial. Most defendants in rape and other sexual assault cases plead not guilty, making a conviction more difficult and many rape cases are subsequently reduced to sexual assault (Zedner 1992; Sampson 1994; Lees 1996). In 1989, 3,305 recorded cases of rape resulted in 613 cautions or convictions, and 15,376 indecent assaults on females led to only 4,119 cautions or convictions (Sampson 1994). In cases of child sexual abuse, the child's evidence is crucial. There are also arguments that diversionary strategies are more effective in these cases as families may be more reluctant to come forward if they have to appear in court and prosecution poses a greater threat to long-term family relationships (Zedner 1992; Sampson 1994). It may therefore not be considered to be in the 'public interest' to prosecute.

Estimating the extent of sexual offending

For all these reasons official figures underestimate the extent of sexual offending. Victim surveys provide a better indication, although their many limitations have also been outlined. While producing varying estimates, they do confirm that sexual offences are far more prevalent than official rates suggest. Even taking a conservative view, Sampson (1994: 36) argues

> at least one quarter of women and perhaps one in ten men have been victims of sexual assaults. Few of those offences will be reported . . . and fewer still of the reports will find their way into the official crime statistics.

As for violent crime, official figures indicate that sexual offences form a very small part of recorded crime – in 1994 in England and Wales they formed only 10 per cent of violent crime recorded by the police. Most indicate an increase, largely attributed to increasing levels of reporting and recording. Some other features of sexual offences revealed by official figures are summarized in Figure 11.1.

Figure 11.1 Characteristics of sexual offences

- *The category of sexual offences is dominated by indecent assaults on women*
  In England and Wales in 1990 these accounted for more than 15,000 of 29,000 sexual crimes recorded by the police, and one survey of violent offences between 1990 and 1994 found that they constituted 79 per cent of sexual offences (excluding rape) (Sampson 1994; Watson 1996). Indecent assault on a male is the next largest category, followed by buggery (Watson 1996). In Scotland the largest category of 'crimes of indecency' is 'lewd and libidinous practices' (mainly offences against children) which exceeded numbers for sexual assault and other offences (Scottish Office 1995).

- *The figures for sexual offences have increased*
  Figures from 1980 to 1990 in England and Wales show a 38 per cent increase, with a further 3.9 per cent increase from 1993 to 1994 (Sampson 1994; Barclay 1995). The increase is greater for rape and indecent assault on a female, whereas figures for unlawful sexual intercourse and indecency between males have declined. In Scotland the figures fell between 1994 and 1995 (Scottish Office 1995).

- *Women are more likely to be victims of sexual assaults than men*
  This is the case with indecent assaults as well as rape (Watson 1996).

- *Young people are more at risk for all categories of sexual assaults*
  Women aged between 10 and 24 have the highest risk of rape. In a survey of cases between 1990 and 1994, more than two-thirds of male victims of indecent assault and buggery were under 16 with a further 16 per cent being between the ages of 16 and 24. Only 1 per cent of male victims was aged over 40 (Watson 1996). Female victims tended to be older, with around half being under 16 and only 5 per cent being aged over 40 (Watson 1996).

- *A high proportion of sexual offences take place in the home*
  In the survey of cases between 1990 and 1994 two-thirds of rapes and half of indecent assaults took place in the suspect's or victim's home (Watson 1996).

- *Sexual assaults are more likely to involve people who know each other*
  In the same survey nearly two-thirds of rapes, three-quarters of indecent assaults on males and two-thirds on females involved people known to the victim. Fifteen per cent of rapes involved spouses and lovers, 15 per cent parents or other family members, 31 per cent acquaintances and 26 per cent strangers. Parents and family were involved in 13 per cent of sexual assaults on men, other acquaintances in 40 per cent, spouses or lovers in 4 per cent and strangers in 27 per cent. Indecent assaults on females were more likely to involve strangers: 37 per cent, with 27 per cent involving acquaintances, 15 per cent parents and family members and 2 per cent spouses or lovers (Watson 1996).

197

As for violent crime, this underlines the smaller risk posed by strangers compared to the home and family, except for indecent assaults on women. Excluding prostitution, a large proportion of sexual offences involve female victims and male perpetrators, although there are growing indications of what is popularly described as 'male rape' (Sampson 1994; Gillespie 1996). Many sexual offences incorporate the gender of offenders in their definition – public indecency, which relates mainly to homosexual activity around public toilets, is dominated by men and prostitution is dominated by women. Men form the majority of offenders in sexual assaults although a small number of women are involved. Further features of sexual offences will be explored in the following sections.

Rape

Many features of rape have already been referred to. While newspaper reports focus on sensational cases involving sex 'fiends' (Soothill and Walby 1991), Figure 11.1 shows that it is more likely to involve acquaintances than strangers, although acquaintance, or date rape is often contrasted with 'real' rape. While estimating the prevalence of rape is extremely difficult, one study estimated that as many as one in six women experience rape in their lifetime (Hall 1985, cited in Walklate 1995: 81). Another study found that one in seven women reported rape in marriage (Painter 1991b, cited in Walklate 1995: 81) while in a survey of Cambridge undergraduates, one in ten reported incidents of 'date rape' (cited in Walklate 1995: 81). This section will look at how rape is defined before going on to explore 'rape myths', the impact of rape and male rape.

Real rape – the definition of rape

Kelly and Radford argue that the image of real rape, reinforced by the police and media, is of an 'attack at night, in a public place, by a stranger who uses force' (Kelly and Radford 1996: 21). Women accept this imagery, as illustrated by the following interviewee:

> 'Well I suppose I thought that rape was something that happens to you out on the street, like with a complete stranger' (ironic laugh).
>
> (Kelly 1988: 148)

This conception of rape is reflected in legal definitions. In England and Wales the offence of rape requires proof that the vagina has been penetrated by a penis. This reflects, argues Walklate, a 'male heterosexual obsession with one object and one opening' (Walklate 1995: 81–2). Absence of consent must also be proved. This definition can be seen as somewhat restrictive. Forced sexual activity which falls short of penetration or which involves oral or anal sex which can attract a life sentence, may be equally serious and rape or attempted rape is often seen not only as a sexual attack, but as life threatening.

The definition also excluded 'male rape' and rape within marriage (Gillespie 1996; Lees 1996). Rape in marriage was excluded on the grounds that the marriage contract included the husband's 'right' to sexual intercourse. In an often cited judgement, Sir Matthew Hale CJ laid down that:

> the husband cannot be guilty of a rape committed by himself upon his lawful wife, for by their mutual matrimonial consent and contract the wife hath given up herself in this kind unto her husband, which she cannot retract.
>
> (Sir Matthew Hale CJ 1736, cited in Zedner 1992: 272)

Arguments in support of the marital exemption illustrate the notion of 'real rape'. It was argued that rape within marriage was not as serious or threatening as stranger rape, and that the wife had consented. The sanctity of the family was seen to be threatened by any suggestion that a wife could accuse her husband of rape. Both English and Scottish Judges argued that if it were an offence, conciliation between partners would be made more difficult (Lees 1996). Against this it was argued that rape in marriage could be persistent and often accompanied by violence. It could, therefore, have a greater subjective impact than a 'one-off' stranger rape (Lees 1996). The marital rape immunity was ended in June 1994 in an amendment to the Criminal Justice Bill making it a statutory offence for a man to rape his wife.

The notion of 'real rape' is also reflected in guidelines for the sentencing of rape which refer to two degrees of rape. Rapes involving the use of excessive violence, a weapon, repeated rape and rape of elderly women or young children are seen as more serious. Thus, according to Kelly and Radford, the majority of rapes are defined as less serious, because, as seen above, more women are raped by someone they know and its impact may be equally as serious (Kelly and Radford 1996).

The mythology of rape

Commonsense understandings of rape incorporate many 'myths' which are illustrated in Figure 11.2. These are often heard in everyday conversation, in the accounts of rapists and in court. In effect they blame the victim by seeing women as really wanting or provoking sexual activity and as able to resist. They absolve the rapist of responsibility for his actions as women have provoked his uncontrollable urges. Women's insistence that they did not consent is denied credibility in the often heard phrase that 'no really means yes'. They also reveal commonsense understandings of what Walklate describes as the 'cultural activity of seduction' (Walklate 1995: 83). A woman's agreement to go to a man's home, for example, is taken to imply a willingness to engage in sexual activity. These notions are so pervasive that wherever victims are known to offenders, consent becomes an issue (Kelly and Radford 1996).

Why are these described as myths? Careful examination raises some important questions (see, for example, Walklate 1995). Why should no *not* mean no? Why should a woman be assumed to 'want it' when she says that she

Figure 11.2 The mythology of rape

Women really want and enjoy rape
'They enjoy it.' 'They want it.'
'Women say no when they mean yes.'
'It wasn't rape, only rough sex.'

Women provoke rape
'They ask for it.' 'They deserve it.'
'Women lead men on.'

It only happens to certain kinds of women
'Nice girls don't get raped.' (Zedner 1992)

Women lie about it
'They tell lies.' 'They exaggerate.' 'Women cry rape.' (Walklate 1995)

Rape can be prevented
'They didn't fight hard enough.'

Rapists are sex fiends
'Men who rape are sick.'

(Adapted from Kelly 1988)

doesn't? How can a woman fight back when this might provoke further violence and injury? Why should women not be free to go anywhere they choose or dress as they choose without seeming to 'ask for' sexual advances? Why would women exaggerate or lie about rape? Many women are deterred from reporting rape precisely because they feel their complaint will not be taken seriously – would they be likely to make it up? These commonsense assumptions reveal, to feminists, the pervasiveness of men's sexual domination. They assume a right to sexual activity even where consent is denied. Another common misconception, which can reassure many women, is that only women who dress or behave like 'tarts' are likely to be raped. Yet women of all ages and social classes can be raped.

However 'mythical' these assumptions may be, they are pervasive and affect how rape is dealt with in the criminal justice process and colour women's feelings about their experiences. Women don't report rape because they fear they will not be believed or will be seen to have provoked it. In court, judges and jurors, female as well as male, may also believe that victims provoked the offence (Lees 1996). To Lees the rape trial is 'a barometer of ideologies of sexual difference, of male dominance and women's inferiority' (Lees 1996: 111). As seen above, trials often hinge around issues of consent. Judges' and juries' belief in male assertions that women's cues have been 'misunderstood' or that a woman's sexual history implies consent, may account for the high attrition rate in rape cases (Lees 1996).

The experience of rape

Survivors' accounts illustrate the effect of these myths. Especially where they know their attackers, women feel that they may have 'asked for' or 'provoked' the attack. This deters women from reporting rape and may put them off further sexual activity. They often experience guilt and blame for what happened (Kelly 1988). One survivor interviewed by Kelly (1988: 204) comments: 'It's the degrading . . . the way people . . . just assume that you must have encouraged it some way.'

Survivors' accounts also show the severe impact of rape. Immediately afterwards, women experience feelings of guilt, shame and worthlessness. Kelly (1988: 171) recounts how interviewees felt 'upset, numb, dirty, ashamed, angry, wanting to forget, abused, guilty and fearful'. Thus, one survivor reports: 'I felt *completely* vulnerable, I felt worthless, like I was shit. I felt like somebody had just kicked me, as though I was completely nothing' (ibid).

Rape has long-term effects and has been associated with post-traumatic stress conditions. Kelly found that it could affect women's attitudes to men and sex, and lead to recurrent flashbacks, dreams and nightmares. Many women try to forget and some have breakdowns. One commented that 'I hated men for years afterwards' and another that 'I hate being touched by any man' (Kelly 1988: 203–5). As many felt that they had provoked the attack, many felt a loss of self-respect.

Male rape

While women are often seen as the main victims of rape, there has been a growing recognition of male rape. Some estimates suggest that around 6,000 cases per year occur in London alone (Sampson 1994). Male rape has remained a largely hidden problem, with men being even more reluctant to come forward. It also has a severe impact – some indeed argue that it is worse for a man. Men may, as seen in Chapter 8, find victimization harder to accept, and, as well as reporting similar feelings to female victims, some experience a 'crisis of masculinity'. They may feel that they have been 'feminized' and degraded. Their feeling of being made to feel like a woman underlines the way in which notions of rape victimization are gendered. It is unlikely however that male experiences can accurately be described as 'worse', but men do experience rape in a different way (Gillespie 1996; Lees 1997).

The 1994 Criminal Justice and Public Order Act amended the definition of rape to include the non-consensual buggery of a male, making the law on rape 'gender blind'. This followed campaigns to change the law against what was seen as the 'last taboo' and was resisted by some feminists who feared that such a change would divert attention from what to them is the key feature of rape – male domination over women. Others argue that male rape does involve relationships of gender and power, and that male suffering from rape justifies its being considered as seriously as female rape (Gillespie 1996; Lees 1996).

This brief exploration of rape shows how it is constructed in the context of sexual relationships, which to feminists illustrate men's dominance over women and their assumed 'right' to women's bodies. Whether or not all men who rape are expressing a desire to dominate is far more complex; however, work by Scully in America suggests that male rapists express these myths, often assume that 'no really meant yes' and experience little guilt (Scully 1990). It has also been found that rape is more common in societies where women have a lower status (Sanday 1981).

Child sexual abuse

Child sexual abuse shares many of the characteristics of rape and violence within the home. It too has been rediscovered in recent decades, is surrounded by a mythology of victim blaming and while often seen as the product of abnormal families is recognized to be far more widespread. In some libertarian arguments sexual relationships between adults and children are seen as healthy, normal and harmless although survivors report severe effects (McLeod and Saraga 1988; Walklate 1989; Sampson 1994).

Defining and discovering child sexual abuse

The problems of the term abuse have already been referred to and the term is not easy to define. It can be restricted to incest which, like rape, involves penetration and specifies a family relationship (McLeod and Saraga 1988; Walklate 1989). But, as for rape, child sexual abuse can involve many other activities ranging from seemingly trivial touching, nudging and kissing – often seen as 'normal' father–daughter petting – to masturbation and oral and anal sex. It is often argued that 'petting' is difficult to separate from abuse but children recognize unwelcome attention (Kelly 1988). The age of the child is also problematic: at what age does 'child sexual abuse' become sexual assault? Sixteen is generally seen as a watershed and child sexual abuse is generally assumed to involve sexual activity between adults and those under 16 (Sampson 1994).

While most societies have some form of 'incest taboo' it was only made a criminal offence in 1908 in England and Wales following campaigns for moral purity. It was seen as a primarily lower-class problem and the law aimed to protect girls in overcrowded slums from the sexual attentions of male relatives. As has been seen, after this time concern focused on children's risks of delinquency and incest, along with 'cruelty', was seen as a 'welfare' rather than a criminal issue (Morgan and Zedner 1992). It was 'rediscovered' after a series of high-profile cases including the so-called 'Cleveland crisis', in which more than 100 cases of sexual abuse were diagnosed in three months in 1987 – compared with two cases in the previous year. Criticism was levelled at doctors' use of a controversial technique to diagnose abuse and at social workers who removed the children from home (Walklate 1989; Morgan and

Zedner 1992). Awareness of child sexual abuse was also heightened by the BBC *Childline* initiative which in part resulted from campaigning by feminists (Walklate 1989). This led to increased reporting and further research.

The many problems of researching child sexual abuse have been referred to earlier. Definitions vary and studies include different kinds of activities such as flashing. In general, most agree that around a fourth of girls and a tenth of boys are likely to experience some form of child sexual abuse either within the family or with adult figures outside the family before the age of 16 (Walklate 1989). Perpetrators are mainly men, with a figure of 95 per cent being most commonly advanced (McLeod and Saraga 1988; Walklate 1989; Kelly 1996). They are typically known and trusted, with one study finding that 9 per cent of cases involved fathers or stepfathers, 9 per cent involved relatives, 4 per cent involved teachers or vicars, and 24 per cent family friends; 49 per cent had no significant relationship. This study included 'flashing' which increases the number of strangers (West 1987, cited in Walklate 1989: 64). Walklate concludes that child sexual abuse is 'most likely to be perpetrated on female children by male adults who are well known to the child' (Walklate 1989: 65).

The mythology of child abuse

A similar mythology to rape surrounds child sexual abuse, illustrated in Figure 11.3 (Kelly 1988). This reflects commonsense views which minimize child abuse. Children fantasize or seduce, there is really little harm, and mothers can be blamed (Walklate 1989). These are also pervasive and affect how allegations of abuse are dealt with. They can also be accepted by survivors.

Figure 11.3 The mythology of child sexual abuse

Children like it
> 'They want it.' 'Girls get pleasure.' 'They don't object so they must like it.'

Children provoke it
> 'They ask for it.' 'Girls are provocative.'

It only happens in some kinds of families
> '. . . girls who come from problem families; large families; rural families.'

Children can't be believed
> 'They tell lies.' 'They exaggerate.' 'Girls fantasize about incest.' 'Girls accuse men to gain attention.'

They could have prevented it
> 'If they had resisted, they could have prevented it.' 'They should have told someone.'

(Adapted from Kelly 1988: 36)

One of Kelly's interviewees was told by a psychiatrist that 'you must realize that you can't blame other people, you must have been a very sexual child' (Kelly 1988: 177).

As for rape myths, close examination prompts several questions. How can children, who have no sexual experience, want or provoke abuse? Walklate points out that it would be difficult for children to make up stories and that while young teenagers may be seen as provocative this is not intentional (Walklate 1989). The notion that victims are not 'harmed' contradicts studies which show long-term effects (Walklate 1989; Morgan and Zedner 1992). The view that it only happens in abnormal families may reassure that 'it can't happen in my family', yet 'it' happens in families across the social spectrum. Blaming the family involves blaming the mother for depriving fathers of sex and 'forcing' them to turn to children, for participating in acts of abuse, or for failing to recognize and stop it. Survivors may blame their mothers, feeling that they ought to have or did know about it (Kelly 1988).

The impact of child sexual abuse

Child sexual abuse has severe short- and long-term effects, which vary according to whether the abuse has been long term or an isolated incident. With the latter the effects may be anxiety, agitation and guilt feelings. Long-term abuse can lead to neurotic disorders, anxiety, appetite and sleep problems and have an adverse effect on school work (Kelly 1988; Zedner and Morgan 1992). Long-term effects include depression, self-destructive behaviour, feelings of isolation, stigma and poor self-esteem (Morgan and Zedner 1992). It can affect later sexual activity, with some avoiding it (Kelly 1988; Morgan and Zedner 1992). Some leave home as soon as they can, which can lead to homelessness or prostitution and involvement in crime (Kelly 1988; Carlen 1996; O'Neill 1996).

Exploring child sexual abuse raises issues about relationships within the family. The dismissal of children's accounts as fantasy or imagination illustrates their powerlessness. Serious abuse typically involves someone they trust but their dependence means that their complaints are rejected. This is further compounded by abusers swearing them to secrecy and threatening family break up should they reveal the abuse (Kelly 1988).

Prostitution

Prostitution is a different kind of sexual offence as it involves consensual as opposed to forced sexual activity. Its economic and public nature forms the basis of the offence and prostitutes are generally regarded with disapproval. Revelation of politicians' involvement with prostitutes is sufficient to end their careers and prostitutes' clients greatly fear disclosure to friends and family (Matthews 1993; McKeganey and Barnard 1996). Prostitutes are commonly described as 'whores' or 'tarts', words generally used as insults to women. Yet sex is sold widely and legally in what is often called the sex industry, which is international. Advertising campaigns use sexual images and a very fine line divides the legitimate use of sexual images from pornography. The criminalization of prostitution may thus seem odd in a world where sex is traded widely and many people use sex to gain favours (McKeganey and Barnard 1996). Like other sexual offences, prostitution is surrounded by myths. Prostitutes are often portrayed as abnormal sexual perverts, yet as with other sexual offences:

> Once one lifts that secrecy what one finds in abundance is not the perverse, the extraordinary, or the exotic but the commonplace, the ordinary and the everyday.
> (McKeganey and Barnard 1996: 1)

This section will firstly explore the legal basis of prostitution before going on to look at a recent study of street prostitutes.

Prostitution and the law

Prostitution has existed throughout history – thus its title as the 'oldest profession'. It has often had an ambiguous legal status which has, in Britain, reflected concerns with public health and the control of sexually transmitted disease along with public order. During the nineteenth century, prostitution was subject to Contagious Diseases Acts following concerns about the health of soldiers who consorted with prostitutes. More recently the spread of AIDS again drew attention to the assumed public health risks of prostitution (McKeganey and Barnard 1996). So-called 'red light' areas are also seen as a public order problem and are associated with kerb crawling and drug trading. There have been many campaigns by residents of these areas to control the problem (Matthews 1993).

While in Britain, prostitution itself is not a crime, keeping a brothel, living on the immoral earnings of prostitution, and soliciting by a 'common prostitute' are criminal (Matthews 1993). This latter offence has been questioned as it involves a label and is seen as sexist as it is the female prostitute and not the male client who is criminalized. Subjecting clients to the criminal law was resisted by arguing that innocent men could be falsely accused. The Wolfenden Committee, which carried out a thorough review of the law in 1957, argued that it would 'enable any woman of bad character to bring charges for the purpose of extortion against male passers-by' (Wolfenden 1957, cited in Heidensohn 1996: 35).

Eventually kerb crawling was made subject to the 1985 Sexual Offences Act. This reflected concerns with public order rather than legal inequality as in some areas 'innocent' women complained of being solicited. While it is now an offence, the nuisance must be persistent, which can be difficult to establish (Matthews 1993).

These laws raise problems for the police. As there is no victim, the main complaints come from residents of red light areas. Action against prostitutes generally takes the form of a number of cautions followed by a court appearance and fine, which is the only available sentence. The fine acts as a licence as following a fine the prostitute generally returns to the street. Police action rarely reduces prostitution although it may limit public nuisance and contain it in clearly designated areas. This can be frustrating for the police although prostitutes, with whom the police build up working relationships, can be a useful source of information about drugs and other forms of crime (Matthews 1993). Police policies vary across localities. One study found, for example, that policing was stricter in Edinburgh, where there have been attempts to remove prostitutes from the streets into 'massage parlours', than in Glasgow where the policy was largely to contain the trade to certain streets and prostitutes were arrested on an informal rota system (McKeganey and Barnard 1996).

It is virtually impossible to estimate the extent of prostitution, some of which is legal and much of which lies in the area between legality and illegality. Some forms of prostitution are highly organized and practised in hotels, saunas, massage parlours and private flats. Some can involve organized crime, especially the trafficking of girls from third world countries lured by the promise of high earnings (Ruggiero 1996a). Given all this, and the highly discretionary nature of police action, official figures are particularly meaningless.

Street prostitutes

A recent study of street prostitutes in Glasgow provides an interesting account of contemporary prostitution (McKeganey and Barnard 1996). The researchers focused on the 'red light' area, interviewing prostitutes and clients. Their initial aim was to explore the risks of HIV, but included other aspects of street prostitution. They calculated that around 425 women were working in the area, a small group frequently and a much larger group infrequently. Some of their main findings are summarized below.

Why work on the streets?

Many women preferred to work on the streets than in saunas, as it was more flexible and allowed them to choose their own hours of work and fit in with child care arrangements.

Why did they turn to prostitution?

While prostitutes are often seen as abnormal 'nymphomaniacs', most studies have found that prostitution has an economic basis and that prostitutes can be described as 'sex workers' (McLeod 1982; Matthews 1993; McKeganey and Barnard 1996). Few women in the study chose prostitution willingly but felt compelled by economic necessity. The money was needed to pay off debts or for Christmas. For those with few educational qualifications or skills prostitution offered a higher income (around £100 per day) than poorly paid alternatives (Matthews 1993). Women who needed money to feed their own or a partner's drug habit tended to participate more intensively. Prostitution was seen as better than theft, which provided uncertain rewards and a higher risk of imprisonment. Drugs and prostitution could both escalate as increased earnings from prostitution enabled higher drug consumption which, in turn, required more earnings. Five of the women in the study died of overdoses.

Learning the tricks of the trade

Many are introduced to prostitution by friends and a supportive network, or subculture introducing women to the 'tricks of the trade' has often been found (O'Neill 1996). In the Glasgow study some had not been introduced in this way and older women reported that this kind of supportive network had been eroded with the influx of drug-using women. There was some conflict between the two groups. 'Junkies' were accused of not using condoms and having lower standards of dress and cleanliness. Overall the women cooperate by having clearly defined spots and, on occasion, working in teams particularly to prevent violence. They indicated elements of professionalism with clear strategies for negotiating with clients and controlling transactions. Most refused some kinds of sexual activity such as anal sex, and all insisted that they always used condoms.

Violence

This cooperation was particularly important given the ever-present risk of violence (McKeganey and Barnard 1996; O'Neill 1996). Most had experienced violence in a minority of encounters and two were murdered during the course of the study (McKeganey and Barnard 1996). Violence ranged from name calling by people travelling through the red light area to physical attacks and rape (Matthews 1993; McKeganey and Barnard 1996; O'Neill 1996). Prostitutes also tend to blame themselves for not being careful enough. Many took routine precautions, staying in clearly defined areas, refusing to work with anyone 'suspicious', not going with more than one client or not working at specific times. They cooperated with each other by noting car numbers or keeping an eye out on alleys where transactions were taking place and others had partners nearby. Very little violence was reported to the police as women felt that they would not be taken seriously.

Coping with the stigma of prostitution

While they saw prostitution as a job, its stigma affected aspects of their lives. Coping strategies represented an attempt to separate their job from the rest of their lives. Many changed clothes and bathed when they got home and

207

encounters with clients were depersonalized. This could involve 'switching off' when they had sex with clients. Asked how they differentiated sex with clients from sex with boyfriends, one reported: 'Well the best way to explain is like a wee switch I've got in ma head that I can completely switch off' (McKeganey and Barnard 1996: 84). Another commented: 'Quite fuckin' easy, look the other way and think o' the money, ye know what I mean' (ibid: 86).

Most resisted attempts by clients to place the transaction on anything other than an economic footing, and some activities, such as kissing or fondling, were avoided. This could upset clients – to which one woman responded: 'Listen hen, you're wi' a prostitute; you want to make love, you go with someone else' (ibid: 87).

These efforts were not always successful in preventing damage to other relationships. Some felt that it did affect their enjoyment of sex with partners – sometimes through being too tired, or by devaluing sex. Partners found prostitution difficult to deal with as it challenged dominant views that relationships should be sexually exclusive.

UNDERSTANDING SEXUAL OFFENDING

The perspectives used to analyse sexual offending are similar to those outlined for violent crime. Sexual offenders have typically been seen as abnormal, although it can be argued that offending is far more widespread and normal than previously assumed. And, like violence, sexual offending can be related to cultural notions of sexual relationships and to the social structure and patriarchal domination. This section will therefore draw on the arguments introduced in Chapter 10 as they relate specifically to sexual violence. In general, approaches have focused on the more serious forms of sexual violence, although, particularly in Britain, much research has taken the form of clinical studies of offenders in prison or in mental hospitals, which has emphasized the individual pathologies of this largely atypical group (Sampson 1994).

The pathological sex offender

Many different kinds of pathologies have been attributed to sex offenders. It has been suggested, for example, that offenders have excessive sex drives or high sex steroid levels, but these only apply to a minority (Sampson 1994). Nor is there significant evidence that offending is related to abnormally high levels of testosterone, which is in any event not related to heightened sexual activity (ibid). Some biological theories have linked sexual offending to men's desire to reproduce, but offences involving children and the elderly and those not involving penetration cannot be linked to reproduction (ibid). There is therefore little evidence to support the commonsense notion that male sexual offending is related to men's uncontrollable urges, reflected in the view that men are not responsible for their actions if provoked (Stanko 1994).

Psychological and psychiatric disorders have also been explored. Clinical studies of sexual offenders portray them as emotionally immature and lacking social skills, as inadequate men who have difficulty with sexual relationships. While this view has much commonsense appeal, it does not apply to all offenders and there is no clear evidence that sexual offenders are any more likely to suffer from mental disorder (Sampson 1994). Offending has also been related to social learning theory which suggests that offenders relate stimuli such as pornographic material or images of women and children to sexual satisfaction. They also learn the widely accepted myths about sexual activity, which are then used to justify offending and minimize guilt (Sampson 1994). This relates sexual offending to the broader cultural values surrounding sexual activity.

Other explanations focus on the 'cycles of abuse' discussed in Chapter 10, drawing on research findings that many abusers have been abused. This may affect individual offenders as the long-term effects of abuse include a lack of self-esteem and a reduced ability to enjoy sex. Abusive behaviour can also be learnt, and many prostitutes report having been abused as children (Matthews 1993; O'Neill 1996). But, as with violence, previous abuse cannot fully explain abusive behaviour, as not all who abuse were abused and not all who were abused subsequently abuse (Sampson 1994). Moreover, it cannot account for the gendered distribution of offending. Men outnumber women as abusers but women outnumber men as victims. Therefore it is unlikely that all abusive men could have been abused as boys and it cannot explain why most women who have been abused do not subsequently abuse, although some versions suggest that they go on to marry abusers (McLeod and Saraga 1988). Sampson further suggests that abusers may use this explanation to minimize their guilt (Sampson 1994).

Sexual offending, particularly child abuse, has also been related to dysfunctional families. A crucial factor here is the role of the mother who is seen to collude in the abuse (McLeod and Saraga 1988). One text on child abuse, cited by McLeod and Saraga, argues that leaving fathers to care for children increases opportunities for abuse and that a father with low self-esteem brought about by unemployment may assert control by abusing a child (Baker and Duncan 1986, cited in McLeod and Saraga 1988). McLeod and Saraga comment, however, that if opportunity were a factor, mothers, traditionally the main carers, would have far higher rates of abuse. These kinds of arguments also assume men's uncontrollable urges. If this were true, they argue, rates of abuse would be much higher.

Men controlling women?

Feminist criticisms of these approaches focus on their denial of male responsibility and the relationship between sexual violence and male power. To them, 'forced' sex is a further assertion of the male propriety over women seen in Chapters 8 and 10, which is also reflected in the myths surrounding sexual violence which assume men's right to women's bodies. It can also be seen in everyday encounters where women report large amounts of verbal abuse and seemingly routine but unwelcome touching and fondling. Conceptions of 'real rape' and the powerlessness of children reflect the primacy accorded to the patriarchal family. The reactions against social workers' intervention following reports of child abuse further reflects this. Child sexual abuse also reveals generational inequalities in families and the exercise of male patriarchal power.

To radical feminists, as seen in Chapter 8, men use sexual violence as a means of controlling and dominating women. Often cited is Brownmiller's argument that rape: 'is nothing more or less than a conscious process of intimidation by which *all* men keep *all* women in a state of fear' (Brownmiller 1975, cited in Sampson 1994: 9). This is echoed in research in the United States where male rapists did see rape as asserting dominance and used rape myths as justifications for their actions. Rapists' notions were rooted in stereotypical notions of proper female behaviour and rape was seen as a conquest (Scully 1990; Scully and Marolla 1993). To see all rapes as consciously intimidating women may nonetheless be an overstatement. Male rape would appear to contradict it, although this can also be related to power. In prison, for example, heterosexual men rape other men as a means of humiliation and domination (Sampson 1994; Sim 1994). Rape can, however, be an afterthought in a burglary or robbery; it may arise from sexual frustration when a date says no or can be a male bonding activity which is not, argues Levi, so clearly related to domination (Levi 1997). This argument also fails to explain why most men do not rape or sexually abuse their children.

It has been pointed out that a key problem for feminist perspectives is their focus on male violence against women (see Chapters 8 and 10). This makes men's victimization and women's participation in sexual violence difficult to explain (see, for example, Kelly 1996). While some male rape can be linked to male power, race, class and age may also be related to sexual violence. The particular vulnerability of children has already been indicated and while this is related to the patriarchal family, men abuse boys and women also abuse. Race is also important as rape may be racially motivated and, as seen in Chapter 9, black and Asian women face sexual harassment and taunts of being 'black whores'. There are also more reported sexual offences in lower-class households, although this could reflect greater involvement with official agencies. It is also possible, however, that poverty and the stress of unemployment may heighten tensions, reduce self-esteem and make men more sexually aggressive. A combination of gender and other factors is therefore likely. Sexual violence has also been related to changing gender roles. Women's resistance of conventional role models, advances into formerly all male environments and lower tolerance of sexual violence may threaten conceptions of masculinity by making men feel inadequate. Competition at work involving so-called 'liberated' women could be linked to some forms of sexual violence (Bailey and Peterson 1995; Walklate 1995). Linking these broader structural changes to individual experiences is extremely difficult but does raise interesting questions about the link between sexual violence and the wider social structure.

CONCLUDING COMMENTS

This chapter has covered many aspects of sexual offending. As for violent crime, it has revealed the different ways in which it can be approached, ranging from clinical explanations to those looking at the wider context of sexual relationships. The many myths surrounding sexual offending reflect cultural conceptions of these relationships, typically playing on men's assumed rights to women's bodies and the role of the family as a means of regulating sexual activity. This also leads to feelings of guilt and shame among victims and prostitutes. Other perspectives challenge these myths and question the view that sexual offending is the product of aberrant men or perverted women. As McKeganey and Barnard (1996) point out in respect of prostitution, there is a need to 'demythologize' sexual offending. As with the chapter on violence, this chapter has been necessarily selective. Many other forms of sexual offending could have been explored and readers are advised to follow up the key reading and references.

The contrasting approaches also indicate different policy directions. Much attention has recently focused on the greater punishment and surveillance of sexual offenders illustrated in discussions about tracking and registering sex offenders, and stringent laws have been applied in the United States (Hebenton and Thomas 1996). It is understandable that concerns have been raised about the prospect of convicted offenders being released back into the community, but it also raises issues about the rights of these offenders (Hebenton and Thomas 1996). It may also affect only a small proportion of sexual offenders. As for violent crime, approaches focusing on the pathological nature of offending may reinforce victims' feelings of guilt and shame. There is now a more general recognition of sexual abuse and more encouragement, through agencies like *Childline*, for victims to come forward. This can be supported in schools and by social welfare agencies.

Many discussions on policy focus on the more serious elements of sexual offending, involving enforced sex. Forms of consensual sexual activity raise different problems. The many difficulties faced by the police in dealing with prostitution indicate that they cannot hope to reduce it substantially and the law is ambiguous by criminalizing only its public aspects. This has led to calls for legalization, which would remove most controls over prostitution, or decriminalization which would remove the criminal law but leave other means of regulation. Removing all regulation might encourage more women into prostitution and would do little to reduce the dangers they face. Decriminalization, on the other hand, could enable control over the public health and public order aspects of prostitution, provide some protection against violence and prevent prostitutes being subject to prosecution (McKeganey and Barnard 1996).

Review Questions

1. How and why are the victims of sexual violence so often blamed for their own victimization?
2. Outline the feminist argument that sexual violence reflects male power over women. How would you evaluate this argument? This should further develop your answer prepared for Chapter 10.

Key Reading

Hester M, Kelly L and Radford J (eds) (1996) *Women, Violence and Male Power*. Buckingham: Open University Press

Kelly L (1988) *Surviving Sexual Violence*. Cambridge: Polity Press

McKeganey N and Barnard K (1996) *Sex Work on the Streets: Prostitutes and their Clients*. Buckingham: Open University Press

Sampson A (1994) *Acts of Abuse: Sex Offenders and the Criminal Justice System*. London: Routledge

Chapter 12

PROPERTY CRIME

In contrast to violent and sexual offences, property crime dominates officially recorded crime and victim surveys and it was also a major concern of the approaches to crime reviewed in Chapter 3. It encompasses an enormous variety of offences, from minor acts of vandalism or theft to major fraud and armed robbery. It includes very different kinds of offenders, from the largely amateur teenage burglars and joyriders referred to in Chapter 7, to more professional burglars and robbers. While, as seen in Chapter 6, it is often assumed to be economically motivated it also produces the thrills and excitement which were seen to attract young people to crime. As illustrated in Chapter 5, it can involve very trivial losses or can have a severe economic and emotional impact. While many of its forms are unambiguously criminal, others are widely tolerated and a very fine line divides some forms of property crime from culturally tolerated behaviour.

This chapter will focus on the main forms of officially classified and recorded 'property crime' while Chapter 13 will turn to patterns of offending associated with professional and organized crime, although it will be seen that these categories overlap. This chapter will start by looking at how property crime is officially and socially constructed and official statistics on offences, offenders and victims. It will go on to explore some of the varieties and characteristics of property crime before, as with previous chapters, looking at some forms in more detail. It will look firstly at car crime and then at burglary and robbery, outlining the characteristics of these offences and what research reveals about the motivations of offenders. Finally some points will be made about how property crime can be analysed and understood.

WHAT IS PROPERTY CRIME?

Official categories of property crime include burglary (in Scotland, housebreaking), theft, fraud and forgery, robbery and criminal damage. Robbery, as has been seen, is sometimes counted as a violent crime but broadly speaking property crime involves stealing and dishonestly obtaining or damaging another's property, with property including tangible items and money along with intellectual 'property' such as copyright. Like other crimes it tends to be associated with strangers and its public image emphasizes its more serious forms. It conjures up images of ram raiders, burglars trashing houses, muggers and robbers terrifying the elderly and fraudsters depriving people of their savings. As with other forms of crime, these images downplay the more mundane and everyday nature of much property crime. The following questions indicate some difficulties with its definition.

What is theft?

It was seen in Chapter 1 that the borderline between theft and other activities is very narrow. In the workplace, for example, the words 'fiddles' or 'perks' describe a number of activities which are legally theft or fraud, and which are justified as in effect constituting the rewards of a job (Ditton 1977; Mars 1982). Other forms of property crime are widely tolerated. Few who pay for goods or services in cash rather than by cheque see themselves defrauding the Inland Revenue, and few who buy suspiciously cheap goods in market stalls, car boot sales or pubs see themselves as 'handlers of stolen goods' (Henry 1978). Few who tape television programmes or records see themselves as 'stealing' intellectual copyright while inflating insurance claims may be justified by paying high premiums (Gill et al 1994).

What is dishonesty?

Fraud involves 'dishonestly' obtaining money or other goods. Yet how can criminal dishonesty be separated from many everyday commercial exchanges? Sellers aim to persuade buyers that their product or service is better than others through advertising or verbal persuasion. Are all these claims 'true'? When 'conned' by an over-zealous salesperson, at what point do victims see themselves as the victim of a fraud? As the principle of *caveat emptor*, let the buyer beware, is firmly entrenched into assumptions about commercial transactions, many fraud victims feel that they are to blame for not being more cautious (Croall 1992; Levi and Pithouse 1992). Moreover, far from being the province of the 'stranger', fraud is often perpetrated by someone known and trusted, often within the family (Levi and Pithouse 1992).

Who are the offenders?

Property crime is identified with a range of different offenders, usually lower class. The above examples indicate that a far wider range of people engage in forms of theft or fraud, although their activities are not seen as crime. For some kinds of property crime, the status of offenders, rather than the activities involved, determines how they are described. Those whose theft and fraud arise from their legitimate occupations are normally known as, although not officially counted as, white collar offenders – many of whom are treated differently by the criminal law and its enforcement. Most recognize that the term professional and organized crime, although not a legal category, describes a different kind of offender whose involvement in crime is more serious. Many burglars, robbers, thieves or fraudsters do not neatly fall into either of these categories but nonetheless appear to dominate the population of convicted offenders. This is not because they are statistically more numerous but because the other two categories have a lower chance of detection. It is also difficult to separate these different groups as statistics give little information about the involvement or status of offenders.

THE SCOPE OF PROPERTY CRIME

Problems of measurement

Property crime has a large hidden figure. Victim surveys, as already indicated, show that many victims do not report property offences, particularly where losses are trivial. The BCS, with its focus on households, also omits institutional victims such as shops, companies, warehouses, banks and building societies which, as will be seen below, are major targets. Official statistics may also give a misleading picture of offenders' characteristics. As seen in earlier chapters, older, more experienced offenders and those in employment may more easily escape detection, inflating the apparent contribution of younger, lower-class offenders. All of this should be born in mind when looking at official measurements of the main forms of property crime.

Official measurements of property crime

In England and Wales property crime formed 93 per cent of all crimes recorded by the police in 1994 (Barclay 1995), and Figure 12.1 summarizes the main features of offences. It can be seen from this that various forms of theft, particularly theft of and from motor cars, form the largest categories and that a wide range of offences, offenders and victims are involved.

Varieties of property crime

These figures do not reveal the many patterns of offending which are involved. Convicted offenders are normally drawn from lower socio-economic groups although, as has been seen, offending is probably more widely spread. As seen in Chapter 8, men *and* women are involved, although men predominate convictions. Chapter 9 indicated that vandalism can have a racial element and mugging has been particularly subject to racialization. While often associated with young offenders, older offenders may be more likely to escape detection. Different patterns of victimization are also involved. While, in general, risks appear to be higher in lower-class areas, victims are drawn from

Figure 12.1 Forms of property crime

Theft
- In 1996, in England and Wales, vehicle crime formed 26 per cent of notifiable crimes recorded by the police and other thefts formed 23 per cent – accounting for nearly half of all recorded crime (Povey et al 1997).

- In the 1993 SCS, vehicle thefts formed 26 per cent of offences reported by victims in Scotland, with household theft forming 14 per cent and personal theft accounting for 12 per cent – just over half of the total (Anderson and Leitch 1994).

Burglary
- Burglary constituted 23 per cent of notifiable crimes recorded by the police in 1996 in England and Wales (Povey et al 1997). It constituted 10 per cent of offences reported to the BCS in 1994 (Barclay 1995) and housebreaking constituted 12 per cent of offences reported to the SCS in 1993 (Anderson and Leitch 1994). The different proportions reflect the higher rate of reporting burglaries to the police as many officially recorded burglaries are attempts involving no loss (Coleman and Moynihan 1996).

- Those under 30 are more at risk, while those aged over 60 are least at risk.

- Just under one-fifth involved an initial loss of under £100 with a third involving losses of over £1,000 (Mirlees-Black et al 1996).

Robbery
- Robbery and theft from the person formed 5 per cent of offences reported to the 1994 BCS for England and Wales (Barclay 1995).

- Robbery includes armed robberies of shops, post offices, banks and building societies along with street robberies, commonly known as mugging, which is also included in the category of thefts from the person (Coleman and Moynihan 1996).

Fraud and Forgery
- Fraud and forgery accounted for 3 per cent of crimes recorded by the police in 1993 (Coleman and Moynihan 1996).

- This category is dominated by cheque and credit card frauds which are undercounted as continuous offending – for example, the frequent use of one credit card is only counted once (Maguire 1997; Coleman and Moynihan 1996).

- Many forms of fraud are dealt with by regulatory agencies and not by the police, and are therefore not included in the criminal statistics (Maguire 1997).

Damage to property
- Criminal damage, which includes vandalism, amounted to 19 per cent of crime reported to the 1994 BCS and 20 per cent reported to the SCS in 1993 (Anderson and Leitch 1994; Barclay 1995). Vehicle vandalism accounts for just over half of this.

---

across the social spectrum. As will be seen below, for example, the more affluent present more attractive targets for burglars and robbers and high-status, expensive cars are also more desirable targets (Bennett and Wright 1984; Kinsey and Anderson 1992).

Different patterns of involvement in property crime reflect a variety of factors including motivation, skills, experience, organization and illegitimate opportunity structures. In some ways these parallel legitimate occupations with a hierarchy ranging from unskilled through to skilled or professional offenders (Ruggiero 1996a). A very broad distinction can be made:

- *Skilled, professional property crime.* This involves larger rewards and a greater degree of skill and planning. Targets are more likely to be houses or commercial premises offering more lucrative gains. It is more likely to involve older, more experienced offenders and be motivated largely by financial gain. Offenders are more likely to have criminal careers and have been involved in a variety of offences. They may be involved in organized crime networks.

- *Unskilled, amateur property crime.* This is more likely to involve smaller amounts and to be opportunist rather than carefully planned. While often motivated by financial gain, it may also be undertaken for diversion, fun or excitement or to provide cash for an addiction. It is more likely to involve younger offenders with fewer skills and carries more risks of being caught.

These categories are not exhaustive and many fall in between, but they do illustrate the wide variety of offences and characteristics of offenders which are found across the continuum of property crime. Shoplifting can be an easy way of getting goods or money for young thieves or drug takers but it can also be highly organized with shoplifters stealing to order. Robberies can be highly planned raids on wages or security vans, or quick raids on a shop or garage. Burglaries can be planned or opportunistic. As will be seen below, many skills are involved in property crime and offenders may move from one form to another, often from less planned and more opportunistic offences to more highly planned and serious ones. This is often described as a 'criminal career'.

The hidden economy

Property crime is associated with what is often called the hidden or informal economy. Stolen goods have to be converted into cash by selling them, and 'hot money' needs to be laundered. Stolen goods cannot be sold through legitimate retail outlets or in public and the informal economy provides a vast range of alternative opportunities. Stolen goods can be sold in street markets, car boot sales, or any shop where the origins of an article and its 'used' character are not an issue. In some areas pubs are venues for trading stolen goods (Henry 1978; Foster 1990). Others use the services of a professional 'fence', who acts as a middle person between the thief and the consumer. The informal economy provides an illegitimate opportunity structure which can distinguish the professional from the amateur offender. Using fences and having more contacts in the informal economy is more characteristic of professional crime (Wright and Decker 1994). In other offences the stolen goods, for example cars or car parts, have to be disguised and re-created which also involves using networks in the hidden economy.

The informal economy depends on a ready market for stolen goods, which may indirectly affect the level of property crime (Sutton 1995). Many consumer goods such as car radios, audio and video recorders, televisions and computers are relatively easy to steal and sell. Manufacturers regularly update these items, which assists the trade in stolen goods by creating a market for second-hand items as wealthier consumers update models and sell their old ones. These are then available to poorer consumers who cannot afford new ones and the legitimate trade in second-hand goods provides 'cover' for stolen goods. The blow of a burglary may be softened by replacing an older model with a newer one, although this can make victims more susceptible to repeat victimization. Poorer victims, with little insurance, may have to buy cheap second-hand items to replace those that have been stolen (Sutton 1995).

DIMENSIONS OF PROPERTY CRIME

The following sections cover three selected forms of property crime. Firstly, crimes involving motor vehicles, often described as car crime, auto crime or vehicle crime, will be explored. This will be followed by an exploration of burglary, a crime arousing considerable concern and often the target of police initiatives. Finally, robbery will be examined which, while statistically less prevalent, is interesting in that it involves both elements of violence and instrumental gain.

Car crime

As seen above, car theft forms the largest single category of recorded crime. Cars have always been attractive targets for thieves and many features which we now take for granted like registration numbers, log books and using a key to start a car all originated from the need to prevent theft. As far back as 1918, the Commissioner of the Metropolitan Police recommended stricter arrangements for registration, although originally owners were advised not to lock their cars as they frequently had to be moved (Webb and Laycock 1992). The key operated starter was introduced in 1949, and by 1969 all new cars had to be fitted with steering locks (ibid). Until the late 1960s increasing car theft was related to increasing car ownership since when it has exceeded it. This is partly explained by changing recording methods as, previously, cars which were subsequently recovered were counted as unauthorized takings, not theft (ibid).

Car crime or vehicle crime normally includes a range of offences from vandalism, stealing parts of a car, stealing a car primarily for pleasure, so-called joyriding, and stealing a car for economic gain. Some car thefts are arranged by owners to obtain insurance money. Thefts from a vehicle vastly outnumber thefts of a motor vehicle. While statistics do not normally distinguish different forms of car theft, it has been estimated that 'joyriding' accounted for around 65 per cent of car thefts in 1990, with professional car thefts for financial gain accounting for 27 per cent and insurance frauds for the remaining 8 per cent (ibid). It has also been suggested that a higher proportion are being stolen for gain and a lower proportion for pleasure, largely due to improvements in security (ibid). Theft from cars has also increased rapidly, partly due to the growth of audio equipment (ibid). The better off have a higher risk of car crime, presumably because their cars are more worth stealing (Mirlees-Black et al 1996).

Cars can be involved in other kinds of crime. They can be a 'weapon' in crimes such as 'car jacking' and 'ram raiding', in which a car or van is used to smash into warehouses and shops, and they can be 'getaway cars' for burglars or robbers. Drivers are required to be licenced and insured, and drunken or reckless driving are also offences. Garages and salesrooms may also be the sites of offences such as turning back odometers, commonly known as 'clocking', fitting illegally imported and dangerous tyres, fraudulently charging for work which has not been done, reconstructing insurance write offs known as 'cut and shuts', or advising consumers that they require work which they don't (Croall 1997). These kinds of frauds cost consumers millions of pounds and the car industry has for long been seen as 'criminogenic'. They are not normally counted as 'car crime' but are included in the study of white collar crime (Croall 1992, 1997). The often used category of car crime is therefore constructed around a rather narrow range of thefts and a prime folk devil has been the joyrider.

Joyriding

While joyriding has been recognized for many years and was studied in the 1970s (Parker 1974), it gained new attention with highly publicized cases of pedestrians being killed by joyriders. The urban disturbances of the early 1990s were also associated with dramatic displays of joyriding and clashes with the police (Campbell 1993). The term joyriding was initially used to describe stealing cars for pleasure, but was widely criticized given the serious nature of the offence. The offence of 'taking without the owner's consent' was created. This was popularly abbreviated to TWOC, and joyriders often describe themselves, as seen in earlier chapters, as 'twoccers'.

Reflecting concerns with prevention, studies of joyriders have focused on how they operate and which cars are likely to be targeted. Offenders' attitudes and motivation have also been explored in studies in various parts of the country, including areas with high rates of joyriding such as Northern Ireland

and Northumbria (McCullough et al 1990; Spencer 1992; Webb and Laycock 1992). The journalist, Bee Campbell, also conducted fascinating interviews with the participants in the urban disturbances of the early 1990s, some aspects of which have already been referred to (Campbell 1993). Some themes emerge from these many studies.

Joyriders are generally introduced to 'twoccing' by friends and it is seen as exciting, with many recounting the thrill, excitement and 'buzz' involved. In one study, nearly a third gave peer influence as the main reason for getting involved in car crime, with nearly one-fifth citing boredom and another fifth a search for excitement (Light et al 1993). Peer influence includes passing on the skills and knowledge needed to break into cars. These skills were highly valued, offenders in one study boasted that they could break into and drive away a car in less than a minute and took less than 30 seconds to steal a radio cassette (Webb and Laycock 1992). For some, part of the attraction is the subsequent chase with the police, whereas others avoid this. Some take enormous pride in driving skills, and performance driving is an important part of the thrill involved. Campbell vividly describes the spectacle of driving displays in peripheral estates and the thrill of chases with the police. One joyrider reports:

> you see a *bad boy* car and you say to yourself, yeah, yeah, I'll have some of that . . . I'll say to myself that if the police come they can't catch me. If I'm in a stolen car, the police have to be fucking good to catch me.
>
> (Campbell 1993: 258)

For many joyriders high-performance cars are chosen targets. One study found that 'sporty' or expensive models were most attractive whereas cars with an 'uncool' image were avoided (Webb and Laycock 1992).

Some develop a career in car crime, starting with stealing from cars, moving on to joyriding and then to stealing for profit which may involve organized crime (Spencer 1992; Webb and Laycock 1992; Light et al 1993). One study found that, at the peak of stealing cars for fun, offenders stole cars two to three nights per week, with one-fifth claiming they had never come into contact with the police (Light et al 1993). After an 'apprenticeship' of six months to one year, a smaller number, around a tenth, became more interested in stealing for profit and around a fifth became ram raiders. In Tyneside Campbell describes an illegal car culture which was linked to an industrialized trade in stolen cars refashioned in garages across the region, an informal trade in stripped components and participation in the 'incendiary pleasure' of extinguishing car carcasses (Campbell 1993: 259).

Burglary

There are many different kinds of burglary, including commercial and household burglary. Some burglars target homes in affluent areas while others stay close to home. As seen in Chapter 5, it has a number of effects on victims ranging from financial losses and 'nuisance value' to feelings of intrusion and sleeplessness. Repeat victimization can have even more severe effects. In one recent study, victims blamed burglaries for strokes and a nervous breakdown and one retired couple had spent most of their savings fortifying their house (Anderson et al 1995). Much recent British and North American research on burglary has focused on residential burglary and, based on the rational choice model outlined in Chapter 4, on the situational contexts in which the decision to burgle is made. Burglars are assumed to assess the risks and likely rewards of a potential target, and understanding these decisions can suggest preventive measures (Bennett and Wright 1984). Some also look at burglars' motivations and why they choose to burgle (Bennett and Maguire 1982; Wright and Decker 1994). Many recent studies have been based in the United States although their findings are relevant to Britain (Shover and Honaker 1992; Wright and Decker 1994). This section will summarize some of the main themes emerging from these studies.

Financial motivation

Burglars' motivations are largely economic, with burglary being seen as a relatively quick and easy way of getting money (Bennett and Wright 1984; Wright and Decker 1994).

Chasing the high life

This economic motivation does not mean that burglars steal to obtain necessities; rewards are more often used to finance a lifestyle based on stylish clothes, alcohol and drugs (Bennett and Wright 1984; Shover and Honaker 1992; Wright and Decker 1994). This is summed up by the often used phrase 'life is a party', and the pursuit of the 'high life'. In the United States, burglars aspire to a street culture in which status derives from consumption styles (Shover and Honaker 1992; Wright and Decker 1994). This has also been found in Britain where, as seen in Chapter 7, many young offenders are similarly motivated (Collison 1996; Parker 1996). In an earlier study by Bennett and Wright, over half the offenders who indicated an economic motivation said that rewards were spent on 'pleasure seeking' with the remainder saying that they needed the money for daily subsistence (Bennett and Wright 1984).

Why choose burglary?

For many, argue Wright and Decker, burglary is an easy option given the absence of both legitimate and illegitimate opportunities to obtain money. The burglars in their study, as in others in Britain, were largely young with few occupational skills or educational qualifications. Legitimate work was not an option and would not provide anything like the same rewards. Their criminal options were also limited. They had few opportunities for white collar crime and lacked the technical skills to disarm complex security devices or the interpersonal skills necessary for fraud. Burglary requires few skills and little investment in hardware. It does not require a firearm and, while many reported problems in escaping without transport, does not require a car. Some found it more morally acceptable than robbery, which involves face to face interaction and a higher risk of violence.

The attraction of burglary

Like many other offences, burglary can be intrinsically rewarding and satisfying and provides a high and a sense of achievement (Wright and Decker 1994). Bennett and Wright (1984: 135) found that while excitement was rarely a main reason for burglary it was important, and one burglar commented: 'I wouldn't go and burgle specifically for the excitement or for kicks, but I did find it exciting.' Others felt they had beaten 'the system', outwitted the police and obtained personal satisfaction. Another comments (ibid: 137):

> I really do believe that there was a little bit more than just the money. It was using your intelligence and everything else, pitting your wits against the police and the locks and everything else. It definitely gave me an uplift, a charge.

The skill of the burglar

While requiring fewer skills than other crimes, burglars do possess what Wright and Decker describe as a 'range of specialized cognitive abilities' or expertise (Wright and Decker 1994: 204). To be successful they must evaluate the elements of risk and reward in a potential target, know how to enter a dwelling, search targets quickly and efficiently and convert stolen goods into money.

Choosing a target

Some of these skills are involved in selecting a target and burglars use a number of cues to evaluate the risk of being caught. These include assessing the level of surveillance, or how likely they are to be observed. In Bennett's study, this involved looking at how close buildings were to other buildings – detached houses were preferred to terraces or semis. Signs of occupancy, such as lights or cars, were particularly important, and most avoided houses where there was any risk of people being in. Security systems, the presence of dogs and the likelihood of neighbours being in were also deterrents. Potential rewards were assessed by estimating whether there were sufficient goods worth stealing. This could be judged by the overall appearance of a house, whether it was 'scruffy' and the kind of car outside the house. Some avoided council houses with one commenting that: 'That looks like a council home.

They haven't got any money' (Bennett 1989: 185). Nonetheless council homes do have high rates of burglary – a seeming contradiction which Bennett explains by pointing out that this sample contained older, experienced offenders. Younger, less experienced offenders might be less selective.

Contrary to the assumption that burglary involves 'strangers', American studies have found that burglars do steal from people they know, as they provide easier targets. They may know people's habits, how to enter the dwelling and where valuables are kept. This may also explain repeat victimization. Once a burglary has been successfully carried out, it is easier to go back to the same house again. As Anderson et al (1995: 42) point out:

> Burglary victims who still have things worth stealing become super-suitable as victims, since they are still worth burgling, and entry and exit points and house layout are known.

Others base decisions on 'tips', often gathered informally in conversations (Bennett and Wright 1984).

Burglars often choose areas close to where they live. In Wright and Decker's study they stressed the importance of blending into the area and looking as 'normal' as possible. One female burglar took her children and left them in the car, feeling that this appeared less suspicious. Burglars also avoided going into strange areas. Black burglars avoided white areas and white burglars black areas (Wright and Decker 1994). Once in a property, they developed a strategy of maximizing their gains. While often tempted to take too much, searches were carried out quickly.

Cashing in

Finally, stolen goods must be converted into money, and the offender's contacts in the hidden economy are valuable. Burglars in Wright and Decker's study preferred to dispose of stolen goods through a professional fence, as transactions were quick with no questions asked. This distinguished 'high-level' from low-level burglars as many had no such connections. They disposed of their goods less efficiently through pawnshops, drug dealers, friends and informal networks.

Rational choices?

While burglary is assumed to be based on rational choices, many decisions were less rational. Burglaries are often prompted by a cash emergency which led to less careful planning. Burglars were less deterred by any likely sentence than by the immediate risk of being caught, although this itself was often underestimated (Bennett and Wright 1984). While often appearing cool and calculated, the burglars experienced tension and anxiety and many take drink or drugs before a burglary to ease this tension (Wright and Decker 1994; Parker 1996).

Robbery

Robbery includes street robbery, popularly known as mugging, and commercial robbery. Street robbery includes offences of robbery and 'snatch thefts' which are distinguished by the degree of violence involved (Barker et al 1993). Commercial robbery, popularly described as 'armed robbery', includes raids on banks, building societies, post offices and garages and can involve the use of firearms. Offenders tend to be involved in one type or another and are seen as substantially different groups (Matthews 1996). While robbery is far less prevalent than other forms of property crime, the element of violence makes it more threatening. This section will start with street robbery and then look at armed robbery.

Street robbery

Street robbery, or mugging, is the archetypical street crime and has already been seen to be subject to moral panic and racialization (Hall et al 1978; Barker et al 1993). It conforms more than any other offence to the stereotype of 'stranger danger' and street crime. The latest BCS confirms that more than half take place in the street and a further third around transport facilities, with three-quarters involving strangers (Mirlees-Black et al 1996). Mugging is a traumatic experience although serious injury is rare. One study of mugging reported to the police in 1987 found that 28 per cent of victims were injured and the BCS report that one-third resulted in injury. Injuries are most often bruises and scratches to the face, legs and knees, as victims are pulled to the ground during an attack (Barker et al 1993). Victims report anger, fear and shock. Some points about victims, offenders and their motivations are summarized below.

VICTIMS

Young men yet again emerge as most at risk although there is some variation. Older women have a lower risk than young men but a higher risk than for other kinds of crime as snatch thefts are more likely to involve handbags (Mirlees-Black et al 1996). The visibility of handbags does make women more vulnerable to snatch theft but they have a lower rate of injury as stealing men's wallets requires more physical contact. Victimization involves all social classes. In one small study in the south-east of England, being smartly dressed, looking wealthy or wearing jewellery attracted the attention of robbers (Barker et al 1993). Some offenders stated a preference for Asians, not from racist sentiments but because they were assumed to carry a lot of money or wore gold jewellery. Black people, on the other hand, were assumed to be poor. Offenders avoided targeting anyone they knew and some avoided robbing or hurting women, especially old women, which was seen as 'wicked' (Barker et al 1993: 25).

224

OFFENDERS

Victim reports suggest that around 95 per cent of offenders are male and under 24. The study mentioned above interviewed a sample of 45 offenders, two-thirds Afro-Caribbean and one-third white. Many were unemployed, and had experienced problems at school. Like burglars, they had few skills or educational qualifications (Barker et al 1993).

WHY ROBBERY?

In the same study, street robbers were largely financially motivated but, like burglars, they used the cash to achieve a 'street style'. The majority said they robbed for money for expensive clothes, trainers, luxuries and cannabis. In this particular study drugs did not emerge as a major factor, nor did gangs, although many did rob in groups (Barker et al 1993).

Armed robbery

While armed robbery is often associated with major 'heists' like the Great Train Robbery, it is more likely nowadays to be less planned and to involve a desperate attempt to gain ready cash. Chapter 13 will also illustrate the major changes which have taken place in the nature and organization of robbery. Better security has increased the risks and rendered the old style safe cracker largely redundant. A more typical robbery is likely to involve a lone, amateur, opportunistic offender, armed with a gun or a replica, entering premises, threatening staff and quickly exiting with money (Gill and Matthews 1994; Matthews 1996). This requires far less skill and less often involves professional criminals who have turned to other forms of crime (Hobbs 1995; Matthews 1996). While armed robbery is experienced as threatening, physical injuries are relatively rare – a study in London in 1990 found that only 7 per cent of robberies involved physical injury and only a small number of these were caused by firearms being discharged. They were more likely to be caused by being hit by firearms or by punching or kicking (Morrison and O'Donnell 1994). Nonetheless, the psychological effects on victims can be severe. This section will look at some elements of victimization, offending, and the use of firearms.

THE VICTIMS

The target of armed robbers is the cash held in commercial premises. Direct victims are therefore banks, building societies, post offices, shops or garages. Improvements in security have affected the distribution of targets, with increased bank security having led to an increase in robberies involving shops, post offices and garages (Matthews 1996). Staff and members of the public who are caught up in raids are indirect victims although they can be injured and threatened.

OFFENDERS

In general, career robbers can be distinguished from amateurs and those lying somewhere in between (Matthews 1996). This reflects differences in planning, the type of weapon used and the chosen target. According to Matthews, robberies involving wages and security vans are generally more planned and professional, and those involving shops and garages are more associated with amateurs, with the latter accounting for the largest percentage. Matthews (1996: 38) suggests a profile of armed robbers as 'virtually all male, in their mid-twenties, with previous convictions often for burglary and other forms of property crime', and states that professionals are most likely to progress into robbery after other crimes and many are involved in drugs, as is the case for amateurs. In a study of armed robbery in London, around 99 per cent of offenders were male. Three-quarters were white and most others were Afro-Caribbean. Few had educational qualifications, and their average age was 28. The majority were unemployed and around a quarter had no fixed address (Morrison and O'Donnell 1994).

WHY ROB?

Studies of robbers confirm that, like other property offenders, most steal for cash to fund a lifestyle beyond their means. Drug, alcohol or gambling addictions are common, especially among more amateur offenders (Gill and Matthews 1994; Morrison and O'Donnell 1994). Some preferred robbery on moral grounds as commercial organizations are insured, whereas robbing people of their possessions or life savings was seen as immoral. One robber commented: 'Robbery is instant cash . . . I know it sounds funny but I didn't like taking other people's things' (Morrison and O'Donnell 1994: 52). Another commented: 'I don't believe in taking people's earnings, what people have worked hard for. Even villains have morals and I think I'm more moral than most' (ibid).

As with other offences robbers refer to its exciting qualities with one offender commenting that 'It feels good to have this power' and another that 'I really enjoyed them – it was better than drugs – a real buzz' (ibid: 54–5).

ASSESSMENTS OF RISK

Many felt robbery was worthwhile for less than £500 and many underestimate the possibility of being caught (Gill and Matthews 1994). In the London study robbers were aware that the Flying Squad is armed and has used weapons against robbers, on rare occasions with fatal results, but they felt the risk of this was minimal (Morrison and O'Donnell 1994).

THE USE OF FIREARMS

The use of firearms constitutes the most threatening aspect of robbery, but this can be exaggerated. Many avoid carrying firearms or carry only replicas, while 'bluffers' pretend that they have a firearm. Many who do carry firearms have no intention of using them – not only to avoid hurting people but because of the higher sentences they might attract (Gill and Matthews 1994). One study estimated that only around one-third of the weapons used in armed robberies are actually capable of firing a lethal shot (Morrison and O'Donnell 1994; Matthews 1996; O'Donnell and Morrison 1997). More professional robbers tended to carry real firearms and expressed a greater willingness to use them, while more amateur offenders were less likely to carry real firearms and be more motivated by the need to get ready cash for drugs (Morrison and O'Donnell 1994).

UNDERSTANDING PROPERTY CRIME

As property crime forms such a large proportion of officially recorded crime, most theoretical perspectives have been applied to its analysis. The financial motivation of offenders and an absence of clear individual pathologies indicate the limitations of pathological theories. Some are motivated by the need to sustain various forms of addiction; however, this cannot provide a comprehensive explanation. Many offenders, particularly those involved in more serious forms of crime, have no such problems, and not all addicts resort to crime. Property crime is more readily seen as rational and calculated, suggesting the potential strength of rational choice perspectives. These, by focusing on offenders' assessments of risk and reward, have also been used to suggest preventive measures such as CCTV. As argued in Chapter 4, however, this can neglect wider issues such as the cultural and structural context in which decisions to commit crime are made. The financial basis of property crime and the lower-class status of offenders also suggest the relevance of the structural approaches outlined in Chapter 3. The property offender can be seen as the classic 'innovator' who finds alternative means to obtain culturally approved goals, and the examples above also illustrate that property crime can be associated with subcultural styles and elements of status and gender. The social and economic changes outlined in earlier chapters are also relevant as property crime forms part of an alternative economy with its own status hierarchy and career progression. Some of these approaches will be discussed below.

The rational property offender?

Approaches focusing on the rational decisions of property offenders have produced interesting and useful insights. They illustrate the financial basis of offenders' motivations and reveal much about how offenders choose particular offences and targets. Even for offences seen as more threatening and 'personal' such as robbery, offenders' motivations are primarily instrumental and while they may be prepared to harm victims, many avoid it. Their choice of a particular form of property crime often reveals elements of conventional morality, although this may lead to different offences. They also suggest a whole range of preventive strategies involving surveillance and making targets more difficult to enter, which may deter offenders. Security improvements have reduced some opportunistic forms of car crime and have had a major impact on bank robbery. Burglars' assessments of risk and reward also suggest the usefulness of everyday measures of prevention such as signs of occupancy and surveillance (Bennett and Wright 1984).

At the same time many of these studies demonstrate some limitations of this perspective. While financial motivations predominate, property offences also provide excitement and are attractive in themselves. Joyriders are not initially financially motivated, and other property crimes – particularly those involving amateurs – show fewer signs of cool calculated planning. Some robberies are motivated by desperation to obtain ready cash to sustain an addiction and are less carefully planned (Gill and Matthews 1994). Many burglaries are similarly less well planned as their link to street culture, which emphasizes spontaneity, illustrates. To Wright and Decker they are rather part of a flow of action (Shover and Honaker 1992; Wright and Decker 1994). While some offenders are rational and calculate the risks of being caught, others feel invulnerable which makes them more difficult to deter. Studies also reveal the dangers of displacement as, if one target is made more difficult, other, easier targets become vulnerable. Thus the carefully planned bank robbery has become far more difficult whereas the speedy, amateurish 'smash and grab' raid on softer targets has become more common (Matthews 1996). More serious offenders turn to other forms of crime or manage to circumvent different kinds of security. This suggests that many offenders look for criminal opportunities and are therefore predisposed to crime, and if one form of crime becomes more difficult, they will seek another depending on their skills and opportunities. Cultural and structural factors therefore remain relevant.

Criminal careers and pursuing the high life

The studies also reveal the lower-class background of many offenders and their lack of educational qualifications or occupational skills. This suggests the importance of economic disadvantage and property offences are often seen as crimes of 'need', compared with white collar offences which are assumed to be crimes of 'greed'. Such simple generalizations are inappropriate. It has been seen, for example, that the rewards of property crime are often used not to meet immediate 'needs' but to maintain an enhanced lifestyle involving the consumption of stylish clothes, drugs or alcohol. Offenders aspire to live up to an image of 'life as a party' (Shover and Honaker 1992; Wright and Decker 1994; Hobbs 1995). As was also seen in Chapter 7, the buzz, excitement and sense of achievement which can be provided by property crime are also important. Property crime thus emerges as an alternative means of obtaining financial reward, excitement, a sense of achievement and, for some, a career structure.

The majority of offenders studied were male, possibly reflecting their statistical prominence, and gender is a significant feature of property crime. As seen in earlier chapters, for young men, crime can provide an alternative way of expressing masculinity unavailable through legitimate channels. Consumer culture and car culture, for example, may offer alternative ways of expressing masculinity. To Campbell, the compulsions of joyriders lie not in crime but in car culture. The joyrider shares mainstream fantasies with the typical motorway speeder. Driving becomes a dialogue with danger and the car becomes a lethal weapon (Campbell 1993: 262). Joyriders favour the top end of the market, high-performance vehicles which are associated with power, status and masculinity. The police, she argues, are equally captivated by car culture and the car chase has become symbolic of glamorous movies in which both joyriders and the police play out their fantasies. This aggressive masculinity reflects the imagery of the media and advertising. To Campbell, car crime says much about the relationship between young men and power, machinery, speed and transcendence and car culture is macho culture. Other forms of property crime can be related to this hegemonic masculinity, as seen in earlier chapters. Styles of consumption, dress, style, participation in street culture and the pursuit of the 'high life' are all gendered and burglary and robbery can additionally provide a sense of achievement.

Women are involved in these activities, and can also see property crime as a means of participating in consumer culture although, as seen in Chapter 8, some suggest that women's crimes are more a response to immediate need. The involvement of women in property crime clearly requires further research. Race may also be an important element, particularly in respect of the more restricted opportunities available in both legitimate and illegitimate economies for minority ethnic groups (Ruggiero 1993, 1996a).

The economic and social changes outlined in earlier chapters are also significant. Many offenders have few legitimate means to achieve their desired lifestyle. Previous chapters have suggested that crime can provide an alternative career structure by providing financial rewards and a sense of achievement. This is similar to, and in some ways exceeds, the potential rewards of legitimate low paid, unskilled employment. Skilled joyriders, burglars or robbers may move on into criminal careers, in a labour market which parallels the legitimate one in which unskilled and semi-skilled workers are distinguished from professional, skilled workers (Ruggiero 1996a). These groups face very different risks and rewards, with the amateur or unskilled offender facing higher risks of being caught and fewer rewards. Upward mobility depends on the illegitimate opportunity structures first analysed by Cloward and Ohlin (1960) and introduced in Chapter 3. Some 'graduate' from an apprenticeship to more highly planned offences with higher rewards. Many of the property offences dealt with in this chapter represent the lower end of a criminal career structure, at the top of which lies the world of more serious or organized crime which will be the subject of the next chapter. Contemporary economic conditions may make a career in crime and in the drugs industry increasingly attractive (see Chapter 14).

CONCLUDING COMMENTS

This chapter has focused on a range of selected property crimes and others, which space prohibits exploring fully, reveal similar characteristics. Shoplifting, for example, can also be a potentially easy source of cash or can involve more organized offending and it is often preferred to other forms as it is easy and less morally objectionable. Similarly, criminal damage has not been extensively explored although some of its aspects were referred to in Chapter 7. It too can be motivated by a search for fun or can be carefully planned to defraud insurance companies. Fraud, which will be referred to in Chapter 15, similarly ranges from relatively minor offences to multi-million pound highly organized offences. Convicted property offenders are largely lower class, many are male and they are primarily financially motivated not necessarily by immediate need but by a desire for conspicuous consumption. Property crime can involve rational choices, although not all offenders are rational or readily deterrable.

Different ways of analysing property crime are also relevant to policy. As has been seen, the rational choice perspective is associated with the development of crime prevention policies, many of which have had some success. They are limited, however, by the recognition that offenders' motives may be more complex and by the problem of displacement. If offenders are predisposed to commit crime, better security may merely lead to alternative criminal opportunities being exploited. The thrill or excitement of, for example, joyriding is also difficult to replace by legitimate alternatives (Webb and Laycock 1992; Light et al 1993). Even the provision of legitimate employment opportunities might not prevent some offenders who lack the skills to take up such opportunities, and for whom employment might not provide as much money or excitement (see, for example, Wright and Decker 1994). It is nonetheless important to recognize that crime prevention should be supplemented by policies tackling the many forms of disadvantage, addictions and lifestyles associated with property crime.

Review Questions

1. Choose any one form of property crime and investigate its nature and extent, looking at official figures and victim surveys. To what extent does it display the different patterns of offending discussed in this chapter?
2. Is property crime better approached from a rational choice perspective or from structural and cultural perspectives?

Key Reading

Morrison S and O'Donnell I (1994) *Armed Robbery: A Study in London*. Centre for Criminological Research, University of Oxford

Shover N and Honaker D (1992) 'The Socially Bounded Decision Making of Persistent Property Offenders', *Howard Journal of Criminal Justice*, Vol 31, No 4, November: 276–94

Webb B and Laycock G (1992) 'Tackling Car Crime: The Nature and Extent of the Problem.' Home Office Crime Prevention Unit, Paper No 32. London: HMSO

Wright R and Decker S (1994) *Burglars on the Job*. Boston: Northeastern University Press

CHAPTER 13

PROFESSIONAL AND ORGANIZED CRIME

The godfathers, drug barons, criminal cartels and organized crime syndicates on whom the 'war' against professional crime is waged are popularly depicted as being at the top of the criminal labour market. Their activities are surrounded by myths which persist because they are relatively inaccessible to investigators. Informed accounts suggest a very different picture. Much so-called organized crime is in fact relatively disorganized and includes mundane and everyday economic transactions, many on the margins of legality and illegality in the informal economy outlined in Chapter 12. Like legitimate industry, the crime industry has changed enormously. It has also been affected by the processes of globalization, internationalization and the deskilling and casualization of labour. Like any other profession or business, criminal businesses need to adapt to technological, financial and economic change.

Professional and organized crime cannot be approached in the same way as other forms of crime. It is not officially categorized in statistics and rarely features in victim surveys. Successful criminals avoid detection and capture and are not found in samples of convicted offenders. This chapter will start by considering the distinctive features of professional and organized crime before exploring some of its characteristics. Selected aspects of this vast area of crime will then be outlined, starting with its changing organization. This will be followed by a brief exploration of the multi-million pound industry of counterfeiting before looking at the close parallels between illegitimate and legitimate business enterprises. Finally these themes will be drawn together by looking at how professional and organized crime can be analysed. A major part of professional and organized crime is the illegal drugs industry, which will be the subject of Chapter 14.

WHAT IS PROFESSIONAL AND ORGANIZED CRIME?

While the terms professional and organized crime are used popularly and in academic literature, they are difficult to define. Professional criminals are generally distinguished by their criminal identity, involvement in a criminal subculture and possession of criminal skills. They are 'full time' as opposed to 'part time' criminals and crime is their way of making a living (Mack 1972). Sutherland, in his classic work *The Professional Thief*, likened professional theft to a legitimate profession with its own distinctive system, language, laws, history, traditions, customs, methods and techniques (Sutherland 1987, cited in Fijnaut 1990). Crafts are associated with occupational identities such as the 'thief', the cheque forger or the 'safe breaker'. Professional criminals may work on their own or in small groups or be organized for a series of one-off 'heists', as popularized in many movies and illustrated by the notorious Great Train Robbery. Craft crime, which has existed throughout the centuries and includes pickpockets and different kinds of thieves, has been distinguished from 'project' crime, in which an entrepreneur organizes a group of people with different skills for a major project such as a bank or art robbery (McIntosh 1975; Hobbs 1994). Professional crime has also been linked to the 'underworld', which enables stolen goods to be converted into cash and functions as a labour market. It is also a means of passing on skills and information along with a set of values and moral and ethical codes. The criminal subculture has often been associated with, for example, the notion of 'honour among thieves', although, as will be seen below, these images are now somewhat romanticized and dated (Hobbs 1995).

The term organized crime is more often used to describe the activities of criminal syndicates such as the notorious Mafia or the Chinese Triads. Their activities include supplying prohibited goods and services such as drugs or gambling along with a variety of protection rackets, intimidation and extortion. Their position is maintained by neutralizing law enforcement through corruption. A key characteristic of organized crime is that it deals with the 'provision of goods and services which are officially defined as illegal' thus filling in gaps left by legal agencies (Ruggiero 1996a: 28). It can, therefore, be seen as an industry – distinguished from legitimate industry by the illegal nature of its activities.

Distinguishing professional and organized crime from other forms of crime is not straightforward, and the following questions can be asked about the definitions outlined above.

How 'professional' are professional criminals?

Professional criminals engage in the same activities as other offenders and their offences are not officially categorized. How can they be identified? Chapter 12 illustrated the wide variety of involvements in crime and it is difficult to draw a line between the amateur and the professional. This also indicated that some of the crafts associated with professional crime have become redundant, and, as will be seen below, it can be argued that professional crime has become increasingly fragmented and its boundaries with the legitimate economy increasingly blurred. Hobbs prefers to use the phrase 'serious crime community' which implies a far looser form of organization (Hobbs 1994).

How organized is organized crime?

Many approaches to organized crime are heavily influenced by the example of the Mafia, which is organized around the family, and emphasize the role of secretive organization and strong loyalty among participants (Ruggiero 1996a). The Mafia is not, however, a typical example of organized crime, which has been found to be far less organized and indeed disorganized (Ruggiero 1996a; Fijnaut 1990).

How are professional offenders different from white collar offenders?

Professional offenders have generally been distinguished from white collar offenders by the primarily criminal nature of their occupation or business. Professional employees who commit crime, such as solicitors who defraud their clients, have betrayed the trust vested in their occupational role. Professional criminals have no such trust, or status, to betray. In practice, however, it is not easy to differentiate the legitimate from the illegitimate business as the two are often closely related.

How can the crime industry be distinguished from legitimate industry?

The criminal nature of a profession or business may be difficult to separate from its legitimate activities. Organized crime relies on the sale of commodities and needs a base for customers to access its services. This may involve setting up a legitimate business 'front' behind which illegal transactions are concealed (see, for example, Levi 1981). Money gained illegally can be 'laundered' by investing in legal businesses. Thus, the borderline between legitimate and illegitimate businesses is very blurred. Illegal businesses, like legal ones, expand, and diversifying into legal businesses carries a lower risk of detection, conviction and imprisonment. Therefore successful criminal enterprises may move from illegitimate to legitimate business spheres (Ruggiero 1996a). To Ruggiero, corporate and organized crime are variants of the same form as they involve similar activities.

THE SCOPE OF PROFESSIONAL AND ORGANIZED CRIME

Problems of measurement

Estimating the nature and extent of professional and organized crime is particularly difficult and official statistics or victim surveys cannot even provide a starting point. It was seen in Chapter 12, for example, that figures on property crime provide few clues about the professional or amateur status of offenders. The most successful serious criminals are less likely to be caught and may delegate more risky and visible activities to lower-level employees (Ruggiero 1996a). Studies of convicted offenders are therefore extremely unrepresentative. Victimization is often indirect and, where the offences involve willing suppliers and consumers, there is no clear victim. Other forms of research are also difficult – professional criminals are even more unlikely than most offenders to welcome sociological or criminological investigation and a host of ethical difficulties, such as becoming involved in criminal activity or fears for personal safety, surround any form of covert research. There is therefore a lack of ethnographies or in-depth studies of offenders (Hobbs 1994, 1995). Some have used biographies of known offenders along with life and oral histories. These, while yielding much useful and interesting qualitative information, can be unreliable. Hobbs (1994, 1995) points out that memoirs are often written towards the end of an offender's career and may be unreliable. Academic literature is dominated by studies from the United States, which may not be applicable to Britain. The media, particularly investigative journalism, can be a useful source of information, as can enforcement agencies (Hobbs 1995; Ruggiero 1996a).

Varieties of professional and organized crime

There are therefore few figures to estimate the extent and impact of this form of crime. Some indication of its potential scope is given in Figure 13.1 which lists the wide variety of activities included in the category and the range of illegal goods and services involved. While not exhaustive, it does illustrate the widespread nature of its activities. It is involved in many forms of property crime, frauds and in the disposal of goods stolen in burglaries and robberies and it can involve extortion and protection rackets. It supplies an enormous range of prohibited services and commodities and produces, distributes and sells a range of products from drugs to counterfeit tea bags. People as well as drugs can be 'trafficked' and illegal immigrants are provided with passages and often employed in a variety of illegal enterprises (Ruggiero 1997). Some trading involves goods subject to taxation and contraband cigarettes and alcohol are smuggled across borders to avoid taxes. Any one organization may be involved in a variety of enterprises. Drugs money is laundered in a variety of illegal and semi-legal enterprises such as counterfeiting. Some activities are international in scope and organized crime has spread its tentacles into the internet and cyberspace. Goods banned in one country may be produced in or exported to countries with less stringent safety or health regulations and cross-border crime exploits differences in the laws of different countries. One example of this is the disposal of toxic waste in countries with less stringent controls (Van Duyne 1993). The scale of these activities can be staggering with some, such as illegal arms, drugs or counterfeiting, being multi-national, multi-million pound industries. At a more local level 'cottage industries' produce illegal goods for sale in many local outlets.

Figure 13.1 Criminal enterprises

- Organizing robberies, car thefts or shoplifting where items may be stolen to order

- Selling stolen goods

- Protection rackets – in which businesses are asked to pay to 'protect' themselves from violence, arson or other forms of damage

- Organized frauds – for example, social security or excise frauds

- Long firm frauds

- The drugs market – the manufacture, distribution and sale of prohibited drugs

- The illegal arms market – obtaining and distributing prohibited arms

- The sex industry – including prostitution and pornography

- Illegal drinking clubs – selling alcohol outside normal licensing arrangements

- Providing and arranging venues for other banned or controlled leisure pursuits – for example, rave parties; boxing and wrestling bouts

- 'People trafficking' – providing transport for illegal immigrants. This can also involve employing illegal immigrants as servants or labourers and 'sex trafficking' where women are employed in the sex industry

- Arranging for the theft and sale of art works

- Organizing illegal gambling

- Arranging for the illegal disposal of industrial waste

- The manufacture, distribution and sale of counterfeit goods

- The distribution and sale of goods banned in one country to another country

- Dealing in goods subject to import controls or health and safety regulations – for example, trading in meat unfit for human consumption; frauds on the European Union

- Money laundering

- Corruption – paying law enforcers and other state agencies and politicians to avoid investigation

- The distribution and sale of goods subject to excise – for example, contraband cigarettes and 'bootleg' alcohol

- Sales frauds and the transmission of pornography via the Internet

- PIN frauds

Offenders

It is impossible to make any generalizations about offenders as so few are convicted or available for research. It is generally argued that the Mafia is less prominent in Britain than in the United States or other European countries, although it has been involved in recent British cases (Hobbs 1994). Other criminal syndicates operating in Britain include Chinese Triad gangs and secret societies originating from Hong Kong who are involved in extremely violent protection rackets, drug dealing, extortion, money laundering and fraud. Colombian groups involved in the cocaine trade are also active in the UK along with the Japanese Yakuza and Indian and Pakistani groups involved in heroin importation and money laundering and, as we have seen, the Jamaican Yardies, although their involvement has been said to have been overestimated (Ruggiero 1993). Hells Angels chapters, involved in the trafficking of cannabis, LSD and amphetamines, are also active in England. Police sources also identify groups from the former Soviet Union and Turkey. Terrorist groups such as the IRA or UVF are also involved in a variety of organized criminal activities from bank robbery, protection rackets, drug dealing and trading in counterfeit, contraband and stolen goods, largely to finance arms purchases (Maguire 1993).

The crime industry is assumed to be dominated by men, largely, as seen in earlier chapters, older than the youthful offenders who dominate other areas of criminal activity. The gender of offenders is more difficult to assess. Public images of professional and organized crime are heavily gendered. There are few depictions of 'Godmothers', drug baronesses or Mrs Bigs to match their male equivalents (see, for example, Heidensohn 1996), and the most notorious convicted offenders have been male. Nonetheless women are involved in serious offending. Shoplifting can be highly organized and women may be employed for gender specific reasons. They are employed in the sex industry and there are also women drug dealers (Hobbs 1995). Hobbs argues that professional crime can be an equal opportunities employer while, on the other hand, women can be exploited in the drugs or sex industries just as much as in legitimate industry (Hobbs 1995; Ruggiero and South 1995). Involvement in professional crime has also been related to working-class, male subcultures, making women's equal participation less likely.

Organized crime has often been seen as an alternative route to upward mobility for lower-class individuals. Again it is difficult to generalize, particularly in view of the increasingly blurred boundaries between legitimate and illegitimate businesses. Criminalization may also play a role with some kinds of business activities being more subject to criminal law and enforcement (Ruggiero 1996a). The race or ethnicity of offenders is not well documented, although there has been a tendency to attribute organized crime to 'outsiders' and immigrants. In the United States, it was assumed to be dominated by the Mafia and Italian immigrants and much has been made of the involvement of Chinese Triad gangs both in the United States and in Britain, and more recently Irish terrorists, Colombians and Jamaican Yardies have also been identified with a range of activities (Keith 1993; Ruggiero 1996a). While these groups do exist, indigenous groups across the country are also involved and indeed black groups may find it as difficult to penetrate illegitimate organizations such as the drugs industry, as they do legitimate ones (Ruggiero 1993; Ruggiero and South 1995).

Victimization

Victimization is far more complex than for other forms of crime as it is often indirect and diffuse. Some forms, such as extortion, robberies and theft, do have direct victims. Other forms involve no direct harm to an individual victim as they depend on the sale of goods or services to willing consumers. These consumers may become victims as illegal drug users may be exploited by being sold harmful, substandard products and illegal immigrants may end up in illegal employment or in the sex industry. Legitimate industry loses sales and the government loses considerable revenue. This indirectly affects other taxpayers and consumers who may have to pay more to make up the shortfall. Jobs may also be lost through the massive trade in counterfeit goods. Organized crime also leads to corruption which may damage trust in business and local and national governments (see, for example, Ruggiero 1994).

VARIETIES OF CRIMINAL ORGANIZATION

Given the enormous diversity and impact of professional and organized crime, it has been subject to relatively little research. This section will look at some recent work on different aspects of criminal organization. Firstly, the changing nature of professional crime will be explored in more depth with accounts from recent research focusing on offenders. This will be followed by a brief examination of the rapidly growing industry in counterfeit goods which illustrates the increasingly blurred boundaries between legitimate and illegitimate industry. Finally, the importance of looking at criminal organization will be outlined, drawing on arguments in previous chapters which have stressed the significance of the criminal labour market.

The changing organization of crime

The intricate relationships between professional and organized crime and the legitimate economy can be seen in the way in which it has developed and adapted to a changing economic and technological environment, which includes changes in social control and policing. To Hobbs (1995: 13), 'professional crime evolves in tandem with the dominant practices of the legitimate economic order and also changes in social control'. In less developed economies, with less centralized police and poorer communications, forms of professional crime such as highway robbery or piracy were enabled by the carriage of goods and money with little security, poor communications and badly organized policing. Travellers on stage coaches, for example, could scarcely phone for help and robbers could more easily escape to sanctuaries for 'outlaws', literally outside the reach of the law. This became more difficult with the growth of a centralized state and police organization. Money was increasingly lodged in safes and banks which in turn became the targets for new forms of robbery requiring new skills (see, for example, McIntosh 1975). As has already been seen, these skills in turn became redundant. Professional thieves have now adapted to electronic banking with some turning to computer crime and more sophisticated international frauds.

The organization of criminal activity has changed considerably during this century. In Britain, a major characteristic of organized crime was its localized nature with local 'firms' in areas such as London, Manchester, Birmingham, Bristol and Glasgow (Hobbs 1994). Before the Second World War these operated in racecourses and during the Second World War expanded their activities to incorporate the black market in goods rationed as part of the war effort. Local firms created monopolies for organizing protection rackets, illegal gambling and prostitution. Firms in different cities coexisted with little competition, a situation which changed little until the 1980s. They were dominated by a few 'elder statesmen' (ibid). New opportunities were exploited on a largely local basis. The rise in home entertainment produced a major market for cheap copies of audio, then video cassettes and new means of transmitting pornography. Violence has always played a major role as maintaining monopolies and extortion rely on the explicit or implicit threat of violence, although serious violence tends to be avoided as it attracts the attention of the police. Nonetheless, argues Hobbs, it is significant and can cause the downfall of criminal gangs. The spectacular murders carried out by the Kray twins, motivated by expressive rather than instrumental violence, led to their capture (ibid).

The somewhat conservative nature of British organized crime conjures up an almost romantic picture of the traditional underworld characterized by codes of honour and pride in craft and skill, often looked on with nostalgia by ageing offenders. It is now an outmoded image and Hobbs (1995: 28) comments that 'if the unwritten code of the underworld ever existed, it is now as outdated as an Ealing comedy'. A number of factors contributed to this change. The growth of the drugs market led to diversification into drug trafficking which produced more competition and increasing violence. The international nature of the drugs industry placed considerable pressure on the neighbourhood firms who had to compete with outsiders. The growth of the enterprise culture eroded traditional loyalties and encouraged the development of a variety of legitimate, semi-legitimate and illegitimate 'entrepreneurial activities' (Hobbs 1995). While the post-war period can be described as the 'golden age' of robbery, robbers have grown old and turned to new money-making opportunities – principally the drugs market but also counterfeiting and gold bullion. Changes in financial markets in the 1980s allowed organized crime to participate in financial crimes. Professional crime has now, therefore, fragmented into a number of different activities (ibid). Old crafts have been deskilled and new opportunities have emerged just as in legitimate industry (ibid). The local 'firm' is still important but, argues Hobbs, local identities are reinvented in the context of global markets. Professional crime has thus moved from an occupational foundation of neighbourhood-oriented extortion and individualistic craft-based larcenies towards an entrepreneurial trading culture driven by localized interpretations of global markets (ibid). Hobbs develops these arguments through extended interviews with 'serious criminals'. These are not the 'Mr Bigs' of popular imagination but include a variety of different kinds of offenders. Some aspects of this are summarized below.

Changing criminal crafts

The decline of traditional skills is illustrated in the reminiscences of a 'craftsman', a safe breaker who recounted pride in his craft and reputation along with his knowledge of explosives and the dangers and risks of his trade. Talking about the demise of his craft, he comments:

> Well, I think because of me they got better safes, and I knocked over 200 safes and they were so easy to knock over . . . people graduated during my time from safes to banks, or to jugs as they'd call them. It was the easy way, where doing it in the safe, you had to take a bit of time, lot of effort, lot of noise, and it took longer to do.
>
> (Hobbs 1995: 18)

Another offender, described as an all-purpose thief, graduated from burglary to armed robbery. He now has a legitimate business but is still involved in criminal dealings and remains a 'thief':

> If you say to me what am I, what do I do, I got to say to you that I am a thief. That's what I do. I see what people got, take it, and sell it . . . We all change as we get older, but really we are the same. I am still a thief . . . All right, in a different way, but it's to do with thieving, sort of low key; you might call it receiving.
>
> (Hobbs 1995: 22)

This offender, argues Hobbs, is now a 'dinosaur' as specialist 'blaggers' are few and far between.

These reminiscences, argues Hobbs, illustrate a continuity with images of traditional crafts and skills, of shipyards and mines. They contrast sharply with the new breed of younger serious criminals who embrace profit rather than the 'macho blag speak' of balaclavas and sawn-off shotguns (Hobbs 1995: 23). This is exemplified in a female drug dealer who dresses smartly, uses a mobile phone and would not look out of place in a merchant bank or city finance house. Looking smart is part of her business method and she uses her gender to 'fool' clients and police officers, who assume that as an attractive woman she is less competent. Thus:

I get away with a lot more in terms of not having any sort of police attention because the way I look, the way I dress, the way I carry on my life is not the sort of way that anybody would think that was particularly dodgy . . . (men) think they can get one over on you, which is an advantage in a way, because they do treat me like I'm a bit dumb occasionally, which is quite funny because I'm not, but that's quite a laugh because they do underestimate my intelligence at times. 'Cos they think they're dead smart about the money, they can cut up the money, but in fact I can cut it up a lot quicker, and that's when I manage to get one over on people . . .

(Hobbs 1995: 25)

The diversity of criminal enterprises

In place of the specialized crafts and skills of the past, contemporary professional crime is heterogeneous and involves a variety of illicit pursuits exploiting a plethora of money-making opportunities. Legal enterprises are often indistinguishable from illegal ones. Whereas older criminals specialized, contemporary serious criminals participate in many different activities. One offender, described by Hobbs as involved in 'mutant' enterprise, leads an apparently respectable lifestyle as a businessman. He owns a video hire shop and has a share in a used car business. He also deals in amphetamines and cocaine, previously imported pornography and began his criminal career by dealing in stolen car parts and acquiring a reputation as a good businessman. His girlfriend is in prison for her part in a conspiracy involving forged foreign currency. His various business activities have evolved from the economic and ideological foundations of late twentieth-century British enterprise culture (Hobbs 1995).

Diversification

Reference has already been made to the need for diversification. One example of this is seen in the careers of two former football hooligans, previously part of a hooligan 'firm'. They became bouncers in illegal raves signalling a shift from overt violence to a more mellow style. The development of rave culture created a marginal, semi-deviant market in which emergent entrepreneurs needed their own form of policing. According to Hobbs, they looked to the old neighbourhoods for employees with 'muscle'. This led to their involvement in the amphetamine trade which made some former football hooligans 'seriously rich'. Others ended up in prison while others turned to more mundane forms of 'villainy'.

The high life

Like other forms of crime, professional crime is attractive. It is set apart from the mundane rhythms of legitimate employment and, to Hobbs, the straight world cannot offer the same financial rewards or excitement. He describes one drug dealer as part of an urban élite at play. His involvement in criminal entrepreneurship is driven by a desire to pursue an extravagant lifestyle, well illustrating the 'life is a party' theme (Shover and Honaker 1992; Hobbs 1995). Conspicuous consumption rather than pure economic necessity is an important part of offenders' motivations. These kinds of offenders take more risks and make fewer efforts to pretend that their enterprises are legitimate than more business-like offenders.

Lower-class violent subcultures

The key role played by violence has already been referred to and Hobbs links this to working-class male cultural expectations in which the fighter carries a high status. Part of the informal order of the illegitimate marketplace is that men doing business also do violence. Power is exercised by instilling fear. To Hobbs it is linked to the patriarchal family. Two of the offenders in his study are a father and son and their relationship and reminiscences are coloured by accounts of the father's violence towards his son and their tolerance of the repeated use of violence.

Counterfeiting

The trade in counterfeit goods illustrates many features of contemporary organized crime. Its scope is indicated in estimates that each year it may cost industry more than one billion pounds along with losing 100,000 manufacturing jobs (*The Scotsman* 8/12/94; Crime Concern 1994). It has been estimated that around one in three audio tapes sold world wide are fake (Ruggiero 1996a). The Federation Against Software Theft has estimated that 49 per cent of computer software in Britain consists of illegal pirate copies, although much of this is due to individual computer owners illegally copying programmes and software (*Independent on Sunday* 2/4/95). It is fraudulent, with consumers paying for falsely represented and substandard goods and can also result in injury. The chemicals used in counterfeit perfume and soap powder, for example, have burnt consumers, in some cases leading to lasting disfigurement, and children have been endangered by fake toys, like power rangers, which use lead paint or have unsafe spikes (Croall 1997).

Counterfeiting is closely related to the legitimate economy. Manufacturers rely on the possession of a 'brand name' which may lead to a monopoly position which enables them to charge higher prices (Ruggiero 1996a). This means that cheap counterfeits have a ready market among consumers who cannot afford the full price. While 'designer' goods are highly vulnerable, an astonishing range of goods is subject to counterfeit, from luxury items such as jewellery, watches or perfume, designer clothes and football strips, trainers and sports gear to more everyday items like soap powder, shampoos, cleaning products and even tea bags (Hennessey 1994; Wassell 1994; Croall 1997). Technological advance has enabled audio and video tapes, compact disks and computer software to be easily copied and fakes are often difficult to detect.

The production, distribution and sale of these goods clearly require considerable organization and have attracted organized crime firms. Fake tea bags found in Glasgow in 1995 were said to provide an example of 'conventional criminals crossing over to the world of commercial crime, which they perceive as a more lucrative and softer option' (*The Scotsman* 8/6/95).

Counterfeit goods are sold in a variety of outlets such as markets, street stalls, pubs and car boot sales. Some are manufactured and distributed on a global scale, often being produced in third world countries. There are also a variety of local, 'cottage' industries. In one case investigators found video machines which produced up to 738 Walt Disney films per day, worth around £8,000. This was a local branch of a firm located in the Far East (*Daily Mail* 22/4/95). In other cases, counterfeit soap powder was produced in a legitimate factory using government-sponsored YTS workers, and sports goods worth around £100,000 per annum were produced in a farmhouse (Hennessey 1994). Production has increasingly shifted to Europe with Britain being a major manufacturing site. Operations have been found in disused mills in the post-industrial north of England (Hennessey 1994; Ruggiero 1996a). Counterfeiting is a useful way of laundering drugs money and it provides a source of income for both professional criminals and terrorists. It has been alleged by investigators that the IRA are involved in the sale of counterfeit videos, audio tapes and compact disks, whereas the UVF has been associated with the sale of counterfeit clothes (*The Scotsman* 8/12/94).

As with many forms of professional and organized crime, complex patterns of offending and victimization are involved. Victimization can be direct and involve physical injury. On the other hand, the question of '*cui bono?*', 'who benefits?', often asked in organizational theory can be applied to counterfeiting with interesting results (Ruggiero 1996a). Legitimate manufacturers and consumers are generally considered to be the main victims. Yet manufacturers charge high prices and counterfeiting enables those who cannot afford these prices to obtain similar goods. Manufacturers' losses can be offset by the enhanced reputation and status as 'market leaders' which they gain from widespread counterfeiting. There have even been cases where they have produced their own counterfeit versions to compete with the fakes (Ruggiero 1996a). Moreover, argues Ruggiero, production has moved to Europe to prevent the enormous profits being left in the Far East (ibid). The counterfeiting industry arguably provides employment and income for the unemployed. Many, therefore, benefit although it could also be pointed out that the largely poorer consumers who provide the main market for counterfeiters – the affluent would tend to buy the 'real thing' – may lose out by buying shoddy, and on occasion dangerous, goods (Croall 1997).

Criminal organization

It has been seen that organized crime can be likened to, and interacts with, legitimate industry. It adapts to market opportunities and has its entrepreneurs, investors, senior managers and employees who aspire to a career. It is related to legitimate industry in many different ways and can be analysed using similar organization theories. From research on organized and corporate crime across Europe, Ruggiero provides an interesting analysis of many aspects of organized crime including the status of entrepreneurs, the changing nature of the criminal labour market and links between legitimate and illegitimate industry (Ruggiero 1996a).

The entrepreneur

The significance of the enterprise culture for organized crime was illustrated above. The term entrepreneur has generally been used to describe individuals who take risks and develop new and innovative commercial activities (Ruggiero 1996a). Entrepreneurs have often been perceived as mavericks and, argues Ruggiero, there has for long been a relationship between economic innovation and deception, reflected in Merton's use of the term innovator to describe the criminal response. Entrepreneurs legitimate profits by taking risks and initiating and coordinating the production and distribution of goods, which is very similar to organized crime. The success of entrepreneurship depends on minimizing risks. For the criminal entrepreneur, Ruggiero argues that these risks include apprehension and detection, and the need to minimize them crucially affects how criminal businesses are organized.

In most business enterprises, the entrepreneur employs labourers to carry out different tasks. To Ruggiero, therefore, a key element of organized crime is the mobilization of criminal labour by recruiting employees who are paid a wage. Employees, however, pose a threat to the criminal entrepreneur as they learn about the business and can pass on information to authorities or engage in blackmail and extortion. This threat can be neutralized by the moral codes of the underworld – 'honour among thieves' – or by, as in the Mafia, relying on the loyalty of family members. Organized crime in immigrant communities may rely on similar group loyalties. It has been seen, however, that these models are not typical of organized crime in general, especially in the era of the supergrass. Another way of minimizing the threat posed by employees is to keep them at a distance from the organization and to employ them for only one small task. Criminal businesses therefore increasingly rely on a variety of semi-skilled and unskilled criminal labour, effectively creating a mass, Post-Fordist labour force (Ruggiero and South 1995).

The criminal labour market

There are many examples of such employment. Former joyriders who have proven skills in car stealing may be recruited to steal cars for organized criminals trading in car components or high-status cars, and others may be employed to strip the car and conceal its origins. Drug users are employed as local dealers. Women in poor countries in the third world are employed as drug couriers or prostitutes. Other employees may be recruited from the ranks of the unemployed. Former miners have been employed to import bootleg beer, and, as seen above, YTS trainees to produce counterfeit goods (Ruggiero 1996a). Thus, argues Ruggiero, there is considerable deskilling and casualization at the bottom of the organized crime hierarchy with increasing specialization at the top. Employees are kept at a distance and know little about other participants or their employers, as will be seen in respect of the drugs industry in Chapter 14.

For the most successful organized criminals, going 'legit' by developing a legitimate business is a form of upward mobility (Ruggiero 1996a). It provides a means of laundering profits and minimizes the risks of detection. Many of the serious criminals in Hobbs' study developed legitimate enterprises, with the boundaries between the legitimate and illegitimate aspects of their activities being extremely blurred. Involvement in the 'upperworld' as well as the 'underworld' develops therefore out of the need to diversify and to conceal illegitimate activities.

Blurring the boundaries – legitimate and illegitimate business

Ruggiero (1996a) describes and gives examples of different relationships between legitimate and illegitimate businesses, which are summarized below.

ORGANIZED CRIME PROVIDES A SERVICE TO LEGITIMATE ENTERPRISES

In some cases, organized crime serves legitimate industries. In, for example, the trade in stolen art works, private individuals, art traders and auction firms become the customers of art thieves. Organized groups act as 'go betweens' between customers who commission works and thieves who are employed for specific thefts. The illegal trade in arms, discussed at more length in Chapter 16, is used by governments and the legitimate arms industry to supply arms to countries banned from obtaining legal supplies. Increasing restrictions on the disposal of chemical and toxic waste have created a market for the speedy and cheap processing of industrial waste. In the Netherlands, firms offer a package of services for disposal including false invoices, chemical reports, transportation and permits to dump waste (Van Duyne 1993). The head of an English legal waste disposal firm was convicted for running a parallel illegal dumping business (Ruggiero 1996a). The contemporary 'slave trade' of trafficking in illegal immigrants provides a further example. In 1993, 81 immigrants were found working in a Kent fruit farm. They had paid to get to England where they were illegally employed and paid £15 per day (cited in Ruggiero 1996a: 141). Young women from developing countries are recruited as servants by apparently legal recruitment agencies who charge them enormous fees (Ruggiero 1996a). In some European countries, trades in importing Asian women for marriage, in adopting children from Russia or

Romania, and in supplying organs for transplant surgery have been reported (ibid). Organized crime therefore performs an ancillary role for the official economy, providing a clandestine 'tertiary' sector.

Legitimate business may knowingly or unknowingly assist organized crime. A good example of this is money laundering, which inevitably requires the involvement of legitimate concerns. Major armed robberies have included plans to launder money through legitimate businesses (ibid). The need to launder the enormous profits from the drugs market has made money laundering a key part of the illegal economy. Traditionally banks, with their codes of secrecy – especially the notorious 'numbered accounts' in Switzerland – have been a major means of doing this. The tightening up of these arrangements created a greater need to generate legitimate business fronts or to divert money to less regulated areas (Levi 1991). This can be done by diversifying into other illegal industries such as counterfeiting, or by diverting large amounts of capital into the less tightly regulated areas of offshore financial markets, popularly known as flight capital (Ruggiero 1996a).

JOINT ENTERPRISES

In some cases organized crime and legitimate industry work together. This is seen in the case of frauds on the European Union, whose agricultural subsidies have provided a major source of finance for both legitimate and criminal enterprises. The enormously complex regulations have provided many opportunities for fraud and partnerships are useful as illegitimate entrepreneurs require access to officials and to legitimate business activities (Ruggiero 1996a). In another case 'clean' financial advisers and 'wheeler dealers' with a criminal record were involved in a major fraud. Three million pounds were raised by selling goods which offenders were only supposed to store for customers. The two main offenders were a business adviser and a second-hand car dealer with a previous criminal record. Ruggiero (1996a: 149) comments that it was impossible to establish which had transmitted to the other the techniques and 'subcultural rationalizations' which facilitated the offence.

UNDERSTANDING PROFESSIONAL AND ORGANIZED CRIME

These arguments suggest that many of the theoretical approaches which have been applied to other forms of crime, particularly pathological or deficit theories, are inappropriate. While many of these focused on non-professional offenders, some did touch on professional and organized crime. Indeed many, as seen in Chapter 3, developed in the prohibition era when organized crime was prominent in the United States and it provides a good illustration of Merton's 'innovator' response. It was linked to the blocked opportunities for upward mobility, with one sociologist, Daniel Bell, describing it as a 'queer ladder of social mobility' (Bell 1953). The criminal subcultures supporting it were seen as pathological or a sign of disorganization, particularly those flourishing among immigrants (Ruggiero 1996a). To these deficit theories organized crime is pathological and is often likened to a cancer (ibid). Rather than being pathological, however, professional and organized crime has been seen to be a form of rational economic activity and as a normal part of economic life. To Lombroso indeed, the Mafioso lacked the stigma of criminality (ibid). To Hobbs professional criminals want to earn money, live in the same world as anyone else, have families, worry about the future and have to cope with a rapidly changing world (Hobbs 1995). Ruggiero (1996a: 33) argues that deficit theories

> . . . can hardly explain the types of organized crime which have developed over the last decades in many European countries. Organized illegal activities seem less the result of poverty, underdevelopment or lack of self control than of its opposite: affluence, development and the control of resources.

This is not to argue that structural approaches are not relevant. It has been seen that involvement in professional and organized crime does provide an alternative way of earning a living and appears to be an attractive means of pursuing an enhanced lifestyle for those without legitimate alternatives. Like other forms of property crime it can provide a sense of achievement and, for men, status as 'a man'. Furthermore, it can be increasingly attractive in the current economic situation. To Hobbs, the decline in employment opportunities for working-class males is a significant factor, as in many local areas the crafts, skills, traditional trades and unskilled work which were crucial in defining and shaping images of masculinity have now disappeared. These also provided a patriarchal base of recruitment to employment which organized crime can replace. To Hobbs crime is a 'boys' game', exploiting local opportunities and drawing on a male working-class culture which has always adapted to formal and informal economies. What he sees as a 'residue' of traditional masculine working-class culture with a potential for violence and instrumental physicality provides a cultural inheritance ideally suited for engagement with serious crime and it represents an intersection of old neighbourhood values and new global markets (Hobbs 1995).

Advancement in criminal careers may, however, be difficult to achieve and may be affected by similar inequalities of class and power to those which constrain legitimate career opportunities. The mass labour market described by Ruggiero may in reality provide few opportunities and is affected by the deskilling and casualization which has affected legitimate industry. For those with few skills, occupational mobility may be limited and the criminal labour market parallels the exploitation and inequality of the legitimate labour market.

Black people may be excluded by the predominance of existing neighbourhood firms and competition with international organizations, and those employed as unskilled labour are kept at a distance from the centre and run a higher risk of detection. Those closer to the centre and more powerful organizations can more easily expand into the legitimate market, although some forms of organized crime have a greater 'pariah' status than others. Crime, argues Ruggiero, is an option open to all individuals who are presented with opportunities from both legal and illegal markets. The availability of these options varies according to status and income. While those with lower status and few resources have fewer legitimate or illegitimate opportunities, higher status wealthy individuals have more (Ruggiero 1996a).

CONCLUDING COMMENTS

This chapter has looked at only a small segment of the vast area of professional and organized crime, which, given its scale and impact, has been surprisingly neglected in both popular and academic discussions of the crime problem. The chapter has focused on its development and its links to legitimate economic activity which, it has been argued, provides a more fruitful approach than seeing it as pathological or abnormal. From the activities of local criminal entrepreneurs to large criminal syndicates, professional and organized crime, like legitimate business, exploits a variety of economic opportunities. It also poses particular policy problems. While vast resources are directed to the so-called war against organized crime, it often remains relatively impenetrable to conventional policing and criminal justice strategies. As crime becomes international, so too must policing and it requires a very different kind of policing to many other forms of crime, involving international policing and intelligence departments. Few major offenders are convicted and its potential rewards in relation to the chances of being caught and convicted make deterrence difficult. Its attractions are difficult to replace by legitimate options. Its market for goods and services comes from the prohibition of some commodities – drugs or prostitution for example. It was seen in Chapter 11 that decriminalizing prostitution might make prostitutes less exploited, and the decriminalization of drugs has also been suggested as a means of curtailing organized crime.

Review Questions

1. Outline the difficulties of defining and researching professional and organized crime. How might a victim survey be designed?
2. In what ways is the criminal industry related to its legitimate counterpart?
3. Is professional and organized crime better analysed as pathological or as a normal feature of economic life?

Key Reading

Hobbs D (1994) 'Professional and Organized Crime in Britain', in Maguire M, Morgan R and Reiner R (eds) *The Oxford Handbook of Criminology*. Oxford: Clarendon Press

Hobbs D (1995) *Bad Business: Professional Crime in Modern Britain*. Oxford: Oxford University Press

Passas N (ed) (1995) *Organized Crime*. Aldershot: Dartmouth

Ruggiero V (1996a) *Organized and Corporate Crime in Europe: Offers That Can't be Refused*. Aldershot: Dartmouth

CHAPTER 14

DRUGS AND CRIME

The illegal drugs market is, as seen in Chapter 13, a major part of organized crime and also affects other forms of crime. Drugs are popularly associated with violent crime, a large proportion of property crime is said to be drugs related and Chapter 11 also revealed that drug use can lead to prostitution. Many kinds of offenders are involved, from the 'Mr Bigs' or drugs 'barons' of popular imagination to the dealers and pushers at the lower end of the criminal labour market. Users of illegal drugs are also offenders and there is now a growing concern about the increasing use of illegal drugs among young people across the social spectrum. Many questions are raised when considering drugs and their link to crime. What is meant by the 'drugs problem'? Which drugs are legal and which are illegal? How is drug use related to crime? How is the drugs industry organized? Who supplies drugs? Who consumes them?

This chapter will start by discussing how the 'drugs problem' is defined and how drug use is related to the criminal law. It will then look at estimates of the extent of illegal drug use before exploring the organization of the drugs industry using studies of trafficking, distribution and the organization of local drug markets. This will be followed by an outline of the relationship between drugs and other forms of crime before discussing how drug use and abuse have been analysed by sociological and criminological perspectives.

DEFINING THE 'DRUGS PROBLEM'

While discussions of drugs often imply a 'drug problem', the consumption of drugs, from caffeine to pain killers, is an everyday activity. What, therefore, is the problem? Does it lie with particular drugs? With drug 'abuse'? When does drug use become defined as abuse? How are 'drug problems' related to 'crime problems'? Why is the use of some drugs illegal while the use of others is not? Exploring these and other questions illustrates how conceptions of drug use and 'abuse' are socially constructed.

What is a drug?

Technically, a drug is any substance which modifies the functions of an organism, and many drugs have the positive function of healing or alleviating diseases (Whittaker 1987). Many substances, from everyday foods to chemical mixtures, have different effects which vary according to the particular drug. In general, alcohol, barbiturates, tranquillizers and heroin have a depressant effect, whereas caffeine, amphetamines, cocaine and tobacco are stimulants. Others such as cannabis, LSD and MDMA distort perceptions (South 1997). The physical properties of a drug or its effects are not, however, related to whether they are socially approved.

Why are drugs used?

Drugs are used for a variety of reasons. Medically they are used to treat diseases and to relieve pain. Drugs are also used in everyday life – many readers, for example, will 'need' doses of caffeine to wake up in the morning, to survive a day's work or to read books like this one! Other drugs, such as alcohol, may be used for relaxation and sociability. Having a 'cup of tea' in Britain is a ritual which accompanies having a break or being sociable, as is, for many, having a drink. Some use 'uppers' to keep them going through a stressful job or to enhance the excitement of leisure activities. Others use 'downers', which numb the senses, to relax or to escape from the grim reality of everyday life.

Normal and abnormal drug use

Many forms of drug are therefore seen as perfectly normal, indeed the person who avoids all drug use may be seen in some circles as deviant. A very fine line divides normal from abnormal drug use which varies between and within cultures. What is seen as a normal intake of alcohol in one household or cultural setting may be seen as verging on alcoholism in another, and alcohol is encouraged in some settings and prohibited in others. Using drugs to treat an illness is seen as beneficial, while using the same drugs for non-medical purposes is seen as abnormal.

Using drugs for pleasure

Strong reactions against drug use are often provoked by the recreational use of drugs among young people. This was seen in the 1960s in relation to cannabis, LSD and heroin, and in the late 1980s and 1990s with the growing use of Ecstasy and ketamine and poly drug use. Yet not all recreational drug use is seen as a problem, as going to the pub remains a popular pastime across the social spectrum. Reactions against recreational drug use may therefore be related to similar fears about young people's activities to those illustrated in Chapter 7.

Drug use and abuse

Normal and abnormal drug use are often associated with concepts of drug use and abuse, although these are difficult to distinguish. While having one or two drinks might be seen as normal drinking, 'excessive' drinking is associated with abuse. This is generally related to the adverse health effects of a drug or to its addictive effects. While some drugs are addictive in that they lead to physical dependency, induce a need to consume more of the drug to experience its effect, and cause withdrawal symptoms, their physical effect works alongside psychological and social factors. A drug may be part of someone's lifestyle and an automatic part of their everyday routines, thus 'coming off' a drug by ending physical dependency is much easier than staying off it. The psychological and social nature of addiction is also seen in the use of addictive language for activities as opposed to substances; thus gambling is seen as an addiction and some people are popularly described as 'workaholics'.

Which drugs are a 'problem'?

Approval and disapproval are not always related to the physical properties or effects of a drug and this is also the case with regulation. It might be assumed that the criminal law would be used to regulate drugs with more serious effects but this is not the case. As is so often pointed out, legal drugs such as alcohol and nicotine have enormously damaging effects, yet cannabis has been found to have fewer negative effects and some positive ones. These contrasts direct attention to the circumstances in which drugs are criminalized.

The criminalization of drugs

The law regulates drugs in different ways. Some are available through prescription by medical practitioners and others, such as alcohol or cigarettes, are subject to licensing arrangements and are legally available only to those above a particular age. Other laws regulate activities, like driving, which are adversely affected by drugs. Some drugs, such as cannabis or heroin, are prohibited by laws making their manufacture, distribution, sale or use a criminal offence. The use of the criminal law to regulate drugs illustrates the way in which different drugs, at different times, have been subject to different forms of regulation.

Some historical examples illustrate shifting conceptions of drug use. In the seventeenth century, coffee houses were seen as 'dens of sedition' and in the eighteenth, commentators talked about a tea drinking 'plague' (Whittaker 1987). Opium was widely on sale throughout the nineteenth century, was cheaper than alcohol, and widely used as a medicine or tonic (Whittaker 1987; Ruggiero and South 1995). Florence Nightingale, Charles Dickens, Byron and Disraeli were all reported to have been regular opium users and it was also used for recreational purposes in industrial regions (Whittaker 1987; Ruggiero and South 1995). Britain was involved in the 'opium wars' in the nineteenth century to protect trading in opium (South 1997). By the end of the nineteenth century, contrasting conceptions of drug use as a 'disease requiring treatment' or as a 'sin requiring punishment' emerged with the medical profession defining opium and cocaine use as a medical problem while the use of opium and alcohol among the lower classes was seen as sinful (South 1997). During the First World War there were concerns about the adverse effects of cocaine on the efficiency of troops and of alcohol on the productivity of factory workers (Ruggiero and South 1995; South 1997). Heroin and cocaine were controlled through emergency war legislation in 1916 which made their possession an offence, except when prescribed by medical practitioners, and regulations also introduced licensing laws restricting the opening of public houses (Ruggiero and South 1995; South 1997).

In Britain, the regulation of drugs other than alcohol was largely through medical prescriptions. The so-called 'British system' relied less on the use of criminal law than that of the United States where the sale of alcohol was prohibited during the 'prohibition era'. Britain appeared to have fewer problems with drug addiction and illegal drug use until the 1960s when numbers of addicts increased and the recreational use of drugs among young people emerged as a new 'problem'. In both the United States and Britain drugs like LSD, cannabis and heroin played a part in youth culture and the popular music scene – reflected in songs like *Lucy in the Sky with Diamonds* (LSD). Subsequent legislation controlled amphetamine and LSD and the Dangerous Drugs Act of 1967 required new addicts to be notified to the Home Office. Currently, illegal drugs are graded in relation to their assumed effects and the severity of sentences (South 1997). Class A drugs include heroin, cocaine, LSD and MDMA, popularly known as Ecstasy; Class B covers cannabis, amphetamines and barbiturates; and Class C, tranquillizers and some mild stimulants (South 1997).

The effects of criminalization will be seen throughout this chapter. Prohibiting a drug makes those who use it subject to the criminal law. It also creates a vast amount of secondary crime related to the manufacture and sale of illegal drugs which, as seen in Chapter 13, is now a vast industry. For users, the high cost of illegal drugs may lead to participation in many different crimes which will be discussed in a later section of this chapter. This has led to arguments that some drugs should be 'decriminalized'.

THE SCOPE OF ILLEGAL DRUG USE

Research problems

Estimating the extent of illegal drug use is extremely difficult as most is unrecorded. Official statistics indicate numbers of addicts notified to the Home Office and numbers cautioned and convicted for drug offences. Neither of these accurately indicates the extent of illegal drug use, as many addicts do not register, large numbers of illegal drug users are not addicted and much illegal drug use does not come to the attention of the police (Plant 1989). Self-report studies have become the most commonly used means of assessing how many people have experimented with and regularly use different kinds of drugs. The BCS now includes estimates of illegal drug use and a growing number of surveys have been carried out with young people. All of these are limited by the nature of self-report surveys and by problems of comparison. Illegal drug use varies according to what drugs are available, which in turn may differ across the country, producing local and regional variations. Surveys use different questions, cover different age groups and it is also recognized that the 'drugs scene' changes rapidly and that studies may become outdated. Nonetheless they do give some indications of the extent and changing pattern of illegal drug use.

The extent of illegal drug use

It is generally agreed that the use of drugs among young people has increased to a point where, by the mid-1990s, it has been 'normalized' (Measham et al 1994). The increase in recreational drug use in the 1960s was followed by the so-called 'heroin epidemic' of the late 1970s and early 1980s. This increase is reflected in official figures which indicate that whereas, in 1945, only 300 drug offences were recorded, in 1985, 26,596 cautions and convictions were recorded with over 80 per cent involving cannabis (Plant 1989). The numbers of addicts increased from 1,426 in 1970 to 7,052 in 1985 (Plant 1989). The rise in heroin use was associated with the increasing availability of cheaper forms of the drug from Iran, Pakistan and Afghanistan, which could be smoked rather than injected, making it more attractive. The drugs scene changed again in the 1990s with the emergence of a 'poly drug' culture which saw the re-emergence of LSD and amphetamine and the emergence of Ecstasy and ketamine, with a range of drugs being used in a 'pick and mix' culture (South 1997). Patterns of use have also changed in that illegal drug use now involves a wider social spectrum of young people, with girls 'catching up' with boys (Measham et al 1994). Figure 14.1 summarizes some recent figures about the nature and extent of drug use among young people.

The rise of illegal drug use is also indicated in estimates that as many as 46 per cent of young people have tried illegal drugs by the time they are 20, figures which have increased since the 1980s (Dale 1996). These figures refer to lifetime usage, with figures for using in the last year or month, shown in Figure 14.1, being substantially smaller. Young people report more usage than older people, and cannabis is the most popular illegal drug. Cocaine, and its much-feared derivative 'crack', appear to be less available and less popular with most users being poly drug users, and metropolitan centres showing the highest concentrations of cocaine use (South 1997). Figure 14.1 also indicates some regional variations. These kinds of figures reflect the changing scene in the 1990s. On the basis of a study of 776 14–15 year olds in the metropolitan north-west, Measham and Parker argue that, in comparison with similar surveys during the 1980s, the prevalence of drug use among 14–15 year olds has risen substantially and that when race, gender and class are taken into

Figure 14.1 Illegal drug use among young people in the 1990s

- The 1994 BCS found that 50 per cent of males aged between 16 and 29 reported ever having used illegal drugs while 28 per cent reported using them in the last year and 18 per cent in the last month (Dale 1996).

- According to the BCS cannabis is the most popular illegal drug, followed by LSD, amphetamines and Ecstasy (Dale 1996).

- A recent survey found higher levels of use of all illegal drugs in Scotland than England with up to 60 per cent of 15–16-year-old schoolboys surveyed in Scotland reporting trying an illicit drug compared to 43.5 per cent in England, 37.8 per cent in Northern Ireland and 35 per cent in Wales (Miller and Plant 1996; Robertson 1996).

- The rates for girls were lower – in Scotland 50 per cent of girls reported trying an illicit drug, compared to 39 per cent in England, 18 per cent in Northern Ireland and 32 per cent in Wales (Miller and Plant 1996; Robertson 1996).

- In a survey of 14–15 year olds in the metropolitan north-west, nearly one-third reported having used cannabis, and one-tenth reported experimenting with at least one of nitrites, LSD, solvents, magic mushrooms and amphetamine. One in 17 had used Ecstasy, and only 1 per cent cocaine (Measham et al 1994).

- This survey showed few overall gender differences but more boys than girls had used magic mushrooms and amphetamine, whereas more girls had used solvents.

- Those at working-class schools were more likely than those at middle-class schools to have used and continue to use a drug.

- Black and white respondents were much more likely to have used and to continue to use drugs than Asians.

---

account, it is spreading to all sections of young people. It is starting at an earlier age and involves a wider range of drugs. Thus they suggest that gender and class boundaries are fragmenting and that recreational drug use is becoming 'normal' (Measham et al 1994). To others, however, such conclusions are exaggerated (South 1997).

Widespread illegal drug use has to be placed in context. More teenagers experiment with alcohol than with illegal drugs, with one major survey reporting that only 5.8 per cent of teenagers reported never having tried alcohol and 77 per cent reported having been drunk at some time; 67 per cent also reported having smoked with one-third reporting smoking in the last 30 days (Miller and Plant 1996; Robertson 1996). Alcohol consumption is reported to be twice as high as in the mid-1950s, although lower than in the eighteenth and nineteenth centuries (South 1997). It could also be pointed out that mortality rates from alcohol are much higher than those for illegal drugs (South 1997), and that there are over 200,000 convictions per annum for public drunkenness and drunken driving (Plant 1989). Tobacco also has a severe impact, with World Health Organization figures estimating that there are around 100,000 premature deaths in the UK each year, and that around one-third of people over 16 smoke (Plant 1989; South 1997). It has also been estimated that approximately 625,000 people are dependent on Valium and 14,000 on barbiturates (Whittaker 1987; Plant 1989). In addition, the sale of alcohol and cigarettes is accompanied by illegal trading to evade taxes (South 1997).

CRIME AND THE DRUGS MARKET

Like many forms of organized crime explored in Chapter 13, the drugs market can be likened to a legitimate business. It is a multi-million pound, global industry and its enormous profits necessitate money laundering, diversifying into other businesses and operating with legitimate 'fronts'. Illegal drugs are often grown in less well-developed countries from where they must be transported or 'trafficked', often across the globe, before being imported and distributed to customers at the street level. This involves: entrepreneurs who purchase supplies from growers and organize their distribution; traffickers who are involved with transportation; and importers and wholesalers who pass the drugs on to retailers or 'dealers' who sell to consumers. Different levels of this organization will be explored below before exploring how drug use is related to crime.

The drugs industry

While it is often assumed that the drugs industry is dominated by highly organized criminal syndicates, these are relatively few, and the industry largely consists of smaller enterprises organized around different functions (Ruggiero and South 1995). Traffickers specialize in secreting drugs and evading customs and law enforcement in the countries through which they pass. International political changes may affect these routes and political instability can assist distribution as it lessens the efficiency of law enforcement. The Balkans, for example, remains a major trade route (ibid). Traffickers have developed a variety of ingenious ways of concealing drugs by, for example, secreting them in car batteries or frozen meat, or even sending them through the post! (ibid). Legitimate import and export businesses also provide excellent 'cover' for transporting drugs. There are distinct production, importation and distribution sectors of the industry with the mass criminal labour force being involved at the lower levels, in the most high-risk activities of street level dealing. This section, which draws on recent research, will look at trafficking and distribution (Dorn et al 1992; Ruggiero and South 1995).

Trafficking

While researching the world of drug distribution is far from easy, Dorn et al (1992) carried out an innovative study based on the accounts of convicted traffickers, police and customs officials. On the basis of this they were able to look at changes in the organization of drug trafficking, which are related to the need to adjust to changing patterns of law enforcement (Dorn and South 1990; Dorn et al 1992; see also Ruggiero and South 1995; South 1997). A number of different groups involved in trafficking were identified as follows:

- *Trading charities* are loosely organized groups ideologically committed to drug use such as hippies and Rastafarians. They imported drugs directly from producer countries, using for example, the 'Afghan Trail'. They aimed to circulate drugs among their group rather than to make profits, thus their description as 'charities'. Tougher law enforcement has, however, largely rendered these groups redundant.

- *Mutual societies* are small groups largely based on friendship networks of user dealers who supply and support each other. Again, intensive policing has reduced these groups and the days of both trading charities and mutual societies are often looked back on with nostalgia.

- *Business sideliners* are primarily involved in legitimate businesses but 'side-line' in drug trafficking. They are normally import–export businesses with social and economic ties to areas of production such as Pakistan.

- *Criminal diversifiers* are those professional criminals who, as seen in Chapter 13, moved from property or professional crime into drugs, enabled by their networks in the informal economy. Their involvement is said to have led to growing violence around the drugs market as different groups compete for territory.

- *Opportunistic irregulars* are largely made up of property and professional criminals involved in a range of illegal activities. They are less organized and can be seen as 'hangers on'.

- *Retail specialists* are relatively stable organizations who employ people to sell drugs and are considered to be less common in Britain than in the United States.

- *State-sponsored enterprise* is involved where drugs enter the market through the activities of corrupt police officers or state officials attempting to obtain cash for private or other gain.

Law enforcement has affected the operations of these groups, with the more loosely organized trading charities and mutual enterprises being forced out by heavier policing. These gave way to the more organized criminal diversifiers and business sideliners who are currently most prevalent in Britain (Ruggiero and South 1995). Thus, far from consisting of the highly organized syndicates of public imagination, the drugs market involves diverse groups and further divisions are illustrated when other aspects of importation and distribution are explored.

Importation and distribution

As indicated above, those involved in import–export businesses with links in producer countries have more opportunity to become involved in importing drugs, which partly accounts for the involvement of immigrant groups. In addition, the closed and solidaristic nature of minority ethnic or expatriate communities provides a basis for group loyalty (Ruggiero and South 1995). In London, for example, the Chinese were dominant the 1960s and 1970s, Iranians were active in the 1980s, and Pakistanis are said to have become increasingly involved since the mid-1980s when Pakistani heroin began to dominate the market. Indian entrepreneurs have also acted as importers and Nigeria is a key staging post for heroin. Many couriers are Nigerian women, known as 'mules'.

Importation is often separated from distribution and, in London, large-scale distribution is dominated by indigenous white groups of English criminal diversifiers who previously monopolized the distribution of other illegal goods. Their links with lower level distributors in local communities and in the local irregular economy are crucial to the development of local markets and an efficient drugs economy (Ruggiero 1993; Ruggiero and South 1995). These groups are also prepared to protect their territory from competition, leading to the use of violence.

Importers are therefore distinct from distributors, and the middle range is also separated from the lower level. This increases security along with distributors' profits as their monopoly in local areas enables them to negotiate good terms with importers, who, having less knowledge of the local irregular economy, would have more difficulty distributing drugs, which would increase their chances of being caught with drugs waiting for distribution. Distributors also use a chain – thus one informant reported that:

> There are about 12 middle range distributors who never go out on the street in this area. They take between 50 per cent and 70 per cent of the street value of the drugs sold. In turn, they buy in other areas. It is very rare that distributors here are in direct contact with importers, or are importers themselves. Those who buy from importers live in more respectable white areas and are usually white British.
>
> (Ruggiero and South 1995: 117)

It is difficult for other groups to break into this monopoly. Thus the so-called Yardies – despite being portrayed as a highly organized gang – consisted of around 30–40 loosely organized illegal immigrants and found it impossible to 'break into' the market dominated by largely white criminal diversifiers (Ruggiero 1993; Ruggiero and South 1995). Ruggiero and South argue that prejudice is as common in the drugs economy as in the legal one

– black people are employed but often at lower levels and for riskier tasks. All low level dealers – the mass labour force referred to in Chapter 13 – face higher risks of detection and violence from other groups.

The local market

After importation and distribution, drugs are sold to the 'end users', the consumers. This street level market is the most visible and vulnerable to law enforcement as consumers must know where to obtain a supply, knowledge which is more likely to come to the attention of the police. Local patterns of consumption are strongly related to the availability of different drugs and to the local drug-using subcultures which affect how people use drugs (South 1997). As seen above, patterns of use have changed in recent years in relation to age, race, gender and class, the changing drugs 'scene' and drug subcultures. This section will focus on the consumers and on the nature of local drug markets.

The consumers

Like many of the activities covered in previous chapters, drug taking is surrounded by popular mythology. Drug takers are often depicted as pathological or crazed 'junkies', as the passive victims of unscrupulous pushers preying on potential young users. A growing number of studies have challenged these myths. Most drug users are introduced to drugs not by pushers or dealers but by friends and associates, and many continue to be provided with drugs within their own network (Pearson 1987a; Parker et al 1988; Ruggiero and Vass 1992). They initially experiment with drugs because they are curious, and their initial experience is often pleasurable (Pearson 1987a; Parker et al 1988). They carry on taking drugs because they are enjoyable rather than through addiction. Indeed addiction is not an inevitable feature of drug use even for addictive drugs like heroin, as some heroin users continue to use without becoming addicted, especially if they have a job (Pearson 1987a). Despite the negative image of the 'junkie' used in much anti-drug propaganda, addicts can enjoy a high status within some drug subcultures (Burr 1987; Pearson 1987a). Nor is the experience of withdrawal as horrendous as it is often portrayed, having been likened to a mild dose of 'flu (Ruggiero and Vass 1992).

Who consumes drugs? As indicated above patterns of drug use are strongly related to age, gender, race and class and these relationships are outlined below.

AGE

It was seen earlier that the recreational use of drugs by young people has increased in recent years (Measham et al 1994; Dale 1996), and it was also seen in Chapter 7 that drug use is attractive to young people and plays an important role in different subcultures. Young people tend to dismiss the risks of drug taking, seeing their choice of drugs, which are taken largely for pleasure, as informed (Measham 1995). It has also been argued that concerns about young people and drugs may be related to the broader concerns about youth cultures and behaviour discussed in Chapter 7, although this does not lessen the adverse effects of drugs. It could indeed be argued that the equally damaging consumption of alcohol, nicotine and tranquillizers by older people are less likely to be surrounded with social disapproval and subject to the attention of the police and the criminal law. Moreover, as is the case with many other forms of youth crime, it is more visible and vulnerable to police and public attention.

GENDER

Young men have in the past been considered more likely to use illegal drugs and it was argued that women were less likely to be involved, particularly with heroin, as it was seen as 'unfeminine'. Female heroin addicts may suffer greater stigma both within and without drug subcultures (Ruggiero and South 1995). It was seen above, however, that recent research suggests that girls, while still reporting lower levels of drug use, are 'catching up' with boys and that they do use Ecstasy (Measham et al 1994; Dale 1996). It was also seen in Chapter 11 that many prostitutes were addicts and women form an increasing proportion of the addict population (South 1997). It has often been assumed that girls and women are often introduced to drugs by their male partners, but women can also see drug taking as providing excitement and purpose (Taylor 1993; Ruggiero and South 1995).

Whether or not girls are catching up, patterns of drug use continue to reflect gendered roles and stereotypes. Collison associates the consumption of drugs, like other forms of crime, with a particularly masculine concern for risk taking and life at the edge (Collison 1996). Measham (1995) argues that young women use drugs in different ways to young men. 'Dance drugs', she argues, are associated with dancing, fitness, fun and sociability, making them especially attractive to young women who are less likely to become involved in dependency or the intravenous use of opiates and tranquillizers. She goes on to argue that:

> There are also clear gender differences in attitudes surrounding excessive drug use. The social taboos and restrictions surrounding women's alcohol consumption, combined with concern for physical health and appearance, appear to be relevant in the illicit drugs arena . . . thus we may find that whilst young women's drug use during the 1990s reaches equal lifetime prevalence with men, it will remain less excessive.
>
> (Measham 1995: 10)

As seen in Chapter 13, women are also involved in the drugs market, and on the basis of an ethnographic study of women drug users in Glasgow, Taylor argues that for women, as for men, such involvement can provide them with a meaningful and structured life style and engagement in entrepreneurial and innovative abilities. One interviewee reports proudly that 'I was dripping in jewellery . . . two rings on each finger and chains round my neck. Leather jackets, hundreds of clothes' (Taylor 1993: 69). In the domestic sphere, it forms a different function by helping women meet the demands and stresses of family life. Thus a single mother reported that, following post-natal depression and living alone with a baby, one 'hit' relieved her stress (Taylor 1993). As mothers, drug users faced enormous social disapproval and the threat of having their children taken away, which was often a spur to give up.

RACE

Drug use has also been racialized and the assumed association of ganja or cannabis with black youth attracted heavy policing which was associated with some of the urban disturbances of the 1980s (South 1997). Cannabis appears to be the most widely used drug in the Caribbean community, although this community shows far lower rates of amphetamine or heroin use and black youth rarely featured in the 'heroin epidemic' of the 1980s (South 1997). While there have also been suggestions that Asian youth are using more drugs than previously, survey figures indicate far lower rates of usage of both legal and illegal drugs among Asians than either white or black youth (Webster 1996). In addition, as has been seen, while Asians have been involved in importing, the profitable distribution sector of the drugs market in Britain tends to be dominated by white groups.

SOCIAL CLASS

As with other forms of crime, there are no simple relationships between class and illegal drug use. While it is generally argued that illegal drug use crosses social classes, it has also been associated with poverty and deprivation. In the past there have been many addicts from the professional classes, particularly among doctors who have easier access, and others became addicted following medical treatment (South 1997). The use of cocaine was also associated with 'yuppies' and young executives, although recent research suggests more widespread use (Ruggiero and South 1995). While higher numbers of notified addicts do originate from deprived areas, this is often where the agencies are located and snowball samples have discovered addicts from more affluent areas (Parker et al 1988; Forsyth et al 1992). Middle-class youth were also involved with the use of cannabis and LSD during the 1960s and, as seen above, the latest rise in drug use has also involved middle-class youth; indeed South (1997) suggests that it has caused more concern because of this.

Despite the involvement of all social classes, the 'drugs problem' is generally constructed around lower-class youth and drug use has a different impact on users from different social classes. Middle- and upper-class drug users, while posing a problem to themselves and their parents, are less likely to be seen as a social problem than lower-class users. They can more easily afford to purchase drugs and, when addicted, are more able to afford expensive treatment. It is often recommended that addicts do not return to the environment in which their habit developed, but few unemployed addicts have little choice other than to return to it (Pearson 1987b). Lower-class drug users are more likely to have to resort to crime to support a drug habit and are more reliant on state-supported treatment programmes; they are thus more likely to be seen as a 'social' problem. Local markets are also more likely to be located in lower-class neighbourhoods, further damaging the quality of life in these areas.

The local drugs economy

The close relationship between the informal economy and the drugs market largely accounts for the location of local drugs markets in areas of higher social deprivation. A study in Glasgow found that people travelled from less deprived to more deprived areas to 'score', and that the most deprived areas were the best for obtaining drugs (Forsyth et al 1992). This may exaggerate the association of deprived areas with numbers of users, as many of the users come from outside these areas. Illegitimate markets can become an important part of the local economy in deprived areas. Pearson, for example, points out that economic exchanges within a drugs market can amount to a weekly turnover of thousands of pounds (Pearson 1987b). In a subsistence economy where many have little spending money, this is a significant sum which fuels local businesses. The dealer, who controls this turnover, can become a figure of local standing and a status symbol (Pearson 1987b; Forsyth et al 1992). The drugs market thus becomes part of the innovative businesses which, as seen in Chapter 13, flourish in areas of high deprivation where legitimate employment is scarce (Parker et al 1988; Hobbs 1994). Apart from employment in the drugs market itself, the activities related to drug use can mirror those of employment. One user in Pearson's study describes a typical day:

> Like you get up, you've gotta go out, get your money, get your smack, come back, use it . . . You're alright for ten minutes, go back out again get money . . . you're turkeying after a couple of hours, can't get nothin', whatever, back out again . . .
> (Pearson 1987b: 88)

Attractive as the drugs economy and its associated subculture may be, its appeal can wear off, particularly as lower-level users and dealers run the highest risks of being caught and captured. Profits are relatively small, particularly for user dealers, and poorer users often receive lower-level, adulterated or dangerous substances (Ruggiero 1993). The drug subcultures of the 1960s were often portrayed as supportive and co-operative, with drug users ideologically committed to drugs forming a 'counter culture'. This togetherness has, in some areas, given way to a subculture characterized by mutual suspicion, competitiveness and aggression, particularly if drugs are scarce. Life at the lower end of the market is also stressful as participants always have to be on the lookout for the police, other users and back stabbers. If heroin is scarce, most refuse to share it (Ruggiero and South 1995). Ruggiero and South found that this experience of hassle, competition and dishonesty were cited by many as a reason for giving up heroin.

Drugs and crime

Although the need to buy drugs has been seen in previous chapters to affect some forms of crime, the often assumed association between drug use and crime is complex and drugs are related to crime in different ways. In the first place selling, producing or using some drugs is in itself criminal as is driving under the influence of drugs. While these account for many offences, greater fears are aroused by the extent to which drug taking leads to secondary crime. This can happen in several ways. It has been seen that the drugs industry is associated with other forms of organized crime, money laundering and violence. It might also be assumed that drug taking contributes to crimes as a result of the physical effects of the drug which might, for example, increase aggression. It was seen in Chapter 10, however, that although many violent offenders are also drunk, there is little evidence that alcohol in itself leads to someone becoming violent, and this is also the case with other drugs. A different kind of relationship is involved where drug takers resort to crime and prostitution to finance their habit. This raises a number of questions. How much property crime is drugs related? To what extent does the use of illegal drugs lead to crime? It could also be suggested that the relationship takes a different form and that involvement in crime may lead to consumption of illegal drugs. Alternatively, it could be hypothesized that other factors lead to both drug use and crime.

It is difficult to assess how much property crime is 'drugs related' although the amount is often exaggerated. In a recent review carried out for the Home Office, Hough points out that while more drug use and crime are carried out by young men, the vast majority of drug users and the vast majority of young male criminals have little serious involvement with either drugs or crime, thus 'most recreational drug use lacks obvious links with crime' (Hough 1996: 4). For the minority who are involved in *both* drugs and crime, different relationships may be involved. Some have found that drug use is an extension of delinquency and becomes attractive as a way of spending the extra income from theft (Burr 1987). This may lead to an escalation of *both* drug use and crime with more crime fuelling more drug use. As seen in Chapter 11, many prostitutes reported an increase in drug use financed by their earnings. In addition, many addicts prefer not to turn to crime (Pearson 1987a). Many start by stealing or 'borrowing' money from friends and family and others turn to drug dealing. For women, prostitution may be a more morally acceptable option which carries less risk of imprisonment. Some are unskilled in criminal techniques and a knowledge of the hidden economy (Ruggiero 1993). Those who do turn to crime may avoid crimes with direct victims, turning to shoplifting for example, where stores are preferred as more impersonal targets (Pearson 1987a; Jarvis and Parker 1989).

All of this reduces the amount of crime which could be said to be a result of drug taking. In a sample of property offenders in the north-west, Jarvis and Parker (1989) identified three distinct groups – offenders who did not have a drugs habit, user-offenders whose criminality had preceded their offending and drug users who were new to offending. While some crime is therefore attributable to drug users seeking to gain cash for their habits, it is extremely difficult to estimate how much. Hough (1996) estimates that it is responsible for a significant minority of crime in England and Wales – numbering hundreds of thousands of offences.

The complex relationship between drug use and crime is illustrated in Parker's study of young adult offenders aged between 18 and 25 years, all of whom were repeat offenders with alcohol problems. Almost all had grown up in poor, urban neighbourhoods and few had qualifications or had ever had a job. One-fifth saw poverty and unemployment as the sole reason for their offending (Parker 1996). Parker argues that drinking, crime and drug taking all formed part of these offenders' lifestyle and that their relationship changed over time. This was illustrated in one case where the offender's drinking had led to more and more crime. He had drunk for twelve hours a day, every day, when he was 16 and 17. He turned to crime to support this habit and amassed a string of offences involving drunkenness and violence. To this offender, drink was related to his offending:

> it makes you worse if you've had a drink . . . Feel like robbing something . . . I was drinking before and after all my offences . . . I tend to fight more when I've been drinking, if someone looks at me weird. You get paranoid when you've been drinking.

> (Parker 1996: 294)

In an attempt to stay out of trouble he turned to cannabis – not, according to Parker, an atypical pattern. Thus another offender comments: '. . . draw (cannabis) is better than alcohol because it calms you down – less likely to commit crime on draw' (ibid: 294). Yet another offender, a car thief, took amphetamine at night to stay awake for taking cars and used tranquillizers for bringing him down and sleeping during the day. Thus, respondents 'interchanged alcohol and illegal drugs such as cannabis and amphetamine for different purposes at different times' (ibid: 296).

UNDERSTANDING ILLEGAL DRUG USE

Many perspectives on crime are relevant to the study of illegal drug use. Individual and pathological theories focus on the individual drug user and addict and, while these are useful in treating the individual offender, it has already been seen that the pathological image of the 'driven' junkie is far from reality. It has also been pointed out that the physical properties of a drug are mediated by the social and cultural context in which it is used, thus individual factors, while important, must be seen in a broader social context. Many sociological approaches have been applied to drug use and the criminalization of drugs was of particular interest to theories critical of pathological approaches as they illustrated the relative nature of criminal law and a labelling process in which drug takers, labelled as deviant, were cast in the role of 'outsiders' (see Chapter 4). More recent approaches have re-examined these and suggest that the contemporary drugs scene requires different forms of analysis (Ruggiero and South 1995).

To early subcultural theorists, drug subcultures were examples of retreatist subcultures as they appeared to imply a rejection of mainstream culture and the adoption of a retreatist lifestyle associated with, for example, hobos, tramps or bohemian musicians and artists. Later subcultural theories saw drug taking as part of youthful rebellion, and the hippies and other drug users of the 1960s and early 1970s were seen as part of a counter-culture expressed through underground magazines which gave advice, among other things, on how to grow marijuana. The development of the trading charities and mutual societies described by Dorn and his colleagues was associated with this culture, which, as seen, has given way to a culture characterized by competition and distrust (Ruggiero and South 1995).

Drug users and subcultures also provided a good illustration of the central themes of labelling theory, and Becker's original work was based on marijuana using jazz musicians (Becker 1963). Later writers also took up the theme of drugs, paying particular attention to the relationship between drug users and the police. Young, writing in the early 1970s, argued that police reaction against hippies translated a 'fantasy' into reality. At that time hippies, characterized by their style of dress, were associated with frequent drug taking and with an assumed escalation from softer to harder drugs. Young found, however, that drug taking was not a central feature of the subculture but became so in reaction to police activity. The police also restricted the informal supply routes, forcing them to participate in the more organized illegal drugs market which, for some, meant an escalation to harder drugs (Young 1971a, 1971b). To critical criminologists the criminalization of drug use was a further example of the use of the criminal law against groups whose alternative lifestyles were perceived as a threat. It was also argued that the criminal law amplified the problem of illegal drug use by encouraging the involvement of professional and organized crime. Many of these approaches, developed during the liberal climate of the 1960s, were associated with arguments for decriminalization.

The heroin 'epidemic' of the 1980s led to more research into aspects of illegal drug use, which, while informed by earlier sociological approaches, also provided the basis for a critical appreciation of them. Ruggiero and South, for example, argue that recent work on the drugs market suggests the need to re-think the traditional approaches of anomie and subcultural theory. Rather than being a retreatist subculture peopled by passive drug users who have opted out of a search for material goals, drug subcultures can involve intense activity. Instead of representing escapism, involvement in drugs provides a form of activity which functions as an equivalent to legitimate employment. The daily activity of the addict, illustrated above, thus provides an alternative set of activities, rewarded at the end of the day by enjoying the drug (Pearson 1987b). In addition, as seen above, drugs can be part of subcultures based on activity and risk taking (Collison 1996). Ruggiero and South further argue that while the notion of subculture remains powerful, the contemporary drugs market involves many diverse groups who cannot be identified with one specific subculture. Rather, they argue, there are different subgroups whose membership and cultural styles are continually shifting. To them, 'the static image that the idea of "subculture" implies seems increasingly less applicable and relevant to youth trends in late- or post-modern society' (Ruggiero and South 1995: 203). Poly drug use, a variety of cultural styles, commercialization and depoliticization all figure in the contemporary drug scene.

They also discuss explanations linking crime and drugs to poverty and disadvantage, links which have been seen to be far from simple, as illegal drug use spreads across social classes. Nonetheless inequality and structural factors create the conditions in which the drugs economy flourishes in the most disadvantaged areas, and provides an alternative form of employment. As seen above, however, the drugs market, like legitimate industry and organized crime, has involved 'deskilling' and the growth of the 'mass labour market'. The mass labourers in the drugs market may be as disadvantaged in this as in any other form of employment. Mobility is limited and casual labour predominates. While women do participate in the drugs market, female couriers from poor regions are exploited and others face organizations dominated by white male working-class subcultures. This also disadvantages black and other ethnic minority groups – although some have managed to gain some ascendancy in limited segments of the drugs market. This kind of 'labour market analysis' can further assist an understanding of many aspects of the drugs industry (Ruggiero and South 1995).

CONCLUDING COMMENTS

It has been seen in this chapter that the relationship between drugs and crime involves many complex issues. Only some drugs are criminalized and studies of illegal drug use reveal that they are widely used in different settings, from the dance scene to cultures in which heroin use can be an alternative status symbol. The drugs market produces enormous profits for participants, from growers, producers and traffickers to local, street level dealers. It also produces a large amount of secondary crime although the extent of this can be exaggerated. For consumers, drugs are attractive although continued involvement in some forms of drug abuse may be less so, and employees in the drugs industry may find that they run high risks and gain less rewards than they had hoped.

Analyses of the drugs market have several important policy implications. To date, despite intensive policing and the so-called 'war on drugs', the drugs market continues to flourish and supplies largely willing users. Enforcement has been targeted at all the different levels – at the growers, transportation routes, at entry into the country, and at the local street level. Despite much publicized raids it has had relatively little effect. While low-level policing may cut off one source of supply, another emerges. This is partly due to the segregation of the participants. Given this, and the amounts of secondary crime created by illegal drug use, some argue that dangerous drugs should be regulated by the medical profession and subject to licensing arrangements similar to those for tobacco and alcohol. Against this it can be argued that it would vastly increase the use of these drugs and thus have a greater social cost (South 1997). Others argue that cannabis alone should be legalized, on the grounds that it has few adverse effects, some medical use and that legalization would save considerable resources. While this may be a more powerful argument, it has recently been rejected by the government.

The research and analyses outlined also have implications for policies which aim to prevent illegal drug use by targeting potential consumers. Successive campaigns have aimed to educate young people about the dangers of drug use. While few dispute that these campaigns, along with better education about the risks of drug taking, are important, their nature has aroused considerable controversy. Some argue that they should take an uncompromising stand against drugs around the theme of 'just say no' whereas others argue that this kind of campaign is likely to be ineffective as many young people believe that they are making an informed choice about drugs. To them, more education about the dangers of drugs is necessary. This, however, involves providing information about drugs, which others see as implying a tolerance of drug taking.

Review Questions

1. Compile a list of situations in which drug use is seen to be 'normal' and in which it seen to be 'abnormal', including both legal and illegal drugs.
   (a) How does this reveal the social construction of different aspects of drug use and abuse?
   (b) Why do you think that some drugs are criminalized while others are not?
2. South argues that 'enforcement and other drug-control policies must confront the likelihood that the "war on drugs" is not one that can be won' (South 1997: 951). In what ways might an understanding of the organization of the drugs industry lead to this conclusion?
3. Based on the material in this chapter and your key reading, compile a list of points which support and criticize arguments for the decriminalization of all drugs. If working in a group, this can be structured as a debate.

Key Reading

Dorn N, Murji K and South N (1992) *Traffickers: Drugs Markets and Law Enforcement*. London: Routledge

Ruggiero V and South N (1995) *Eurodrugs. Drug Use, Markets and Trafficking in Europe*. London: University College of London Press

South N (1997) 'Drugs: Use, Crime, and Control', in Maguire M, Morgan R and Reiner R (eds) *The Oxford Handbook of Criminology*, 2nd edition. Oxford: Clarendon Press

CHAPTER 15

WHITE COLLAR AND CORPORATE CRIME

White collar crime is generally associated with wealthy and powerful offenders, and a series of recent high-profile cases such as the collapse of Baring's bank and the Bank of Credit and Commerce International (BCCI), along with the Maxwell pensions fraud, have prompted suggestions that it, too, is rising. A spate of transport accidents and 'disasters' in the late 1980s also drew attention to the possible liability of companies when safety rules are broken. These major cases are only the tip of the iceberg as crime committed at work ranges from the 'fiddles' of employees at all levels of employment to multi-million pound financial frauds. It involves small businesses, corner shops and multi-national corporations, salespersons and senior executives. It was also seen in Chapter 13 that it is increasingly difficult to separate legitimate from illegitimate businesses.

This chapter will start by considering how white collar crime is defined before exploring the difficulties of researching this area. It will look at the extent of offences and at some characteristics of offending and victimization. Subsequent sections will investigate specific aspects. Earlier chapters have referred to the neglected area of corporate or institutional 'violence' which will be explored before turning to one of the biggest frauds in recent years, the BCCI case, and at some work looking at why managers might commit or conspire in illegal acts. Finally, as with other chapters, different approaches to understanding white collar crime will be outlined before concluding with some points about controlling this form of crime.

WHAT IS WHITE COLLAR AND CORPORATE CRIME?

The definition of white collar crime has always been contentious (Croall 1992; Langan 1996; Nelken 1997). It was first defined by Edwin Sutherland in 1941 as 'crime committed by persons of high social status and respectability in the course of their occupations' (Sutherland 1949: 9). He questioned the existing focus on lower-class offenders by pointing to the illegal activities of those involved in business and commerce, sparking off a long debate about the definition and status of white collar crime. The following are some of the many issues which have been raised.

269

Is white collar crime 'crime'?

In his research Sutherland included activities, such as false advertising or food adulteration, which were not at the time covered by the criminal law but which he argued were equally as harmful as many crimes. He was attacked, however, on the grounds that criminologists should not include acts which were not crime nor should they imply that some acts *should* be crime (Tappan 1977). This led to extensive debates over whether white collar crime was 'really' crime, and its criminal status has always been contested (Nelken 1997). This prompted critical criminologists to ask why 'criminal' activities of the 'powerful' were not subject to the same kind of criminalization.

Is white collar crime 'real' crime?

Many business activities are subject to the criminal law but are often seen as 'not really crime', making their criminal status ambiguous (Aubert 1977; Croall 1992; Nelken 1997). While some forms of white collar crime, such as embezzlement or fraud, are generally accepted as 'real' crime, others, such as breaches of health, safety or environmental law, are more likely to be seen as 'quasi' or 'technical' crimes, descriptions used by offenders in court to argue that they are 'not really criminal' (Croall 1988). Many of these offences are not enforced by the police but by other agencies whose role is to ensure compliance with regulations. This can involve persuading offenders to comply, setting up educational programmes and providing advice, with prosecution often being seen as a last resort (see, for example, Croall 1992). A different language surrounds these 'regulatory' offences. The literature often refers to 'regulation' rather than 'policing' or 'controlling', 'wrongdoing' rather than 'crime', 'violations' or 'breaches' rather than 'offences', and 'sanctions' rather than 'punishment' (Cook 1989; Croall 1992). The 'problems' involved are not seen as 'crime problems' but may be described as, for example, problems of 'ethics' or 'standards' in business or as problems of occupational health and safety, food safety, consumer protection or environmental policy. And, as seen earlier, events in which death, injury or disease result from inattention to regulations are generally described as 'incidents', 'accidents' or even 'disasters' rather than 'crimes' (Wells 1993).

Who are the offenders?

Another set of problems surrounds Sutherland's inclusion of the high status and respectability of offenders (Shapiro 1990; Croall 1992; Ruggiero 1996a). This directs attention to the offenders rather than to their activities and creates difficulties for researchers. How can the rather vague terms 'high status' or 'respectable' be defined and operationalized? Employees at all levels steal from their employers, defraud consumers and neglect or circumvent regulations (Levi 1987; Croall 1989). Are only some to be counted as white collar offenders? If so where is the line to be drawn?

Crime at work

To some, the most important aspect of Sutherland's definition is its emphasis on legitimate occupations, and white collar crime can be seen as a breach of the trust involved in an occupational role (Shapiro 1990; Croall 1992). People are employed to carry out work which employers or clients cannot do themselves, in some cases because they lack the specialist skills, technological expertise or professional knowledge. This means that the employer or client must trust the employee or service provider, as, in many cases, they cannot assess the quality or value of the service provided. This is the case whether the offender is a building labourer or a large corporation; thus some prefer to define white collar crime as occupational crime.

Individual, corporate and organizational crime

One difficulty with this conception, and indeed with Sutherland's, is the wide variety of activities which it includes and there have been attempts to develop subcategories. A major distinction is often made between crimes *against* organizations where offences are carried out individually or in groups by employees or service providers for their own personal gain, and crimes *for* organizations in which the motive is not personal gain but the profitability or survival of the organization. The former is often described as 'occupational crime' and the latter as corporate crime. As not all organizations are 'corporations' but can be public sector organizations, the term organizational crime is often used in preference. While this distinction is widely used, it is not watertight – some crimes, like corruption or tax evasion, could fall into either category, and the phrase 'crimes for organizations' may be misleading as organizational offences do not always benefit the organization. It could rarely be said, for example, that the deaths or injuries of workers or consumers or the defrauding of pensions funds benefit the organization (see, for example, Punch 1996).

The characteristics of white collar and organizational crime

Given the diverse nature of this area of crime, can it be clearly distinguished from what is often described as 'conventional' crime? A number of characteristics, summarized below, have been identified which, while not unique to white collar crime, taken together do differentiate it from many other forms of crime (Clarke 1990; Croall 1992; Langan 1996).

- Offences tend to be *invisible*. Their relationship to offenders' occupational roles makes them easier to conceal – as Clarke (1990) points out, offenders are legitimately present at the scene of the crime. Victims may be slow to realize that anything is wrong and concealment may rely on offenders' 'inside knowledge' of organizational procedures (Clarke 1990; Croall 1992).

271

- They are often extremely *complex* as they rely on technical or scientific knowledge. Many participants may be involved and it may not be easy to trace how the offence was carried out and by whom. This may take months and even years of investigation.

- Within organizations a *'diffusion of responsibility'*, in which functions and responsibilities are delegated, makes it difficult to legally or morally identify a 'guilty' person. While one person may have broken a rule, others are responsible for issuing instructions and monitoring compliance. Individuals can therefore 'pass the buck' up or down the chain of responsibility with employees 'blaming' employers for not preventing offences and employers blaming employees for failing to comply with instructions (Croall 1992; Fisse and Braithwaite 1993; Wells 1993).

- *Victimization* is also *diffuse*. As seen in Chapter 5, many white collar offences have what Sutherland described as a 'rippling effect', affecting individuals very little but yielding considerable profits (Sutherland 1949). In other cases there is no direct relationship between the offender and victim as where, for example, an employee's failure to check a safety device causes an injury.

- The invisibility and complexity of offences makes them difficult to *detect*.

- They are also difficult to *prosecute* due to the difficulties of obtaining sufficient evidence and establishing who is the 'guilty party'.

- This means that white collar offences are often characterized as enjoying *lenient treatment*, with few being prosecuted and even fewer ending up in prison.

- This in turn is related to their *ambiguous criminal status*, outlined above.

THE SCOPE OF WHITE COLLAR AND CORPORATE CRIME

Research problems

Many of the difficulties of researching and assessing the extent of this area of crime can be inferred from the preceding discussion. Official statistics are particularly unreliable as so few offences are detected, reported and prosecuted. They do not fit legal offence categories and regulatory offences, being non-indictable, are not all listed separately. These are dealt with by a vast range of enforcement agencies and Inspectorates including those dealing with, for example, financial, customs and excise, health and safety, consumer protection and pollution regulations, whose records, which are not all widely available, do not always indicate numbers of known and detected offences. It was pointed out in Chapter 5 that victim surveys do not cover white collar and corporate crime although some surveys, such as the third Islington Crime Survey, have included questions on commercial and health and safety at work offences (Pearce 1992), and others have carried out surveys of institutional victims (Levi 1988). These are inevitably limited to offences of which many victims are aware but, as seen earlier, some are not.

Other forms of research are also difficult. Samples of offenders are difficult to obtain and, as so many offences are hidden in occupational routines, can only be studied by participant observation or in-depth interviewing (see, for example, Ditton 1977; Mars 1982). Researchers, however, are rarely in a position to carry out such research, especially in financial and commercial enterprises. The complexity of offences also means that considerable financial, scientific or legal expertise is required to fully analyse them (Levi 1987). Enforcement agencies are more approachable and have been the subject of many revealing studies which have explored how offences and offenders are typified and how enforcement decisions are made (see, for example, Carson 1971; Hawkins 1984; Hutter 1988; Cook 1989). As is the case for professional and organized crime, a variety of other sources are used including individual case studies, investigative journalism, court observation and reports, cases reported in the mass media, and interviews with enforcers.

The nature and extent of offences

Given all these difficulties it is virtually impossible to estimate the extent of white collar crime, although many so-called 'guesstimates' argue that it probably exceeds the costs of conventional crime. Levi (1987), for example, estimated that in 1985 the total cost of fraud reported to fraud squads amounted to £2,113 million, which was twice the cost of theft, burglary and robbery in that year. In a survey of 56 large corporations he also found that almost 40 per cent reported at least one fraud costing over £50,000. As will be seen below, major frauds involve billions of pounds, and the BCCI case was initially estimated to have involved £5–15 billion (*Sunday Times* 14/7/91). Recent publicity has also surrounded the high cost of frauds on the National Health Service with the Healthcare Financial Management Association having recently estimated that 'tens of millions of pounds' are being lost by prescriptions frauds and false claims of payment by doctors, dentists, pharmacists and opticians (*The Guardian* 24/6/97: 8). As with professional and organized crime, its potential effect can be indicated by listing some of its major forms, as in Figure 15.1, which is not exhaustive.

It has also been argued that white collar crime has increased in recent years, with the high-profile cases referred to above and many other smaller pensions and financial frauds. While, as Nelken (1997) points out, it is impossible to estimate if white collar crime has increased as its extent has never been established, a number of factors have been associated with a possible increase. Punch (1996) argues, for example, that the deregulation and globalization of financial markets in the 1980s increased opportunities for crime, the declining

Figure 15.1 Forms of white collar and corporate crime

Occupational crime

- Employee theft which includes money, goods or intangibles such as 'computer time' (Mars 1982).
- Frauds on consumers, including abstracting money from accounts, overcharging or charging for work which has not been done.
- 'Fiddling' expenses.
- Tax evasion, which includes 'moonlighting' (working outside formal employment but not declaring this to tax authorities), failing to disclose all earnings, evading VAT.
- Frauds on the NHS, including prescriptions frauds.
- Sales frauds including those perpetrated through telecommunications networks.

Computer crime

Includes many of the above activities in which computers are used and also includes crimes specific to computers such as computer hacking, stealing competitors' mailing lists and the many sales frauds now perpetrated via the Internet.

Corporate/organizational crime

Crimes against consumers include

- 'Food frauds' – adulterating or falsely describing the contents of food.
- Manufacturing or selling food 'unfit for human consumption', which includes food poisoning.
- Selling goods with short weight, which includes food, alcohol and other goods.
- Offences under the Trade Descriptions Act, which includes car 'clocking' (turning back the odometers of cars), counterfeiting and otherwise misdescribing the quality or contents of goods.
- Manufacturing or selling dangerous goods, including toys (this may also involve some counterfeit goods).

Health and safety offences include

- Failure to comply with health and safety regulations covering all industrial or commercial premises and also transport. These include considerations of:
  - passenger safety
  - the safety of workers
  - the safety of consumers
  - the safety of the general public – for example, in leisure centres, adventure centres, fairs and playgrounds, football matches and as residents

Environmental offences include breaking regulations to prevent pollution such as those involving:

- the safety of water for consumers;
- rivers and coastal waters;
- the control of toxic emissions and toxic waste.

Financial frauds, including those involving

- The sale of financial services such as pensions or savings plans.
- Insurance frauds, including those where companies 'torch' or set fire to premises to claim insurance where the business is failing.

Corruption

---

power of trade unions and the climate of deregulation which curtailed the resources of enforcement agencies hindered detection and the growth of the 'spirit of enterprise' created a moral climate encouraging the prioritization of profits at the expense of consumers and workers.

Offenders

As so few offenders are prosecuted it is difficult to determine their characteristics, although there are some indications that they are not from such high-status backgrounds as is often assumed (Croall 1989; Langan 1996). For example, Levi (1987) argues that prosecutions for fraud more often involve 'mavericks' than 'elite insiders' and Clarke (1989) found that businesses resorting to arson as a form of insurance fraud were mainly small businesses with financial difficulties. Cook (1989) found that the Inland Revenue tend to prosecute moonlighting builders and small video stores whose offences are cheap and easy to investigate, and in a study of consumer protection legislation, the majority of convicted offenders were small rather than large businesses – butchers, bakers, grocers and corner shops – rather than large multi-national corporations who formed only a small minority (Croall 1989). Other studies have also found many offenders whose businesses lie on the margins of legality and illegality – often described by enforcers as 'rogues' or 'cowboys' – who are more akin to 'shady operators' (Sutton and Wild 1985; Croall 1989).

This, as with other forms of crime, can reflect the activities of enforcement agencies and the vulnerability of different kinds of offenders to detection and prosecution. It was pointed out above that enforcement agencies tend to prosecute only a small number of known offenders and deal with others by persuading them to comply or negotiate out-of-court settlements. 'Rogues', 'cowboys' and other small businesses may be perceived to be either unwilling or unable to change their operations and therefore more 'deserving' of prosecution. Their offences are more visible as they are more often involved in selling directly to the public – the white collar equivalent of street crime – whereas large organizations can more easily conceal their operations (Hutter 1988; Croall 1989). Small businesses may also be vulnerable in that their operations are less complex and the proprietor is more readily identifiable as the responsible person (Croall 1989).

Wealthy offenders or large corporations can more easily avoid breaking the law as they can employ expert advice on how to stay within the 'letter' of the law while flouting its 'spirit' (McBarnet 1988). Tax accountants specialize in finding legal loopholes for clients to avoid paying taxes, and legal, scientific, financial and technical advisers may be employed to find ways around the law (McBarnet 1988). Smaller businesses are less able to afford this advice. If larger businesses do break the law, they may also use expert advisers to negotiate with enforcers and to contest cases in court – producing more lenient outcomes (Croall 1989). As with other forms of crime, there is therefore no simple relationship between social status and offending although the relative absence of wealthy and powerful offenders does not imply that they are intrinsically more law abiding.

Far less is known about the age, gender and 'race' of offenders although, as seen in Chapter 7, it is reasonable to assume that white collar offenders are older as some degree of age and experience is necessary to commit offences. The race or ethnicity of offenders has not been systematically explored, although as with other forms of crime offences may be associated with 'outsiders' and 'mavericks', with immigrants and foreigners whose commercial ethics are assumed to be inferior. There is little evidence, however, to substantiate this. It has also been seen that white collar and corporate offending is assumed to be male dominated. While women's share of fraud is higher than for other crimes, this is attributable to non-white collar forms of cheque and credit card fraud (Levi 1994). In very general terms there have been few 'notorious' female white collar offenders to compare with the male defendants in the *Guinness* trials, the BCCI executives, or the managing directors of firms who have been charged with corporate manslaughter (Levi 1994). This may be because women are less often found in positions with so many opportunities to commit high-profile white collar or corporate offences. Nonetheless women are convicted for white collar offences and a small proportion of small business offenders were female proprietors and employees (Croall 1989). More research is needed, however, to establish whether women do, as is sometimes suggested, have more business integrity (Levi 1994).

Patterns of victimization

There has been less systematic exploration of victimization from white collar than from other forms of crime and, as seen earlier, it is not easy to capture in victim surveys. Some offences, such as insider trading or corruption, are seen as victimless although the former adversely affects investors and lack of trust in financial markets or standards in public life can adversely affect business and government (Croall 1992). Institutional victims such as the government or companies may be seen as 'able to afford it' although the public pays higher prices and taxes to make up for losses from white collar crime. White collar crime also involves power. It was seen earlier that offences often involve an abuse of an occupational role, involving scientific, technical or professional expertise. Thus some offences involve the power of the knowledgeable seller, producer or service provider over the less knowledgeable client or consumer. This need not imply a class relationship – the employer who lacks computer skills may be powerless in the face of the computer expert and the middle-class car owner powerless in the face of the garage mechanic. On the other hand, as for other forms of crime, the more affluent may more easily avoid risks as they can choose not to work in dangerous workplaces, live near polluting industries and are less likely to employ 'cowboy' builders (Croall 1997). In addition, poorer victims may suffer disproportionately.

Victims of organizational crime are generally described as consumers, workers or the general public, but other forms of inequality, as indicated in Chapters 5 and 8, can be involved. While some offences do affect people indiscriminately, others affect specific groups. Producers and sellers design and 'market' products for specific groups and, for example, cheap, substandard and often counterfeit goods will most often be targeted at poorer consumers. Gender is involved as many products and services, reflecting idealized images of masculinity and femininity, are targeted specifically at men or women. Some of the most notorious examples of corporate crime have involved products designed to alter women's bodies either through cultural representations of 'beauty' or through controlling their reproductive capacities (Szockyj and Fox 1996). The notorious Dalkon Shield contraceptive was marketed world wide on the basis of falsified test results, and led to many deaths, infertility and illness. Current concerns include 'cosmetic surgery' and the use of silicone breast implants which can cause permanent damage and whose side effects are not emphasized (Croall 1995; Szockyj and Fox 1996). Many women follow intensively marketed diets, many of which do not work and some of which carry health risks (Croall 1995). While these latter are not 'criminal' offences, there have been calls to subject some of the worst abuses to the Trade Descriptions Act as they are inherently misleading (Croall 1995).

Workers, as will be seen below, are victimized by occupationally related diseases contracted from the substances they work with, by being paid low wages or by being endangered, killed or injured through neglect of safety regulations. As seen in Chapter 8, many fatalities and injuries are associated with traditionally male-based industries, and in such 'man's work' 'accidents' are often attributed to the intrinsic risks and dangers rather than to the neglect of safety precautions which may be the immediate cause of the 'accident' (Carson 1981). Women, on the other hand, can be the victims of long-term health risks in, for example, the food industry. They are also particularly vulnerable to low pay, harassment and illegal discrimination (Croall 1995; Szockyj and Fox 1996). It was also seen in Chapter 8 that women's assumed financial or technical incompetence may make them vulnerable to, for example, car repair and service and financial frauds (Croall 1995). Age is also relevant, as illustrated by the abuse of the elderly or young in institutions and the exploitation of the middle aged and elderly by pensions frauds, the most dramatic example being the plundering of the pension funds of Maxwell employees (Punch 1996).

Victimization by white collar crime can compound victimization from other forms of crime and can also be repeat victimization – most people are probably the victims of several white collar offences each month. It can also have widespread and often devastating effects on local communities – as happens, for example, in major pollution incidents or so-called 'disasters'. This illustrates the point made by Box that, while the effects of corporate crime are often seen as trivial, or economic rather than physical, corporate crime can kill and injure (Box 1983).

DIMENSIONS OF WHITE COLLAR AND CORPORATE CRIME

'Institutional violence'

The high toll of so-called institutional violence has already been referred to, and while many deaths and injuries result from corporate misconduct, it is difficult to identify an organization as a 'killer' 'guilty' of murder or assault. This section will outline the impact of some forms of what we shall call 'corporate misconduct', because many of the cases explored have not resulted in criminal convictions although they involve breaches of criminally enforced regulations. It will then go on to explore how and why these cases are often not dealt with or constructed as crime.

Corporate victimization

What has been described as the world's worst industrial accident took place in the Indian town of Bhopal in December 1984, where an explosion released the poisonous gas, methyl isocyanate, into the atmosphere. This killed between 3,000 and 5,000 people, more than 200,000 were injured and, in the areas most affected, at least 90 per cent of families were affected by the death or severe incapacitation of at least one parent (Pearce and Tombs 1993; Punch 1996). While the 'cause' of this disaster has never been fully established, it emerged that the plant, run by Union Carbide, was poorly designed and run down and had less adequate safety systems than equivalent plants in the United States. The case illustrates how Western companies operate in third world countries with more lenient regulations, a problem which also affects the export of pharmaceutical and other products found to be unsafe in the West (Braithwaite 1984). Companies often justify this by claiming that they are providing much needed employment or medicines to the third world (Ruggiero 1996a).

In Britain a large but unknowable number of deaths result from failure to comply with safety regulations. Figure 15.2 lists some of the best-known cases in the last decade. The inquiries following many of the transport 'disasters' found evidence of sloppy safety procedures and a neglect of safety. Around 500 people each year are also killed at work, and while it is difficult to ascertain how many of these deaths are the result of offences, this is assumed to be a major contributing factor (Tombs 1990; Wells 1993; Slapper 1994). Reports carried out by the Health and Safety Executive in the 1980s indicated that, in at least two-thirds of fatal accidents, managers had violated the Health and Safety at Work etc. Act (Tombs 1990). Yet only around one-sixth of these deaths result in prosecution (ibid), and prosecutions and convictions for corporate manslaughter are rare – until 1994, none had been successful (Slapper 1994). These kinds of incident affect different groups, for example:

Figure 15.2 Deaths as a result of institutional misconduct

- 192 passengers died when the *Herald of Free Enterprise* sank near Zeebrugge in 1987. The company and several of its directors and employees were charged unsuccessfully with corporate manslaughter (Wells 1993).

- In 1987, 31 people died in a fire in King's Cross Station, London. No prosecutions followed although a subsequent report was critical of management safety policies (Wells 1993).

- In 1987, 34 people died in a rail crash in Clapham, London, which was subsequently found to have been due to faulty signal wiring. British Rail was convicted for failing to ensure the safety of employees and passengers (Wells 1993).

- 51 people died in a collision involving a pleasure boat, the *Marchioness*, in 1989 – Department of Transport safety policies were severely criticized (Wells 1993). Private prosecutions followed without a successful conviction.

- In 1994, four teenagers were drowned in Lyme Regis Bay while staying at an adventure centre. The two directors of the company were convicted of manslaughter – the company had used unqualified staff and ignored safety warnings (*The Independent* 9/12/94, cited in Croall 1997).

- Six passengers were killed at Ramsgate when a ferry passenger walkway collapsed – four companies were prosecuted in 1995 (Croall 1997).

- At least two local authorities have been convicted and fined following the deaths of tenants from carbon monoxide poisoning caused by inadequately maintained gas appliances. In 1995 the London Borough of Greenwich was fined £5,000 following the deaths of two tenants; and one resident died and at least 800 were endangered when Manchester City Council fitted gas heaters incorrectly (Slapper 1994; Croall 1997).

WORKERS

Workers are not only affected by safety regulations but can also die as a result of diseases contracted at work, most notably from asbestos but also from lung disease and occupationally related cancers (Tombs 1998). While these may not involve criminal offences they raise important issues about employers' concern for workers' health. A variety of less fatal illnesses have also been attributed to exposure to inadequately tested substances. In the chemicals industry, for example, workers are exposed to potentially toxic mixes of chemicals whose effects may be unknown (Tombs 1998). In the food industry workers, many of them women, face dangers from working with high concentrations of food additives which cause a variety of reactions as workers are subjected to higher concentrations of substances than consumers (Miller 1985).

CONSUMERS

Consumers can be endangered by a range of common, everyday items. Prosecutions under food laws reveal a variety of injuries caused by 'foreign objects' in food which include glass, bits of wood, sticking plasters and even caustic soda. These enter the food during preparation and often result from inattention to quality or safety controls (Croall 1992). Food poisoning, recently the subject of much attention, can kill and cause considerable discomfort – although it is difficult to establish the 'chain of evidence' linking an outbreak to a particular shop or restaurant (Croall 1992). Increases in food poisoning have been attributed to the growth of take-aways, fast food and eating out. While prosecutions are rare because of evidential difficulties, in 1992 Environmental Health Officers issued 156,000 written warnings to food establishments and prosecuted 2,253 cases, of which 1,760 led to convictions. More than 700 outlets were closed and in 6,500 cases contaminated food was seized or surrendered (Croall 1997). Issues of food safety and compliance with regulations are also raised in connection with BSE and the recent outbreak of *E. coli* food poisoning in Scotland, responsible for the deaths of 20 consumers. In this latter case investigations and legal action are still under way and following one unsuccessful prosecution of the butcher who sold the infected meat, there have been calls for a Public Inquiry (*The Scotsman* 28/10/97: 1). Consumer safety has also been seen to be an issue in relation to the production and sale of counterfeit goods, dangerous toys and cheap, fake perfume (Croall 1997).

POLLUTION

Neglect of regulations can also lead to pollution which can cause a variety of illnesses, allergic reactions and aggravates respiratory conditions. It can also kill wild life and fish. In its thirty-fourth conviction since privatization in 1990, Severn Trent was convicted following a chemical leak which killed 33,000 salmon (Croall 1997). Dirty beaches and rivers have been associated with a variety of diseases and sickness, and consumers in Camelford suffered a variety of problems including skin rashes, nausea and vomiting following the discharge of aluminium sulphate into the water supply (Croall 1992).

Are corporations and institutions criminal?

How can this toll of death, disease and injury be related to 'crime'? Or, to put the question in a different way – why is it *not* widely regarded as crime? While some companies are prosecuted it is often for lesser offences than that of manslaughter. Many prosecutions fail and many companies are not prosecuted at all, even for breaches of regulations that have been identified. This is related to the way in which the criminal law defines offences. Popular and legal conceptions of crime, as seen, rely on the guilty individual who knowingly and intentionally commits an offence (see, for example, Wells 1993).

Corporations are not individuals, they have no mind, and therefore cannot intend harm, although they are legally liable for some offences of their employees. In addition, those within corporations or organizations do not intend to kill or injure workers or consumers and, as seen above, the diffusion of responsibility makes it difficult to pinpoint the 'guilty' party, although recklessness about the results of actions can and does form the basis of prosecutions. Nonetheless, the immediate cause of an offence may not be the root cause as many other factors are involved. The case of the sinking of the *Herald of Free Enterprise* provides a useful illustration.

The immediate cause of this 'disaster' was the failure by the assistant bosun to close the bow doors of the ferry as he had fallen asleep. The chief officer and the captain should both have checked that the doors were closed, but had not done so. There was also no system to check that the doors were closed and a proposal to install alarm bells had been rejected. This directs the 'blame' to senior executives and to the company itself. The Sheen Report into the incident concluded that:

> All concerned in management, from the members of the Board of Directors down to the junior superintendents, were guilty of fault in that all must be regarded as sharing responsibility for the failure of management. From top to bottom the body corporate was infected with the disease of sloppiness.
>
> (Sheen Report 1987: para 14.1, cited in Wells 1993: 47)

While the immediate cause of this disaster was therefore relatively straightforward, attributing responsibility was far more complex. The speed at which the ferry had to turn around to maximize trips, the long shifts which the assistant bosun had to work, repeated warnings about previous occasions when ferries had sailed with open doors and the inherent design weaknesses of roll on–roll off ferries have all been advanced as contributory factors (Wells 1993; Tombs 1998). Corporate offences therefore involve far more complex cause and effect relationships than conventional crimes.

This makes prosecution both risky, in terms of securing a conviction, and expensive – the failed prosecution against P&O, the company involved in the *Herald* case, was estimated to have cost £1 million (Wells 1993). In addition, regulatory agencies are less skilled than the police in gathering evidence for major criminal and murder trials. While major incidents involving multiple deaths do lead to prosecutions, they are often for relatively minor charges which are easier to prove and attract lower penalties. The diffusion of responsibility also enables defendants to claim that it was 'someone else's fault' and the absence of intent enables them to claim that they intended no harm (Croall 1988). While organizations may therefore accept their legal responsibility, they can deny any moral fault. A further problem is that companies and organizations cannot be punished in the same way as other offenders. They cannot be sent to prison, and closing them down or fining them too punitively could affect 'innocent' shareholders and employees. Punishment, like criminal responsibility, relies on the notion of the individual offender and companies can less easily be 'rehabilitated' or put on probation. While, as will be seen below, some of these problems can be overcome, they illustrate some of the reasons why institutional 'violence' lies outside the social and legal construction of crime.

The biggest fraud: BCCI

The global nature of financial frauds and the blurred boundaries between white collar and organized crime are well illustrated the case of BCCI, more jocularly described as the 'Bank of Crooks and Criminals International', or the 'Bank of Cannabis and Cocaine International', which was closed in 1991 amidst revelations of widespread fraud and corruption. Founded by Agha Hasan Abedi, who aimed to make it the largest third world bank to serve 'little countries' and 'little people', it grew rapidly and attracted investments on a global scale from major investors in Arab countries, small businesses, British local authorities and third world countries (Passas 1995). When it was closed, its liabilities were estimated to be around $10 billion owed to 800,000 depositors in 1.2 million accounts in over 70 countries (Passas 1995). One indictment spoke of a $20 billion swindle, UK local authorities were said to have lost up to £100 million, and the Western Isles council lost around £24 million (Croall 1992). At his trial, one of the participants, Abbas Ghokal, was said to have run up a £795 million debt to the bank and to have been involved with a series of swindles, false documents, and a sham financial structure which funded his lavish lifestyle (*The Guardian* 3/4/97).

Within the bank, said by the Governor of the Bank of England to have been dominated by a 'criminal culture', illegal activities included nepotism, money laundering, mismanagement, bribery, corruption of politicians, evasion of foreign exchange regulations, false accounting, misappropriation of depositors' money, blackmail, massive fraud and the provision of finance for illegal arms deals (Punch 1996; Passas 1995). It involved what Punch describes as a 'litany of villains', including Manuel Noriega who used it to launder funds from drug smuggling and fraud in Panama, and was also used to launder money for major drug cartels, illegal arms dealers, terrorists and secret service organizations (Punch 1996). It was also used by thousands of legitimate businesses and depositors. The bank made losses in stock market trading, using clients' money to cover a series of fictitious loans, and money was shifted around from one account to another, from country to country, thereby evading the regulators of any one country.

The scope of the frauds defies simple explanation (Passas 1995). According to Punch, a number of factors were involved. Often mentioned is the personal autocratic style of the bank's founder, traditional Asian banking practices and the strong bonds between many employees. These banking practices included providing services to clients such as favourable treatment, nepotism and lavish hospitality. Abedi is said to have drawn in unscrupulous operators and serious criminals and to have had a cavalier attitude to paper and accounts. There were ample opportunities for corruption and internal critics were bought off. The bank had a fragmented structure which included a 'bank within a bank' registered in the Cayman Islands, and shell companies in the Cayman Islands and the Netherlands Antilles. This made the bank difficult to control, gave almost total power to Abedi and enabled it to evade international controls. There were many signals that the bank was suspect – but regulators were slow to react. To Punch, it was protected by the involvement of security services and the limited resources of regulators who focused on money laundering rather than the bank itself. The frauds were extremely complex and difficult to unravel. In addition it involved middle eastern money, which may have made Western governments reluctant to threaten investment and political relationships (Punch 1996).

This case illustrates many of the characteristic features of white collar crime. The frauds were enormously complex, particularly in view of the global nature of the operation and the involvement of so many different groups. Regulatory agencies, including the Bank of England, were criticized for their slow response. The bank became a basically criminal organization, in which cooking the books became a way of life. It circumvented regulation and thrived in the absence of global regulation. The case also provides a good example of the interconnections between legitimate businesses, organized crime, terrorists and security services – for whom the bank provided an essential service.

Why do managers break the law?

In a recent text based on studies of managers in the United States and Europe, Punch (1996) explores the circumstances in which managers resort to law breaking, which he relates to the nature of organizations themselves. While organizations maintain a 'front' of orderliness and rationality, behind this, he argues, are shadow organizations in which organizations use 'dirty workers' to do 'dirty tricks' like undermining competition or industrial espionage. Managers therefore have to manage the duality between 'clean' and 'dirty activities'. The diffusion of responsibility also means that they feel removed from the consequences of their actions and, when breaking the law, can draw on a variety of ideological rationalizations, like the techniques of neutralization outlined in Chapter 3 (Sykes and Matza 1957; Punch 1996). These include claiming that they were 'only following orders', that 'business is business' or that breaking regulations is justifiable as 'government is stifling enterprise'.

Punch draws a portrait of the 'managerial mind and personality structure'. Rather than seeing managers who break the law as 'bad people' he argues that the conditions in which they work shape their moral consciousness and induces ordinary people to violate laws and rules. The search for profits, often seen as a source of offending, is important – while managers are not daily obsessed by profits they underpin decision making at key moments. Managers may also be persuaded to commit crimes for 'the good of the organization' in situations where not doing so would indicate an absence of loyalty – some crimes may be 'crimes of obedience' (Punch 1996: 241). Within organizations, individual feelings give way to organizational 'group think' as managers are socialized into an identification with the company. This may lead to a form of tunnel vision where the interests of the organization override personal morality and individuals engage in self-deception by denying the immorality of the group's actions. They may, for example, receive evidence that a product they are marketing is unsafe, but continue to believe in the product as damaging evidence is filtered out in a form of 'cognitive dissonance'. They thus experience a conflict between personal and organizational morality, which, when combined with a realization that achievement is not sufficient for success, leads to their becoming 'calculating, manipulative, devious, heartless amoral chameleons' (Punch 1996: 244). Like other offenders, law-breaking managers may have different 'moral careers'. Some break the law instrumentally and only temporarily, others blunder into misconduct, and yet others engage in lengthy conspiracies. In extreme cases, such as BCCI, the organization becomes a criminal organization although most businessmen rarely see what they are doing as illegal, unethical or criminal (Punch 1996).

Some forms of organizational crime can, like violent or property crime, provide fun, excitement and 'sneaky thrills'. Business culture values risk takers and gamblers – like the entrepreneurs discussed in Chapter 13 (Punch 1996; Ruggiero 1996a). As seen in Chapter 8, elements of masculinity may also be reflected in the businessman's aggressive pursuit of profits and success. Thus, argues Punch, business is often likened to war and gendered images are common. Takeovers are described as love affairs or marriages, with aggressive ones likened to rape or warfare. The acquiring company is depicted as 'macho' and the target company as female. A mythology of toughness surrounds corporate heroes and vendettas and personal battles illustrate the importance of power and control. Levi similarly points to the gendered images of aggressive masculine executives in films such as *Wall Street*, and to the sentiments voiced by merchant bankers that the 'City is a place for men, not for boys' (Levi 1994: 241). He also points out, however, that linking white collar crime to masculinity would over-predict crime, as many male executives or managers do not turn to crime, and many resort to crime not to satisfy a taste for the high life or to display aggressive masculinity, but from a perception that bankruptcy is imminent or a business will not survive (Levi 1994).

UNDERSTANDING WHITE COLLAR AND CORPORATE CRIME

It has been more difficult to apply many of the traditional theories of crime to white collar crime, particularly as so many focused on the lower-class offender. Pathological theories are particularly limited – as Sutherland (1949: 257–8) commented, criminologists

> would suggest in only a jocular sense that the crimes of the Ford Motor Company are due to the Oedipus complex, those of the Aluminium Company of America to an inferiority complex, or those of the US Steel Corporation to frustration and aggression, or those of du Pont to traumatic experience.

Similarly anomie theory was more difficult to apply, with greed, rather than need, often seen to be at the heart of white collar offending (Box 1983; Punch 1996). The cultural tolerance of many offences also made subcultural theory appear less appropriate and, as offenders are by and large not seen as deviant, labelling perspectives were similarly not applied (Box 1983; Croall 1992). Radical and critical criminologists focused less on offenders and offences than on the relationship between business power and the law implied in the lesser criminalization of white collar crime (see Chapter 4). Recent work on white collar and corporate crime reflects a variety of perspectives, some informed by earlier theories and others looking at the organizational aspects of offences.

Criminogenic organizations?

As white collar and corporate crime rely on occupational and organizational roles, attention has turned to the organization, which has often been characterized as 'criminogenic' (Croall 1992; Punch 1996). To Punch, the organization is the offender, the means, the setting, the rationale, the opportunity and also the victim of corporate deviance (Punch 1996). The diffusion of responsibility can, as seen above, assist offending by distancing individuals from responsibility and thereby from guilt. In addition, the source of much corporate crime lies, as indicated in the P&O case, in organizational systems and standard operating procedures which should ensure the prevention of law breaking. These may not be fully enforced, and in some organizations the prioritization of profits or, in non-profit-making organizations, efficiency has often been seen to lead to systems being ignored in the face of, for example, competitive pressure or the pressure for increasing output or sales (Croall 1992).

Occupations and organizations also provide different kinds of 'illegitimate opportunity structures'. Not all employees have the opportunity to evade taxes or handle cash and some occupations are particularly criminogenic or 'fiddle prone' (Mars 1982). These include those relying on the use of specialist knowledge where the 'ignorant' consumer or employer is particularly vulnerable. Professional occupations who have the power to 'diagnose' problems and suggest solutions are particularly criminogenic, as are occupations like car sales and services (see, for example, Croall 1992). Other occupations are fiddle prone because workers have autonomy in their work, are not closely overlooked and handle money – thus the sales representative has more opportunities for fiddling than the supermarket cashier (Mars 1982). 'Gatekeepers', a category which includes actual gatekeepers and occupations such as brokers, are responsible for introducing clients to service providers, which provides many opportunities for corruption (Mars 1982).

The economic environment within which organizations operate can also be related to offending. Some forms of white collar crime increase during recessions where the need to prioritize profits or to survive can take precedence over compliance with regulations. This can increase costs and crimes may be committed to raise necessary cash, or desperate business proprietors may burn their premises to gain the insurance money. In this situation businesses face a form of anomie – with opportunities for success being blocked and crime being an 'innovative' response (Box 1987). Other forms of offending flourish in boom times – insider dealing, aggressive takeovers and many financial crimes may expand with the increasing opportunities offered by a buoyant market (ibid). The law and its enforcement also form a key part of the business environment. A 'rational' decision to offend may be affected by calculations of how great the chances are of being caught, prosecuted and sentenced. The small chance of prosecution and the scarce resources of enforcers have been seen to provide a favourable regulatory environment (Box 1987; Croall 1992).

This can also be affected by economic policies which, as seen in Chapter 6, have been dominated by 'free market' principles discouraging intervention in the industrial sphere. This, along with the 'spirit of enterprise', arguably provided an ideal moral climate for many forms of business crime as the aggressive pursuit of profits became morally acceptable (Punch 1996). It also led to what has been described as 'deregulation', which constrained the powers and resources of law enforcers. In respect of tax evasion, Cook points to the conflict of values between *laissez-faire* and welfarism. Under *laissez-faire* values taxation is seen as unfair and over-taxation is resisted. In this climate, 'beating' the Inland Revenue becomes a legitimate 'sport' whereas taking from what is 'given' by the state is seen as a serious crime (Cook 1989). Economic priorities may also be important. In his work on health and safety in the North Sea oil fields, Carson argues that a 'political economy of speed', in which governments were eager to maximize the revenues from oil, made them reluctant to subject oil companies to tougher regulation (Carson 1981).

Criminalization and white collar and corporate crime

This latter example points to the complex issue of criminalization in relation to white collar and corporate crime. To what extent does the criminal status of offences reflect the power of business groups over the law? It could alternatively be argued that white collar and corporate crime are treated differently because they are different and pose different problems for control. This can be seen by looking at the development of laws and law enforcement.

While business groups do exert considerable influence over the laws regulating their activities, it is difficult to substantiate any 'conspiracy theory'. Some business activities are criminalized, thus business groups are not always successful in resisting regulation. Moreover, business groups do not always represent a cohesive set of interests (see, for example, Croall 1992). Work on the origins of nineteenth-century legislation like the early Factory and Food and Drugs acts suggests that some business groups agreed to regulation as it was seen as being in their best interests to do so. Larger manufacturers, for example, calculated that smaller competitors might be priced out of the market by regulation. In the first instance laws were often 'symbolic', making few provisions for enforcement. The eventual form of law emerged out of a long process of negotiation between government, industry and enforcers in which different industrial groups represented their own interests, and in which stricter enforcement was accepted but the status of offences was differentiated from other forms of crime (Carson 1971; Paulus 1974). In his work on North Sea oil referred to above, Carson also found that the state, enforcers and businesses, which might have all been seen to represent 'establishment interests', often disagreed (Carson 1981).

Law enforcement has also been seen to be a crucial part of the process of criminalization, and the enforcement of white collar and corporate offences has often been characterized as lenient. To enforcers and some commentators, however, the compliance strategies outlined above are a more cost-effective way to protect the public than prosecution (Hawkins 1990; Pearce and Tombs 1990). It has been argued, for example, that as prosecution is expensive and may often fail and often leads only to a small fine, advice, persuasion, negotiation and out-of-court settlements are cheaper and more effective. Agencies may have a continuous relationship with regulated businesses and taking an overly tough stance could antagonize them, reducing the chances of compliance (Hawkins 1984). On the other hand, this can be challenged. How, for example, is cost effectiveness to be measured in relation to crime? Is it cost effective to prosecute a burglar? Or, as Stephen Box once asked, would it be seen as appropriate to write several letters to a burglar asking that burglar to desist from breaking into people's houses? (Box 1983). Moreover, it can also be asked why enforcement agencies so often proceed against 'easier' targets instead of the 'richer pickings' to be gained from, for example, more affluent tax payers – which might also be more cost effective (Cook 1989). To some, therefore, arguments about cost effectiveness reflect ideological constructions.

CONCLUDING COMMENTS

This chapter has explored many aspects of the vast area of white collar and corporate crime and has illustrated the many ambiguities which, to Nelken, pervade discussion of the subject as its ambiguous criminal status creates considerable disagreement about its explanation and control (Nelken 1997).

This has included questions about whether it is really crime and, if so, whether it can be approached and explained in the same way as other crimes. It also involves questions about whether it *should* be dealt with as 'crime'. These questions are ultimately unanswerable, although they do illustrate the nature of social and ideological constructions of crime and suggest very different approaches to the control of white collar crime.

To some, as seen above, this requires different laws and different enforcement to conventional crime, whereas to others any such suggestions imply more lenient treatment. Criticisms of this imply a need for tougher enforcement policies, more prosecution and stricter punishment. While these differences may appear irresolvable, some suggestions can be made. Pearce and Tombs, for example, have suggested that companies, like drivers, could be charged with dangerous or reckless employing, and others have argued that individuals within companies could be given clear responsibilities for safety and other forms of compliance, making them individually liable for blame and prosecution (Pearce and Tombs 1990; Wells 1993). In other countries companies are given probation or community service orders specially adapted for companies (Croall 1992; Wells 1993). To Braithwaite, there is little point in arguing for tougher prosecution policies as this would overburden the courts, and he suggests a mixture of strategies including tackling the cultures of organizations to emphasize the interests of consumers and workers and encourage 'whistle blowing'. Companies who break laws can be 'shamed' by requirements that their convictions are given publicity. Sanctions, he argues, should take the form of an enforcement pyramid, ranging from milder sanctions and agreements to comply, through probation and community service, to tougher sentences, including what he has described as corporate 'capital punishment' which need not disadvantage employees and shareholders as companies could be run for a period of time by the state (see, for example, Braithwaite 1989; Braithwaite and Pettit 1990; Fisse and Braithwaite 1993). The criminal law, however, is not the only means of controlling corporate crime and it should also be exposed and public intolerance expressed through wider social movements on the part of consumers, workers and the environment (Braithwaite 1995).

Review Questions

1. As for professional and organized crime, consider how you might design a 'victim' or 'crime' survey of white collar and corporate crime. What difficulties would you encounter? Taking account of all the forms of white collar, corporate and organizational crime described in this chapter, consider how many times, and in what ways, you have been victimized by it in the last three months. How does this compare with victimization from other forms of crime?

2. Why is the analysis of white collar and corporate crime surrounded by ambiguity? Consider whether white collar and corporate crime can and should be dealt with as crime.

Key Reading

Croall H (1992) *White Collar Crime*. Buckingham: Open University Press

Langan M (1996) 'Hidden and Respectable: Crime and the Market', in Muncie J and McLaughlin E (eds) *The Problem of Crime*. London: Sage

Nelken D (1997) 'White Collar Crime', in Maguire M, Morgan R and Reiner R (eds) *The Oxford Handbook of Criminology*, 2nd edition. Oxford: Clarendon Press

CHAPTER 16

STATE AND
POLITICAL CRIME

While the state, law makers and law enforcers play a major role in defining crime, they may also commit crime. The activities of governments are subject to international laws and conventions which deal with violent activities such as torture and war crimes. These offences are committed by state officials who, along with politicians, may also engage in bribery and corruption. Where these are committed on behalf of, and are effectively condoned by, the state, they can be seen as state sponsored or state organized, although, as with white collar crime, a very fine line divides this from many individually deviant acts for personal benefit. Many forms of state, government or political crime are not, however, dealt with or constructed as 'crime'. State 'violence' is often seen as an issue of human rights or civil liberties and bribery and corruption on the part of state officials and politicians is treated as an issue involving the standards of public life. Looking at state and political crime, therefore, raises issues about the construction of crime as well as revealing many activities not generally regarded as crime.

This chapter will start by considering how state and political crime are defined and their relationship with 'crime'. The problems of researching and assessing their potential extent will be outlined before examining three very different forms of state and political crime, starting with 'state violence'. It will then discuss political corruption and the significance of 'sleaze' before looking at an example of the interrelationship between government, white collar and organized crime in the operation of the illegal market in arms. Finally, some recent work which has developed analyses of state crime will be explored.

WHAT IS STATE AND POLITICAL CRIME?

There are few official, legal or criminological definitions of this category. One major American text entitled *Elite Deviance* includes chapters on political deviance (Simon and Eitzen 1993) and another collection is entitled *Corporate and Governmental Deviance* (Ermann and Lundman 1978). Some early critical criminologists argued somewhat polemically that state activities such as economic exploitation and institutionalized racism or sexism should be dealt with and analysed as crime, although this was not widely accepted (Schwendinger and Schwendinger 1970). More recently, Cohen has argued persuasively that many forms of state crime are justifiably part of the agenda of criminologists (Cohen 1996). Some of the issues in defining and conceptualizing this category are outlined below.

State, political and criminal violence

Political crime, terrorism and state violence are interrelated, as McLaughlin (1996) argues that similar acts are differently described depending on who perpetrates them. The state holds a monopoly on the legitimate use of force, which can be distinguished from the illegitimate use of violence (McLaughlin 1996, and see Chapter 10). State agencies such as the military or the police can legitimately use force where it is defined as being in the public interest and is sanctioned by the state. This covers wars, anti-terrorist campaigns, public order and situations in which 'reasonable force' can be used. State officials can therefore legitimately kill, injure, intimidate or harass people, actions which would otherwise be considered to be violent or brutal although it is often difficult to differentiate between legitimate or 'reasonable' force and 'unreasonable' and illegitimate violence (McLaughlin 1996). 'Terrorists' also kill or injure people and are widely condemned, although to them their violence is legitimated by their cause. Some legitimacy is accorded to some terrorists in situations where, for example, prisoners are accorded the 'special status' of 'political prisoners'. In other cases terrorists are criminalized by describing them as 'no better than common criminals', which denies the legitimacy of their cause (Hillyard 1987; McLaughlin 1996).

From criminals to terrorists to freedom fighters

The definition of what is 'political' and 'legitimate' violence is therefore highly contested and ideologically constructed. This can be seen in the very fine distinctions between the words, often used in the media and by governments, to describe politically motivated violence such as 'terrorists', 'guerrillas' or 'freedom fighters'. These terms indicate degrees of censure which reflect judgements about the legitimacy of the groups involved, and groups may be described differently depending on who is defining their activities – terrorists in one country may be described as 'freedom fighters' in another. Descriptions may change as political perceptions alter, with some 'terrorists' ending up as legitimate governments. The most notable example of this is the transformation of the African National Congress (ANC) from terrorist group to legitimate government and Nelson Mandela, who underwent a long period of imprisonment, from dangerous criminal to widely respected world statesman.

State terror and war crimes

While the actions of terrorists are condemned because they use terror for political ends and target 'innocent civilians', similar tactics of 'terror' are used by governments, particularly in war. As McLaughlin points out, a major feature of twentieth-century warfare has been the targeting and terrorizing of 'innocent civilians' as a legitimate military strategy, especially with the development of air warfare and saturation bombing (McLaughlin 1996). This happened during the Second World War with the destruction of Dresden and the use of atomic bombs on the Japanese cities of Hiroshima and Nagasaki. While justified as being necessary to defeat the Germans and Japanese, each responsible for appalling crimes against humanity, their military justification has subsequently been challenged and they too have been seen as crimes against humanity. While individuals from the defeated states were tried for war crimes, those responsible for saturation bombing were not (ibid). What is defined as a war crime may therefore be determined by the victor rather than by agreed objective standards (ibid). The failure to define saturation bombing as a war crime led to its subsequent use in the Vietnam and Gulf Wars although in the latter, press reports of 'collateral damage' disguised the killing of thousands of civilians (ibid).

State crime

Is state crime 'crime'?

War crimes, along with other violent activities such as genocide or torture, are not generally included within the study of crime. Yet, as Cohen points out, the use of force by the state is covered by criminally enforced laws (Cohen 1996). National and international laws on human rights define such activities as crime and war crimes are subject to procedures which use the language of criminal justice. He further argues that victimization is widespread – not only from state violence but from seemingly victimless crimes such as corruption, which can be seen to undermine trust in the democratic process. Thus, he argues, the study of state crime is justifiably part of criminology (Cohen 1996).

Who are the criminals?

As with corporate crime, state crime raises problems about who is morally and legally responsible. Can a state or government, for example, be characterized as 'criminal'? To what extent is the state or its agencies responsible for the 'deviant' acts of individuals? The diffusion of responsibility is reflected in the typical justification for state crime that the accused person 'was only following orders'.

State-organized crime

As is the case with white collar and corporate crime, the 'deviant' acts of individuals for personal benefit or gratification can be distinguished from those which are seen to benefit the state, the public or the national interest.

Chambliss argues that some crime can be described as state organized, arguing that:

> the most important type of criminality organized by the state consists of acts defined by law as criminal and committed by state officials in the pursuit of their job as representatives of the state.
>
> (Chambliss 1995: 256)

Under this heading he includes a variety of activities including piracy, smuggling, assassination, criminal conspiracies and violations of laws limiting state activities. State agencies can also divert illegal campaign contributions and sell arms to countries who have been internationally prohibited from receiving arms, and states have also supported terrorist activities against legitimate governments. This he distinguishes from acts which benefit individuals, such as the acceptance of bribes or the illegal use of violence by police or military personnel – unless these acts violate existing criminal law and are sanctioned by official policies (Chambliss 1995). While this provides a useful distinction, it may be difficult in practice to determine whether activities are institutionalized in policy. One example of this is where the police, anxious to obtain a conviction, obtain evidence illegally. While they are expected to stay within the law, they are also expected to obtain sufficient evidence to convict the guilty, and courts have accepted illegally obtained evidence (see, for example, Davies et al 1995). Similarly, as will be seen below, the fight against terrorism or the need to defeat an enemy may justify overstepping the limits of the law.

THE SCOPE OF STATE AND POLITICAL CRIME

Research issues

State and political crime pose considerable difficulties for the researcher. As they are not generally regarded as crime there are no official statistics or victim surveys. Like white collar crimes they are often invisible, an invisibility which is exacerbated because they often involve the covert activities of security services and other agencies whose activities are shielded from public view. Governments and their agencies are ideally placed to 'cover up' their activities and to silence the press, with one recent case, discussed below, having involved the use of Public Immunity Certificates to withhold key documents 'in the public interest'. Offences may be revealed by investigative journalists; however, press reports may not always be reliable (Chambliss 1995) and the role of the media is constrained by the need to provide strong enough evidence to withstand libel suits. Government reports and inquiries can be of some use although they are also limited as governments are naturally reluctant to order inquiries which may reveal their own wrongdoing. Inquiries may be given narrow agendas and may engage in what cynics describe as a 'whitewash' or, according to McLaughlin, a process of 'deconstruction, reconstruction and depoliticization' which obscures the truth (McLaughlin 1996). Reports are often contested, new evidence is offered and the full picture may take many decades to emerge. Many analyses have therefore been based on exposures of individual incidents or 'scandals' which may be not be representative. Much recent work has been dominated by cases in the United States such as the Watergate and Irangate scandals which are atypical and based on one country, which, argues Cohen (1996), diverts attention from their relationship to 'normal politics'. The segregation of war and other state crimes to the realms of human rights and civil liberties further restricts awareness of their extent, although some indications can be given by reports of specific interest groups such as Amnesty International and INQUEST (see, for example, Cohen 1996; Ryan 1996).

The extent of state crime

Assessing the extent of state crime is therefore virtually impossible and it is also difficult to compare with 'conventional' crime. It can however far outstrip most forms of crime in terms of victimization. Cohen argues that if reports such as those of Amnesty International are used an enormous worldwide toll of genocides and mass political killings is revealed, including:

> The Turkish genocide of at least a million Armenians; the Holocaust against six million Jews and the hundreds of thousands of political opponents, gypsies and others; the millions killed under Stalin's regime; the tribal and religious massacres in Burundi, Bengal and Paraguay; the mass political killings in East Timor and Uganda; the 'autogenocide' in Cambodia; the 'ethnic cleansing' in Bosnia; the death squads and disappearances in Argentina, Guatemala, El Salvador.
>
> (Cohen 1996: 493)

To add all this up and compare it to conventional crime would, he asserts, be an insult to the intelligence. To this could be added torture, which, while illegal, is widely practised in democratic societies including Great Britain and Northern Ireland and is particularly serious because the agent responsible for upholding the law is responsible for the crime. For a large part of the world's population, therefore, state agents are the normal violators of 'legally protected interests' (Cohen 1996).

DIMENSIONS OF STATE AND POLITICAL CRIME

State violence

As seen above, the definition of state violence is highly subjective and can take many different forms. This section will outline some of its main forms, while analyses of this and other forms of state crime are incorporated into the section on understanding state crime.

War crimes

As seen above, war crimes, as legally defined, cover a vast area. The International Military Tribunal at Nuremberg, for example, included within its definition the murder, ill treatment or torture, and deportation to slave labour, of civilians in occupied territory or prisoners of war. Other crimes include the killing of hostages, the plundering of property, the wanton destruction of human settlements and devastation not warranted by military necessity (McLaughlin 1996). Crimes against peace have also been identified including the planning, preparation or waging of a war of aggression in violation of international treaties. As indicated above, considerable problems are encountered in attributing responsibility, and individuals can be judged and punished whether or not they were ordered by commanding officers or political leaders, although commanding officers are responsible for violations carried out by troops (ibid). They are thus, like other crimes, subject to trial and punishment. Typical defences deny individual responsibility by using the defence that the accused was 'only following orders', although this may not be accepted. If it is not, however, it may lead to defendants claiming that they have been scapegoated and can turn them into martyrs (ibid).

State-directed terror

Under the heading of state violence McLaughlin (1996) details different forms of what he describes as 'state-directed terror'. Terrorism generates 'counter terrorist' measures, many of which involve a variety of illegal activities and repressive measures justified as necessary to combat terrorism. These may generate further terror such as the use of death squads to kill terrorists identified by covert means, and the use of torture or intimidating interrogation against those suspected of being terrorists or able to identify them. It has been alleged that such practices have been used in Northern Ireland and that sections of the security forces have financed and colluded with terrorist groups engaged in 'retaliatory' killings with the aim of terrorizing the terrorists (Hillyard 1996; McLaughlin 1996). Combating terrorism also justifies the introduction of special powers to enable the conviction and imprisonment of terrorists, which may undermine citizens' rights and dispense with the normal due process of law. These special powers are normally seen as 'emergency' powers, to be used only for a short period but can be 'normalized' and their use may criminalize groups who are assumed to be associated with terrorists, as was seen in Chapter 9 in respect of the use of the Protection against Terrorism Act which Hillyard (1993) argues resulted in the 'criminalization' of the Irish population in parts of mainland Britain.

Torture

To McLaughlin torture is the 'ultimate form of individualized terror' (McLaughlin 1996: 288). While illegal it is commonplace in many countries and has, he argues, been refined and modernized with the growth of a lucrative global market in internal security equipment and the expansion of expertise in the technologies of political and social control. Torture is generally used to extract information, to prepare 'enemies' or internal dissidents for show trials and public confessions, to end the political effectiveness of the detainee and to deter others by generating fear (McLaughlin 1996). McLaughlin argues that it can also be used in conjunction with the extra judicial arrest or abduction of dissidents, often known as 'disappearances', occasionally followed by torture and secret execution. It is estimated that 10,000–30,000 people 'disappeared' in Argentina between 1976 and 1983.

Genocide

Perhaps the ultimate crime that can be committed in peace time as well as war is genocide, which involves seeking systematically and deliberately to eradicate, or attempt to eradicate, a national, ethnic, racial or religious group by mass murder. This is often accompanied by torture and mass rapes and often aims not only to eradicate human beings but also history, memory and culture (McLaughlin 1996).

Piracy

Chambliss details other examples of 'state organized' crime including the involvement of states in piracy, drug smuggling, state assassination and the use of human beings as 'guinea pigs' (Chambliss 1995; see also Simon and Eitzen 1993). He also provides an interesting account of state-organized piracy. During the period of colonialization and exploration, emerging states were anxious to amass capital to fund these activities. While Portugal and Spain financed explorations, other states, including France and England, wanted to share the rewards but did not want to wage war against Portugal and Spain. At this time piracy was widespread and was viewed by all nations as an extremely serious crime. Pirates were, argues Chambliss, similar to today's property or organized criminals – they were drawn from the ranks of the poor who had few alternatives save servitude and slavery, making piracy a dangerous but attractive option. While not legalizing piracy, states encouraged the plundering of Portuguese and Spanish vessels thus securing some of the rewards. The French Government, for example, instructed colonial governors to allow pirates to use their harbours in return for a share of the merchandise. England was also involved – Francis Drake was ensured a safe passage and was said to be acting under the orders of the Crown. On one voyage alone, Drake returned to England with enough gold and silver obtained from piracy to meet the government's expenses for seven years. Drake was knighted, but subsequently tried and convicted for piracy, and the Queen denied any involvement.

The violence of state agencies

State or institutional violence also includes the activities of state agencies such as the army, the police or prison service. Of particular concern has been the deaths of suspects, prisoners and immigrants in custody and the use of firearms by the police (see, for example, Biles 1991; Ryan 1996). Deaths in custody occur in a variety of situations – some are related to alcohol, some occur as a result of suicide and others result from fights and scuffles during arrest or in the police station (Ryan 1996). Not all of these involve misconduct, as some are due to natural causes, but they do raise issues about the standard of care accorded to those in custody, about the use of 'reasonable force' and about how deaths are subsequently investigated.

Deaths occurring as a result of alcohol or suicide have attracted criticisms of neglect, and in England and Wales, coroners' juries have returned verdicts of 'lack of care' (Ryan 1996). Deaths as a result of violence during arrest and questioning raise issues about the extent to which violence is justified in individual circumstances such as, for example, cases in which arrest is violently resisted. Particular issues have been the police use of strategies of restraint and control such as 'headlocks' and, most recently, of CS gas sprays (Ryan 1996). In a still unresolved case in London in 1994, a black man was arrested by the police for 'acting suspiciously'. He was reported to have struggled so violently that he was kicked in the head and officers applied a neck hold with so much force that he died. Various explanations were offered, including that he had been accidentally suffocated by his clothing. Following protracted investigations, in which the man's family and their representatives challenged police versions, a coroner's jury returned a verdict of 'unlawful killing' which led to the initial decision not to prosecute being overturned (Ryan 1996; Coles et al 1997). Concerns about shootings by the police were prompted by a number of high-profile cases in the 1970s and 1980s where the victims were not 'dangerous' convicted criminals. These incidents have often involved black people, leading to additional criticisms of racism. While it is impossible to estimate the number that are the result of 'crime' or 'misconduct' and, if so, whether they result from individually 'deviant' acts, they can be seen as institutionalized when the difficulties of establishing 'blame' or responsibility are considered.

It is often very difficult, following deaths in custody, to establish exactly 'what happened' and attribute responsibility. Families of those killed can face enormous problems obtaining information and challenging the police version of events and the interest group INQUEST was set up following a number of cases where police misconduct was alleged but was difficult to establish (Ryan 1996). Inquests play a significant role as, until the inquest, investigations are handled by the police or other relevant agencies. These investigations should attribute responsibility and take appropriate action against any misconduct or law breaking. Their deliberations are, however, not publicly available and families are often not given adequate information before the inquest, which, as Ryan (1996) points out, often begins with the assumption that if no misconduct has been revealed in police investigations, none has occurred. The inquest is therefore an open forum in which evidence can be questioned, but in order to do so, families have to gather independent evidence and secure legal representation, all of which is costly and legal aid is not available. Against this, state agencies have enormous advantages as 'expert witnesses' and lawyers are financed by public funds and are well acquainted with the results of police investigations (Ryan 1996; Coles et al 1997). Nonetheless coroners' verdicts have, as indicated above, found the police or prison service to be responsible, and have led to new investigations and prosecutions although subsequent action may be slow and few police officers have been prosecuted. This raises crucial issues about the public accountability of state agencies to the law and about their ability to control investigations.

Sleaze, scandals and cover ups: political crime and deviance

The public accountability of politicians and members of local and national governments has also been questioned and a general moral panic about 'sleaze' made this a major issue in the General Election of 1997 and beyond. This incorporates a variety of issues involving the conduct of politicians and public servants, including the legally defined offences of bribery and corruption. In Britain the criminal offence of bribery involves:

> the transaction of soliciting or receiving inducements or rewards to local government politicians (but not to MPs) and all public officials for decisions or actions – or, conversely, the failure to act or to make a decision – that favours the donor or their organization.
>
> (Doig 1996: 36)

The term corruption is more widely used to describe:

> any use of official position, resources or facilities for personal benefit, or . . . possible conflict of interest between public position and private benefit.
>
> (ibid: 36)

This involves offences of misconduct in public office and is also covered by a variety of internal regulations. In general terms the phrase 'standards of conduct' is used to encompass a mixture of law, regulations, culture, attitudes and traditions (Doig 1996).

Defining activities as 'corruption' is highly subjective and, as Levi and Nelken point out, 'corrupt' acts in some countries are seen as normal elsewhere and conceptions of what is considered to be unacceptable change and can be challenged by anti-corruption campaigns (Levi and Nelken 1996; Hodgkinson 1997). Anti-corruption campaigns are therefore closely linked to corruption and are politically and ideologically constructed. Typically, for example, to right wing parties corruption involves the waste of public money, often in local government, to which the solution is privatization and the introduction of competition. To others, however, as will be seen below, privatization and competition encourage corruption, and left wing parties typically see corruption as being motivated by personal gain and to provide favours for the business elite (Levi and Nelken 1996). Allegations of corruption are often politically motivated and used by oppositions to challenge governments or by governments to discredit opposition (ibid).

Political corruption is often seen as an intrinsic feature of political life, in which politicians and others seek personal aggrandizement, influence and power. To Levi and Nelken, allegations of corruption in Europe in the 1980s are linked to political parties' need to finance election campaigns coupled with the ability of the victorious party to grant favours and positions. In the United States the so-called 'political machine', where elected political leaders appoint non-elected persons to key positions, opens the door to bribery and corruption (Simon and Eitzen 1993). Even where advantage may less tangible, it is often assumed that politicians and public officials are 'worth knowing' due to their contacts, knowledge or influence.

Standards of public life

Britain has generally been associated with less corruption than other countries – compared with Italy, for example, Britain's politicians have been seen as 'minnows' (Leigh and Vulliamy 1997). As with other forms of crime, there is a tendency to see corruption as 'foreign' and to associate it with countries with less rigorous standards of pubic life (Levi and Nelken 1996; Hodgkinson 1997). This assumption has permeated successive discussions and official reports on the subject, which have tended to reflect a faith in the personal integrity of public servants and politicians (Doig 1996). This has been the case since the nineteenth century which saw the emergence of a 'shared culture', a code of 'gentlemen', in which private gain was eschewed in favour of public responsibility and the public interest (ibid). Scandals did, however, occur. In the Marconi Scandal in 1911, for example, it was revealed that the Prime Minister David Lloyd George and another minister bought shares in Marconi before they went on sale to the public but after they knew that the British Government had signed a large contract with the company. Their purchase was concealed although, when it was revealed, the ministers suffered few repercussions and went on to higher office (Leigh and Vulliamy 1997). The Prime Minister did accept that 'rules of prudence' may not have been observed and went on to reiterate these. Scandals were generally seen as individual 'atypical' cases which reinforced the belief in the generally high standards of public life (Doig 1996).

This confidence continued in the face of 'scandals' in the 1970s, when the activities of the architect John Poulson were revealed. He was implicated in a web of corrupt activities in relation to building contracts with local government, police and health services. Following a series of much publicized trials, T Dan Smith, then leader of Newcastle Council and William Pottinger, a senior civil servant at the Scottish Office were prosecuted and imprisoned (Doig 1996; Leigh and Vulliamy 1997). Inquiries into these and other matters made many recommendations for improving law and procedures but Parliament was reluctant to act and their recommendations were not implemented. By the late 1980s and early 1990s, however, a series of events contributed to the developing moral panic about 'sleaze'.

The development of 'sleaze'

Two reports, which did not at the time receive much public attention, revealed problems across a range of public services. In 1994 the Public Accounts Committee issued a report in which it suggested a departure from long-established standards and detailed a range of problems across public sector organizations including inadequate financial controls, failure to comply with rules and inadequate stewardship of public money and resources (Doig 1996; Hodgkinson 1997). Reports by the Audit Commission into probity in local government and the National Health Service also revealed limitations in systems for preventing fraud and argued that ethical standards and an anti-fraud culture were needed as the ethical environment had become more demanding following the delegation of financial services and management responsibilities brought about by Conservative reforms (Doig 1996).

There were also increasing concerns about the conduct of politicians, particularly in respect of their 'outside interests'. Two MPs who were parliamentary aides to Ministers resigned following revelations that they had been prepared to take cash for asking parliamentary questions. It was also revealed that some MPs were being paid retainers by lobbying firms on behalf of clients who sought access to Members of Parliament and Government Ministers to advance their interests. The clients of Ian Greer's firm, for example, included the Serbian Government and a United States tobacco company which wanted to be allowed to market carcinogenic tobacco products aimed at the young (Leigh and Vulliamy 1997). These interrelated 'scandals' also involved allegations of links with arms exports, arms licences and relationships with foreign governments. Many of the sums paid to politicians were subsequently revealed not to have been declared either in the register of MPs interests or to the Inland Revenue, involving a mixture of misconduct and criminal offences (Leigh and Vulliamy 1997). This, together with a series of sexual scandals involving government ministers, made more embarrassing by the then Prime Minister's advocacy of high standards of personal morality, combined to produce a moral panic about 'sleaze'.

In 1994 the Nolan Committee was set up to address the question of standards in public life. In its 1995 report it criticized what it saw as the often opaque descriptions which were routinely entered in the register of MPs interests and found that entering interests was interpreted by some MPs as an indication that the interest was acceptable (Leigh and Vulliamy 1997). It complained of what it saw as a tolerance of corruption in a 'culture of slackness' and of a 'culture of moral vagueness' among the holders of public office (ibid: 44). It acknowledged public anxiety about sleaze which it related to a 'pervasive atmosphere . . . in which sexual, financial and governmental misconduct were indifferently linked' (ibid: 149). It called for a 'respect for the traditions of upright behaviour' and stressed the importance of personal integrity, asked for clearer information to be given to the register and a better system of independent monitoring (Doig 1996: 51). Like many previous reports, however, it had many limitations. Doig argues that by stressing individual and personal characteristics it neglected the deeper roots of corruption and continued the tradition of placing faith in personal behaviour. It did not attempt to assess the extent of corruption, carried out no empirical research, did not look at the reports of the Public Accounts Committee and, while it discussed privatization, did not systematically investigate it (Doig 1996; Hodgkinson 1997).

Concerns about 'sleaze' continued leading to further allegations and further inquiries, such as the subsequent Downey report. This reported that there was 'compelling evidence' that some politicians had misrepresented payments and favours. Some continued to challenge these findings which were recently accepted by the House of Commons Standards and Privileges Committee which found the ex-MP, Neil Hamilton, 'guilty' of a number of activities including staying at the Ritz Hotel owned by Mohammed Al Fayed and failing to declare this and other payments, including those paid in the now famous brown paper envelopes, lying to the Deputy Prime Minister about his relationship with the lobbying firm, and failing to register £10,000 commission fees. This, they concluded, fell 'seriously and persistently' below the standards expected of an MP. Had he still been an MP it would have led to a lengthy period of suspension (*The Guardian* 7/11/97: 1). Since the 1997 General Election other allegations of misconduct have emerged. One MP is currently under investigation, having been alleged to have paid money to an opponent to stand down, and local councillors in Glasgow were alleged to have accepted trips abroad in return for votes. Concerns about 'sleaze' encompass a general feeling of mistrust in the ethical standards of public figures and politicians, leading some to talk about the 'corruption of politics' (Doig 1996; Levi and Nelken 1996). Do these feelings have any basis?

It is ultimately unknowable whether there has been a rise in 'corruption' or a decline in public standards (Levi and Nelken 1996). Some factors have however been associated with creating a climate more favourable to corruption, as suggested by the reports cited above. Conservative government reforms included privatization and the introduction of internal markets into many areas of public service. These were introduced rapidly and public servants were exhorted to embrace market principles in what amounted to a 'cultural revolution' (Hodgkinson 1997). This may well have created a conflict between the profit and efficiency oriented culture of the private sector and the public interest oriented values outlined above, creating a 'criminogenic' situation similar to the organizations described in Chapter 15. It may also, by encouraging profit-making and self-seeking activities, have created a form of 'marketization anomie' in which norms and values became unclear (Hodgkinson 1997). For politicians, a major factor was the growth of professional lobbying which created many potential conflict of interest situations between the interests of the wider electorate and the interests of those who sought to benefit from contacts, paid or otherwise, with MPs.

The arms industry

A good illustration of the interrelationship between the state, organized crime and legitimate industry referred to in previous chapters is provided by illegal trading in arms. The arms industry is important to governments for several reasons. For arms manufacturing countries, export revenues are so important to the economy that they have been said to drive foreign policy and overseas development projects, with aid being granted in the expectation of major arms deals (Ruggiero 1996a; 1996b). Other governments, international 'pariahs', are subject to arms embargoes which prohibit any other country exporting arms to them along with any equipment or technical expertise which could be used for arms manufacture or the development of nuclear or chemical weapons. These governments must therefore rely on illegal supplies. Governments are responsible for ensuring that rules are complied with and they are enforced through a process of international inspection. In Britain, manufacturers seeking to export arms or anything which could be used in their manufacture must obtain export licences. The major players in the arms trade are therefore manufacturers of arms, army officers, state officials and inspectors (Ruggiero 1996b). Mediators are also involved in negotiations between producing and importing countries.

There are several kinds of illegal arms deals. Some involve breaking regulations covering the quality and quantity of arms which can be produced and sold. These are enforced by inspectors who, according to Ruggiero (1996b), are part of an international elite closely allied to manufacturers and are exposed to corruption. Embargoes can be overcome by exporters making false claims about the purpose of goods or the destination of arms and financial institutions can misrepresent the sums involved along with the identity of purchasers and sellers. There is also a clandestine market in arms which involves a trade in light armaments and second-hand weapons, often destined for countries subject to an embargo. Organized crime is heavily involved in this latter trade but is less able to deal with trade involving major quantities of large weapons or manufacturing technologies. The market for these goods is buoyant and there has also been a growing demand for arms from Western countries who have continued to produce large quantities of arms despite the collapse of the Soviet Union (Ruggiero 1996b). This, according to Ruggiero (1996b: 12), has led to the growth of a 'grey market' in arms, which involves government officials and ministers 'innovatively' interpreting official policy which is often characterized by 'confusion'.

This was illustrated in the Matrix Churchill case which involved the export of arms and defence-related equipment to Iraq. Three executives from the firm were prosecuted for illegally exporting defence-related equipment to Iraq, using false 'end user certificates' in which the destination country was entered as Jordan and misrepresenting what the equipment was to be used for, including the export of pipes supposedly to be used in the manufacture of an Iraqi 'super gun' (Ruggiero 1996b). The case collapsed when it was revealed that one of the three executives had been working for the intelligence services and that government ministers knew about and had encouraged the exports, despite official guidelines which discouraged the sale of defence-related equipment to Iraq. Ministers also refused to release essential papers for the defence by using public immunity certificates (PIIs). This also implied that ministers had misled Parliament about the status of arms exports to Iraq because, as it subsequently emerged, they feared a public outcry and did not wish to damage relationships with other Arab states. The subsequent Scott Inquiry substantiated claims that ministers had not revealed any shift in export guidelines (Birkinshaw 1996). They had therefore privately 'relaxed' the rules while publicly insisting they were being complied with (McLaughlin 1996; Ruggiero 1996b). No government ministers were prosecuted, although in similar cases in other countries they have been, and none resigned (Ruggiero 1996b).

UNDERSTANDING STATE AND POLITICAL CRIME

Few of the theoretical perspectives reviewed in earlier chapters have been specifically applied to state crime as it is not generally constructed as 'crime'. Many, however, have considerable relevance and analyses draw on similar themes to those developed in relation to white collar and corporate crime. While terrorists, war criminals or torturers are often described in emotive terms as 'sadists' or 'inhuman', their activities have to placed in the context of the organizations in which they work and the functions which they perform for the state. These often provide justifications for activities which are surrounded by a 'culture of denial' (Cohen 1996). While consideration of the factors that affect governments' participation in state crime involves a vast range of political or historical analyses, state crime, like corporate crime, can also be viewed in terms of the conflicting goals faced by the state and its agencies. In addition, as seen above, a major theme in exploring state crime is the way in which it is socially and ideologically constructed. These themes will be explored below.

It is common to individualize state and political crime which, as seen above, is often attributed to the actions of 'deviants' or, in the often used phrase, 'rotten apples in the barrel' (Doig 1984). As with corporate crime, individuals commit crime within organizations and, as Chambliss (1995) points out, while individuals are the perpetrators of offences, they are not the cause. Torturers are state employees and undergo a period of socialization and training which results in being able to inflict pain with professional detachment (McLaughlin 1996). Thus argues McLaughlin (1996: 297), the

> making of a torturer would appear to have less to do with individual psychology and more to do with the social and political order in which the torture is taking place.

Terrorists are also generally portrayed as psychologically disturbed fanatics but see themselves as soldiers committed to a just cause – a view which may be legitimated if their struggle is successful. In this respect are they any different from soldiers in national armies? Some of these soldiers may also commit extreme acts of violence and atrocities which are justified according to their cause (McLaughlin 1996). Similarly, corrupt politicians or violent or corrupt police officers are generally seen as atypical and 'deviant' but, as seen above, this can serve the function of portraying the organization in a reassuring light. As Doig (1984) points out, describing individuals as 'rotten apples' deflects attention from the barrel.

Denying state crime

To many torturers, terrorists or war criminals, horrific acts become accepted as an almost routine part of their role, as necessary to defeat an assumed enemy. This may involve a process of 'enemy creation' which depersonalizes and dehumanizes victims (McLaughlin 1996). Soldiers who have participated in atrocities often use abusive phrases to describe their victims, often with racist overtones. In Vietnam, American soldiers described the Vietnamese as 'gooks', 'dopes' and 'slopes' and Serbians described their victims as 'gypsies', 'filth' and 'animals' (McLaughlin 1996; Cohen 1996). In activities which have involved genocide, whole populations have been depersonalized – Jews in Nazi Germany, for example, had to wear yellow stars, and coloured labels were also used in the killing fields of Cambodia. Military discipline also enables the diffusion of responsibility discussed in relation to corporate crime. Following the My Lai massacre in Vietnam, in which a whole village of between 400 and 500 were killed by American soldiers, one officer, Lieutenant Calley, used the 'only following orders' defence and is also said to have commented that 'it was no big deal' (Cohen 1996: 503). Cohen argues that when such acts are ordered, normal principles are replaced by a duty to obey. Once the first step has been taken, soldiers carry on without considering the implications, coming to see it as 'all in a day's work' or as routine, illustrated also by the use of euphemisms such as 'surgical strikes' to describe atrocities.

Cohen also describes a 'litany of denials and justifications' which amount to a spiral of denial. In the first place the response of governments is to deny that the event happened at all. Faced with proof that is happening or has

304

happened, they attempt to claim that it is not, or was not, what it appears to be and negative criticisms are denied by interpreting events in a positive light. Atrocities can be euphemistically described as 'transfers of population', aggressive action as 'self defence', and killing massive numbers of citizens by bombing described, as in the Gulf war, as 'collateral damage'. Finally governments resort to a tactic summed up by 'even if it's what you say it is, it's justified' – arguing that the action is or was necessary to protect national security, to advance the war against terrorism or to serve some other cause (Cohen 1996).

This takes place within a 'culture of denial' in which the 'techniques of neutralization' seen in respect of other forms of crime are employed. Governments deny injury by claiming, for example, that 'they exaggerate, they don't feel it, they are used to violence'. The victim is denied by claims that 'they started it', 'they are the terrorists', 'we are the real victims'. Responsibility is denied by claiming that individuals were only following orders, that they were cogs in the machine. The claim that crimes are 'crimes of obedience' is the most pervasive and powerful in defence. Condemners are condemned in what Cohen sees as a vast discourse of official denial – Israel, for example, justifies breaches of international law by claiming that 'the whole world is picking on us', 'everyone is against us' or are Anti-Semitic. Other states claim that 'it's worse elsewhere' or that criticism amounts to racism and cultural imperialism – often by imposing Western values. States and governments also appeal to many higher loyalties – to the nation, the army, a sacred mission or a higher cause (Cohen 1996). Even where new governments take over to reform or overturn oppressive regimes there often follows a form of 'collective amnesia' in which earlier activities are rarely discussed.

Conflicting goals

Many forms of state crime can also be see as arising out of conflicting goals, similar to anomie theory. Chambliss, for example, points out that the goals of the state or its agencies may conflict with law. His analysis of piracy, outlined above, illustrates how the goals of capital accumulation led to the sanctioning of piracy despite its illegal status. The multifarious criminal activities of the Central Intelligence Agency (CIA), which included drug smuggling, intervention into the internal affairs of other countries and attempted political assassinations, can also be related to the contradiction between the law and their aim of 'ridding the world of communism' (Chambliss 1995). It was seen in relation to the arms market that a desire to protect the arms industry and to maximize export revenues conflicted with human rights concerns.

The police also face conflicting goals. Many analyses of the police point to the major conflict between crime control and due process (see, for example, Davies et al 1995). As seen above, the police are expected to stay within the law while enforcing it. This is a central feature of the due process of law under which defendants are presumed innocent until proven guilty and underlies many of the laws, rules and guidelines surrounding police activity – from the need to obtain evidence legally, to rules surrounding how interviews, as opposed to interrogations, should be carried out, and the need to avoid actual or threatened violence. On the other hand, the police are expected to detect crime and to ensure that those guilty are convicted and punished; they can be subject to intense pressure, especially following serious crimes, to find the person responsible. These goals often conflict. Police officers may suspect, or, on the basis of information, may 'know' that a person is guilty, but may not be able to obtain sufficient evidence to secure a conviction. In such situations breaking the rules and guidelines by 'fitting up' a suspect, extracting confessions, using intimidation or violence, or fabricating evidence can be seen as an expedient means of convicting someone they 'know' is guilty, which is justified by their assumption that they are guilty. Obtaining evidence is also time consuming and costly – thus securing confessions or fabricating evidence may save time and money (Ruggiero 1996a). This conflict of goals may underlie miscarriages of justice and some cases of violence. In Northern Ireland, where the security forces have been alleged to engage in killing, a similar conflict may be found. To Hillyard this illustrates the classic dilemma faced by those attempting to pursue an effective social control strategy while at the same time upholding the law. Undercover work, for example, involves secretive, deceptive, manipulative and exploitative activities which are difficult to supervise and render accountable but are justified as being in the national interest (Hillyard 1996).

State crime and criminalization

Many of the points made earlier in this chapter have illustrated the complex relationship between state crime and criminalization. In many ways state crime challenges social and ideological constructions of crime as it is generally not regarded as part of the 'crime problem'. In addition, the state and its agencies, as seen in earlier chapters, are well placed to affect these constructions through their influence on popular representations of crime. This is well illustrated in McLaughlin's questioning of the distinction between terrorism and state terror where similar activities are very differently constructed. To McLaughlin, terrorism is a form of ideological censure – with terrorism as conventionally understood attracting the full force of criminalization – while state terror is justified, unless carried out by states which are accorded little legitimacy. The ideologically constructed nature of crime is also seen in the many ways in which acts are justified as being in the 'public' or the 'national' interest and in the denials which Cohen (1996) details. Subtle shifts in these constructions are also evidenced in the way in which 'war crimes' are defined – often depending on who does the defining. Whether or not it is socially or ideologically constructed, state crime has real victims and involves similar activities to other forms of crime.

CONCLUDING COMMENTS

This chapter has only been able to scratch the surface of the vast area of state and political crime which ranges from atrocities committed across the globe to more localized concerns about 'sleaze'. These offences take many different forms, and it has also been seen that their inclusion within the category of 'crime' is contested, although they involve activities which readily fall within both legal and social constructions of crime. Looking at state crime, however, raises very strong questions about this construction as while many are hidden they cause vast amounts of serious victimization and most are 'criminal' in both commonsense and legal terms. As Cohen argues, they can therefore be justifiably included in the study of crime. In addition, even though there may be some complacency that Britain suffers less from both state violence and corruption than other countries, they can and do occur in Britain and they also illustrate the global context within which crime must be analysed. These, along with other themes, will be drawn upon in the concluding chapter.

Review Questions

1. Draw up a list of the main forms of state crime and political crime.
   (a) Have any examples of these been reported in recent months?
   (b) How many in Britain?
   (c) Are they presented and interpreted in the same way as other crimes?
   (d) Detail any examples you encounter of the 'culture of denial'.
2. Taking any one form or example of state or political crime, illustrate how it can be related to the conflicting goals of the state, its agencies, politicians or government.

Key Reading

Chambliss W (1995) 'State Organized Crime – The American Society of Criminology, 1988 Presidential Address', in Passas N (ed) *Organized Crime*. Aldershot: Dartmouth

Cohen S (1996) 'Human Rights and Crimes of the State: The Culture of Denial', in Muncie J, McLaughlin E and Langan M (eds) *Criminological Perspectives*. London: Sage

Doig A (1996) 'From Lynskey to Nolan: The Corruption of British Politics and Public Service', *Journal of Law and Society*, Vol 23, No 1: 36–56

McLaughlin E (1996) 'Political Violence, Terrorism and Crimes of the State', in Muncie J and McLaughlin E (eds) *The Problem of Crime*. London: Sage

CHAPTER 17

CONCLUSION

This book has explored many issues surrounding the study of crime. It has considered the difficulties of researching and counting crime and assessing its impact and has reviewed many different theories and perspectives which aim to understand it. It has looked at the relationships between crime and social inequalities of class, age, race, gender and power and examined a range of different patterns of crime. In conclusion, this chapter will attempt to draw together some of the themes which have been referred to in successive chapters and return to the questions raised in Chapter 1. It will start by considering the different ways in which crime and different crime 'problems' are constructed and will then review how the relationships between crime and society have been developed. While, as stated in Chapter 1, the emphasis of this book has been on crime in Britain, many chapters have also illustrated the international dimensions of crime, and these will be outlined. Finally, although the stated focus has been on crime, the relevance of the study of crime for criminal justice and social policy will be briefly considered.

CONSTRUCTING THE CRIME PROBLEM

The relationships between legal, social and political constructions of crime, introduced in Chapter 1 have been illustrated in successive chapters. A major question in relation to white collar, corporate and state crime is whether these activities are 'really' crime, a question which presupposes some concept of 'real crime'. Yet with many forms of crime a very fine line divides 'normal' activities from 'criminal'. When do the dishonest or deceptive activities of a business or a politician become defined as 'criminal'? When do 'normal' sexual relationships become 'deviant' or exploitative? When is drug use 'criminal'? These issues are raised across the spectrum of crimes. What is violent crime? Why do popular and official conceptions of violent crime omit the injuries and harm caused by corporate or state 'violence'? What divides legitimate force from illegitimate violence? Why did it take so long for violence in the family to be recognized as a 'real' crime? What is theft or fraud? What is to be considered as 'corrupt'? Exploration of these and many other questions

308

reveals that the criminal status of activities is often contested and involves political and ideological considerations (see, for example, Muncie 1996).

Analyses of different issues has also illustrated how notions of the 'crime problem' or different 'crime problems' are constructed around particular activities and issues. Thus, discussions of being 'tough on crime' often focus only on 'youth crime' which in turn is associated not with 'youth' in general but with lower-class young men living in inner cities and peripheral estates, and in some areas this is also associated with race or ethnicity. The 'drugs problem' is also typically constructed as a problem of recreational drug use among young people. 'Violent crime' is often portrayed as a problem of public violence and 'stranger danger' a conception also seen in relation to some sexual offences as in the construction of 'real rape'. Some other forms of crime are seen as serious problems, hence the 'war' on drugs and organized crime – although these are often portrayed as a 'problem' of major criminal syndicates which may neglect the widespread involvement of many different groups in the criminal labour market.

The questions which academic approaches pose about crime depends in part on whether they accept or challenge these constructions, and in deconstructing them they may construct other 'problems'. To early sociological and criminological theories the crime problem was seen to originate from a series of 'problems' related to individual offenders, individual victims, families, subcultures or the structure of society itself. To the labelling perspective and critical criminology, 'the problem' became the activities of social control agents and criminalization. To some feminists 'the problem' is male violence and male power, whereas to critical 'race' theories, 'the problem' is the racialization of crime. As attention turned away from establishing the 'causes' of crime to its control, an absence of control and discipline became 'the problem', and to administrative criminologists 'the problem' was the immediate situation in which crime occurred.

Given all these questions, it could be asked if 'crime' is a useful category at all as it is difficult to define and encompasses very different activities with few distinguishing or essential characteristics (see, for example, Muncie 1996). It is differentiated from other activities primarily by the application of the criminal sanction, a process which reflects not the inherent properties of actions but political interests and power. Thus it could be argued that 'crime' is a particular form of ideological censure (see, for example, Sumner 1994, 1997). Emphasizing the socially and ideologically constructed nature of crime could, however, be taken to imply that crime is not 'really' a problem but 'merely' a social construction – an implication which prompted the left realist argument that crime 'really' is a problem. Recognizing the socially constructed nature of crime and crime problems need not, however, deny their impact. It suggests that while many activities are harmful, deceptive or dishonest, only some are subjected to the censure of the criminal law. It also suggests that definitions and depictions of the 'crime problem' have to be looked at critically and sceptically before researching and studying crime.

UNDERSTANDING CRIME AND SOCIETY IN BRITAIN

In relating crime and society in Chapter 1, it was pointed out that individuals' decisions to commit crime were shaped by their cultural background and structural position. It was also suggested that crime is affected by technological, economic and social change and by patterns of inequality in society. These themes have recurred at many stages of this book – in looking at how crime can be explained or understood, in exploring how it is related to social inequalities and in examining specific patterns of crime. This has illustrated how attempts to individualize crime may neglect its cultural and structural roots, the effect on crime of social and economic change and the complex relationship between crime and social inequality. These issues will be explored below.

Individual, culture and structure

Individualizing crime

Different chapters have shown that crime is often individualized by relating it to the individual characteristics of offenders, families or victims. Early approaches attempted to establish how criminals, and later, victims were 'different'. Biological and other 'natural' differences were assumed to explain the different conviction rates of men and women. Violent and sexual crime have been 'medicalized' by relating them to the clinical problems of offenders, to excess aggression or sex drives and to 'dysfunctional' families. The family has also been involved in theories relating crime and delinquency to the situation of individual families and to a lack of discipline and control in the family. While it is more difficult to individualize professional and organized white collar, corporate or state crime, offenders are often portrayed as 'mavericks', as atypical 'rotten apples' in an otherwise stable barrel. Organizations themselves may be portrayed as 'deviant'. Problems within social control agencies can also be attributed to the individual acts of prejudiced or atypical officers rather than to the institutional nature of discrimination or violence. To conservative criminologies, crime is a matter of individual responsibility and individual choice, and administrative criminology focuses on the individual situations in which crime occurs.

Individualizing crime has an enormous appeal. It can be reassuring to assume that crime is a product of deviant individuals who can be isolated and cured, rather than being a part of normal life. If victims are assumed to have provoked crimes, 'we' have less to worry about. The promise of the modernist project described in Chapter 3 was that the 'causes' of crime could be identified and a 'cure' developed, and this gave way to arguments that, as crime was a matter of individual choice and responsibility, individuals could be deterred and crime could be reduced by altering the situations in which these choices were made. Identifying risk factors can also place the responsibility on victims to protect themselves.

While it has not been disputed that some crimes are the result of aberrant individuals or that individuals choose to commit crime, many limitations of individualized approaches have been pointed out. They do not clearly differentiate between offenders and non-offenders and associating crime with individual pathologies can also involve labelling and a circular argument. If 'crime' is seen as atypical, criminals are labelled 'abnormal', and abnormalities are then used to explain their behaviour. If there is violence in a family, it is labelled as dysfunctional, which in turn explains the violence (see Chapter 10). Moreover, 'blaming' individuals can divert attention from the relationship between crime and culture and social structure. Attributing violent and sexual crime to aberrant men diverts attention from the 'normal' violence in everyday life. Blaming crime on young people's 'natural' tendency to commit crime avoids looking at their structural position. Attributing corporate crime to 'pathological' corporations or professional crime and corruption to 'mavericks' diverts attention from the 'normality' of crime in many professions and organizations and in the world of politics.

Crime and culture

This indicates the significance of cultures and subcultures within which crime is tolerated. Some offences are so widely tolerated that they are not seen as 'real crimes'. The 'enterprise culture', as will be seen below, has been associated with a wide range of offences. It has also been seen that the culture of 'masculinity' has been associated with a variety of crimes, from violent and sexual crime to property crime, car crime, serious crime and aggressive tactics in the world of business. Other offences are tolerated in subcultures in which status and achievement may be derived from offending – from the youth cultures which were the focus of early subcultural theories to contemporary examples, including the street subcultures in which 'life is a party', the subculture of prostitutes, the poly drug culture, car culture, the criminal culture of the underworld, the subcultural environment of managers in which law breaking is justified, the fraud culture within organizations, and the 'slack' political culture which justifies corruption. Many subcultures have diverse origins and, as we have seen, it now makes little sense to talk of one 'delinquent subculture' (Ruggiero and South 1995).

Like individuals, cultures can be 'blamed' for crime. It was seen in Chapter 3 that the proliferation of different cultures, many of them immigrant cultures, was interpreted as social disorganization and associated with crime. Chapter 6 illustrated how the 'dependency culture' characteristic of the 'underclass' has also been associated with crime and that this follows a tendency to 'blame' the culture of the 'dangerous classes'. Youth cultural styles have, as seen in Chapter 7, for long been considered as threatening. Critical race theories point to the association of crime with the assumed 'weakness' of some minority ethnic cultures and the notion of the 'underclass' has also been associated with race and ethnicity. Culture can therefore be used ideologically as part of the criminalization process and can reflect wider structures of domination. This can also, like individualized notions of crime, divert attention from the structural roots of crime whose exploration involves looking at social change and social inequality.

Crime and social change

Social and economic change has been a major theme in analyses of crime from Durkheim's work, written at the end of the nineteenth century, to contemporary work, at the end of this century, exploring the effect of globalization and de-industrialization. To Durkheim, anomie developed out of the transition from what are often called pre-industrial or pre-modern societies to industrial or modern societies. It was related to the decline of old ways of life and the emergence of a society which appeared to present 'boundless aspirations' (see Chapter 3). So great have been the technological, economic and social changes of recent decades that some have argued that society has undergone a similar transition from 'modern' to 'post-modern' which has affected all aspects of life from work and employment to culture and social structure. The structures, cultures and ideas which characterized modern societies are seen to have fragmented, creating many uncertainties and risks. The casualization and flexibilization of work and the speed with which skills and knowledge become outmoded means that many no longer feel secure in their employment. The social structure, previously characterized by identifiable groups or classes, has also fragmented with divisions emerging between those in and out of work, the skilled and the unskilled, and divisions related to housing, race, ethnicity and area of residence, which leave many, the so-called 'underclass', effectively excluded from participation in wider society. While these changes are widely acknowledged, not all agree that they amount to a fundamental transition, thus the phrase 'late modern' rather than 'post-modern' is often used.

Whatever words are used to describe these changes, they have had a major effect on crime. The effects of unemployment and social exclusion have particularly affected communities in which many can no longer look forward to stable employment. As seen in Chapters 6 to 9, they have affected different groups. For many young people they have led to a period of 'extended adolescence', and for young men to a 'crisis in masculinity' where they can no longer achieve the locally defined goals appropriate to young men. For young women they have not only reduced employment opportunities but created the prospect of impoverished single parenthood. For minority ethnic groups these effects are exacerbated by the experience of discrimination in housing and employment. For some, these problems can make crime an increasingly attractive 'solution', as it may provide excitement, financial rewards and a sense of achievement. It has also been seen that these changes are associated with 'free market' economic policies such as privatization, marketization, the deregulation of industry and an encouragement of the 'enterprise culture', all of which have been associated with different forms of crime. They may provide a moral climate justifying the 'innovative' business solutions of property and professional offenders, the prioritization of profits at the expense of consumers, workers, passengers or the public, which underlie much white collar and corporate crime and various forms of corruption and fraud.

These processes have also affected the illegitimate labour market and have contributed to the increasingly blurred boundaries between illegitimate and legitimate enterprises. In the expanding informal economy trading in second-hand and stolen goods may merge with drug dealing and a variety of other legitimate and illegitimate business ventures on the margins of the legitimate economy. At the higher level of the criminal labour market organized criminals run businesses very much like their legitimate counterparts and the deregulation of financial markets has enabled them to move between legal and illegal businesses, as was seen in relation to organized and white collar crime. The criminal labour market has also been affected by similar changes to those affecting the legitimate labour market. The specialisms and crafts associated with professional crime have become deskilled and a new, flexible, casualized and Post-Fordist criminal labour market has emerged (Ruggiero and South 1995, and see Chapters 13 and 14). Serious, specialized criminals have moved into new forms of crime such as computer crime and drugs creating a hierarchy of entrepreneurs, middle management, specialist operators and mass labour. And in this labour market upward mobility may be as difficult as it is in the legitimate one. Women and minority groups can be exploited and 'ghettoized' into specialist tasks and the unskilled labourer has little hope of high rewards or upward advancement (Ruggiero 1996a).

Social change has also affected attitudes to and worries about crime as rapid change generates a variety of generalized anxieties which can be focused on crime as an identifiable problem (Jefferson and Holloway 1997). Chapter 5 pointed out that fears and worries about crime may express more generalized anxieties about other misfortunes, many of them created by the uncertainties of modern or post-modern society. This can also be seen in the identification of specific crime 'problems' such as the 'dangerous classes', the 'underclass' or the potential lawlessness of the unemployed, the stranger, and the outsider. As seen in Chapter 7, Pearson relates fears about youth to more general anxieties about social change reflected in the tendency to look back with nostalgia to a 'golden age'. Similar anxieties could be reflected in concerns about declining standards of morality in worries about 'sleaze'. These 'fears' can be played upon in the criminalization process, which, by attributing 'crime' to specific groups, focuses attention on these groups, justifies harsher control measures and diverts attention away from wider issues of social inequality.

Crime and social inequality

Successive chapters have also illustrated the complex relationship between crime and social inequalities. While early theories related crime to deprivation, critical and radical criminologists pointed to the differential criminalization of lower-class crime and the crimes of the 'powerful'. Later approaches also introduced the interrelated inequalities of race, age and gender. This suggests many different questions. Is deprivation related to crime and if so how? Are some forms of crime related to structural inequalities between victims and perpetrators? Who suffers most from crime?

While a recurrent theme in many analyses of crime, the relationship between crime and indications of deprivation such as poverty, unemployment or low income is still contested and it could be argued that (a) these are not major 'causes' of crime as statistical correlations cannot be established, (b) the majority of those who are most socially deprived do not turn to crime and (c) people from all social classes engage in crime. Nonetheless there are strong indications that forms of deprivation and disadvantage can be and are related to some forms of crime. This can be seen in the statistical studies outlined in Chapter 6 and in the many subsequent examples of offenders for whom crime provides an alternative to legitimate opportunities. Both absolute and relative deprivation have to be considered. While it was argued in Chapters 4 and 6 that the role of absolute deprivation is problematic, some forms of crime may be what Carlen (1966) describes as 'crimes of survival' in which offenders have few alternatives but to resort to crime. This can be seen in respect of the young homeless with no legitimate income and also in respect of families, particularly single-parent families, who may be trapped in a situation of being unable to pay bills and subsequent fines (see, for example, Chapter 8). The stress of living on low incomes has also been seen to play a part in family and other forms of violence (see Chapter 10 and Levi 1997). It has also been seen that, to left realists, relative rather than absolute deprivation is a major source of crime, particularly as the gap between those on high incomes and those on low incomes has widened (see Chapters 4 and 6). This may partly account for the often mentioned pursuit by offenders across a spectrum of property offences, drugs and serious crime of the 'high life', and of participation in styles of consumption which they cannot legitimately afford but which are widely visible among the more affluent. This echoes the themes of anomie theory which relates crime to boundless expectations and the growth of consumerism (see Chapter 3). It has also been seen, however, that poverty, deprivation or disadvantage cannot explain all crime and the existence of the crimes of the powerful, be they corporate, white collar or state crimes cannot be explained in these terms. Indeed, Ruggiero (1996a) argues that 'wealth' not poverty causes crime.

Some forms of crime exploit inequalities. While it was seen in Chapter 4 that the early ideas of radical criminologists – i.e. that crime represented a form of rebellion in which the poor stole from the rich – were unfounded as property crime is predominantly intra class, nonetheless the possessions of the more affluent are targeted by property offenders while the powerful may, through corporate and state crime, victimize the powerless. Other inequalities are also relevant. To feminists, violent and sexual crime is indicative of women's subordination which is also reflected in the mythology surrounding these offences. Inequalities within, to feminists, the patriarchal family are also illustrated in the vulnerability of the very young and the very old to physical and sexual abuse, and racial inequalities are revealed in the persistence of racially motivated crime and harassment. Other forms of crime exploit different kinds of vulnerability. It was seen in respect of white collar crime that the lay person, whether rich or poor, can be exploited by those for whom knowledge may become power, as professional, scientific or technical knowledge can provide opportunities for many forms of fraud and deceit. State crime also illustrates how governmental, institutional and political power and privilege can be criminally exploited.

While people of all social classes may be victimized, it was argued in Chapter 5 that crime may have a more severe impact on those with fewer resources to protect themselves and who may suffer proportionately more. This may be compounded by repeat victimization and living in areas characterized by higher rates of street crime and public assault which may also attract a drugs market. Such groups may also be more vulnerable to some forms of professional and organized and business crime as they provide the market for the cheap, fake and often dangerous counterfeit goods and for the 'rogues and cowboys' whose businesses may involve dangerous and fraudulent activities. Crime therefore reflects many different kinds of inequalities, to which must be added the greater vulnerability of some groups to criminalization.

CRIME: A GLOBAL PROBLEM?

While, as stated in Chapter 1, the focus of this text has been on crime in Britain, this cannot be isolated from the increasingly international nature of many crime problems. The process of globalization, which affects both economic and cultural life, has already been referred to, and the internationalization of some forms of crime has also been illustrated in many chapters. Cultural goals are increasingly global and, as seen in Chapter 16, international law regulates many forms of crime. Crime in Britain must therefore be placed in an international context, aspects of which will be explored below.

The international crime industry

The chapters on professional and organized crime, the drugs market, white collar, corporate and state crime all provide examples of the significance of international crime as they involve multi-national industries with different operations being carried out in different countries. Drugs and some counterfeit goods are often produced in less developed countries in the Far East, Asia and, for drugs, South America, before being distributed across the globe and imported into Britain for sale in a variety of semi-legal and illegal outlets. Many of the counterfeit cassettes, videos and computer games for sale in local markets and car boot sales in Britain originate in the Far East. It was also seen in Chapter 13 that organized crime may involve smuggling not only goods but also people, with young women and children being 'imported' into the sex industry (Ruggiero 1996a). Organized crime is therefore increasingly becoming international crime.

Some offences, often known as cross-border crimes, exploit the different regulations of different countries. Goods banned in one country may be 'dumped' on other countries with looser regulations. This happens with pharmaceuticals and the drug thalidomide, banned in the West after being related to a variety of birth defects, was sold for many years in third world countries under a different name, as was the Dalkon Shield contraceptive referred to in Chapter 15 (Braithwaite 1984). As seen in Chapter 13, toxic waste can also be dumped and other products controlled in some countries can be illegally exported and imported. Meat frauds, for example, have involved the passing of horse, kangaroo and meat intended for pet food across borders and into the legitimate food chain in Britain and other European countries (Croall 1992). As the Bhopal case outlined in Chapter 15 indicates, companies may operate in some countries with less stringent safety standards. The European Union is said to lose millions of pounds through frauds on subsidies and revenues, many of which similarly exploit different regulations (Croall 1992; Van Duyne 1993).

The globalization of industry and telecommunications has also enabled new forms of international crime. It was seen in Chapters 13 and 15 that the internationalization of banking has enabled money to be passed around the world in seconds, enabling fraudsters to exploit different tax and banking regulations and assisting the laundering of money from illegal enterprises. The BCCI case revealed some of these features and also showed how such international financial frauds can affect local communities and small investors (see Chapter 15). Telecommunications have also led to a proliferation of crimes using telephones, television and computers. The Department of Trade and Industry has noted an increase in 'tele sales' frauds and sales frauds perpetrated via the Internet where the perpetrators are based abroad (Croall 1997). The Internet can also be used for a variety of offences including the distribution of pornographic images, also based on international operations. These can be down loaded and sold with counterfeit games in a variety of sites, including school playgrounds (Croall 1997).

The criminal labour market is also international and involves, as seen in Chapters 13 and 14, criminal enterprises from abroad operating in Britain. These may, like their legitimate counterparts, employ local labour. As Hobbs (1995) points out, the master status of professional criminal can be acquired and retained only by operating within a shadow economic order that, like its counterpart in the straight world, is vulnerable to the whims of multinational corporations with head offices in Europe, Asia and America. Labour from the third world may also be exploited as the examples of 'people trafficking' indicate, and the drugs industry employs women from African countries, often living in poverty, as 'mules' or couriers (Ruggiero and South 1995).

The internationalization of crime is also related to political changes and foreign policy, and historical examples have illustrated the role of states in supporting piracy and their involvement in wars to protect the opium trade. The link between export and trade interests and foreign policy can involve corruption as the example of the arms industry in Chapter 16 illustrates. Changes in what is described as the geopolitical structure may also be important. The collapse of the Soviet Union and other Eastern European countries not only created informal economies and the growth of organized crime in these states, but also affected the supply and distribution of drugs and armaments, fuelling the trade in these goods (Ruggiero 1996a).

Globalization, culture and crime

The globalization of telecommunications has also had an enormous effect on culture, as people across the world watch the same television programmes and images from many countries are transported across the globe. It was seen in Chapter 7 that young people's aspirations to consumer styles are affected by what Collison (1996) described as consumer icons from across the globe. Studies of youth crime, professional crime and the drugs market all illustrate the international theme of 'life is a party'. Images of crime are no longer restricted to local or national cultures, but disseminated through Hollywood blockbusters and high-profile international cases. The trial of O J Simpson was watched throughout the world and the trial of the British girl, Louise Woodward, accused of killing a baby in her charge in the United States, recently dominated British headlines and led to the formation of action groups in both the United States and in Britain. It is important to recognize, however, that the globalization of culture does not mean that it is homogeneous (Sparks 1997). Global influences interact with local ones producing cultures and subcultures drawing on multiple influences. Thus as Hobbs points out, serious criminals draw on local traditions intermingled with imported images (see Chapter 13). Crime in any specific local area is affected by local traditions along with global influences. As some subcultural theories point out, subcultural styles are based on a unique mixture of cultural symbols disseminated through the mass media and influences from the parent culture (see Chapter 3).

Crime in an international context

It is also important to look outwards from Britain to the international context of crime. In respect of state crime, for example, Cohen (1996) warns of the dangers of ethnocentrism – looking inwards and ignoring what happens abroad. This can also involve complacency, illustrated in assumptions that some forms of crime – for example, corruption – are less prominent in Britain than elsewhere. It has also been seen that many other forms of crime have been associated with 'foreignness', and seen as 'un-British'. This can be short sighted as it was often argued that Britain had fewer problems of professional and organized crime and drugs – both of which are now widespread and involve not only foreign 'firms' and syndicates but indigenous employees and entrepreneurs. In addition, while many examples of state crime and violence were drawn from abroad, this does not mean that they are less important or cause less harm. There is a tendency to blot out these events as they happen to other people in other places, but they are nonetheless crimes against 'humanity' and against international laws and therefore deserve attention (Cohen 1996).

CRIME, CRIMINAL JUSTICE AND SOCIAL POLICY

This book has centred on crime rather than criminal justice and this section will not deal with specific policies but will outline some broad issues raised by the study of crime. While it has been seen that the so-called modernist project aimed to establish the causes of and a cure for crime, such grand aims – or as post-modernists refer to them, 'meta narratives' – have now been abandoned and it was seen in Chapter 4 that it has been argued that crime can be prevented without establishing its causes. Against this, however, it is often contested that such policies will be limited if they neglect the structural roots of crime. Nonetheless, sociological theories linking crime to social disadvantage and social exclusion are far less easy to relate directly to policy (Downes and Rock 1995), and they also imply that a wide range of social and economic policies must also be considered. To labelling perspectives, the formal agencies of social control may amplify crime and criminalize specific groups, implying that they should be used less. To critical approaches, less directly concerned with policy, not only should the processes of criminalization be avoided but the constructed nature of crime should be challenged, involving wider political processes. Taken together this suggests a number of questions.

- Can the criminal justice process effectively reduce or prevent crime?

- Should tackling crime be related to other social policies?

- Should the criminal justice process intervene less?

- Should other approaches be adopted?

- What is the role of the criminal law and criminalization?

Although the formal criminal justice process is often seen as the major vehicle for controlling crime, its role is necessarily limited. It has been seen, for example, that only a small proportion of crimes are detected and reported and even fewer offenders are convicted. Many kinds of crime, such as the drugs market, professional and organized, state and white collar, have been seen to be relatively impervious to formal controls. Indeed the success of

318

criminal businesses depends on the avoidance of detection and capture. The formal apparatus of criminal justice also aims to deter offending by increasing the chances of being caught and through deterrent sentencing. While many potential offenders may well be deterred, many others are not. It was seen in relation to property crime that some offenders underestimate their chances of being caught, others calculate that the rewards of the offence outstrip their chances of being caught, and others commit crimes on the spur of the moment with little rational planning. For other offences, such as white collar or corporate crime, the slim chances of being caught mean that little deterrence exists. The criminal justice system on its own is therefore limited in its ability to substantially reduce the total volume of crime, and its more important role is to process offenders who are detected.

These limitations were acknowledged with the growth of crime prevention policies based on the rational choice theories outlined in Chapter 4. An enormous range of these policies have now been developed involving not only the police but community groups, welfare agencies and individual citizens. They range from simple schemes to encourage people to be more aware of security and projects aiming to make streets and residential areas more secure by, for example, installing security equipment and gating alleyways, to the installation of close circuit television (CCTV) in public spaces such as shopping malls, stations, airports and many offices and residential premises. These have had a considerable effect – as seen in Chapter 13, they have reduced the number of bank robberies and many offenders will avoid committing crimes where such security systems have been installed. They have made many environments more secure and have considerably reduced crime in some communities. Their limitations, however, have also been referred to (see Chapters 4 and 12). While they may reduce some forms of crime in some areas, some offenders have turned to other forms of crime or to softer targets. They work better with some kinds of crime than others. They have little effect, for example, on serious crime, as offenders are skilled enough to avoid security and they are limited in respect of violence in the family or state crime. While they make some environments safer they may have less impact on those most at risk, many of whom are less able to afford such measures. This has raised the prospect of the more affluent classes increasingly protecting themselves with locks, bolts and bars from the crimes of the lower classes, leaving lower-income groups to be more victimized (see, for example, Marx 1995). It was also seen in previous chapters that their effects may be limited because they tackle crime at the level of individual environments, and can do little to address the wider structural roots of crime.

These structural roots, seen above as lying in deprivation, disadvantage and in social and economic policies, lie outside the reach of the formal criminal justice process. Tackling these would ultimately involve developing different economic policies which lie well beyond the scope of this text. It can be suggested, however, that reducing or preventing crime also involves looking at a range of economic and social policies. Even though crime may

not be related directly to unemployment, the development of long-term structural unemployment and social exclusion has an effect on crime and social
exclusion is now seen by many as a major social problem to be addressed by
a range of policies dealing with youth unemployment and changes in the
welfare system. Other areas of social policy – as seen in relation to drugs,
education and youth policy – are also important. Left realists and others also
advocate 'multi-agency' policies in which all those concerned about crime,
such as the police, community groups, educational and welfare agencies,
become involved in local policy-making arenas to address local crime problems. While the success of some of these schemes has been limited by lack of
funding, resources and the different perceptions of different agencies, they
nonetheless have some potential (see, for example, Davies et al 1995).

Other approaches are suggested by the insights of the labelling perspective, which imply that intervention by the criminal justice process should be
minimized as it can confirm 'deviant' or criminal identities, stigmatize the
offender and thus lead to secondary deviance or a criminal career. It was
seen in Chapter 4 that left realists advocate minimal intervention: these kinds
of ideas lay behind suggestions that many offenders, particularly young offenders, should be diverted from the criminal justice process at an early stage
by cautioning, informal warnings and other forms of diversion which can
include referral to social welfare agencies and, in a small number of cases,
victim–offender mediation schemes. It was also argued that, where possible,
young offenders should be kept out of custody. It has also been seen that some
forms of crime, particularly white collar crime, are also often dealt with out
of court and some, like Braithwaite, suggest that these kinds of arrangements
could be developed for other forms of crime (Braithwaite and Pettit 1990).
Braithwaite also argues that, as shame is a powerful mechanism encouraging conformity, measures which encourage the 'shaming' of offenders can be
used to express public disapproval, but at the same time seek to 'reintegrate'
offenders into the community, rather than create 'outsiders' (Braithwaite 1989;
Braithwaite and Pettit 1990). As seen in Chapter 15, Braithwaite argues that
this is relevant to corporate offenders and juvenile delinquents alike. Many of
these suggestions are particularly relevant for juvenile offenders, for many of
whom, as seen in Chapter 7, involvement in crime is transitory.

These ideas suggest that the formal processes of criminal law, policing and
punishment may not be the only, or even the most appropriate, way to deal
with some forms of crime and can indeed 'create' crime by criminalizing
activities which can lead to secondary crime. As seen in relation to drug
taking and prostitution, for example, the criminal law creates enforcement
problems, is relatively ineffective in reducing crime and can lead to involvement in other forms of crime. It has also been seen that professional crime
thrives on trading in prohibited goods – if fewer goods were prohibited this
would reduce opportunities for criminal 'enterprises'. Many of these activities could be regulated by licensing arrangements which need not involve the
criminal law. Many forms of youth crime could also, it be argued, be dealt

with outside the formal processes of law. It has also been seen that what is often called the 'criminal law' approach to corporate and white collar crime is severely limited, although against this it could be argued that criminal law is necessary both as a deterrent and as an expression of disapproval of these kinds of activities. While widespread decriminalization is not generally advocated, these questions do raise the issue of whether the criminal law should be used so extensively.

These arguments also suggest that the criminal law is only one among many means of regulating harmful activities, although, as argued above, it remains a powerful form of censure and reflects societal disapproval. Changing the criminal status of activities may, however, only be one strategy for expressing that disapproval, and campaigns which have sought to challenge constructions of crime have often been linked to wider political movements. The greater attention paid to the victim of crime, and particularly to sexual violence, resulted from social and political pressures originating outside the criminal justice process in the women's movement (see Chapters 5 and 8). Changing the cultures in which many forms of crime are tolerated can only, argue some, be achieved by broader social movements. In the United States and elsewhere campaigns about white collar, corporate and state organized crime were initiated by a range of consumer and environmental campaigns (Braithwaite 1995). Civil and human rights organizations have played a role in raising awareness of many forms of state crime, and tackling other forms of this involve wider issues of openness in government and public accountability. Many forms of crime therefore involve a wider range of issues than can be tackled by the criminal justice process.

There are therefore, no simple or straightforward solutions to crime, just as there are no simple or straightforward explanations of it. Crime is, as has been seen, a vast and complex subject, which can be viewed from the many different perspectives introduced in this book. It involves not one crime problem but many different crime problems, many of them not widely defined as 'crime'. Many different questions can be asked about crime, reflecting the many different ways in which these problems are constructed. Many of these questions remain unanswered and require further research and analyses. At the same time, however, the answer to many questions is unknowable and the study of crime remains a fascinating enterprise which seeks to understand many hidden and unresolved issues.

BIBLIOGRAPHY

Aitken L and Griffin G (1996) *Gender Issues in Elder Abuse*. London: Sage

Adler F (1975) *Sisters in Crime*. New York: McGraw Hill

Alba C (1996) 'Hospital Opens Police Station to Curb Violence', *The Herald* 26/8/96

Amir M (1971) *Patterns of Forcible Rape*. Chicago: University of Chicago Press

Anderson D, Chenery S and Pease K (1995) *Biting Back: Tackling Repeat Burglary and Car Crime*. Police Research Group: Crime Detection and Prevention Series. London: HMSO

Anderson S, Grove Smith C, Kinsey R and Wood J (1990) *The Edinburgh Crime Survey*. Edinburgh: Scottish Office

Anderson S, Kinsey R, Loader I and Smith C (1994) *Cautionary Tales: Young People, Crime and Policing in Edinburgh*. Aldershot: Avebury

Anderson S and Leitch S (1994) *The Scottish Crime Survey 1993: First Results*. Scottish Office Central Research Unit Paper. Edinburgh: Scottish Office

Ariès P (1962) *Centuries of Childhood*. London: Jonathan Cape

Ashworth A (1994) *The Criminal Process*. Oxford: Clarendon Press

Aubert V (1977) 'White Collar Crime and Social Structure', in Geis G and Maier R F (eds) *White Collar Crime: Offences in Business, Politics and the Professions – Classic and Contemporary Views*. Revised edition. New York: Free Press, Collier and Macmillan

Bagguley P and Mann K (1992) 'Idle Thieving Bastards? Scholarly Representations of the "Underclass"', *Work, Employment and Society*, Vol 6/1: 113–26

Bailey W and Peterson R (1995) 'Gender Inequality and Violence Against Women: The Case of Murder', in Hagan J and Peterson R (eds) *Crime and Inequality*. Stanford: Stanford University Press

Baker T and Duncan S (1986) 'Child Sexual Abuse', in Meadow R (ed.) *Recent Advances in Paediatrics*. Edinburgh: Churchill Livingstone

Barclay G (ed) (1993) *Digest 2: A Digest of Information on the Criminal Justice System*. London: HMSO

Barclay G (ed) (1995) *Digest 3: Information on the Criminal Justice System in England and Wales*. Home Office Research and Statistics Department. London: HMSO

Barker M, Geraghty J, Webb B and Key T (1993) *The Prevention of Street Robbery*. Home Office Police Research Group Crime Prevention Unit Series Paper 44. London: HMSO

Beck A, Gill M and Willis A (1994) 'Violence in Retailing: Physical and Verbal Victimisation of Staff', in Gill M (ed) *Crime at Work: Studies in Security and Crime Prevention*. Leicester: Perpetuity Press

Becker H (1963) *Outsiders: Studies in the Study of Deviance*. New York: Free Press

Bell D (1953) 'Crime as an American Way of Life', *The Antioch Review*, 13: 131–54; reprinted in Passas N (ed) (1995) *Organized Crime*. Aldershot: Dartmouth

Bennett T and Wright R (1984) *Burglars on Burglary*. Aldershot: Gower

Bennett T (1989) 'Burglars' Choice of Targets', in Evans D and Herbert D (eds) *The Geography of Crime*. London: Routledge

Bennett T and Maguire M (1982) *Burglary in a Dwelling: The Offence, the Offender and the Victim*. London: Heinemann Educational Books

Biles D (1991) 'Deaths in Custody in Britian and Australia', *The Howard Journal of Criminal Justice*, Vol 39/2: 110–20

Birkinshaw P (1996) 'Government at the End of its Tether: Matrix Churchill and the Scott Report', *Journal of Law and Society*, Vol 23/3: 406–26

Bland L (1992) 'The Case of the Yorkshire Ripper: Mad, Bad, Beast, or Male?', in Radford J and Russell D (eds) *Femicide: The Politics of Woman Killing*. Buckingham: Open University Press

Bottomley K and Pease K (1986) *Crime and Punishment – Interpreting the Data*. Milton Keynes: Open University Press

Bowlby J (1953) *Child Care and the Growth of Love*. Harmondsworth: Penguin

Bowling B (1993) 'Racial Harassment and the Process of Victimisation', *British Journal of Criminology*, Vol 33/2: 216–30

Box S (1983) *Power, Crime and Mystification*. London: Tavistock

Box S (1987) *Recession, Crime and Punishment*. London: Macmillan

Box S and Hale C (1983) 'Liberation and Female Criminality in England and Wales', *British Journal of Criminology*, 23/1: 35–49

Box S and Hale C (1986) 'Unemployment, Crime and Imprisonment', in Matthews R and Young J (eds) *Confronting Crime*. London: Sage

Braithwaite J (1984) *Corporate Crime in the Pharmaceutical Industry*. London: Routledge & Kegan Paul

Braithwaite J (1989) *Crime, Shame and Re-integration*. Cambridge: Cambridge University Press

Braithwaite J (1995) 'Inequality and Republican Criminology', in Hagan J and Peterson R (eds) *Crime and Inequality*. Stanford: Stanford University Press

Braithwaite J and Pettit P (1990) *Not Just Deserts: A Republican Theory of Justice*. Oxford: Clarendon Press

Brake M (1985) *Comparative Youth Culture*. London: Routledge & Kegan Paul

Brake M and Hale C (1992) *Public Order and Private Lives*. London: Routledge

Brogden M, Jefferson T and Walklate S (1988) *Introducing Police Work*. London: Unwin Hyman

Brownmiller S (1975) *Against our Will: Men, Women and Rape*. London: Secker & Warburg

Brundson E and May M (1992) 'The Under-Reporting of Workplace Violence in the Care Professions', *Criminal Justice Matters*, No 8 Summer: 6

Burr A (1987) 'Chasing the Dragon: Heroin Misuse, Delinquency and Crime in the Context of South London Culture', *British Journal of Criminology*, Vol 27/4: 333–57

Cain M (1973) *Society and the Policeman's Role*. London: Routledge & Kegan Paul

Campbell A (1984) *Girls in the Gang*. Oxford: Basil Blackwell

Campbell B (1993) *Goliath: Britain's Dangerous Places*. London: Virago

Campbell B (1994) 'The Underclass: Regressive Re-alignment', in *Criminal Justice Matters*, No 18 Winter: 18–19

Carlen P (1976) *Magistrates' Justice*. London: Martin Robertson

Carlen P (1983) *Women's Imprisonment*. London: Routledge & Kegan Paul

Carlen P (1985) *Criminal Women*. Oxford: Polity Press

Carlen P (1988) *Women, Crime and Poverty*. Milton Keynes: Open University Press

Carlen P (1992) 'Criminal Women and Criminal Justice', in Matthews R and Young J (eds) *Issues in Realist Criminology*. London: Sage

Carlen P (1996) *Jigsaw: A Political Criminology of Youth Homelessness*. Buckingham: Open University Press

Carlen P (1997) 'Homelessness, Crime and Citizenship', *Criminal Justice Matters*, No 26 Winter: 24–5

Carlen P and Worrall A (eds) (1987) *Gender, Crime and Justice*. Milton Keynes: Open University Press

Carson W G (1971) 'White Collar Crime and the Enforcement of Factory Legislation', in Carson W G and Wiles P (eds) *Crime and Delinquency in Britain*. London: Martin Robertson

Carson W G (1981) *The Other Price of British Oil*. London: Martin Robertson

Chambers G and Tombs J (eds) (1984) *The British Crime Survey: Scotland*. A Scottish Office Social Research Study. Edinburgh: HMSO

Chambliss W (1995) 'State Organized Crime – The American Society of Criminology, 1988 Presidential Address', in Passas N (ed) *Organized Crime*. Aldershot: Dartmouth

Christiansen, K O (1974) 'Seriousness of Criminality and Concordance among Danish Twins', in Hood R (ed) *Crime, Criminology and Public Policy*. London: Heinemann

Clarke J (1996) 'Crime and Social Order: Interrogating the Detective Story', in Muncie J and McLaughlin E (eds) *The Problem of Crime*. London: Sage

Clarke M (1989) 'Insurance fraud', *British Journal of Criminology*, Vol 29/1: 1–20

Clarke M (1990) *Business Crime: Its Nature and Control.* Cambridge: Polity Press

Clarke R (1980) 'Situational Crime Prevention: Theory and Practice', *British Journal of Criminology*, 20

Clarke R and Mayhew P (1980) *Designing Out Crime.* London: HMSO

Cloward R and Ohlin L (1960) *Delinquency and Opportunity.* New York: Free Press

Cohen A K (1955) *Delinquent Boys.* New York: Free Press

Cohen P (1972) 'Working Class Youth Cultures in East London', *Working Papers in Cultural Studies*, No 2. Birmingham University

Cohen S (1972) *Folk Devils and Moral Panics.* Oxford: Martin Robertson

Cohen S (1979) 'Guilt, Justice and Tolerance: Some Old Concepts for a New Criminology', in Downes D and Rock P (eds) *Deviant Interpretations.* Oxford: Clarendon Press

Cohen S (1996) 'Human Rights and Crimes of the State: The Culture of Denial', in Muncie J, McLaughlin E and Langan M (eds) *Criminological Perspectives.* London: Sage

Coleman C and Moynihan J (1996) *Understanding Crime Data: Haunted by the Dark Figure.* Buckingham: Open University Press

Coles D, Shaw H and Ward T (1997) 'Deaths, Police and Prosecutions', *Criminal Justice Matters*, No 29 Autumn: 10–11

Collison M (1996) 'In Search of the High Life: Drugs, Crime, Masculinities and Consumption', *British Journal of Criminology*, Vol 36/3: 428–44

Connell R W (1987) *Gender and Power.* Oxford: Polity Press

Cook D (1989) *Rich Law, Poor Law: Different Responses to Tax and Supplementary Benefit Fraud.* Milton Keynes, Open University Press

Cook D and Hudson B (eds) (1993) *Racism and Criminology.* London: Sage

Cowie J, Cowie V and Slater E (1968) *Delinquency in Girls.* London: Heinemann

Crime Concern (1994) *Counting the Cost – A Briefing Paper on Financial Losses Arising from Crime.* Crime Concern: The Thames Valley Partnership

Croall H (1988) 'Mistakes, Accidents and Someone Else's Fault: The Trading Offender in Court', *Journal of Law and Society*, Vol 15/3: 293–315

Croall H (1989) 'Who is the White Collar Criminal?', *British Journal of Criminology*, Vol 29/2: 157–74

Croall H (1992) *White Collar Crime.* Buckingham: Open University Press

Croall H (1995) 'Target Women: Women's Victimisation from White Collar Crime', in Dobash R, Dobash R and Noaks L (eds) *Gender and Crime.* Cardiff: Cardiff University Press

Croall H (1997) 'Business, Crime and the Community,' *International Journal of Risk, Security and Crime Prevention*

Crow I et al (1989) *Unemployment, Crime and Offenders.* London: Routledge

Currie E (1991) *International developments in Crime and Social Policy.* NACRO Crime and Social Policy: 107–20; London: NACRO

Currie E (1996) 'Social Crime Prevention Strategies in a Market Society', in Muncie J, McLaughlin E and Langan M (eds) *Criminological Perspectives*. London: Sage

Dale A (1996) 'Surveying the Scene: Young People and Drugs', *Criminal Justice Matters*, No 24 Summer: 10–11

Daly M and Wilson M (1988) *Homicide*. New York: de Gruyter

Davidoff L and Greenhorn M (1991) 'Violent Crime in England and Wales', paper presented at the British Criminology Conference, York.

Davies M, Croall H and Tyrer J (1995) *Criminal Justice: An Introduction to the Criminal Justice System in England and Wales*. London: Longman

Davies P (1996) 'Crime, Victims and Criminal Justice Policy', in Davies P, Francis P and Jupp V (eds) *Understanding Victimisation*. Northumbria Social Science Press

Davies P, Francis P and Jupp V (1996) 'Understanding Victimology: Theory, Method and Practice', in Davies P, Francis P and Jupp V (eds) *Understanding Victimisation*. Northumbria Social Science Press

Ditton J (1977) *Part Time Crime: an Ethnography of Fiddling and Pilferage*. London: Macmillan

Dobash R and Dobash R (1992) *Women, Violence and Social Change*. London: Routledge

Doig A (1996) 'From Lynskey to Nolan: The Corruption of British Politics and Public Service', *Journal of Law and Society*, Vol 23/1: 36–56

Doig A (1984) *Corruption and Misconduct in Contemporary British Politics*. Harmondsworth: Penguin

Dorn N and South N (1990) 'Drugs Markets and Law Enforcement', *British Journal of Criminology*, Vol 30/2: 171–88

Dorn N, Murji K and South N (1992) *Traffickers: Drugs Markets and Law Enforcement*. London: Routledge

Downes D (1966) *The Delinquent Solution: A Study in Subcultural Theory*. London: Routledge

Downes D (1997) 'Law and Order Futures', *Criminal Justice Matters*, No 26 Winter: 3–4

Downes D and Rock P (1995) *Understanding Deviance: A Guide to the Sociology of Crime and Rule Breaking*, revised 2nd edition. Oxford: Clarendon Press

Durkheim E (1964) *The Rules of Sociological Method*. New York: Free Press; first published 1895. Extract 'The Normal and the Pathological' reprinted in Muncie J, McLaughlin E and Langan M (eds) *Criminological Perspectives*. London: Sage

Durkheim E (1970) *Suicide*. London: Routledge & Kegan Paul

Eaton M (1986) *Justice for Women?* Milton Keynes: Open University Press

Edwards S (1981) *Female Sexuality and the Law*. Oxford: Martin Robertson

Ellingworth D, Farrell G and Pease K (1995) 'A Victim is a Victim is a Victim: Chronic Victimisation in Four Sweeps of the British Crime Survey', *British Journal of Criminology*, Vol 35: 360–5

Ermann M and Lundman R (eds) (1978) *Corporate and Governmental Deviance: Problems of Organizational Behaviour in Contemporary Society*. New York: Oxford University Press

Eysenck H (1977) *Crime and Personality*. London: Routledge & Kegan Paul

Farrell G, Phillips C and Pease K (1995) 'Like Taking Candy: Why does Repeat Victimization Occur?, *British Journal of Criminology*, Vol 35/3: 384–99

Farrington D (1994) 'Human Development and Criminal Careers', in Maguire M, Morgan R and Reiner R (eds) *The Oxford Handbook of Criminology*. Oxford: Clarendon Press

Field S (1990) 'Trends in Crime and their Interpretation: A Study of Recorded Crime in Post War England and Wales', Home Office Research Study No 119. London: HMSO

Field S (1996) 'Crime and Consumption', in Muncie J, McLaughlin E and Langan M (eds) *Criminological Perspectives*. London: Sage

Fijnaut C (1990) 'Organized Crime: A Comparison between the United States of America and Western Europe', *British Journal of Criminology*, Vol 30/3: 321–40

Fisse B and Braithwaite J (1993) *Corporations, Crimes and Accountability*. Cambridge: Cambridge University Press

Fitzgerald M (1993) 'Racism': Establishing the Phenomenon', in Cook D and Hudson B (eds) *Racism and Criminology*. London: Sage

Fitzgerald M (1995) 'Ethnic Differences', in Walker M (ed) *Interpreting Crime Statistics*. Oxford: Clarendon Press

Fitzgerald M and Hale C (1996) *Ethnic Minorities, Victimization and Racial Harassment: Findings from the 1988 and 1992 British Crime Surveys*. Home Office Research Study No 154. London: Home Office.

Forsyth A, Hammersley R, Lavelle T and Murray K (1992) 'Geographical Aspects of Scoring Illegal Drugs', *British Journal of Criminology*, 32/3: 292–309

Foster J (1990) *Villains: Crime and Community in the Inner City*. London: Routledge

Fyfe N (1997) 'Crime', in Pacione M (ed) *Britain's Divided Cities: Geographies of Division in Urban Britain*. London: Routledge

Gelsthorpe L (1989) *Sexism and the Female Offender*. Aldershot: Gower

Gelsthorpe L (1997) 'Feminism and Criminology', in Maguire M, Morgan R and Reiner R (eds) *The Oxford Handbook of Criminology*, 2nd edition. Oxford: Clarendon Press

Gelsthorpe L and Morris A (1988) 'Feminism and Criminology in Britain', in Rock P (ed) *A History of British Criminology*. Oxford: Clarendon Press

Gelsthorpe L and Morris A (1990) 'Introduction: Transforming and Transgressing Criminology', in Gelsthorpe L and Morris A (eds) *Feminist Perspectives in Criminology*. Milton Keynes: Open University Press

Gill K, Woolley A and Gill M (1994) 'Insurance Fraud: The Business as a Victim?', in Gill M (ed) *Crime at Work: Studies in Security and Crime Prevention*. Leicester: Perpetuity Press

Gill M and Matthews R (1994) 'Robbers on Robbery: Offenders' Perspectives', in Gill M (ed) *Crime at Work: Studies in Security and Crime Prevention*. Leicester: Perpetuity Press

Gillespie T (1996) 'Rape Crisis Centres and 'Male Rape': A Face of the Backlash', in Hester M, Kelly L and Radford J (eds) *Women, Violence and Male Power*. Buckingham: Open University Press

Gilroy P (1987a) *There Ain't no Black in the Union Jack*. London: Hutchinson

Gilroy P (1987b) 'The Myth of Black Criminality', in Scraton P (ed) *Law, Order and the Authoritarian State*. Milton Keynes: Open University Press

Glueck S and Glueck E (1950) *Unravelling Juvenile Delinquency*. New York: Commonwealth Fund

Goffman E (1968) *Asylums*. Harmondsworth: Penguin

Graef R (1990) *Talking Blues; The Police in their own Words*. London: Fontana

Graham J and Bowling B (1996) *Young People and Crime*. Research Study No 145. London: Home Office Research and Statistics Department.

Graham P and Clarke J (1996) 'Dangerous Places: Crime and the City', in Muncie J and McLaughlin E (eds) *The Problem of Crime*. London: Sage

Gresswell D and Hollin C (1994) 'Multiple Murder: A Review', *British Journal of Criminology*, Vol 34/1: 1–15

Hagell A and Newburn T (1994) *Persistent Young Offenders*. London: Policy Studies Institute

Hall R (1985) *Ask Any Woman*. London: Falling Wall Press

Hall S (1996) 'Drifting into a Law and Order Society', in Muncie J, McLaughlin E and Langan M (eds) *Criminological Perspectives*. London: Sage

Hall S and Jefferson T (eds) (1976) *Resistance Through Rituals*. London: Hutchinson

Hall S, Critcher C, Jefferson T, Clarke J and Roberts B (1978) *Policing the Crisis: Mugging, the State and Law and Order*. London: Macmillan

Hartless J, Ditton J, Nair G and Phillips S (1995) 'More Sinned Against than Sinning: A Study of Young Teenagers' Experience of Crime', *British Journal of Criminology*, Vol 35/1: 114

Hawkins K (1984) *Environment and Enforcement: Regulation and the Social Definition of Pollution*. Oxford: Clarendon Press

Hawkins K (1990) 'Compliance Strategy, Prosecution Policy and Aunt Sally – A Comment on Pearce and Tombs', *British Journal of Criminology*, 30/4: 444–67

Hebenton B and Thomas T (1996) 'Tracking Sex Offenders', *Howard Journal*, Vol 35/2: 97–112

Hedderman C (1995) 'Gender, Crime and the Criminal Justice System', in Walker M (ed) *Interpreting Crime Statistics*. Oxford: Clarendon Press

Heidensohn F (1989) *Crime and Society*. London: Macmillan

Heidensohn F (1992) *Women in Control? The Role of Women in Law Enforcement*. Oxford: Oxford University Press

Heidensohn F (1995) 'Feminist Perspectives and their Impact on Criminology and Criminal Justice in Britain', in Rafter N and Heidensohn F (eds) *International Feminist Perspectives in Criminology: Engendering a Discipline*. Milton Keynes: Open University Press

Heidensohn F (1996) *Women and Crime*, 2nd edition. London: Macmillan

Heidensohn F (1997) 'Gender and Crime', in Maguire M, Morgan R and Reiner R (eds) *The Oxford Handbook of Criminology*, 2nd edition. Oxford: Clarendon Press

Hennessey J (1994) in *The Scotsman* 8/12/94

Henry S (1978) *The Hidden Economy: The Context and Control of Borderline Crime*. Oxford: Martin Robertson

Hentig, H von (1948) *The Criminal and His Victim*. New Haven: Yale University Press.

Hester M, Kelly L and Radford J (eds) (1996) *Women, Violence and Male Power*. Buckingham: Open University Press

Hester S and Eglin P (1992) *A Sociology of Crime*. London: Routledge

Hillyard P (1987) 'The Normalization of Special Powers: From Northern Ireland to Britain', in P Scraton (ed) *Law, Order and the Authoritarian State*. Milton Keynes: Open University Press

Hillyard P (1993) *Suspect Community: People's Experience of the Prevention of Terrorism Acts in Britain*. London: Pluto Press

Hillyard P (1996) 'The Stalker Affair and the Quest of Justice: The Failure of the Law in Northern Ireland', Paper presented to the Law and Society Association Annual Conference, Strathclyde University, 10 July

Hindelang M J, Gottfredson M R and Garofalo J (1978) *Victims of Personal Crime: An Empirical Foundation for a Theory of Personal Victimization*. Cambridge: Ballinger

Hirschi T (1969) *Causes of Delinquency*. Los Angeles: University of California Press

Hirst P (1972) 'Marx and Engels on Law, Crime and Morality', *Economy and Society*, Vol 1/1

Hobbs D (1988) *Doing the Business: Entrepreneurship, the Working Class and Detectives in East London*. Oxford: Clarendon Press

Hobbs D (1991) 'A Piece of Business: The Moral Economy of Detective Work in the East of London', *British Journal of Sociology*, Vol 42: 4

Hobbs D (1994) 'Professional and Organized Crime in Britain', in Maguire M, Morgan R and Reiner R (eds) *The Oxford Handbook of Criminology*. Oxford: Clarendon Press

Hobbs D (1995) *Bad Business: Professional Crime in Modern Britain*. Oxford: Oxford University Press

Hodgkinson P (1997) 'The Sociology of Corruption – Some Themes and Issues', *Sociology* 31/1: 17–35

Holdaway S (1983) *Inside the British Police*. Oxford: Blackwell

Holdaway S (1996) *The Racialization of British Policing*. London: Macmillan

Holdaway S (1997) 'Some Recent Approaches to the Study of Race in Criminological Research', *British Journal of Criminology*, Vol 37/3: 383–400

Hollin C (1989) *Psychology and Crime: An Introduction to Criminological Psychology*. London: Routledge

Holman B (1994) 'A View from Easterhouse', in *Criminal Justice Matters*, No 18 Winter: 12

Hough M (1996) 'Drug Misuse and the Criminal Justice System: A Review of the Literature', *Criminal Justice Matters*, No 24 Summer: 4–5

Hough M and Mayhew P (1983) *The British Crime Survey: First Report*. Home Office Research Study No 147. London: Home Office Research and Statistics Department

Hudson B (1993) 'Racism and Criminology: Concepts and Controversies', in Cook D and Hudson B (eds) *Racism and Criminology*. London: Sage

Hutter B (1988) *The Reasonable Arm of the Law?* Oxford: Clarendon Press

Jacobs P, Brunton M and Melville M (1965) 'Aggressive Behaviour, Mental Subnormality and the XYY male', *Nature*, Vol 208: 1351

Jarvis G and Parker H (1989) 'Young Heroin Users and Crime', *British Journal of Criminology*, 29/2: 175–85

Jefferson T (1990) *The Case against Paramilitary Policing*. Milton Keynes: Open University Press

Jefferson T and Holloway W (1997) 'The Risk Society in an Age of Anxiety: Situating Fear of Crime', *British Journal of Sociology*, Vol 48/2: 255–66

Jefferson T and Walker M (1992) 'Ethnic Minorities in the Criminal Justice System', *Criminal Law Review*, 83–8

Jefferson T, Walker M and Seneviratne M (1992) 'Ethnic Minorities, Crime and Criminal Justice: A Study in a Provincial City', in Downes D (ed) *Unravelling Criminal Justice*. London: Macmillan

Jones T, McClean B and Young J (1986) *The Islington Crime Survey*. Aldershot: Gower

Jupp V (1989) *Methods of Criminological Research*. London: Unwin Hyman

Katz J (1988) *Seductions of Crime: Moral and Sensual Attractions in Doing Evil*. New York: Basic Books

Keith M (1993) *Race, Riots and Policing*. London: UCL Press

Kelly L (1988) *Surviving Sexual Violence*. Cambridge: Polity Press

Kelly L (1996) 'When Does the Speaking Profit Us?: Reflections on the Challenges of Developing Feminist Perspectives on Abuse and Violence by Women', in Hester M, Kelly L and Radford J (eds) *Women, Violence and Male Power*. Buckingham: Open University Press

Kelly L and Radford J (1996) ' "Nothing Really Happened": The Invalidation of Women's Experiences of Sexual Violence', in Hester M, Kelly L and Radford J (eds) *Women, Violence and Male Power*. Buckingham: Open University Press

Kinsey R (1984) *Merseyside Crime Survey: First Report*. Liverpool: Merseyside Metropolitan Council

Kinsey R and Anderson S (1992) *Crime and the Quality of Life: Public Perceptions and Experiences of Crime in Scotland: Findings from the 1988 British Crime Survey*. Scottish Office Central Research Unit. Edinburgh: HMSO

Kitsuse J and Cicourel A (1963) 'A Note on the Uses of Official Statistics', *Social Problems*, Vol 11/2: 132–9

Lacey N, Wells C and Meure D (1990) *Reconstructing Criminal Law: Critical Perspectives on Crime and the Criminal Process*. London: Weidenfeld & Nicolson

Landau S F and Nathan G (1983) 'Selecting Juveniles for Cautioning in the London Metropolitan Area', *British Journal of Criminology*, Vol 23/2: 128–49

Langan M (1996) 'Hidden and Respectable: Crime and the Market', in Muncie J and McLaughlin E (eds) *The Problem of Crime*. London: Sage

Lea J and Young J (1993) *What is to be Done about Law and Order?*, 2nd edition. London: Pluto Press

Lees S (1992) 'Naggers, Whores, and Libbers: Provoking Men to Kill', in Radford J and Russell D (eds) *Femicide: The Politics of Woman Killing*. Buckingham: Open University Press

Lees S (1996) 'Unreasonable doubt: the outcomes of rape trials', in Hester M, Kelly L and Radford J (eds) *Women, Violence and Male Power*. Buckingham: Open University Press

Lees S (1997) 'Naggers, Whores and Libbers: Provoking Men to Kill' (with new postscript), in Lees S (ed) *Ruling Passions: Sexual Violence, Reputation and the Law*. Buckingham: Open University Press

Leigh D and Vulliamy E (1997) *Sleaze: The Corruption of Parliament*. London: Fourth Estate

Lemert E (1951) *Social Pathology*. New York: McGraw-Hill

Leng R, McConville M and Sanders A (1992) 'Researching the Discretions to Charge and to Prosecute', in Downes D (ed) *Unravelling Criminal Justice*. London: Macmillan

Levi M (1981) *The Phantom Capitalists*. London: Heinemann

Levi M (1987) *Regulating Fraud: White Collar Crime and the Criminal Process*. London: Tavistock

Levi M (1988) *The Prevention of Fraud*. Crime Prevention Unit, Paper 17. London: HMSO

Levi M (1989) 'Suite Justice: Sentencing for Fraud', *Criminal Law Review*, 420–34

Levi M (1991) 'Regulating Money Laundering', *British Journal of Criminology*, Vol 31/2: 109–25

Levi M (1994) 'Masculinities and White Collar Crime', in Newburn T and Stanko E (eds) *Just Boys Doing Business?* London: Routledge

Levi M (1997) 'Violent Crime', in Maguire M, Morgan R and Reiner R (eds) *The Oxford Handbook of Criminology*, 2nd edition. Oxford: Clarendon Press

Levi M and Nelken D (1996) 'The Corruption of Politics and the Politics of Corruption: An Overview', *Journal of Law and Society*, Vol 23/1: 1–17

Levi M and Pithouse A (1992) 'The Victims of Fraud', in Downes D (ed) *Unravelling Criminal Justice*. London: Macmillan

Light R, Nee C and Ingham H (1993) *Car Theft: The Offender's Perspective*. Home Office Research and Planning Unit: Home Office Research Study No 130. London: HMSO

Lombroso C (1897) *L'Uomo Delinquente*, 5th edition. Torino: Bocca

Lombroso C and Ferrero W (1895) *The Female Offender*. London: Unwin

Loveday B (1992) 'Right Agendas: Law and Order in England and Wales', *International Journal of the Sociology of Law*, Vol 20: 297–319

McBarnet, D (1988) 'Law, Policy and Legal Avoidance: Can Law Effectively Implement Egalitarian Strategies?', *Journal of Law and Society*, Vol 15/1

McCullough, D, Schmidt T and Lockhart B (1990) *Car Theft in Northern Ireland: Recent Studies on a Persistent Problem*. CIRAC Paper No 2. Belfast: The Extern Organisation

McIntosh M (1975) *The Organization of Crime*. London: Macmillan

McIntosh M (1988) 'Introduction to an Issue: Family Secrets as Public Drama', *Feminist Review*, No 28, January (Spring Special Issue)

McKeganey N and Barnard K (1996) *Sex Work on the Streets: Prostitutes and their Clients*. Buckingham: Open University Press

McLaughlin E (1996) 'Political Violence, Terrorism and Crimes of the State', in Muncie J and McLaughlin E (eds) *The Problem of Crime*. London: Sage

McLaughlin E and Muncie J (1993) 'Juvenile Delinquency', in Dallos R and McLaughlin (eds) *Social Problems and the Family*. Buckingham: Open University Press

McLeod E (1982) *Women Working: Prostitution Now*. London: Croom Helm

McLeod M and Saraga E (1988) 'Challenging the Orthodoxy: Towards a Feminist Theory and Practice', *Feminist Review*, No 28, January (Spring Special Issue)

McRobbie A and Garber J (1976) 'Girls and Subcultures', in Hall S and Jefferson T (eds) *Resistance Through Rituals*. London: Hutchinson

Mack J (1972) 'The Able Criminal', *British Journal of Criminology*, Vol 12/1: 44–54

Maguire K (1993) 'Fraud, Extortion and Racketeering: The Black Economy in Northern Ireland', Paper presented to the Third Liverpool Conference on Fraud, Corruption and Business Crime. University of Liverpool, March.

Maguire M (1997) 'Crime Statistics, Patterns and Trends: Changing Perceptions and their Implications', in Maguire M, Morgan R and Reiner R (eds) *The Oxford Handbook of Criminology*, 2nd edition. Oxford: Clarendon Press

Maguire M, Morgan R and Reiner R (eds) (1994) *The Oxford Handbook of Criminology*. Oxford: Clarendon Press

Maguire M, Morgan R and Reiner R (eds) (1997) *The Oxford Handbook of Criminology*, 2nd edition. Oxford: Clarendon Press

Mama A (1989) *The Hidden Struggle: Statutory and Voluntary Sector Responses to Violence against Black Women in the Home.* London: London Race and Housing Research Unit

Marlow A and Pitts J (1997) 'Taking Young People Seriously', *Criminal Justice Matters*, No 26 Winter: 12–14

Mars G (1982) *Cheats at Work, an Anthropology of Workplace Crime.* London, George Allen & Unwin

Marx G (1995) 'The Engineering of Social Control: The Search for the Silver Bullet', in Hagan and Peterson (eds) *Crime and Inequality.* Stanford: Stanford University Press

Mason D (1995) *Race and Ethnicity in Modern Britain.* Oxford: Oxford University Press

Matthews R (1993) *Kerb-Crawling, Prostitution and Multi-Agency Policing.* Police Research Group; Crime Prevention Unit Series Paper 43. London: HMSO

Matthews R (1996) *Armed Robbery: Two Police Responses.* Police Research Group; Crime Detection and Prevention Series Paper 78. London: HMSO

Matthews R and Young J (eds) (1992) *Issues in Realist Criminology.* London: Sage

Matza D (1964) *Delinquency and Drift.* New York: Wiley

Matza D (1969) *Becoming Deviant.* Englewood Cliffs, NJ: Prentice Hall

Mawby R and Walklate S (1994) *Critical Victimology: The Victim in International Perspective.* London: Sage

Mayhew P (1996) 'Researching Crime and Victimisation', in Davies P, Francis P and Jupp V (eds) *Understanding Victimisation.* Northumbria Socia Science Press

Mayhew P and Mirlees-Black C (1993) *The 1992 British Crime Survey.* Home Office Research Study No 132. London: HMSO

Mayhew P, Elliot D and Dowds L (1989) *The 1988 British Crime Survey.* London: HMSO

Measham F (1995) 'Young Women and Drugs', *Criminal Justice Matters*, No 19 Spring: 10–11

Measham F, Newcombe R and Parker H (1994) 'The Normalization of Recreational Drug Use amongst Young People in North-West England', *British Journal of Sociology*, Vol 45/2: 287–312

Mendelsohn B (1947) 'New Bio-Psychosocial Horizons: Victimology', *American Law Review*, Vol 13: 649

Merton R K (1938) 'Social Structure and Anomie', *American Sociological Review*, Vol 3: 672–82

Messerschmidt J (1995) 'From Patriarchy to Gender: Feminist Theory, Criminology and the Challenge of Diversity', in Rafter N and Heidensohn F (eds) *International Feminist Perspectives in Criminology: Engendering a Discipline.* Milton Keynes: Open University Press

Miles R (1989) *Racism.* London: Routledge

Miller M (1985) *Danger! Additives at Work.* London: London Food Commission

Miller P and Plant M (1996) 'Drinking, Smoking and Illicit Drug Use among 15 and 16 year olds in the United Kingdom', *British Medical Journal*, Vol 313: 394–7

Miller W B (1958) 'Lower Class Culture as a Generating Milieu of Gang Delinquency', *Journal of Social Issues*, Vol 14/3

Mills C W (1970) *The Sociological Imagination*. Harmondsworth: Penguin

Mirlees-Black C, Mayhew P and Percy A (1996) *The 1996 British Crime Survey: England and Wales*. Home Office Statistical Bulletin Issue 19/96. London: HMSO

Mitchell B (1990) *Murder and Penal Policy*. Basingstoke: Macmillan

Morgan J and Zedner L (1992) *Child Victims: Crime, Impact, and Criminal Justice*. Oxford: Clarendon Press

Morrison S and O'Donnell I (1994) *Armed Robbery: A Study in London*. Centre for Criminological Research, University of Oxford.

Muncie J (1984) *The Trouble with Kids Today*. London: Hutchinson

Muncie J (1996) 'The Construction and Deconstruction of Crime', in Muncie J and McLaughlin E (eds) *The Problem of Crime*. London: Sage

Muncie J, McLaughlin E and Langan M (eds) (1996) *Criminological Perspectives*. London: Sage

Muncie J and McLaughlin E (eds) (1996) *The Problem of Crime*. London: Sage

Murray C (1990) *The Emerging Underclass*. London: Institute of Economic Affairs

Murray C (1996) 'The Underclass', in Muncie J, McLaughlin E and Langan M (eds) *Criminological Perspectives*. London: Sage

Naffine N and Gale F (1989) 'Testing the Nexus: Crime, Gender and Unemployment', *British Journal of Criminology*, Vol 29/2

Nelken D (1997) 'White Collar Crime', in Maguire M, Morgan R and Reiner R (eds) *The Oxford Handbook of Criminology*, 2nd edition. Oxford: Clarendon Press

Newburn T (1995) *Crime and Criminal Justice Policy*. London: Longman

Newburn T and Stanko E (1994) 'When Men are Victims: The Failure of Victimology', in Newburn T and Stanko E (eds) *Just Boys Doing Business?* London: Routledge

O'Donnell I and Morrison S (1997) 'Armed and Dangerous? The Use of Firearms in Robbery', *Howard Journal of Criminal Justice*, 36/3: 305–20

O'Neill M (1996) 'Researching Prostitution and Violence: Towards a Feminist Praxis', in Hester M, Kelly L and Radford J (eds) *Women, Violence and Male Power*. Buckingham: Open University Press

Painter K (1991a) 'Violence and Vulnerability in the Workplace: Psychosocial and Legal Implications', in Davidson M and Earnshaw J (eds) *Vulnerable Workers: Psychosocial and Legal Issues*. Chichester: Wiley

Painter K (1991b) *Wife Rape, Marriage and the Law: Survey Report: Key Findings*. University of Manchester, Department of Social Policy and Social Work

Pantazis C and Gordon D (1997) 'Television Licence Evasion and the Criminalisation of Female Poverty' *Howard Journal of Criminal Justice*, 36/2: 170–86

Park R and Burgess E (eds) (1925) *The City*. Chicago: University of Chicago Press

Parker H (1974) *The View from the Boys*. David & Charles

Parker H (1996) 'Young Adult Offenders, Alcohol and Criminological Cul-de-sacs', *British Journal of Criminology*, Vol 36/2: 282–98

Parker H, Newcombe R and Bakx K (1988) *Living with Heroin: The Impact of a Drugs 'Epidemic' on an English Community*. Milton Keynes: Open University Press

Parton N (1985) *The Politics of Child Abuse*. Basingstoke: Macmillan

Passas N (1995) ' "I Cheat, Therefore I Exist?" The BCCI Scandal in Context', in Passas N (ed) *Organized Crime*. Aldershot: Dartmouth

Patrick J (1973) *A Glasgow Gang Observed*. London: Eyre Methuen

Paulus I (1974) *The Search for Pure Food: A Sociology of Legislation in Britain*. London: Martin Robertson

Payne D (1992) *Crime in Scotland: Findings from the 1988 British Crime Survey*. Central Research Unit Paper. Edinburgh: Scottish Office

Pearce F (1976) *Crimes of the Powerful*. London: Pluto Press

Pearce F (1992) 'The Contribution of "Left Realism" to the Study of Commercial Crime', in McLean B and Lowman J (eds) *Realist Criminology: Crime Control and Policing in the 1990's*. Toronto: University of Toronto Press

Pearce F and Tombs S (1990) 'Ideology, Hegemony and Empiricism: Compliance Theories and Regulation', *British Journal of Criminology*, Vol 30/4: 423–43

Pearce F and Tombs S (1993) 'US Capital versus the Third World: Union Carbide and Bhopal', in Pearce F and Woodiwiss M (eds) *Global Crime Connections: Dynamics and Control*. London: Macmillan

Pearson G (1983) *Hooligan: A History of Respectable Fears*. London: Macmillan

Pearson G (1987a) *The New Heroin Users*. Oxford: Blackwell

Pearson G (1987b) 'Social Deprivation, Unemployment and Patterns of Heroin Use', in Dorn N and South N (eds) *A Land Fit for Heroin?* London: Macmillan

Pearson G (1994a) 'Youth, Crime, and Society', in Maguire M, Morgan R and Reiner R (eds) *The Oxford Handbook of Criminology*. Oxford: Clarendon Press

Pearson G (1994b) 'Moral Blinkers: Crime and Social Exclusion', in *Criminal Justice Matters*, No 18 Winter: 3–4

Pease K (1997) 'Crime Prevention', in Maguire M, Morgan R and Reiner R (eds) *The Oxford Handbook of Criminology*, 2nd edition. Oxford: Clarendon Press

Piliavin I and Briar S (1964) 'Police Encounters with Juveniles', *American Journal of Sociology*, Vol 70/2: 206–14

Pitts J (1988) *The Politics of Juvenile Crime*. London: Sage

Pitts J (1996) 'The Politics and Practice of Youth Justice', in McLaughlin E and Muncie J (eds) *Controlling Crime*. London: Sage

Plant M (1989) 'The Epidemiology of Illicit Drug Use and Misuse in Britain', in MacGregor S (ed) *Drugs and British Society: Responses to a social Problem in the 1980's*. London: Routledge

Plummer K (1979) 'Misunderstanding Labelling Perspectives', in Downes D and Rock P (eds) *Deviant Interpretations*. Oxford: Clarendon Press

Polk K (1994) 'Masculinity, Honour and Confrontational Homicide', in Newburn T and Stanko E (eds) *Just Boys Doing Business?* London: Routledge

Pollak O (1961) *The Criminality of Women*. New York: A S Barnes

Povey D, Prime J and Taylor P (1997) *Notifiable Offences: England and Wales, 1996*. Home Office Statistical Bulletin, Issue 3/97 March. London: HMSO

Punch M (1996) *Dirty Business: Exploring Corporate Misconduct*. London: Sage

Pyle D (1994) 'Crime, Unemployment and Economic Activity', in *Criminal Justice Matters*, No 18 Winter: 6–7

Pyle D and Deadman D (1994) 'Crime and the Business Cycle in Post War Britain', *British Journal of Criminology*, Vol 34/3: 339

Radford J (1992) 'Introduction', in Radford J and Russell D (eds) *Femicide: The Politics of Woman Killing*. Buckingham: Open University Press

Rafter N and Heidensohn F (eds) (1995) *International Feminist Perspectives in Criminology: Engendering a Discipline*. Milton Keynes: Open University Press

Reiner R (1989) 'Race and Criminal Justice', *New Community*, Vol 16/1: 5–22

Reiner R (1992) *The Politics of the Police*. London: Harvester Wheatsheaf

Robertson R (1996) 'Teenagers Pick Up Worst Kind of Habit', *The Herald* 16/8/96: 8

Rock P (1990) *Helping the Victims of Crime: The Home Office and the Rise of Victim Support in England and Wales*. Oxford: Clarendon Press

Rock P (1991) 'The Victim in Court Project at the Crown Court at Wood Green', *Howard Journal*, Vol 30/4: 301–10

Rock P (1997) 'Sociological Theories of Crime', in Maguire M, Morgan R and Reiner R (eds) *The Oxford Handbook of Criminology*, 2nd edition. Oxford: Clarendon Press

Ruggiero V (1993) 'Brixton London: A Drug Culture Without a Drug Economy?', *The International Journal of Drug Policy*, Vol 4/3: 83–90

Ruggiero V (1994) 'Corruption in Italy: An Attempt to Identify the Victims', *Howard Journal of Criminal Justice*, Vol 33/4: 319–38

Ruggiero V (1996a) *Organized and Corporate Crime in Europe: Offers That Can't be Refused*. Aldershot: Dartmouth

Ruggiero V (1996b) 'War Markets: Corporate and Organized Criminals in Europe', *Social and Legal Studies*, Vol 5: 5–20

Ruggiero V (1997) 'Trafficking in Human Beings: Slaves in Contemporary Europe', *International Journal of the Sociology of Law*, Vol 25: 231–44

Ruggiero V and South N (1995) *Eurodrugs. Drug Use, Markets and Trafficking in Europe.* London: University College London Press

Ruggiero V and Vass A (1992) 'Heroin Use and the Formal Economy: Illicit Drugs and Licit Economies in Italy', *British Journal of Criminology,* Vol 32/3: 273–91

Ryan M (1996) *Lobbying from Below: INQUEST in Defence of Civil Liberties.* London: UCL Press

Sampson A (1994) *Acts of Abuse: Sex Offenders and the Criminal Justice System.* London: Routledge

Sampson A and Phillips C (1992) *Multiple Victimization: Racial Attacks on an East London Estate.* Police Research Group Crime Prevention Unit Series: Paper No 36. London: Home Office Police Department

Sampson R and Wilson W J (1995) 'Toward and Theory of Race, Crime and Urban Inequality', in Hagan J and Peterson R (eds) *Crime and Inequality.* Stanford: Stanford University Press

Sanday P (1981) 'The Socio Cultural Context of Rape: A Cross-cultural Study', *Journal of Social Issues,* 37/4: 5–27

Saraga E (1993) 'The Abuse of Children', in Dallos, R and McLaughlin E (eds) *Social Problems and the Family.* London: Sage

Saraga E (1996) 'Dangerous Places: The Family as a Site of Crime', in Muncie J and McLaughlin E (eds) *The Problem of Crime.* London: Sage, pp 183–227

Scarman OBE, Rt Hon The Lord (1981) *The Brixton Disorders, 10–12 April 1981.* London: HMSO

Scheff T (1966) *Being Mentally Ill.* London: Weidenfeld & Nicolson

Schwendinger H and Schwendinger J (1970) 'Defendants of Order or Guardians of Human Rights', *Issues in Criminology,* Vol 7: 72–81

Scottish Office (1995) *Recorded Crime in Scotland.* Scottish Office Statistical Bulletin CrJ/1995: 2

Scraton P and Chadwick K (1991) 'The Theoretical and Political Priorities of Critical Criminology', in Stenson K and Cowell D (eds) *The Politics of Crime Control.* London: Sage

Scully D (1990) *Understanding Sexual Violence.* London: Harper Collins

Scully D and Marolla J (1993) ' "Riding the Bull at Gilleys": Convicted Rapists Describe the Rewards of Rape', in Bart P and Moran E G (eds) *Violence against Women: The Bloody Footprints.* London: Sage

Shacklady-Smith L (1978) 'Sexist Assumptions and Female Delinquency', in Smart C and Smart B (eds) *Women, Sexuality and Social Control.* London: Routledge & Kegan Paul

Shah R and Pease K (1992) 'Crime, Race and Reporting to the Police', *The Howard Journal,* Vol 31: 192–9

Shapiro S (1990) 'Collaring the Crime, Not the Criminal: Re-considering the Concept of White Collar Crime', *American Sociological Review,* Vol 55: 346–65

Shaw C (1930) *The Jack-Roller: A Delinquent Boy's Own Story*. Chicago: University of Chicago Press

Shaw C and McKay H (1942) *Juvenile Delinquency and Urban Areas*. Chicago: University of Chicago Press

Sheen Report (1987) *M.V. Herald of Free Enterprise: Report of the Court No. 8074*. Department of Transport. London: HMSO

Sheldon W (1949) *Varieties of Delinquent Youth*. New York and London: Harper

Shover N and Honaker D (1992) 'The Socially Bounded Decision Making of Persistent Property Offenders', *Howard Journal of Criminal Justice*, Vol 31, No 4: 276–94

Sim J (1994) 'Tougher than the Rest? Men in Prison', in Newburn T and Stanko E (eds) *Just Boys Doing Business?* London: Routledge

Sim J, Scraton P and Gordon P (1987) 'Crime the State and Critical Analysis: An Introduction', in P Scraton (ed) *Law, Order and the Authoritarian State*. Milton Keynes: Open University Press

Simon D and Eitzen D (1993) *Elite Deviance*, 4th edition. Boston: Allyn & Bacon

Slapper G (1994) 'Crime without Punishment', *The Guardian* 1/2/94

Smart C (1977) *Women, Crime and Criminology*. London: Routledge & Kegan Paul

Smart C (1979) 'The New Female Criminal: Reality or Myth?', *British Journal of Criminology*, Vol 19/1

Smith D J and Gray J (1985) *Police and People in London: The PSI Report*. Aldershot: Gower

Smith D J (1997) 'Race, Crime and Criminal Justice', in Maguire M, Morgan R and Reiner R (eds) *The Oxford Handbook of Criminology*, 2nd edition. Oxford: Clarendon Press

Solomos J (1993) 'Constructions of Black Criminality: Racialisation and Criminalisation in Perspective', in Cook D and Hudson B (eds) *Racism and Criminology*. London: Sage

Solomos J and Rackett T (1991) 'Policing and Urban Unrest: Problem Constitution and Policy Response', in Casmore E and McLaughlin E (eds) *Out of Order? Policing Black People*. London: Routledge

Soothill K and Walby S (1991) *Sex Crime in the News*. London: Routledge

South N (1997) 'Drugs: Use, Crime, and Control', in Maguire M, Morgan R and Reiner R (eds) *The Oxford Handbook of Criminology*, 2nd edition. Oxford: Clarendon Press

Sparks R (1997) 'Recent Social Theory and the Study of Crime and Punishment', in Maguire M, Morgan R and Reiner R (eds) *The Oxford Handbook of Criminology*, 2nd edition. Oxford: Clarendon Press

Spencer E (1992) *Car Crime and Young People on a Sunderland Housing Estate*. Home Office Police Research Group Crime Prevention Unit Series: Paper No 40. London: HMSO

Stanko E (1990a) *Everyday Violence: How Women and Men Experience Sexual and Physical Danger*. London: Pandora

Stanko E (1990b) 'When Precaution is Normal: A Feminist Critique of Crime Prevention', in Gelsthorpe L and Morris A (eds) *Feminist Perspectives in Criminology*. Milton Keynes: Open University Press

Stanko E (1994) 'Challenging the Problem of Men's Individual Violence', in Newburn T and Stanko E (eds) *Just Boys Doing Business?* London: Routledge

Stanko E and Hobdell K (1993) 'Assault on Men: Masculinity and Male Victimization', *British Journal of Criminology*, Vol 33/3: 400–15

Steffensmeier D and Allan E (1995) 'Age-Inequality and Property Crime: The Effects of Age-linked Stratification and Status-Attainment Processes on Patterns of Criminality across the Life Course', in Hagan J and Peterson R (eds) *Crime and Inequality*. Stanford: Stanford University Press

Stevens P and Willis C (1979) *Race, Crime and Arrests*. Home Office Research Study No 58. London: HMSO

Sudnow D (1965) 'Normal Crimes: Sociological Features of the Penal Code in a Public Defender Office', *Social Problems*, Vol 12/3: 255–76

Sumner C (1994) *The Sociology of Deviance: An Obituary*. Buckingham: Open University Press

Sumner C (1997) 'Censure, Crime, and State', in Maguire M, Morgan R and Reiner R (eds) *The Oxford Handbook of Criminology*, 2nd edition. Oxford: Clarendon Press

Sutherland E (1947) *Principles of Criminology*, 4th edition. Philadelphia: Lippincott

Sutherland E (1949) *White Collar Crime*. New York: Holt, Rinehart & Winston

Sutherland E (1987) *The Professional Thief: By a Professional Thief*. Chicago: University of Chicago Press

Sutton A and Wild R (1985) 'Small Business: White Collar Villains or Victims?', *International Journal of the Sociology of Law*, Vol 13: 247–59

Sutton M (1995) 'Supply by Theft: Does the Market for Second-hand Goods Play a Role in Keeping Crime Figures High?', *British Journal of Criminology*, Vol 35/3: 400–16

Sykes G and Matza D (1957) 'Techniques of Neutralization: A Theory of Delinquency', *American Sociological Review*, Vol 22: 664–70

Szockyj E and Fox J G (eds) (1996) *Corporate Victimization of Women*. Northeastern University Press

Tappan P (1977) 'Who is the Criminal?', in Geis G and Maier R F (eds) *White Collar Crime: Offences in Business, Politics and the Professions – Classic and Contemporary Views*, revised edition. New York: Free Press, Collier and Macmillan

Taylor A (1993) *Women Drug Users: An Ethnography of a Female Injecting Community*. Oxford: Clarendon Press

Taylor I (1991) 'The Concept of "Social Cost" in Free Market Theory and the Social Effects of Free Market Policies', in Taylor I (ed) *The Social Effects of Free Market Policies*. Hemel Hempstead: Harvester Wheatsheaf

Taylor I (1997) 'The Political Economy of Crime', in Maguire M, Morgan R and Reiner R (eds) *The Oxford Handbook of Criminology*, 2nd edition. Oxford: Clarendon Press

Taylor I, Walton P and Young J (1973) *The New Criminology*. London: Routledge & Kegan Paul

Thomas W I (1923) *The Unadjusted Girl*. Boston: Little Brown

Thrasher F (1927) *The Gang*. Chicago: Phoenix Press

Toch H (1969) *Violent Men*. Harmondsworth: Penguin

Tombs S (1990) 'Industrial Injuries in British Manufacturing Industry', *Sociological Review*, 324–43

Tombs S (1998), 'Health and Safety Crimes and the Problem of "Knowing"', in Davies P, Francis P and Jupp V (eds) *Invisible Crimes*. London: Macmillan

Travis A (1997) 'Crime Fears Lead to Street Anxiety', *The Guardian* 26/5/ 97: 6

Utting D, Bright J and Henricson C (1993) *Crime and the Family: Improving Child Rearing and Preventing Delinquency*. Occasional Paper 16. Family Policy Studies Centre

Van Dijk J and Mayhew P (1993) *Criminal Victimization in the Industrialised World: Key Findings of the 1989 and 1992 International Crime Surveys*. The Hague: Ministry of Justice

Van Duyne P (1993) 'Organized Crime and Business Crime Enterprises in the Netherlands', *Crime, Law and Social Change*, Vol 19/2: 103–42

Virdee S (1997) 'Racial Harassment', in Modood T et al (eds) *Ethnic Minorities in Britain: Diversities and Disadvantage*. London: Policy Studies Institute

Walby S (1989) 'Theorising Patriarchy', *Sociology*, Vol 23/2: 213–34

Walby S (1990) *Theorizing Patriarchy*. Oxford: Blackwell

Walker M (1987) 'Interpreting Race and Crime Statistics', *Journal of the Royal Statistical Society*, Part 1: 39–56

Walker M (1988) 'The Court Disposal of Young Males, by Race, in London in 1983', *British Journal of Criminology*, 28/4: 441–59

Walker M (1989) 'The Court Disposal and Remands of White, Afro-Caribbean and Asian Men in London in 1983', *British Journal of Criminology*, 29/4: 353–67

Walker M (1995) 'Statistics of Offences', in Walker M (ed) *Interpreting Crime Statistics*. Oxford: Clarendon Press

Walklate S (1989) *Victimology: The Victim and the Criminal Justice Process*. London: Unwin Hyman

Walklate S (1995) *Gender and Crime: An Introduction*. London: Prentice Hall/ Harvester Wheatsheaf

Walklate S (1996) 'Can there be a Feminist Victimology?', in Davies P, Francis P and Jupp V (eds) *Understanding Victimisation*. Northumbria Social Science Press

Walklate S (1998) *Understanding Criminology*. Buckingham: Open University Press

Walmsley R, Howard L and White S (1992) *The National Prison Survey 1991: Main Findings*. Home Office Research Study No 128. London: HMSO

Wassell T (1994) in *The European* 24/6/94

Watkin H et al (1977) 'XYY and XXY Men: Criminality and Aggression', in Sarnoff A et al (eds) *Biosocial Bases of Criminal Behaviour*. New York: Gardner Press

Watson L (1996) *Victims of Violent Crime Recorded by the Police, England and Wales*, 1990–1994. Home Office Statistical Findings, Issue 1/96. London: HMSO

Webb B and Laycock G (1992) 'Tackling Car Crime: The Nature and Extent of the Problem', Home Office Crime Prevention Unit Paper No 32. London: HMSO

Webster C (1996) 'Asian Young People and Drug Use', *Criminal Justice Matters*, No 24 Summer: 11–12

Webster C (1997) 'The Construction of British "Asian" Criminality', *International Journal of the Sociology of Law*, Vol 25: 65–86

Wells C (1988) 'The Decline and Rise of English Murder: Corporate Crime and Individual Responsibility', *Criminal Law Review*, 789–801

Wells C (1993) *Corporations and Criminal Responsibility*. Oxford: Clarendon Press

Wells J (1995) *Crime and Unemployment*. Employment Policy Institute Economic Report, Vol 9/1 February

West D (1965) *Murder Followed by Suicide*. London: Heinemann

West D (1969) *Present Conduct and Future Delinquency*. London: Heinemann

West D J (1987) *Sexual Crimes and Confrontations*. Aldershot: Gower

West D J and Farrington D (1973) *Who becomes Delinquent?* London: Heinemann

West D J and Farrington D (1977) *The Delinquent Way of Life*. London: Heinemann

White P (1995) 'Homicide', in Walker M (ed) *Interpreting Crime Statistics*. Oxford: Clarendon Press

Whittaker B (1987) *The Global Connection*. Cape

Whyte W (1943) *Street Corner Society*. Chicago: University of Chicago Press

Williams J and Taylor R (1994) 'Boys Keep Swinging: Masculinity and Football Culture in England', in Newburn T and Stanko E (eds) *Just Boys Doing Business?* London: Routledge

Williams K (1994) *Textbook on Criminology*, 2nd edition. London: Blackstone

Willis P (1977) *Learning to Labour: How Working Class Kids get Working Class Jobs*. Gower: Farnborough

Wilson H (1980) 'Parental Supervision: A Neglected Aspect of Delinquency', *British Journal of Criminology*, Vol 20: 20

Wilson W J (1987) *The Truly Disadvantaged: The Inner City, the Underclass and Public Policy*. Chicago: University of Chicago Press

Wolfgang M (1958) *Patterns in Criminal Homicide*. Philadelphia: University of Pennsylvania Press

Wolfgang M and Ferracuti F (1967) *The Subculture of Violence*. London: Tavistock

Wooton B (1959) *Social Science and Social Pathology*. London: George Allen & Unwin

Worrall A (1990) *Offending Women*. London: Routledge

Worrall A (1995) 'Troublesome Young Women', *Criminal Justice Matters*, No 19 Spring: 6–8

Wright R and Decker S (1994) *Burglars on the Job*. Boston: Northeastern University Press

Yablonsky L (1962) *The Violent Gang*. New York: Macmillan

Young J (1971a) *The Drugtakers*. London: Paladin

Young J (1971b) 'The Police as Amplifiers of Deviancy', in Cohen S and Taylor L (eds) *Images of Deviance*. Harmondsworth: Penguin

Young J (1975) 'Working Class Criminology', in Taylor L, Walton P and Young J (eds) *Critical Criminology*. London: Routledge & Kegan Paul

Young J (1986) 'The Failure of Criminology: The Need for a Radical Realism', in Matthews R and Young J (eds) *Confronting Crime*. London: Sage

Young J (1994) 'Incessant Chatter: Recent Paradigms within Criminology', in Maguire M, Morgan R and Reines R (eds) *The Oxford Handbook of Criminology*. Oxford: Clarendon Press

Young J (1997) 'Left Realist Criminology: Radical in its Analysis, Realist in its Policy', in Maguire M, Morgan R and Reiner R (eds) *The Oxford Handbook of Criminology*, 2nd edition. Oxford: Clarendon Press

Young J and Matthews R (eds) (1992) *Rethinking Criminology: The Realist Debate*. London: Sage

Zedner L (1997) 'Victims', in Maguire M, Morgan R and Reiner R (eds) *The Oxford Handbook of Criminology*, 2nd edition. Oxford: Clarendon Press

Zedner L (1992) 'Sexual Offences', in Casale S and Stockdale E (eds) *Criminal Justice under Stress*. London: Blackstone

NAME INDEX

SUBJECT INDEX